Making Precious Things Plain

Volume 8
Old Testament Study Guide, Pt. 2
Deuteronomy—Solomon

Randal S. Chase

Making Precious Things Plain, Vol. 8:
Old Testament Study Guide, Pt 2.
Deuteronomy—Solomon
(2ⁿᵗ Edition)

© 2010 Randal S. Chase

Send inquiries to:
Plain and Precious Publishing
3378 E. Sweetwater Springs Drive
Washington, UT 84780

Send e-mail: info@makingpreciousthingsplain.com

For more copies visit www.makingpreciousthingsplain.com

For a listing of all Plain and Precious Publishing products, visit www.makingpreciousthingsplain.com or call 435–251–8520.

Printed in the United States of America

ISBN: 978-1-937901-08-0

Cover Photo: es-Sakhara (©David Harris, all rights reserved, used by permission). This is the rock within the Dome of the Rock. Upon this rock Abraham nearly sacrificed his son Isaac; the Ark of the Covenant sat upon it within the Holy of Holies of Solomon's Temple; and King David made sacrifice to God before going into battle; and Muslims believe that the prophet Mohammad ascended into heaven.

Making Precious Things Plain
Volume 8
Old Testament Study Guide, Pt. 2
Deuteronomy—Solomon

Table of Contents

Acknowledgments

This book is dedicated to Church members everywhere who hunger and thirst for an understanding of the scriptures. It has been my privilege to teach literally thousands of such souls in gospel classes, as well as in CES Institute and Adult Education classes, over the years. They have all inspired me with their dedication to reading, pondering, and feasting upon the word of God. I have learned much from them in the process.

I acknowledge the help and encouragement of my sweet wife Deborah, who has assisted me in all of my endeavors to teach and to write concerning the gospel of Jesus Christ. I acknowledge the encouragement of many friends and students to write these study guides, the patient and meticulous assistance of my editor and son, Michael Chase, who has assisted in this work, and other Church scholars who have provided solid counsel about its form and substance, and who have offered invaluable insights on many topics.

I acknowledge other knowledgeable gospel scholars and teachers who have written similar study guides in the past, which I have quoted time and time again in this volume:

The *Old Testament Student Manual*, Vols. 1–2 [Church Educational System manuals, 2003] is an invaluable tool for all students of the Old Testament, and many of the cultural, linguistic, and other ideas presented herein were first obtained from this manual.

Kent Jackson's *The Restored Gospel and the Book of Genesis* [1989], Chapters 6–10, is helpful in understanding how the restored gospel informs our understanding of Old Testament events. Rasmussen's *Latter-day Saint Commentary on the Old Testament* [1994] does the same in a verse-by-verse format. The *Studies in Scripture* series, Volumes 2–4 [1985–1989], edited by Kent Jackson and Robert L. Millet, provides excellent scholarly commentary on the Old Testament and the Pearl of Great Price from a variety of LDS researchers and authors.

Daniel H. Ludlow wrote *A Companion to Your Study of the Old Testament* [1986], as part of a series of such companions to our study of all the scriptures. These perhaps come closer to the spirit of what this book is all about—making the history and revelations plain to those who just need a little help with their gospel studies. I have had some of Brother Ludlow's family in my classes, and I cherish his personal encouragement to me and a personally-signed copy of his *Selected Writings* that he provided to me a few years ago.

Skousen's series of books on the Old Testament, *The First Two Thousand Years* [1953], *The Third Thousand Years* [1964], and *The Fourth Thousand Years* [1964] were instrumental years ago in sparking my personal interest in Old Testament studies. Written in narrative format, with insightful comments, his works have been both celebrated and challenged over the years. I, for one, appreciate them.

Most, if not all, of the above-named volumes are now out of print. I am hoping that the portions of them that I have quoted in this volume will continue to spread their insights for years to come.

Foreword

The Old Testament is one of the most vivid and memorable of all our books of scripture. Many, if not most, of the exciting stories we learned as children from the Bible come from the Old Testament: Adam and Eve in the garden, Noah and the flood, Abraham nearly sacrificing Isaac, Joseph in Egypt, Moses parting the waters and receiving the ten commandments, Joshua and the battle of Jericho, Samson and Delilah, the loyalty of Ruth, the suffering of Job, David and Goliath, Solomon's wisdom, Daniel in the Lion's Den, Esther rescuing Israel from execution, and so many other stories have thrilled us with their heroic acts of faith.

The "First Testament" of Christ

More importantly, the Old Testament is the "First Testament" of Christ. The Savior said: "Search the scriptures; for in them ye think ye have eternal life: and they are they which testify of me" (John 5:39). Clearly, when He said "the scriptures," He meant the Old Testament, since that was the only volume of scripture available to them. And He plainly said that the Old Testament testified of Him—the Savior. Thus, the Old Testament could more properly be thought of as the "First Testament of Jesus Christ." For that reason alone, it is worth serious study.

Elder Mark E. Peterson said: "[Jesus] never would have said that, if the scriptures available to the people of that day did not testify of Him. He urged them to read the scriptures that they might see how the prophets whom they adored, but now long since dead, actually did foretell His coming. They testified of Him ... The Lord quoted ... Moses and the other prophets ... 'in all the scriptures the things concerning himself.'"[1] .

Again and again throughout the Old Testament, the Messiah's coming is predicted through profound symbols, compelling stories, and remarkably accurate prophecies. The major purpose of all testaments, old or new, is to bear witness of Christ. As a result, to the spiritual eye and ear, the Old Testament (more accurately, the "First Testament") is like a giant hand pointing forward to the coming of the Lord Jesus Christ. If we are led by the Holy Spirit we will see the unmistakable mark of the Messiah in every book we read in these scriptures.

President Brigham Young said: "The Old and New Testaments, the Book of Mormon, and the Book of Doctrine and Covenants, ... are like a lighthouse in the ocean, or a finger-post which points out the road we should travel. Where do they point? To the fountain of light. . . That is what these books are for. They are of God; they are valuable and necessary: by them we can establish the doctrine of Christ"[2] .

The author's sincere desire is to make the Old Testament plain as a powerful witness of the Messiahship of Jesus Christ.

How to Use This Book

To facilitate learning, students and teachers may use this study guide in a variety of ways. I have suggested two below, in no particular order of preference. Choose the method that works best for you, but whatever method you choose, complete the assigned scripture reading for each week's lesson *before* you go to class.

Option 1. Prayerfully read the scriptures associated with the current lesson *first*, and then read the chapter in this book that corresponds to those scriptures.

Option 2. Carefully and prayerfully read the scriptures associated with the current lesson, using this study guide as a reference to help you understand the context and consequences of the scriptures *while you are reading them*. To do this, you would keep this book open and use it as a guide and commentary alongside your scriptures.

This study guide comments on many, but not all, of the scriptures in the Old Testament. Rather than a verse-by-verse analysis, I have provided a summary restatement of events, divided into scripture blocks with attached explanations and quotes. An example of how these scripture blocks and comments are organized is shown below:

● **Genesis 2:16–17 The consequence for eating was mortality, meaning eventual physical death.** The Lord God gave Adam instruction concerning the tree of knowledge of good and evil, and He prescribed the penalty for eating its fruit: "in the day that thou eatest thereof thou shalt surely die" (v. 17).

President Joseph Fielding Smith said: "What did Adam do? The very thing the Lord wanted him to do, and I hate to hear anybody call it a sin, for it wasn't a sin. Did Adam sin when he partook of the forbidden fruit? I say to you, no, he did not! … The Lord said to Adam, here is the tree of the knowledge of good and evil. If you want to stay here then you cannot eat of that fruit. If you want to stay here then I forbid you to eat it. But you may act for yourself and you may eat of it if you want to. And if you eat it you will die"[3].

The Prophet Joseph Smith said: "Adam did not commit sin in eating the fruit, for God had decreed that he should eat and fall. But in compliance with the decree, he should die … [That] he should die was the saying of the Lord; therefore, the Lord appointed us to fall and also redeemed us"[4].

Adam and Eve's "transgression" was the very thing the Lord wanted them to do. Had they not done so, the entire plan of salvation would have failed. In giving Adam and Eve the two commandments, the Lord placed them in a position to choose between a higher law and a lesser law, thus preserving their agency and allowing them to choose. Adam and Eve were then responsible for the consequences of their choices. They could not blame the Lord for the outcome. God had not, in any way, violated their agency. He let them choose.

Some Chapters Are Thematic, Not Chronological

While the order of presentation of these chapters on the Old Testament is roughly chronological, it is not strictly so. There are a number of "topical" chapters that provide a more general understanding of the context within which events occurred, such as chapters on how to study the Old Testament, the Wilderness Tabernacle, Animal Sacrifices, and Old Testament laws of mercy and righteousness.

In every chapter, I have provided an historical setting for the scriptures discussed. I have also freely included other scriptural references that provide additional light on the topic. In the end, understanding the doctrine is more important than the history, though I believe it is possible to understand both, and it is better if we do.

Note to Teachers

For the convenience of readers, the chapters in this study guide are organized around the lesson topics for the Church's Gospel Doctrine classes. However, teachers should remember that this study guide is not intended to become a substitute for the official lesson manuals of the Church. Your lessons should follow precisely the organization found in your lesson manual, and should be centered on the assigned scriptures for each lesson. Teachers should read their lesson manuals first and take note of the main doctrinal points that are listed there. After doing this, teachers may use this book as a way of enhancing their own personal understanding of the events and scriptures covered in a particular lesson, just as any other gospel scholar might do. But you should never use this book as a guide to teaching your lessons.

Notes

1. *Moses: Man of Miracles* [1977], 148–149

2. In *Journal of Discourses*, 8:129

3. "Fall-Atonement-Resurrection-Sacrament," address delivered at Institute of Religion, 14 Jan. 1961, 2

4. *The Words of Joseph Smith: The Contemporary Accounts of the Nauvoo Discourses of the Prophet Joseph,* Andrew F. Ehat and Lyndon W Cook, eds. [1980], 63

CHAPTER 17

Moses' Exhortations to Obedience

(Deuteronomy)

ཨོཾ

INTRODUCTION

The Book of Deuteronomy

Deuteronomy is the Greek name for this book. It means "Repetition of the Law." It is also familiarly known to the Jews as *mishneh hattora*, meaning "copy of the law." The Hebrew name of the Book, "These Are the Words", is taken from the first words of Deuteronomy. It was written at or near Mt. Nebo, which overlooked the promised land.

- **Author:**   Moses (1 Nephi 5:10–11; 2 Nephi 3:17; Moses 1:40–41).

- **Position:**   Fifth book of the Pentateuch—the five books of Moses.

- **Purpose:**   A review and exposition of the law of God—sometimes called the "Gospel of Moses."

- **Length:**   34 chapters.

Deuteronomy is quoted more often by the Old Testament prophets than any other book of the Law. It is also quoted frequently in the New Testament. For example: Matt. 4:4 (Deut. 8:3); Matt. 4:7 (Deut. 6:16); Matt. 4:10 (Deut. 6:13); Mark 12:30 (Deut. 6:5); and 2 Cor. 13:1 (Deut. 19:15)

The Setting for the Sermons

Deuteronomy consists of a series of three sermons which Moses delivered to the Israelites in Moab, just before they entered the promised land.

- Chapters 1–4   <u>First Speech.</u> A recitation of the events that took place between the departure from Sinai and arrival east of the Jordan River.

- Chapters 5–25   <u>Second Speech.</u> Moses' account of the events that took place at Sinai, and the instructions that Israel received there, often called the Deuteronomic Law (chapters 12–26). Moses here reviews and explains the law by providing examples of their application.

- Chapters 26–30   <u>Third Speech.</u> Moses' final instructions to his people, including blessings and curses that he promised to them, based on their behavior.

- Chapters 31–34   <u>The Last Acts of Moses.</u> An appendix to the book, including exhortations to Joshua and a final celebration before the departure of Moses

The following three chapters discuss these speeches, one and a time, reviewing these last words of Moses to the children of Israel in some detail. Most gospel classes, including the Gospel Doctrine class, do not attempt to cover all of this material. But for those who are reading these *Making Precious Things Plain* study guides this is useful information when trying to grasp both the spirit and the letter of the laws given to Israel by Moses.

Moses' First Speech:
Israel's Experiences and Choices

(Deuteronomy 1–4)

೮つೞ

A REVIEW OF EVENTS IN THE WILDERNESS

Moses' first speech was a recitation of the events that took place between the departure from Sinai and arrival east of the Jordan River.

- **Deuteronomy 1:1–3 "Moses spake unto the children of Israel."** They were located on the west side of the Jordan River, in the plain between Mt. Nebo and Heshbon, near the Jordan River (v. 1).

  This was their 40th year since leaving Mt. Sinai, in the eleventh month, on the first day of the month (v. 3)—sometime around January in our present-day calendar.

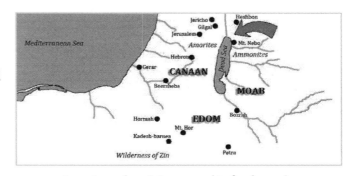

Location where Moses gave his final speeches

"Moses spake unto the children of Israel, according unto all that the Lord had given him in commandment unto them" (v. 3).

- **Deuteronomy 1:5–8 The Lord gave the promised land to the Israelites.** At Mt. Sinai the Lord commanded them to go to the land of the Amorites and the Canaanites, including Lebanon and all the territory north to the river Euphrates (vv. 5–7). "Behold, I have set the land before you," said the Lord. "Go in and possess the land which the Lord sware unto your fathers, Abraham, Isaac, and Jacob, to give unto them and to their seed after them" (v. 8).

- **Deuteronomy 1:9–11 The Israelites had multiplied greatly while in the wilderness.** Moses told the Lord at Sinai that he was not able to bear the responsibility of the Israelites alone (v. 9). And since that time they had become "as the stars of heaven for multitude" (v. 10). Moses prayed for them to become "a thousand times so many more as ye are, and bless you, as he hath promised you!" (v. 11).

- **Deuteronomy 1:12–18 Moses had organized them with leaders over 10s, 50s, 100s, and 1000s** (v. 15). This was according to the wise advice of his father-in-law Jethro and also the Lord's commands (v. 13). The Israelites had accepted these leaders (v. 14), who had been charged to "hear the causes between your brethren, and judge righteously between every man and his brother, and the stranger that is with him" (v. 16). They were charged not to "respect persons in judgment; but ye shall hear the small as well as the great; ye shall not be afraid of the face of man; for the judgment is God's: and the cause that is too hard for you, bring it unto me, and I will hear it" (v. 17). By this means Moses had guided them in "all the things which ye should do" (v. 18).

- **Deuteronomy 1:19–31 When they arrived at the promised land they were afraid to enter it.** The journey from Mt. Sinai to Kadesh-barnea was only 11 days long according to verse 2. So they had not been in the wilderness all that long when they came to the land of the Amorites and were commanded to "go up and possess it, as the Lord God of thy fathers hath said unto thee; fear not, neither be discouraged" (v. 21). They first wanted to send in spies to ascertain what lay ahead of them, which Moses did (vv. 22–24).

The spies returned with good reports on the fruitfulness of the land, but the Israelites refused to take possession of it out of fear of the Amorites (vv. 25–27). Moses tried to encourage them, saying, "Dread not, neither be afraid of them. The Lord your God which goeth before you, he shall fight for you, according to all that he did for you in Egypt before your eyes" (v. 30). He also reminded them that the Lord had protected and blessed them "as a man doth bear his son" in all their travels in the wilderness (v. 31).

STORY OF THE BIBLE, IMAGE 62, P.153, 1873, 1877, 1884

Spies return with fruits of promised land

- **Deuteronomy 1:32–46 Why the Lord refused to let them enter at that time.** They knew that what Moses told them was true, "yet in this thing [they] did not believe the Lord [their] God" (vv. 31–32). Hearing this, the Lord "was wroth, and sware, saying, surely there shall not one of these men of this evil generation see that good land, which I sware to give unto your fathers" (vv. 33–35). The Lord is just. They did not want to go in, and He would not force them. Instead, he gave them what they wanted—never to go into the land of promise. The only exceptions were Caleb and Joshua, the only two of twelve leaders who wanted to obey the Lord's command to enter the land (vv. 36, 38).

Not even Moses would enter the promised land (v. 37). Only their children, "which in that day had no knowledge between good and evil, [would] go in thither, and unto them will I give it, and they shall possess it" (vv. 38–39). Realizing their error, they then wanted to go into the land, but it was too late to do so with the Lord's blessings. They were warned not to try, but were disobedient again and went into the land, where they were smitten by the Amorites and driven out (vv. 40–44). They sorrowfully wept at their loss, "but the Lord would not hearken to your voice, nor give ear unto you" (v. 45).

- **Deuteronomy 2:1–3:20 Moses reviewed all of the significant events from Israel's forty years of wandering in the wilderness.** We will not rehearse those events here, but suffice it to say that for 40 years God had been with them and they had "lacked nothing" (2:7). He fed them every day and protected them from enemies who could otherwise have easily destroyed them.

- **Deuteronomy 3:23–27 Moses will be allowed to see the promised land, but not to enter it.** As the Israelites camped on the plains east of the Jordan River, ready to enter the promised land, Moses sought the Lord in prayer: "O Lord God, thou hast begun to shew thy servant thy greatness, and thy mighty hand: for what God is there in heaven or in earth, that can do according to thy works, and according to thy might? I pray thee, let me go over, and see the good land that is beyond Jordan, that goodly mountain, and Lebanon" (vv. 24–25). But because of the disobedience of the Israelites in the wilderness, he did not intend to let Moses guide them into their promised land (v. 26). He told Moses to be satisfied with seeing it, commanding him, "Get thee up into the top of Pisgah, and lift up thine eyes westward, and northward, and southward, and eastward, and behold it with thine eyes: for thou shalt not go over this Jordan" (v. 27).

- **Deuteronomy 3:28, 21–22 The appointment, ordination, and charge to Joshua by Moses.** The Lord commanded Moses, saying, "charge Joshua, and encourage him, and strengthen him: for he shall go over before this people, and he shall cause them to inherit the land which thou shalt see" (v. 28). Moses said unto Joshua, "Thine eyes have seen all that the Lord your God hath done unto these two kings: so shall the Lord do unto all the kingdoms whither thou passest. Ye shall not fear them: for the Lord your God he shall fight for you" (vv. 21–22).

Clear Choices for Israel

- **Deuteronomy 4:1–2 Moses charges Israel to hear and obey the laws he will give them.** Moses charged the Israelites to be obedient "unto the statutes and unto the judgments, which I teach you, for to do them, that ye may live, and go in and possess the land which the Lord God of your fathers giveth you" (v. 1). He also said: "Ye shall not add unto the word which I command you, neither shall ye diminish ought from it, that ye may keep the commandments of the Lord your God which I command you" (v. 2). If read out of context, this scripture would appear to restrict any further revelation or scripture after it. But that is not true; it speaks only of the book of the law that Moses was reading to them. He wanted no alterations, additions, or deletions to be made to the commandments the Lord had given him. The same is true of the verse in the Revelation of John, where he says a similar thing.

Elder Mark E. Petersen said:

> Of course, a careful reading of this text shows very clearly that John the Revelator was speaking only of the book of Revelation and not of any collection of other sacred writings. Moses used a similar expression in speaking to ancient Israel when he said: "Ye shall not add unto the word which I command you, neither shall ye diminish ought from it, … " This is found in the fourth chapter of the book of Deuteronomy (verse 2). In the 12th chapter of the same book Moses said this: 'What thing soever I command you, observe to do it: thou shalt not add thereto, nor diminish from it.' (Verse 32.)

Can anyone suppose that in these words Moses laid down a prohibition against all subsequent revelations and against all books which might be called scripture in years to come? Did he have the power to silence all future prophets and forbid them to speak or write as God intended that they should? Of course not, or we would be without most of the Old Testament and would have none of the New Testament at all.

It was the same with John the Revelator. In warning against additions to the book of Revelation he spoke of that book only, insisting that no one attempt to change or corrupt what he had said. The Bible was not compiled when John wrote the book of Revelation, so he could not possibly have referred to it.

Furthermore, scholars tell us that the Gospel of John was written after the book of Revelation, and if this be true it becomes another indication that John had no thought of precluding other writings but only of protecting this particular book of Revelation from change or corruption.[1]

- **Deuteronomy 4:3–4 God had preserved the lives of the righteous.** By this time "all the men that followed Baal-peor" (the false god of the nations that surrounded them), had been "destroyed … from among you" (v. 3). "But ye that did cleave unto the Lord your God are alive every one of you this day" (v. 4).

The false god Baal

- **Deuteronomy 4:5–8 By following God's commands, they will become a wise and understanding people.** Moses said to them, "Behold, I have taught you statutes and judgments, even as the Lord my God commanded me, that ye should do so in the land whither ye go to possess it" (v. 5). By living these laws, they would become an example of wisdom and understanding to all the nations surrounding them (v. 6). He asked them, "what nation is there so great, who hath God so nigh unto them, as the Lord our God is in all things that we call upon him for?" (v. 7), and "what nation is there so great, that hath statutes and judgments so righteous as all this law, which I set before you this day?" (v. 8).

Elder Mark E. Petersen said: "Some people have the idea that the Ten Commandments were first given by Moses when he directed the children of Israel and formulated their code of laws. This is not the case. These great commandments are from the beginning and were understood in righteous communities in the days of Adam. They are, in fact, fundamental parts of the gospel of Jesus Christ, and the gospel in its fullness was first given to Adam (*Doctrines of Salvation*, 1:94–96)" (*Adam: Who Is He?* [1976], 58).

Consider the following table which shows how they were given in our own day:

No.	Commandment	Then	Now
1.	Thou shalt have no other gods before me.	Exodus 34:10–14; Deuteronomy 5:6–7	D&C 76:1–4
2.	Thou shalt not make unto thee any graven image.	Exodus 34:17; Deuteronomy 4:15–19	D&C 1:15–16
3.	Thou shalt not take the name of the Lord thy God in vain.	Leviticus 19:12; Deuteronomy 5:11	D&C 63:61–62
4.	Remember the Sabbath day to keep it holy.	Exodus 31:12–17; Deuteronomy 5:12–15	D&C 59:9–13
5.	Honor thy Father and Mother	Exodus 21:15, 17; Deuteronomy 21:18–21	D&C 27:9
6.	Thou shalt not kill.	Exodus 21:12–14; Deuteronomy 5:17	D&C 42:18–19,79
7.	Thou shalt not commit adultery.	Exodus 22:16–17; Deuteronomy 5:18	D&C 42:22–26,74
8.	Thou shalt not steal.	Leviticus 19:13; Deuteronomy 5:19	D&C 42:20,84–85
9.	Thou shalt not bear false witness.	Psalms 101:7; Deuteronomy 5:20	D&C 42:21,27,86
10.	Thou shalt not covet.	Proverbs 28:16; Deuteronomy 5:21–22	D&C 19:25–26

George Albert Smith said, "It was a long time ago that the Lord gave to Moses the Ten Commandments. If the people of the world had observed the Ten Commandments from that time until now, we would have a different world. There would be millions of people who would live longer than they have lived and be happier. The Ten Commandments are in force today, and if we are good Latter-day Saints and are observing what the Lord has advised, among other things, we will honor the Sabbath day and not make it a day of pleasure. The Constitution guarantees us liberty that no other nation enjoys. Most of the nations are losing the liberties they have had because they have not kept the commandments of the Lord."[2]

● **Deuteronomy 4:9, 23–24 Israel is warned to remember their promises to God.** Men, with a veil of forgetfulness drawn over their minds, are prone to forget things. Moses therefore warned them to never forget the great things the Lord had done for them and for their fathers: "Take heed to thyself, and keep thy soul diligently, lest thou forget the things which thine eyes have seen, and lest they depart from thy heart all the days of thy life: but teach them thy sons, and thy sons' sons" (v. 9). They were also to never "forget the covenant of the Lord your God, which he made with you, and make you a graven image, or the likeness of any thing, which the Lord thy God hath forbidden thee" (v. 23). With all the nations surrounding them doing these things, it would be too easy to accept their customs and practices. But their god—the only true and living God—would not tolerate such idolatry. "For the Lord thy God is a consuming fire" [He will destroy them] and a "jealous God" [He will not tolerate worship of false gods] (v. 24).

- **Deuteronomy 4:25–28 Moses prophesies that Israel will eventually turn to idolatry in the promised land, and be scattered and destroyed.** After three generations, when "ye shall have remained long in the land, [ye] shall corrupt yourselves, and make a graven image … and shall do evil in the sight of the Lord thy God, to provoke him to anger" (v. 25). Moses then called "heaven and earth to witness against you this day, that ye shall soon utterly perish

Household idols and shrines found among Israelite settlements

from off the land whereunto ye go over Jordan to possess it; ye shall not prolong your days upon it, but shall utterly be destroyed" (v. 26). The Lord would then "scatter you among the nations, and ye shall be left few in number among the heathen, whither the Lord shall lead you. And there ye shall serve gods, the work of men's hands, wood and stone, which neither see, nor hear, nor eat, nor smell" (vv. 27–28).

Elder LeGrand Richards said concerning this verse, "Today, Israel does not worship gods of 'wood and stone' who can 'neither see, nor hear, nor eat, nor smell,' but they have turned, as has the Christian world, to the worship of a spirit god or spirit essence which is said to be everywhere present in the universe, a god that can no more 'see, nor hear, nor eat, nor smell,' than could the gods of 'wood and stone' to which Moses referred. This is truly a departure from the worship of the true and living God, the God of Abraham, Isaac and Jacob, with whom Moses communed 'face to face as a man speaketh unto his friend (Exodus 33:9-11.)'[3]

- **Deuteronomy 4:29–31 Even after they are scattered, God will not forsake nor destroy them, nor forget the covenant he made to Abraham, Isaac, and Jacob.** When Israel found herself scattered among the nations, "if from thence thou shalt seek the Lord thy God, thou shalt find him, if thou seek him with all thy heart and with all thy soul" (v. 29). Though they would suffer tribulation among the nations, in the "latter days" the Lord would gather them again (v. 30; Isaiah 49:14–16). Thus, their "jealous" God is also "a merciful God" who "will not forsake thee, neither destroy thee, nor forget the covenant of thy fathers which he sware unto them" (v. 31).

- **Deuteronomy 4:33–36 The uniqueness of Israel's experience with God.** The nations of the world call upon their gods of wood and stone and imagine that they are being blessed by them. But the God of Israel—being the only true and living God in all the universe—had appeared to them and spoken to them. "Did ever people hear the voice of God speaking out of the midst of the fire, as thou hast heard, and live?" Moses asked (v. 33). Did any other God rescue a people from slavery among a powerful enemy as the Lord had done for the children of Israel in Egypt? (v. 34). All this was done "that thou mightest know that the Lord he is God; there is none else beside him" (v. 35). He had spoken to them out of heaven, and on earth had guided them by a pillar of fire from which He also spoke (v. 36). He was no imaginary God; He lives, and they knew it from personal witness. They had, indeed, been treated as a blessed and chosen people.

- **Deuteronomy 4:41–43 Moses established three cities of refuge** for persons guilty of involuntary man-slaughter until their cases could be judged or until the high priest died.

These were established on the east side of the Jordan River "that the slayer might flee thither, which should kill his neighbour unawares, and hated him not in times past; and that fleeing unto one of these cities he might live" (vv. 41–42; see also Deuteronomy 19:1–10).

These three cities of refuge were Bezer in the wilderness territory of the Reubenites; Ramoth in Gilead in the land of the Gadites; and Golan in Bashan in the land of the Manassites (v. 43).

Fleeing to a city of refuge

STORY OF THE BIBLE, IMAGE 68, P173, 1873, 1877, 1884

Notes

1.   In *Conference Report*, Oct. 1964, 121.
2.   *The Teachings of George Albert Smith*, Robert and Susan McIntosh, eds. [1996], 97.
3.   *Israel! Do You Know?* [1954], 18.

Moses' Second Speech: Reviewing and Explaining the Law

 (Deuteronomy 5–25)

෨෬

REVIEWING THE COMMANDMENTS RECEIVED AT SINAI

Moses' second speech was an account of the events that took place at Sinai, and the instructions that Israel received there, often called the Deuteronomic Law (chapters 12–26). This speech constitutes Moses' explanation and commentary on law, showing with examples how the law was applied in everyday Israelite life.

The Ten Commandments

● **Deuteronomy 5:1–6:3 Moses reiterates the Ten Commandments to the rising generation.** He reminded this younger generation that "the Lord our God made a covenant with *us* in Horeb. The Lord made not this covenant with our fathers, but with *us, even us, who are all of us here alive this day*" (vv. 2–3, emphasis added). So, in a very real sense, though they may not have been physically present at the time (or, if they were, they were little children) "the Lord talked with *you* face to face in the mount out of the midst of the fire" (v. 4, emphasis added). This could also be said of us today in the latter days. The commandments given to Moses are eternal—applicable to all generations and dispensations of time.

After hearing these commandments, the Israelites had voluntarily promised to be obedient to God's laws (v. 27). The Lord had heard this promise and was pleased by their commitment (v. 28), and said: "O that there were such an heart in them, that they would fear me, and keep all my commandments always, that it might be well with them, and with their children for ever!" (v. 29). This reveals much about the loving character of the Lord. He gives us commandments for our own good—that it might be well with us and with our children forever.

Such well-being is contingent upon our keeping the commandments, so the Lord charged the children of Israel, "Ye shall observe to do therefore as the Lord your God hath commanded you:

ye shall not turn aside to the right hand or to the left. Ye shall walk in all the ways which the Lord your God hath commanded you, that ye may live, and that it may be well with you, and that ye may prolong your days in the land which ye shall possess" (vv. 32–33).

Remembering and Loving God

● **Deuteronomy 6:4–5 The Jewish "shema."** This passage, called the "*shema*" ("hear"), is the most important statement of Jewish faith found in the scriptures. The Jews repeat it on special occasions and at the moment of death:

> *4 Hear, O Israel: The Lord our God is one Lord:*
> *5 And thou shalt love the Lord thy God with all thine heart, and with all thy soul, and with all thy might.*

● **Deuteronomy 6:6–9; 11:18–21 The origin of Jewish phylacteries and mazuzahs.**

Moses commanded the Israelites to keep the Lord's commandments in their hearts, to "teach them diligently unto thy children, and ... talk of them when thou sittest in thine house, and when thou walkest by the way, and when thou liest down, and when thou risest up" (vv. 6–7). (This is repeated in Deuteronomy 11:18–21).

He then used figures of speech to indicate how total their commitment to keeping the commandments should be:

— "Thou shalt bind them for a sign upon thine hand" (v. 8). The hand was a symbol of action. Thus, the commandments should be remembered and kept in all that they did each day.

— They shall be as frontlets between thine eyes" (v. 8). Frontlets were strips of parchment on which were written four passages of scripture ... and which were rolled up and inserted into two square leather boxes attached to the forehead or arm with bands of leather. The key word in this passage is "as." The commandments were to be remembered as surely "as if" they had bound them between their eyes or on their arms.

— "Thou shalt write them upon the posts of thy house, and on thy gates" (v. 9). Their homes were to be places where their spiritual heritage and commitment to the commandments were obvious. These *mezuzah*s (Hebrew for "doorpost") were scriptural passages written on parchment and inserted into a tiny, cylindrical box. This was then attached to the door frame, and Jews would touch or kiss it each time they left or entered the home. Often, a mezuzah would contain the shema prayer described above. The doorpost in Jewish culture symbolized the portal through which they moved when interacting with their fellows. Passing through the doorpost and acknowledging the mezuzah (on the way out or in) would serve as a continuous reminder to do the will of God.

Eventually, as Israel fell into apostasy some believed these frontlets and mezuzahs were intended to fend off evil spirits. Thus, the Greeks called them *phylacteries*, which means "safeguards." But they were really intended to be interpreted symbolically and to teach important principles.

President Ezra Taft Benson said: "[People who are] captained by Christ will be consumed in Christ. … Enter their homes, and the pictures on their walls, the books on their shelves, the music in the air, their words and acts reveal them as Christians"[1].

● **Deuteronomy 6:10–12 We are to remember the Lord under all circumstances, even when things are going well for us.** After the Israelites took possession of the "great and goodly cities, which thou buildedst not," with all their "houses full of all good things, which thou filledst not, and wells digged, which thou diggedst not, vineyards and olive trees, which thou plantedst not," they were to be careful not to become complacent (vv. 10–11). When their bellies were full, their houses secure, their flocks and herds expanding, and their silver and gold multiplied, they were to "beware lest thou forget the Lord, which brought thee forth out of the land of Egypt, from the house of bondage" (v. 12).

● **Deuteronomy 8:10–20 We are to remember the Lord under all circumstances, even when things are going well for us.** It would be too easy under such comfortable circumstances to "forget the Lord thy God, which brought thee forth out of the land of Egypt, from the house of bondage; who led thee through that great and terrible wilderness, wherein were fiery serpents, and scorpions, and drought, where there was no water; who brought thee forth water out of the rock of flint; [and] who fed thee in the wilderness with manna" (vv. 14–16), especially since many of these things had happened to their parents, not so much to them. But even this generation might be tempted to say, "My power and the might of mine hand hath gotten me this wealth" (v. 17). The Israelites (and we) need to remember that it is the Lord "that giveth thee power to get wealth," and He does so to keep His covenants "which he sware unto thy fathers" (Abraham, Isaac, and Jacob). And if they (or we) forget the source of our blessings, we will "surely perish" (vv. 18–19).

President Brigham Young said: "The worst fear that I have about [members of this Church] is that they will get rich in this country, forget God and His people, wax fat, and kick themselves out of the Church and go to hell. This people will stand mobbing, robbing, poverty, and all manner of persecution, and be true. But my greater fear for them is that they cannot stand wealth; and yet they have to be tried with riches, for they will become the richest people on this earth."[2]

● **Deuteronomy 6:13, 16; 8:3 These three scriptures were later quoted by the Savior in thwarting temptation.**

— When Satan tempted Him to turn the stones into bread, He countered: "It is written, man shall not live by bread alone, but by every word that proceedeth out of the mouth of God" (Matt. 4:4). "And he humbled thee, and suffered thee to hunger, and fed thee with manna, which thou knewest not, neither did thy fathers know; that he might make thee know that man doth not live by bread only, but by every word that proceedeth out of the mouth of the Lord doth man live" (Deut. 8:3).

— When Satan challenged him to cast Himself down from the pinnacle of the temple, He said: "It is written again, Thou shalt not tempt the Lord thy God" (Matt. 4:7). "Ye shall not tempt the Lord your God, as ye tempted him in Massah" (Deut. 6:16).

— When Satan offered Him the kingdoms of the world, he said: "Get thee hence, Satan: for it is written, Thou shalt worship the Lord thy God, and him only shalt thou serve" (Matt. 4:10). "Thou shalt fear the Lord thy God, and serve him, and shalt swear by his name" (Deut. 6:13).

Remembering Their Blessings and Covenants

● **Deuteronomy 7:6–8 The Lord is a loving God who keeps His promises.** Moses reminded the children of Israel that they were "an holy people unto the Lord thy God … a special people unto himself, above all people that are upon the face of the earth" (v. 6). He did not do this "because ye were more in number than any people; for ye were the fewest of all people" (v. 7). The Lord did it because He "loved you, and because he would keep the oath which he had sworn unto your fathers" (v. 8). From this we can see that the Lord is a loving God and one that keeps His word when He makes promises.

● **Deuteronomy 7:25–26 The idols of other nations were to be destroyed entirely, and neither the idols themselves nor the precious metals on them were to be taken into the homes of the Israelites.** They were commanded to "not desire the silver or gold that is on them, nor take it unto thee, lest thou be snared therein" (v. 25). These idols of false gods were "an abomination to the Lord thy God," which were not to be tolerated in their homes (v. 26). They should "utterly detest it, and … utterly abhor it; for it is a cursed thing" (v. 26). There was good reason for this warning, because, in the end, their love of these false gods destroyed them individually and as a nation.

● **Deuteronomy 8:2–6 Moses reminds them of all the ways in which the Lord had "led thee these forty years in the wilderness."**

— The Lord fed them daily with manna for 40 years, so that they might understand that "man doth not live by bread only, but by every word that proceedeth out of the mouth of the Lord" (v. 3).

— Their clothes "waxed not old upon thee, neither did thy foot swell [their shoes wear out], these forty years" (v. 4). This was needed because they had limited means for producing clothing.

— The Lord had chastened them "as a man chasteneth his son" (v. 5), that they might learn to "keep the commandments of the Lord thy God, to walk in his ways, and to fear him" (v. 6).

● **Deuteronomy 11:1–3, 7–8 Moses reviews the great acts of the Lord seen by the children of Israel in the wilderness.** These included those listed in the scripture above and many more, including but not limited to:

— Hearing their prayers, keeping faith with their forefathers, and delivering them from Egyptian captivity.

— Dividing the Red Sea and saving them from Pharaoh's army.

— Providing daily bread and water.

— Manifesting Himself at Sinai with power and an audible voice.

— Revealing holy and wise laws so they could govern themselves.

— Calling them to be holy people, like Himself.

— Giving them the land of promise, showing that He keeps His covenants.

● **Deuteronomy 8:2 The purpose of their wilderness wanderings was** "to humble thee, and to prove thee, to know what was in thine heart, whether thou wouldest keep his commandments, or no."

— D&C 98:14 He does the same with us today. "I have decreed in my heart," the Lord said to the Saints early in this dispensation, "that I will prove you in all things, whether you will abide in my covenant, even unto death, that you may be found worthy."

● **Deuteronomy 9 "Ye have been rebellious against the Lord from the day that I knew you."** In this chapter, Moses reminds Israel of their many gross sins in the wilderness. He reminded Israel that it was not because of their righteousness that they were now allowed to enter the promised land. In fact, Moses said: "Ye have been rebellious against the Lord from the day that I knew you" (v. 24). The Lord had threatened to destroy them for their idolatry at Mt. Sinai, and would have done so if Moses had not "[fallen] down before the Lord forty days and forty nights, as I fell down at the first" and "prayed … unto the Lord, [saying] destroy not thy people and thine inheritance, which thou hast redeemed through thy greatness, which thou hast brought forth out of Egypt with a mighty hand" (vv. 25–26). He had reminded the Lord of His promises to Abraham, Isaac, and Jacob, and asked Him to "look not unto the stubbornness of this people, nor to their wickedness, nor to their sin" (v. 27), because "they are thy people and thine inheritance, which thou broughtest out by thy mighty power and by thy stretched out arm" (v. 29).

● **Deuteronomy 10:1–5 At Mt.** Sinai, Moses created a new (second) set of tablets and an "ark" [of the covenant] in which to place them. Moses had destroyed the first set of tablets, which contained the higher law. Thus, he "made an ark of shittim wood, and hewed two tables of stone like unto the first, and went up into the mount, having the two tables in mine hand" (v. 3). On these, the Lord wrote "the ten commandments, which the Lord spake unto you in the mount out of the midst of the fire in the day of the assembly" (v. 4). Then Moses "put the tables in the ark which I had made; and there they be, as the Lord commanded me" (v. 5). All of this was done to "save the words of the everlasting covenant of the holy priesthood" that they had received (JST Deut. 10:2).

JAMES J. TISSOT, 1904

● **Deuteronomy 10:12–15 All that God requires of Israel (or us) is to love and serve Him with all our hearts and souls.** Those who think that the God of the Old Testament is a fierce, demanding, and vengeful God have simply not read the Old Testament entirely and in its proper context. Perhaps no other scripture captures the nature of Jehovah better than this one, which asks, "And now, Israel, what doth the Lord thy God require of thee, but to fear the Lord thy God, to walk in all his ways, and to love him, and to serve the Lord thy God with all thy heart and with all thy soul, [and] to keep the commandments of the Lord, and his statutes ... for thy good?" (vv. 12–13). The great Creator God of the universe and of the earth "with all that therein is, ... had a delight in thy fathers to love them, and he chose their seed after them, even you above all people, as it is this day" (vv. 14–15).

- **Deuteronomy 11:7–9 If Israel serves the Lord, they will possess the land of Canaan and prosper.** Many of the blessings contained in this chapter were discussed earlier in association with the blessings listed in chapter 8 (above). Moses reminded them that "your eyes have seen all the great acts of the Lord which he did" and they should therefore "keep all the commandments which I command you this day, that ye may be strong, and go in and possess the land" (vv. 7–8). If they do, the Lord will "prolong your days in the land, which the Lord sware unto your fathers to give unto them and to their seed" (v. 9).

- **Deuteronomy 11:9–15 The blessedness of the land of Canaan.** Moses describes the land as "a land that floweth with milk and honey" (v. 9). Unlike Egypt, where they had to water their crops, "the land, whither ye go to possess it, is a land of hills and valleys, and drinketh water of the rain of heaven" (vv. 10–11). Throughout the year, "the eyes of the Lord thy God are always upon it" (v. 12). If the Israelites will "hearken diligently unto my commandments ... [and] love the Lord your God, and to serve him with all your heart and with all your soul, ... [the Lord] will give you the rain of your land in his due season, the first rain and the latter rain, that thou mayest gather in thy corn, and thy wine, and thine oil. And I will send grass in thy fields for thy cattle, that thou mayest eat and be full" (vv. 13–14).

"The first or former rain [was] that which fell in Judea about November, when they sowed their seed, and this served to moisten and prepare the ground for the vegetation of the seed. The latter rain fell about April, when the corn was well grown up, and served to fill the ears, and render them plump and perfect ... "[3]

- **Deuteronomy 11:18–21 They are to keep the Lord in their thoughts, desires, and actions, and teach His commandments to their children.** They were to keep their covenants constantly in their minds and hearts (*as if* they had them inscribed on frontlets between their eyes), and in everything that they did ("bind[ing] them *[as] a sign* upon [their] hand[s]") (v. 18, emphasis added). This is the same gospel that the Lord Jesus Christ taught during His ministry. Unfortunately, instead of binding these things in their hearts, minds, and actions, they took the command literally and wrote them on frontlets which they tied to their foreheads and hands—substituting the temporal act for the spiritual teaching of Moses.

They were to "teach them [to] your children, speaking of them when thou sittest in thine house, and when thou walkest by the way, when thou liest down, and when thou risest up" (v. 19). They were to be as evident in their homes as if they had written the commandments on their gates and doorposts (v. 20). And if they did these things, "your days may be multiplied, and the days of your children, in the land which the Lord sware unto your fathers to give them, as the days of heaven upon the earth" (v. 21).

- **Deuteronomy 11:22–23, 25 If they are righteous, no nation, though "greater and mightier" will be able to stand before them.** If they will "diligently keep all these commandments which I command you, to do them, to love the Lord your God, to walk in all his ways, and to cleave unto him; then will the Lord drive out all these nations from before you, and ye shall possess greater nations and mightier than yourselves" (vv. 22–23). "There shall no man be able to stand before you: for the Lord your God shall lay the fear of you and the dread of you upon all the land that ye shall tread upon" (v. 25). Thus, as he had done for Enoch's people, the Lord will protect them from their enemies.

- **Deuteronomy 11:24 The extent of the promised land.** The Lord promised them that "every place whereon the soles of your feet shall tread shall be yours: from the wilderness and Lebanon, from the river [Nile], [to] the river Euphrates, even unto the uttermost [Mediterranean] sea shall your coast be."

Elder Mark E. Peterson said:

> The Knox Roman Catholic Bible gives this rendering of that descriptive passage: "All shall be yours, wherever your feet shall tread; the desert, and Lebanon, and the western sea and the great river Euphrates shall be your frontiers."
>
> The Jerusalem Bible reads: "Wherever the sole of your foot treads shall be yours; your territory shall stretch from the wilderness [desert] and from Lebanon, from the river, the river Euphrates, to the western sea."
>
> That language is almost identical to the modern render- ing in the Torah.
>
> The Complete Bible, an American Translation, by Goodspeed and Smith, reads: "Every place on which the sole of your foot treads shall be yours; the region from the desert as far as Lebanon, from the River, the river Euphrates, as far as the Western Sea shall be your domain."[4]

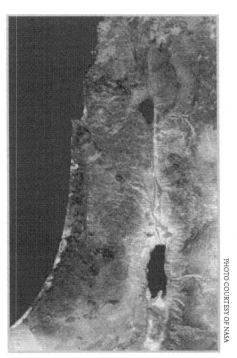

Satellite photo of extent of the promised land of Israel

The Moffatt Bible, translated in modern terms, reads: "Every foot of ground you tread shall be your own, and your frontier shall stretch from the desert to Lebanon, from the River, the river Euphrates, to the Mediterranean Sea."[5]

There can be no doubt, then, as to the extent of the area promised to Abraham and his descendants, the Twelve Tribes. It went from the Nile to the Euphrates and from the Arabian desert to the Mediterranean Sea, and was a rich land, the best part of the Fertile Crescent.

How rich was it? Would the Lord give a dry and barren land to Abraham? Would he call it a good land if it were not so? And what about minerals, so necessary to a civilized way of life?

The scripture speaks for itself:

> *For the Lord thy God bringeth thee into a good land, a land of brooks of water, of fountains*
> *and depths that spring out of valleys and hills;*
> *A land of wheat, and barley, and vines, and fig trees, and pomegranates; a land of oil olive, and*
> *honey;*
> *A land wherein thou shalt eat bread without scarceness, and thou shalt not lack any thing in it;*
> *a land whose stones are iron, and out of whose hills thou mayest dig brass. (Deut. 8:7–9).*

What more could they ask? The modernized Torah reads:

For the Lord your God is bringing you into a good land, a land with streams and springs and lakes issuing from plain and hill, a land of wheat and barley, of vines, figs, and pomegranates, a land of olive oil and of honey; a land where you may eat food without stint, where you will lack nothing; a land whose rocks are iron and from whose hills you can mine copper. When you have eaten your fill, give thanks to the Lord your God for the good land which He has given you. (Deut. 8:7–10).

And the Jerusalem Bible reads:

But Yahweh your God is bringing you into a prosperous land, a land of streams and springs, of waters that well up from the deep in valleys and hills, a land of wheat and barley, of vines, of figs, of pomegranates, a land of olives, of oil, of honey, a land where you will eat bread without stint, where you will want nothing, a land where the stones are of iron, where the hills may be quarried for copper. You will eat and have all you want and you will bless Yahweh your God in the rich land he has given you.

Then it was obviously a rich land, rich in water, agriculture, copper, iron, and all else they would need. So when the Lord said it was a good land, he meant just that.

Not even irrigation was needed in Palestine at that time, [see Deut. 11:10–12 above].

…

But what about the milk and honey with which it would flow? Much has been said about the honey, but what of the milk?

When the Israelites scanned the land, "behold the place was a place for cattle." (Num. 32:1). And when the scouts sent out by Moses returned and reported to him,

they said: "We came unto the land whither thou sentest us, and surely it floweth with milk and honey; and this is the fruit of it," showing him what they had brought. (Num. 13:27. See also Deut. 1:35; 3:25).

But as is always the case, the Lord expected the Israelites to be worthy of such a good place in which to live; and he told them frankly that if they failed to keep the commandments, he would withdraw his blessings from the land.

The Canaanites in the land were a wicked and filthy people, and the Lord decreed that they should be swept off the face of this good land, even as were the Sodomites. According to the best references available, they too were sex perverts, and were so disgusting before the Lord that he would no longer allow them to live there. (Deut. 9:4; 12:1; Lev. 18:24).

He would not destroy them by fire as he did the Sodomites, but he would eliminate them by warfare so that his Twelve Tribes could have the land with a minimum of damage.[6]

Just how depraved were the Canaanites? Rushdoony, a noted Bible scholar gave some details of their excesses: "The Canaanites against whom Israel waged war were under judicial sentence of death by God. They were spiritually and morally degenerate. Virtually every kind of perversion was a religious act: and large classes of sacred male and female prostitutes were a routine part of the holy places. Thus, God ordered all the Canaanites to be killed (Deut. 2:34; 3:6; 20:16–18; Josh. 11:14), both because they were under God's death sentence, and to avoid the contamination of Israel"[7].

Landmarks to Remind Them of Their Choices

● **Deuteronomy 11:26–29 Landmarks are established to remind them of their options and their consequences.** If the Israelites obeyed the commandments of the Lord they would receive a blessing; if they were not obedient they would be cursed (vv. 26–28). To remind them of their choices, the Lord commanded them to designate Mt. Gerizim a mount of blessing and Mt. Ebal a mount of cursing (v. 29).

"The two mountains mentioned were selected … because they were opposite to one another, and stood, each about 2500 feet high, in the very centre of the land not only from west to east, but also from north to south. (Keil and Delitzsch, *Commentary on the Old Testament*, 10 vols. [1996], 1:3:349–350).

This place was also the place of Abraham's first altar in the land of promise, and it was the place of Jacob's first camp upon arriving back from Haran, where he also built an altar.

The area there was called the "plains of Moreh." Moreh means "director, teacher," just as torah means "direction, or doctrine." Both are from yareb, "to point out, give guidance." It was thus a place where the Lord gave guidance and direction to Abraham, Jacob, and their descendants.

Mt. Gerizim on the left and Mt. Ebal on the right

The Utter Destruction of Wicked People and Their Practices

● **Deuteronomy 12:1–7 Upon entering the promised land, Israel was to destroy the Canaanite places of worship and erect altars to Jehovah** at designated spots. The idol worshipers had established places of worship "upon the high mountains, and upon the hills, and under every green tree" (v. 2). In these groves, they would engage in impure sexual practices in celebration of fertility. The Lord commanded the Israelites to "overthrow their altars, and break their pillars, and burn their groves with fire; and ye shall hew down the graven images of their gods, and destroy the names of them out of that place" (v. 3). They were never to worship the Lord in this way (v. 4).

Instead, they were to establish holy altars in places "which the Lord your God shall choose … to put his name there," and only to these sacred place should they come to worship (v. 5). "And thither ye shall bring your burnt offerings, and your sacrifices, and your tithes, and heave offerings of your hand, and your vows, and your freewill offerings, and the firstlings of your herds and of your flocks" (v. 6). They should by this means "rejoice in all that … the Lord thy God hath blessed thee" (v. 7).

● **Deuteronomy 16:21–22 They are not to plant groves nor erect idols near their places of worship.** This would prevent them from becoming shrines of fertility cults, which was the cultural norm among the Canaanites.

● **Deuteronomy 12:15–28 They may eat the meat of their offerings, but not the blood, and not things that had been given to the Lord as a tithe.** They were to pour out the blood of slain animals "upon the earth as water" (v. 16) because "the blood is the life; and thou mayest not eat the life with the flesh" (v. 23). There were reasons of health for this prohibition, but also a respect for the life of animals. These things they were to do in their households as they desired, but "only … holy things which thou hast, and thy vows, thou shalt take, and go unto the place which the Lord shall choose … [for] burnt offerings, the flesh and the blood, upon the altar of the Lord thy God" (vv. 26–27).

In these cases, "the blood of thy sacrifices [was] poured out upon the altar" [thus consuming it in the fire], and then they were allowed to "eat the flesh" (v. 27). Thus, except in certain types of offerings where the entire offering was to be consumed in the fire, the priests and the offerer ate the cooked meat that came off the altar. This is what the Lord meant when he said in verse 7: "And there ye shall eat before the Lord your God, and ye shall rejoice in all that ye put your hand unto, ye and your households, wherein the Lord thy God hath blessed thee." Sacrificial meals were meals of thanksgiving unto God.

- **Deuteronomy 12:29–32 The nations they were driving from the promised land were guilty of every abomination, including sacrificing their children to their gods.** They were not to permit themselves to even be curious, saying, "How did these nations serve their gods?" or to imitate them in any way (v. 30).

Living children sacrificed to the white-hot arms of Molech

The Canaanites committed "every abomination to the Lord, which he hateth … for even their sons and their daughters they have burnt in the fire to their gods" (v. 31). The Israelites were to keep the Lord's commandments and "not add thereto, nor diminish from it" (v. 32).

- **Deuteronomy 13:1–5 False prophets are to be detected and destroyed.** "If there arise among you a prophet, or a dreamer of dreams, and giveth thee a sign or a wonder, and the sign or the wonder come to pass, whereof he spake unto thee, saying, Let us go after other gods, which thou hast not known, and let us serve them," they were not to believe nor follow him (vv. 1–2). Any such false prophet "shall be put to death; because he hath spoken to turn you away from the Lord your God" (v. 5). "So shalt thou put the evil away from the midst of thee" (v. 5).

- **Deuteronomy 13:6–11 Family members who apostatize are also to be put to death.** Whether it be "thy brother, the son of thy mother, or thy son, or thy daughter, or the wife of thy bosom, or thy friend, which is as thine own soul," if they "entice thee secretly, saying, Let us go and serve other gods, which thou hast not known … Namely, of the gods of the people which are round about you, nigh unto thee, or far off from thee, … Thou shalt not consent unto him, nor hearken unto him; neither shall thine eye pity him, neither shalt thou spare, neither shalt thou conceal him" (vv. 6–8). "But thou shalt surely kill him [and] thine hand shall be first upon him to put him to death, and afterwards the hand of all the people. And thou shalt stone him with stones, that he die; because he hath sought to thrust thee away from the Lord thy God" (vv. 9–10).

By our modern standards, this may seem extremely harsh. But we must ever keep in mind the vicious and sensual nature of the practices of these idolaters. If tolerated, they would corrupt the entire Israelite nation and make them guilty of the same abominable deeds as those perpetrated by the nations they were driving out of Canaan. Indeed, in hindsight, we can see that because they did not take these measures seriously, they were eventually corrupted and destroyed for embracing these practices. By the Lord's command, "All Israel shall hear, and fear, and shall do no more any such wickedness as this is among you" (v. 11).

- **Deuteronomy 13:12–17 They are to utterly destroy cities that practice these abominations, including all people, animals, and possessions.** Even if some Israelite cities were among those participating in these abominations, "Thou shalt surely smite the inhabitants of that city with the edge of the sword, destroying it utterly, and all that is therein, and the cattle thereof, with the edge of the sword" (v. 15). Then, when the battle is over, "thou shalt gather all the spoil of it into the midst of the street thereof, and shalt burn

The Canaanites were to be utterly destroyed

  with fire the city, and all the spoil thereof every whit, for the Lord thy God: and it shall be an heap for ever; it shall not be built again" (v. 16). They were not to keep any "cursed thing" as a spoil. "Cursed thing" refers to anything sacrificed to idols or made to represent an idol or made to be used in the worship of idols. Cursed things were to be avoided by the Israelites altogether.

- **Deuteronomy 17:1 Their animal sacrifices are to be "without blemish."** As symbols of the ultimate sacrifice—Jesus Christ—these sacrificial animals, whether cattle or sheep, were to be without "blemish, or any evilfavouredness." Making such inappropriate offerings was considered an abomination by the Lord, as Cain learned to his great anger thousands of years before this time.

- **Deuteronomy 17:2–7 Worshipers of false gods are to be put to death.** Any Israelite—man or woman—who left the true worship of the God of Abraham and went off to serve and worship other gods—"either the sun, or moon, or any of the host of heaven"—were, upon conviction for their crimes, to be stoned to death (vv. 2–5). But such accusations would have to be substantiated by two or three witnesses; a single witness is not sufficient for conviction. Then, after conviction, the witnesses themselves were to be the first to cast stones, "and afterward the hands of all the people" (vv. 6–7).

- **Deuteronomy 18:9–14 The evil practices of Israel's neighbors are forbidden.** Such things as "mak[ing a] son or his daughter to pass through the fire, or … us[ing] divination, or [being] an observer of times, or an enchanter, or a witch, or a charmer, or a consulter with familiar spirits, or a wizard, or a necromancer" were all forbidden practices in Israel (vv. 9–11). These abominable practices were the very reason why the Lord was destroying them and driving them out of the promised land (v. 12). But the children of Israel were commanded to be "perfect with the Lord thy God" and not suffer these evil practices to exist among them (vv. 13–14).

- **Deuteronomy 18:20–22 The test for a true prophet of God.** If a man purported to be a prophet—either for Jehovah or for any other god—who was not, in fact, called by the Lord to prophesy, "that prophet shall die" (v. 20). So, how would they know if a prophecy did not come from the Lord? (v. 21). It was as simple as the following test: "When a prophet speaketh in the name of the Lord, if the thing follow not, nor come to pass, that is the thing which the Lord hath not spoken, but the prophet hath spoken it presumptuously: thou shalt not be afraid of him" (v. 22).

President Joseph Fielding Smith said: "When is a prophet a prophet? Whenever he speaks under the inspiration and influence of the Holy Ghost … When prophets write and speak on the principles of the gospel, they should have the guidance of the Spirit. If they do, then all that they say will be in harmony with the revealed word. If they are in harmony then we know that they have not spoken presumptuously. Should a man speak or write, and what he says is in conflict with the standards which are accepted, with the revelations the Lord has given, then we may reject what he has said, no matter who he is"[8].

LIVING THEIR RELIGION

- **Deuteronomy 14 Israel was to become a holy people by observing dietary laws and the law of tithing (JST Deuteronomy 14:21).** Verses 22–29 explain that the tithe, or tenth of all increase, was to be contributed "in kind"; but if the contributor lived too far from the central place for making the contribution, he could sell the material and carry the money instead to the place of offering. There, he could convert it back into whatever kinds of goods he desired to use in making his in-kind contribution.

Celebrating the Jubilee year

- **Deuteronomy 15:1–5 "The Lord's release."** Every 7 years Israelites were to be released from their debts (but not strangers). "Of a foreigner thou mayest exact it again: but that which is thine with thy brother thine hand shall release" (v. 3). This would not be required when the time came that "there shall be no poor among you" (when they become a Zion people), which could happen for them. "The Lord shall greatly bless thee in the land which the Lord thy God giveth thee for an inheritance to possess it" (v. 4). But this would be possible "only if thou carefully hearken unto the voice of the Lord thy God, to observe to do all these commandments which I command thee this day" (v. 5).

- **Deuteronomy 15:6 They may lend to other nations but they may not borrow from them.** By this rule they "shalt reign over many nations, but they shall not reign over thee."

- **Deuteronomy 15:7–11 Generosity, not criticism, is to be manifest by the rich toward the poor.** Just as King Benjamin taught the Nephites, "if there be among you a poor man of one of thy brethren … thou shalt not harden thine heart, nor shut thine hand from thy poor brother" (v. 7). Rather they were commanded to "open thine hand wide unto him, and … lend him sufficient for his need, in that which he wanteth" (v. 8). They were not to withhold help to the poor just because the 7th year was nigh (v. 9). "Thou shalt surely give him, and thine heart shall not be grieved when thou givest unto him," said the Lord, who promised in return to " bless thee in all thy works, and in all that thou puttest thine hand unto" (v. 10). This is the Lord's "own way" (D&C 104:16)—He blesses the rich so that they may bless the poor—and if they fail to do so they will be damned (D&C 104:18). The Lord warned the Israelites that "the poor shall never cease out of the land," and that they were always required to "open thine hand wide unto thy brother, to thy poor, and to thy needy, in thy land" (v. 11).

- **Deuteronomy 15:12–18 Indentured Hebrew servants (slaves) are also to be set free every 7th year.** Thus indenturedness—working off a debt through labor, but not slavery—was permitted for a limited amount of time. "And when thou sendest him out free from thee, thou shalt not let him go away empty: Thou shalt furnish him liberally out of thy flock, and out of thy floor, and out of thy winepress: of that wherewith the Lord thy God hath blessed thee thou shalt give unto him" (vv. 13–14). They were to always remember that they, themselves, had been slaves in Egypt and the Lord set them free (v. 15). Now, if a servant desired to stay with them after seven years "because he is well with thee … [and] loveth thee and thine house," that was permitted—but only by the servant's choice (vv. 16–17). They were not to consider this a hard requirement, since they had received more than six years of service (twice the amount of a hired servant), and "the Lord thy God shall bless thee in all that thou doest" if they kept this commandment (v. 18).

- **Deuteronomy 15:19–23 The firstlings of the flocks are to be sanctified to the Lord.** The were not to work these animals, nor shear them, because they belonged to the Lord (v. 19). After sacrificing them, they could enjoy a ceremonial meal featuring some of the sacrifice's meat, if they wished (v. 20). A portion of the meat was also given to the priests for their sustenance. But if the animal was "lame, or blind, or have any ill blemish, thou shalt not sacrifice it unto the Lord thy God" (v. 21). They could keep such animals and eat them at home without condemnation (v. 22). But in no case were they to eat the blood of any animal; they were to "pour it upon the ground as water" (v. 23).

- **Deuteronomy 16:1–17 The feasts of Israel—Passover, Unleavened Bread, Weeks, and Tabernacles—were to be rigorously observed by all Hebrew males, but they were actually family affairs.** Moses instructed the people not to "appear before the Lord empty" (at the Tabernacle) on such occasions, but to "rejoice before the Lord" (vv. 2, 11, 16). The four most important feasts (or holidays) for Israel were: the feast of Passover, the feast of Pentecost, the Day of Atonement, and the feast of Tabernacles. The feasts of Passover, Pentecost, and Tabernacles were joyous events tied to important historical events. The Day of Atonement was a time of contrition and repentance for all of Israel. These holy days were set down for Israel by the Lord. During these days every male Israelite was commanded to appear "before the Lord thy God" (meaning at the tabernacle, or, later, the temple) as a symbol of his allegiance to Jehovah (Deuteronomy 16:16; Leviticus 16:29–34). In this way, Israel was reminded four times a year to pause and reflect on their blessings from God. At the same time, each feast or holy day symbolized one or more aspects of the mission of Jesus Christ.

Regular Jewish celebrations included the following:

Sabbath	Lk 4:16; 6:6; 23:56	Weekly
Passover	John 18:39	Spring
Feast of Pentecost	Acts 20:16	50 days after Passover
Feast of Tabernacles	John 7:2	Fall
Day of Atonement and fasting	Acts 2:1; 27:9	Fall
Hanukkah or Feast of Dedication	John 10:22	Winter
New moon	Col 2:16	Monthly

| Sabbath Year | Leviticus 25 | Every 7 years |
| Jubilee Year | Leviticus 25 | Every 50 years |

—Adapted from Charting the New Testament, *© 2002 Welch, Hall, FARMS Chart 1-5*

John Tvedtnes said, "In 1972, I mentioned to President and Sister Harold B. Lee (then on a visit to Jerusalem) that our April and October conferences corresponded with the timing of the ancient festivals of Passover and Tabernacles. Sister Lee noted that she recalled, as a little girl, that the Salt Lake Tabernacle was always decorated with tree branches during October Conference. I have been yet unable to confirm this from other sources"[9]

"Israel's seasonal reminders came in the triennial festivals of Passover (Pesah), Weeks (Shavuot, or Pentecost), and Tabernacles (Sukkoth). These were held in the spring and fall—naturally timed with the agrarian cycle of planting and harvesting (Deut. 16; see also Deut. 11:13-17). Not only was the timing significant, but the activities themselves "commemorated the great events of Israel's history, the occasions when in an unmistakable way God had stepped in to deliver his people"[10]. Neusner observes that these three festivals typify three roles of the Messiah. 'Passover is the festival of redemption and points toward the Torah-revelation of the Feast of Weeks; the harvest festival in the autumn celebrates not only creation, but especially, redemption'[11]."

THE ROLE OF PRIESTS AND LEVITES

● **Deuteronomy 17:8–13 Difficult disputes were to be brought before the priests for judgment.** During their sojourn in the wilderness, the Israelites brought their difficult matters to Moses for judgment. He now instructed them, "If there arise a matter too hard for thee in judgment … then shalt thou arise, and get thee up into the place which the Lord thy God shall choose; And thou shalt come unto the priests the Levites, and unto the judge that shall be in those days, and enquire; and they shall shew thee the sentence of judgment: And thou shalt do according to the sentence, which they of that place which the Lord shall choose shall shew thee; and thou shalt observe to do according to all that they inform thee" (vv. 8–10). They were not to vary from the sentence or instruction given "to the right hand, nor to the left," and any man who did so "shall die" so that they can "put away the evil from Israel" (vv. 11–12).

Levite priests sat in judgment

- **Deuteronomy 18:1–8 Priests and Levites were to be supported by all other Israelites.** Because "the priests the Levites, and all the tribe of Levi, shall have no part nor inheritance with Israel: they shall eat the offerings of the Lord made by fire" (v. 1). Thus the meat of sacrifices, part of which was consumed by the offerer, would sustain the Levite priests who spent their full time administering sacrificial ordinances at the tabernacle or temple. Their portion was "the shoulder, and the two cheeks, and the maw [stomach]" (v. 3). They were also to receive "the firstfruit also of thy corn, of thy wine, and of thine oil, and the first of the fleece of thy sheep, shalt thou give him" (v. 4). Thus, these non-animal offerings were a form of tithing or payment-in-kind that would also benefit the Levites.

Levite   High Priest   Priest

STORY OF THE BIBLE, #60, P147, 1873, 1877, 1884

If a Levite moved from one place to another, when he began working in his new place of residence the existing Levites would have to take him in and share with him (vv. 6–7). Levites could also receive unofficial payment for services—not a requirement but kind of like a tip from a willing offerer—which is referred to here as "patrimony" (v. 8).

- **Deuteronomy 18:15–19 A prophet "like unto Moses" (Christ) will rise up, and Israel is commanded to obey him in all things (3 Nephi 20:23).** Notice that the word "Prophet" is capitalized in this case. The Lord said unto Moses, "I will raise them up a Prophet from among their brethren, like unto thee, and will put my words in his mouth; and he shall speak unto them all that I shall command him. And it shall come to pass, that whosoever will not hearken unto my words which he shall speak in my name, I will require it of him" (vv. 18–19).

RULES OF GOVERNMENT

Rules for Kings

- **Deuteronomy 17:14–20 Counsel for future kings.** Moses here prophesies that after they have settled in the holy land they will ask for "a king … like as all the nations that are about" (v. 14). Although this is not a wise thing to do, nevertheless they are permitted to appoint a king who meets the Lord's standards.

  — He shall be chosen by the Lord (v. 15).

  — He shall be chosen from among the Israelites, not a foreigner (v. 15).

— He shall not seek to increase his power ("horses") (v. 16). In the ancient Middle East, horses were used primarily in warfare. A king who sought to increase his military power will have forgotten the need to trust in the strength and protection of God.

— He shall not seek to return the people to Egypt (v. 16).

— He shall not multiply wives to himself (v. 17). Kings had multiple wives for political as well as personal reasons. Foreign wives risked an enticement to false gods and were forbidden, "that his heart turn not away." This situation led to Solomon's fall from God's favor (1 Kings 11:4).

— He shall not seek to multiply his wealth (v. 17), which leads to oppression and unjust taxation of the people.

— His basis for rule was to be the law of God. He must obtain a copy of the book of the law and "read therein all the days of his life: that he may learn to fear the Lord his God, to keep all the words of this law and these statutes, to do them" (v. 19).

— He shalt not become arrogant, thinking he is better than the people (v. 20).

— By doing these things he will lengthen the lives of himself and his people (v. 20).

Rules of Civil Government

● **Deuteronomy 19:1–10 Moses established three cities of refuge.** See Deuteronomy 4:41–43 above for an explanation of the purpose of these cities. In this case, Moses is talking about what to do when a murderer flees to a city of refuge. People guilty of manslaughter or accidental death might find refuge there until their case can be heard. This "Lest the avenger of the blood pursue the slayer, while his heart is hot, and overtake him, because the way is long, and slay him; whereas he was not worthy of death" because the act was not intended—he "hated him not in time past" (v. 6).

● **Deuteronomy 19:11–13 Murderers may not be protected in cities of refuge.** If a murderer flees to a city of refuge "the elders of [the] city shall send and fetch him thence, and deliver him into the hand of the avenger of blood, that he may die" (v. 12). Murderers were not to be pitied, they were to be executed in order to "put away the guilt of innocent blood from Israel, that it may go well with thee" (v. 13).

● **Deuteronomy 19:14 Respect for people's property rights.** "Thou shalt not remove thy neighbour's landmark," Moses said. When a man inherits property he should honor the boundaries which "they of old time have set."

Intentional murder was not forgiven

- **Deuteronomy 19:15 The law of witnesses—2 or 3 are required.** As mentioned earlier in Deuteronomy 17:2–7, accusations have to be substantiated by two or three witnesses; a single witness is not sufficient for conviction.

- **Deuteronomy 19:18–20 False witnesses are to be punished for the crime they falsely accused another of committing.** There is consummate justice in this principle. If "the witness be a false witness, and hath testified falsely against his brother; Then shall ye do unto him, as he had thought to have done unto his brother: so shalt thou put the evil away from among you" (vv. 18–19). Falsely accuse a man of murder and you will be put to death yourself just as he would have been if convicted, and so on with every conceivable crime and punishment. Thus, people will fear to bear false witness and "commit no more any such evil among you" (v. 20).

- **Deuteronomy 19:21 "An eye for an eye, a tooth for a tooth."** This is one of the most famous of the laws of Moses and also one of the most misunderstood. It does not suggest that we should avenge every wrong done to us with equal actions in return. It is speaking specifically of the punishment for false witnesses (see above) and the fact that they should be punished in precisely the same way that the falsely accused would have been if their false witness had succeeded in deceiving the judges. Thus, in the case of a false witness there should be no pity; "but life shall go for life, eye for eye, tooth for tooth, hand for hand, foot for foot."

Rules of Military Law

- **Deuteronomy 20 The rules of miliary law in Israel.** Rushdoony, a noted Bible scholar gave some excellent insights into the principles in the Mosaic code related to warfare.[12] The following is an adaptive summary of his much more extensive discussion.

High priest addresses Israelite troops

1. Wars are to be fought only in defense of justice, the suppression of evil, and in defense of the homeland against an enemy.

2. Since warfare against evil is godly and serves God's task of restoration, God promised to protect His warriors if they maintained their faith and obedience.

3. All able-bodied men 20 years old and up were eligible for military service (Num. 1:2, 3, 18, 20, 45; 26:2, 3), though it was still a selective service (Num. 31:3–6) and not every man was required to serve in any particular war. Their eligibility was thus established only to assert their availability in an extreme crisis.

4. Exemption from military service was granted for various circumstances:

    (a) Those who had built a new house and had not dedicated nor enjoyed it.

    (b) Those who had planted a vineyard and had not yet enjoyed its fruit.

(c) Newlywed men, because they would have a divided mind in battle. "He shall be free at home one year, and shall cheer up his wife [whom] he hath taken" (Deut. 24:5).

(d) Those who were "fearful and faint-hearted," because they would be dangerous to army morale (Deut. 20:5–9). The purpose of an army should be to fight God's battles without fear (Deut. 20:1–4).

(e) Levites were also exempt from military service. They very often fought anyway, but they were exempt from a draft.

"From these exemptions, a general principle appears: the family has a priority over warfare. The young bridegroom cannot serve; the new home must come first. The new farmer similarly gains exemption. Important as defense is, the continuity of life and godly reconstruction are more important."

5. Cleanliness in the camp is required (Deut. 23:9–14). Their latrines should be located outside the camp, and a spade "to cover up your filth" (Deut. 23:13, Moffatt) so that the Lord may not see anything indecent "and turn away from you" (Deut. 23:14, Moffatt).

6. Prior to a declaration of war or an attack, an offer of peace must be extended to the enemy. The offer of peace cannot be an offer to compromise. The cause, if it be just, must be maintained (Deut. 20:9–14). A "sneak attack" after a declaration, in Gideon's manner, is legitimate because hostilities are already in progress. But, prior to a declaration of war, an attempt to negotiate with honor is required.

7. Some enemies were to be annihilated. The Canaanites against whom Israel waged war were under judicial sentence of death by God. They were spiritually and morally degenerate. Virtually every kind of perversion was a religious act: and large classes of sacred male and female prostitutes were a routine part of the holy places. Thus, God ordered all the Canaanites to be killed (Deut. 2:34; 3:6; 20:16–18; Josh. 11:14), both because they were under God's death sentence, and to avoid contamination of Israel.

8. Since the normal purpose of warfare is defensive, Israel was forbidden to use more than a limited number of horses (Deut. 17:16)—the offensive weapon of ancient warfare.

9. No "scorched earth" tactics were to be used—thus, these rules regarding trees when sieging a city. When "besieg[ing] a city a long time … thou shalt not destroy the trees thereof by forcing an axe against them: for thou mayest eat of them, [but] thou shalt not cut them down … to employ them in the siege" (Deut. 20:19). In other words, war is not to be waged against the earth, but against men. Life must go on. The fruit tree and vineyard are an inheritance and a heritage for the future. They are not to be destroyed.

10. The laws of booty provide a reward to soldiers (Num. 31:21–31, 42; Deut. 20:14). This provides a legal ground for soldiers' pay and also a pension, a reward for their services. Also, war indemnity was an aspect of the penalty imposed on an enemy (2 Kings 3:4) as penalty for their offense, and to defray the costs of the war.

Other Civil Laws and Practices

● **Deuteronomy 21:1–9 Unsolved murders were to be expiated through a special blood sacrifice.** The leaders of the city where the murder occurred were to take an un- used (fresh and healthy) heifer into a location that is not used for cultivation of any kind and cut off the head of the heifer there (vv. 1–4). The Levites were to be present at this sacrifice, and "all the elders of that city, that are next unto the slain man, shall wash their hands over the heifer that is beheaded in the valley" while they say, "Our hands have not shed this blood, neither have our eyes seen it" (vv. 5–7). They were then to ask the Lord to be merciful and "lay not innocent blood unto thy people of Israel's charge," and then the responsibility for the murder "shall be forgiven them" (v. 8) and they will thus "put away the guilt of innocent blood from among you" (v. 9).

● **Deuteronomy 21:15–17 Laws concerning inheritances for children.** The Israelites were not to show favoritism toward one child over another. The very strict rules of primogeniture were to be followed (see following).

The Rules of Primogeniture
(Rules of Inheritance in Israel)

1. All sons are entitled to an equal portion of inheritance to begin with.

2. The oldest son then receives an extra portion (to care for the family).

3. The oldest son of each wife in turn has birthright before all others.

4. Thereafter, the order of birth prevails, according to mother.

5. Daughters inherit through their husbands' families only.

6. Children of handmaidens are considered children of the owning wife.

7. Natural-born children inherit before children of a wife's handmaiden.

8. For Abraham's descendants, righteousness was also required for the birthright.

9. Marrying outside the pure blood of the patriarchs disqualified all children of such wives from birthright, though not from inheritance.

10. The right of patriarchal presidency was granted only on condition of the keeping of all these requirements.

● **Deuteronomy 21:18–20 Rules of dealing with rebellious and extremely wayward children.** If a man had "a stubborn and rebellious son, which will not obey the voice of his father, or the voice of his mother, and … when they have chastened him, will not hearken unto them," he can bring that son before the elders of the city and testify concerning him—"This our son is stubborn and rebellious, he will not obey our voice; he is a glutton, and a drunkard" (vv. 18–20). Then "all the men of his city shall stone him with stones, that he die: so shalt thou put evil away from among you; and all Israel shall hear, and fear" (v. 21).

Remember that this is only <u>one</u> option (and the most extreme one) open to the father. He must first attempt to "chasten" the child and redeem him from his wayward ways (v. 18). He is not forced to bring the child to be stoned, but has that option if the child is utterly unredeemable. Who better to know this than the father and mother? And what righteous parent would seek the death of their child if the sins were not monumental and unrelenting?

STORY OF THE BIBLE, #58, p143, 1873, 1877, 1884

Death by stoning

● **Deuteronomy 21:22–23 Executed criminals' bodies were not to be left hanging overnight.** "If a man have committed a sin worthy of death, and he be … put to death, and thou hang him on a tree: His body shall not remain all night upon the tree, but thou shalt … bury him that day … that thy land be not defiled, which the Lord thy God giveth thee for an inheritance." This is the commandment which caused such concern in Jesus' day about removing His body from the cross before the Sabbath day began.

● **Deuteronomy 22:1–12 A series of miscellaneous rules.** These would be similar to our present-day misdemeanors and neighborhood maintenance requirements. Some were for obvious practical purposes; some reminded Israel of principles of purity.

— Laws against keeping lost animals or possessions (vv. 1–3).

— Laws against passing by a brother or his animal who needs help (v. 4).

— Laws against transvestite behavior (v. 5).

— Laws against robbing a nest or killing its occupant (vv. 6–7).

— Laws against failing to protect against hazards at home (v. 8).

— Laws against sowing mixed seeds (v. 9).

— Laws against plowing with a mixed team of animals (v. 10).

— Laws against mixing fabrics in a garment (v. 11).

— Laws requiring "fringes" on garments as reminders of covenants (v. 12).

● **Deuteronomy 22:13–29 Punishments for various forms of sexual misdeeds.** If a man violated a woman the punishment depended on the circumstances. Keil and Delitzsch provided the following summary in their *Commentary on the Old Testament*,[13] which is edited here for purposes of brevity:

— If a man violates a woman who is betrothed (vv. 23–27):

   vv. 23–24   If a betrothed virgin allowed a man who was not her bridegroom to have intercourse with her, they were both to be led out to the gate of the town, and stoned to death—the woman because she consented to it, and the man because he humiliated a "neighbour's wife." Thus, a betrothed woman was considered on a par with a married woman.

vv. 25–27   If a man violated a betrothed woman in the field [raped her], the man alone was to die, and nothing was to be done to the woman. In the open field, if the girl had called for help no one could have helped her. It was therefore considered a forcible rape.

- **If a man violates a woman who is not betrothed (vv . 28–29):**

  vv. 28–29   If a virgin was not betrothed, and a man had sex with her, and they were found [discovered or convicted of the deed], the man was to pay the father of the woman 50 shekels of silver for the reproach brought upon him and his house, and to marry the girl whom he had humbled, without ever being able to divorce her. It is assumed as self-evident here, that the father had the right to refuse to let him marry the woman.

- **Deuteronomy 22:30 Prohibition against incest.** To "discover his father's skirt" is a Hebrew euphemism similar to "uncovering one's nakedness" and means to have sexual relations. Thus, this prohibition probably referred to incest with a stepmother. The law prohibited all forms of incest (Leviticus 18), and Moses is illustrating one of them here.

- **Deuteronomy 23:1–8 The rights of citizenship in Israel.** Edom and Egypt warred openly with Israel and tried to destroy them, but Ammon and Moab worked to pervert Israel [Numbers 22:2–5; 31:16], after Israel showed them forbearance [Deut. 2:9, 19, 29]. Thus, Ammonites and Moabites were denied citizenship in Israel. One notable exception was Ruth, a Moabite and an ancestor of the Lord Jesus Christ.

- **Deuteronomy 23:9–14 Laws concerning cleanliness of a military camp.** See rule 5 in the discussion of the rules of military law above.

- **Deuteronomy 23:15–25 Another miscellaneous list of laws.**

  — Providing sanctuary for refugees (vv. 15–16).

  — Forbidding male and female prostitution, or the use of money thus obtained to make an offering unto the Lord (vv. 17–18).

  — Forbidding usury (lending with interest) to any Israelite for any purpose [victuals are food]. Usury to people of other nations is allowed (vv. 19–20).

  — Forbidding failure to pay vows (v. 21). Refusing to make a vow is not a sin (v. 22), but every vow that is made must be kept (vv. 22–23).

  — Forbidding illicit harvesting of a neighbor's crops (vv. 24–25).

- **Deuteronomy 24:1–22 More miscellaneous laws explained.**

— Divorce (vv. 1–4). A man can divorce a woman who has become "unclean" [adulterous or spiritually wavering] by giving her a "bill of divorcement." The purpose of a bill of divorcement was that a woman divorced by her husband could remarry if she desired. The restriction here is that one who has divorced his wife may not later remarry her, thus forbidding frivolous divorces.

— Military exemption for newlyweds (v. 5). See rule 4c of Israelite military law above.

— Pledges (collateral) should not be taken of a man's means of making a living (v. 6).

— Stealing is a capital crime (v. 7).

— Leprosy requires quarantine and the intervention of Levite priests (vv. 8–9).

— Laws about lending (vv. 10–13). Going into a man's house or property to retrieve pledges is forbidden. So, too, is taking a pledge from a poor man.

— Laws about oppressing servants, whether Israelite or not (vv. 14–15). They are to be paid promptly for their services every day.

— Laws about personal responsibility (v. 16). Individuals shall be punished only for their own sins and not the sins of their fathers.

— Laws about fairness in dealings with others (vv. 17–18). They were not to "pervert judgment" against the most vulnerable among them: strangers, the fatherless, or the widow, remembering always that they were once thus treated in Egypt.

— Laws about gleaning (vv. 19–21). Leftovers in the field after harvesting, or fruit remaining on the tree after picking, were to be left there to benefit the poor, the fatherless, and the widow. They should be allowed to glean them freely.

● **Deuteronomy 25:1–3 Forty stripes are the most that can be laid upon a man as punishment for sin.** In order to prevent a miscount, 39 lashes were usually administered. The Apostle Paul reported, "Of the Jews five times received I forty stripes save one" (2 Corinthians 11:24).

● **Deuteronomy 25:4 They were not to muzzle their oxen.** They were to treat their animals with kindness and a minimum of discomfort while they worked for them in "tread[ing] out the corn."

Working with unmuzzled oxen

● **Deuteronomy 25:5–10 The Levirate law of marriage provided that a dead man's brother should marry the widow and raise a family to the dead man.** The word "levirate" has nothing to do with the tribe of Levi. Rather, it is taken from the Latin word *levir*, meaning "husband's brother." The Sadducees used this law in trying to trap Jesus when they asked whose wife such a woman would be in the Resurrection (Matt. 22:23–33).

"The custom [ensured] the security of a widow who might otherwise be left destitute and friendless ... If no brother existed, some more distant male relative was required to perform this duty. Whichever relative married the widow became her *go'el* (redeemer or protector). The first son born to the widow by the new marriage was counted as a child of the dead husband and inherited his property"[14].

- **Deuteronomy 25:13–16 Honesty and fairness in business dealings is required.** Having inaccurate or "diverse" [varying] weights and measures (vv. 13–14) is called "an abomination" (v. 16). They were always to use "a perfect and just weight, a perfect and just measure" in all their business dealings (v. 15).

- **Deuteronomy 25:17–19 The Amalekites are to be utterly destroyed by the Israelites.** They were not to forget what the Amalekites did to the Israelites while they were traveling in the wilderness (Exodus 17:8–16). They "smote the hindmost of thee, even all that were feeble behind thee, when thou wast faint and weary; and [they] feared not God" (v. 18). When they are secure in their new land, enjoying "rest from all thine enemies round about," they are to "blot out the remembrance of Amalek from under heaven" (v. 19).

Notes

1. In Conference, Oct 1985, 6; or *Ensign*, Nov 1985, 6–7.
2. *Brigham Young: The Man and His Work*, 4th ed. [1960], 128.
3. Clarke, *Bible Commentary*, 1:770.
4. Edgar J. Goodspeed and J. M. Powis Smith, eds., *The Bible: An American Translation* [1931]. 2nd edition [1935].
5. James Moffatt, *A New Translation of the Bible, Containing the Old and New Testaments* [1926]. Revised edition [1935]. Reprinted [1995].
6. *Moses: Man of Miracles* (1977), 34–36.
7. *Institutes of Biblical Law* [1973], 277–2810.
8. *Doctrines of Salvation*, comp. Bruce R. McConkie, 3 vols. [1954–56], 1:187.
9. John Tvedtnes, "King Benjamin and the Feast of Tabernacles," in *By Study And Also By Faith: Essays in Honor of Hugh W. Nibley* [1990], 2:230, n. 20.
10. Alexander, David, and Pat Alexander, eds. *Eerdmans' Handbook to the Bible* [1973], 180.
11. Jacob Neusner, *The Way of Torah: An Introduction to Judaism*, 2nd ed. [1974], 39.
12. *Institutes of Biblical Law* [1973], 277–281.
13. 10 vols. [1996], 1:3:412.
14. *Great People of the Bible and How They Lived* [1979], 132.

Moses' Third Speech: Prophecies, Blessings and Cursings

(Numbers 26–27; Deuteronomy 26–30)

୨ଠଓଃ

THE LAST DAYS OF MOSES

As Moses delivered his third and final speech, he was approaching the end of his mortal life. Some of the historical details of this period are contained in the book of Numbers, while his teachings are primarily found in the book of Deuteronomy. We will make use of both of these books to understand in context what was happening and being taught during this crucial period.

Moses Bas relief, U.S. House of Representatives

Preparing to Receive Their Inheritances

● **Numbers 26 A second census of the house of Israel is taken.**

— After 40 years in the wilderness, the people numbered 601,730 compared to 603,550 when they began. The Levites had increased from 22,000 to 23,000.

— No original Israelites remained. Except for three people—Joshua, Caleb, and Moses—not one person over 20 years of age who had been numbered at the beginning of the desert wanderings 38 years earlier was left among the children of Israel.

● **Numbers 27:1–11; 36 Laws concerning inheritances are given, including a provision for daughters to inherit a father's earthly goods when no living son exists.** The daughters of Zelophehad, who had died in the wilderness without a male heir, came to Moses asking that his inheritance be given to them (vv. 1–4). Moses took the matter to the Lord, who confirmed that these women should receive "a possession of an inheritance among their father's brethren; and thou shalt cause the inheritance of their father to pass unto them" (vv. 5–7). He clarified the rules of inheritance as follows:

— "If a man die, and have no son, … his inheritance [shall] pass unto his daughter" (v. 8).

— "If he have no daughter … ye shall give his inheritance unto his brethren" (v. 9).

— "If he have no brethren … give his inheritance unto his father's brethren" (v. 10).

— If his father have no brethren … ye shall give his inheritance unto his kinsman that is next to him of his family" (v. 11).

Moses Views the Promised Land

● **Numbers 27:12–14 Moses climbs Mt.** Nebo for a look at the promised land. Mt Abarim [Nebo] was in Moab (present-day Jordan) very near where the children of Israel would cross over the river into the promised land.

The Lord said to Moses that after he had seen it he would be "gathered unto thy people" (usually means to die). The Lord said the reason he could not enter was because of his own rebellion in the wilderness of Zin, where he struck the rock to obtain water and took the credit personally for its happening (vv. 13–14).

Moses views the promised land from Mt. Nebo

Joshua Is Called to Succeed Moses

● **Numbers 27:15–23 Joshua is presented to the people and ordained.** The Lord commanded Moses, "Take thee Joshua the son of Nun, a man in whom is the spirit, and lay thine hand upon [ordain] him" (v. 18). He was to do this in the presence of "Eleazar the priest, and … all the congregation," giving him his "charge in their sight" (v. 19). As he did so, he was to confer "some of thine honour upon him, that all the congregation of the children of Israel may be obedient" (v. 20). He also made it clear that while Joshua was to be their new leader, he was to "stand before Eleazar the priest, who shall ask counsel for him [with the] Urim [and Thummim] before the Lord [meaning at the tabernacle] (v. 21). All of this Moses did with exactness (vv. 21–23).

Elder Bruce R. McConkie said: "Special blessings, anointings, sealing of anointings, confirmations, ordinations, callings, healings, offices, and graces are conferred by the laying on of hands by the Lord's legal administrators. As with all of the Lord's prescribed procedural requisites, the proffered blessings come only when the designated formalities are observed.[1] … Ordination to offices in the priesthood is performed by the laying on of hands. (Alma 6:1; Acts 6:5–6; 1 Tim. 5:22). Setting apart to positions of presidency, administration, or special responsibility comes in the same way"[2].

Offering the
Firstfruits
of the
Land of Promise

● **Deuteronomy 26:1–11 Israel is to express gratitude to God by offering a basket of firstfruits upon entering the promised land** and by paying tithes while in the land. These "firstfruits" were to be "the first of all the fruit of the earth, which thou shalt bring of thy land that the Lord thy God giveth thee" (vv. 1–2). They were to take them in a basket to the priest at the altar of the tabernacle (v. 3).

There they were to profess how Israel had gone to Egypt, become enslaved, and were led out "with a mighty hand" (v. 8) by the Lord to "a land that floweth with milk and honey" (v. 9). They were to thus worship the Lord while also rejoicing "in every good thing which the Lord thy God hath given unto thee, and unto thine house" (vv. 10–11).

- **Deuteronomy 26:16–19 One of the clearest statements found in scripture of the covenant between God and Israel.** Moses had just finished reviewing the law with them in his first two speeches, now they were to keep them by covenant. The people covenanted:

  — To do these statutes and judgments with all their hearts and souls (v. 16).

  — To confess that the Lord is their God (v. 17).

  — To hearken unto His voice in all things (v. 17).

  — To be his peculiar people by keeping all his commandments (v. 18).

  In return, the Lord covenanted to "make thee high above all nations … in praise, and in name, and in honour … an holy people unto the Lord thy God" (v. 19).

- **Deuteronomy 27:1–7 Upon entering the land, Israel was to build an altar of uncut stones and also a monument inscribed with the words of God given to Moses.** Notice that He did not want them to make statues or idols of any kind. They were to memorialize the commandments by carving them in stone on a plastered monument on Mt. Ebal (vv. 1–4). They were also to build an altar there of uncut stones on which they could offer appropriate offerings unto the Lord (vv. 5–7).

The Choice for Israel: Blessings or Cursings

Inside the promised land, there were two nearly-identical mountains with a valley between them—Mt. Gerizim and Mt. Ebal. The Lord declared these two mountains to be symbolic of Israel's choices while they remained in the promised land.

- **Deuteronomy 27:8–12 Upon Mount Gerizim representatives of 6 tribes were to stand and bless Israel for obedience**—Simeon, Levi, Judah, Issachar, Joseph, Benjamin. The words of the law were to be inscribed there on stone monu- ments (v. 8). The blessings the Lord promised them if they would be faithful were as follows (Deut. 28):

  — Their land and possessions will be blessed (vv. 1–5).

Mt. Gerizim on the left

— Their lives will be protected (vv. 7, 9–10).

— There will be peace (v. 6).

— They, their land, and their animals will all be fruitful and multiplied (vv. 8, 11–14).

- **Deuteronomy 27:13–28:64 Upon Mount Ebal representatives of 6 tribes were to stand and curse Israel if they became disobedient**—Reuben, Gad, Asher, Zebulun, Dan, Naphtali. The curses that disobedience would bring upon them were as follows (Deut. 28):

Mt. Ebal on the right

— Land, flocks, and people cursed with pestilence and sickness (vv. 16–24, 38–39).

— People overcome by enemies (vv. 25, 49–53).

— Children lost through famine, captivity, disease (vv. 32, 41, 52–53, 60–62).

— God will scatter them around the earth (vv. 63–64).

- **D&C 41:1 The same blessings and cursings have been pronounced in our own day.** The Lord delights to bless us "with the greatest of all blessings" when we hear Him, but He will curse those who will not hear Him "with the heaviest of all cursings."

Elder Bruce R. McConkie said: "Cursings are the opposite of blessings, and the greater the opportunity given a people to earn blessings, the more severe will be the cursings heaped upon them, if they do not measure up and gain the proffered rewards. Failure to pay tithing, for instance, brings condemnation upon the covenant people, whereas the people of the world—not being specifically obligated to keep this law—do not suffer the same penalties for non-tithe paying ..."[3].

- **Numbers 28–30 Moses establishes regulations for worship and vows.** Sacrifices were to be offered regularly as follows:

— Each morning and evening.

— On the Sabbath.

— On the first day of each month.

— At Passover (15th day of the first month).

— On each day of the Feast of Unleavened Bread (following Passover).

— At the Feast of Firstfruits (the day of Pentecost—50 days after Passover).

— At the Feast of Trumpets (1st–2nd day of the seventh month).

— At the Feast of Tabernacles (15th day of seventh month).

Vows and oaths must be kept, but fathers may disallow vows of daughters, and husbands may disallow vows of wives.

● **Deuteronomy 29:1–15 The covenant made with the children of Israel at Moab.** This covenant was in addition to the one the Lord made with them at Mt. Sinai (v. 1). Moses reminded them of all the Lord had done for them since leaving Egypt (v. 2), and the great temptations, signs, and miracles they had witnessed (v. 3). And despite all of this, they had not had "an heart to perceive, and eyes to see, and ears to hear, unto this day" (v. 4). The Lord had fed and preserved them for 40 years in the wilderness "that ye might know that I am the Lord your God" (v. 6).

Now the Lord wanted them to covenant with Him to be obedient in the land of promise. This covenant, in the form of an oath, would establish them as "a people unto himself, and that he may be unto thee a God, as he hath said unto thee, and as he hath sworn unto thy fathers, to Abraham, to Isaac, and to Jacob" (v. 13). It applied not only to those there on that day but also with those who would follow who are "not here with us this day" (vv. 14–15).

THE LAST PROPHECIES OF MOSES

The Scattering of Israel

● **Deuteronomy 29:16–28 Following after other gods will bring destruction.** They had already seen the abominations of the people they were driving out of Canaan "and their idols, wood and stone, silver and gold, which were among them" (v. 17). If any Israelite, male or female, should turn away from the Lord and "go and serve the gods of these nations" (v. 18), though they may think they shall have peace "the Lord will not spare him, but … the anger of the Lord and his jealousy shall smoke against that man, and all the curses that are written in this book shall lie upon him, and the Lord shall blot out his name from under heaven" (vv. 19–20).

The Lord predicted that their "children" [posterity] would do these things and that the destruction He would bring upon the land—plagues, sicknesses, brimstone, salt, and burning—would become a wonderment to other nations who saw it (vv. 22–23). They would know that it was done "because they have forsaken the covenant of the Lord God of their fathers" and "went and served other gods, and worshipped them, gods whom they knew not, and whom he had not given unto them" (vv. 25–26). The Lord will then "[root] them out of their land in anger, and in wrath, and in great indignation, and cast them into another land" (v. 28).

● **Deuteronomy 29:29 This revelation belonged to them and their posterity.** This principle—that secret things "belong unto the Lord" but what has been revealed "belongs unto us" is true for every dispensation of the gospel, including ours.

● **Deuteronomy 28:45–57 The brutality of their destruction is described**—including cannibalism of children. The predicted curses "shall pursue thee, and overtake thee, till thou be destroyed; because thou hearkenedst not unto the voice of the Lord thy God, to keep his commandments and his statutes which he commanded thee" (v. 45). Because they will choose not to serve the Lord "with joyfulness, and with gladness of heart" (v. 47), they will "serve thine enemies which the Lord shall send against thee, in hunger, and in thirst, and in nakedness, and in want of all things: and he shall put a yoke of iron upon thy neck, until he have destroyed thee" (v. 48).

The utter destruction of Jerusalem, called the abomination of desolation by the prophets

The enemy that destroys them (Babylon) will come "from far, from the end of the earth, as swift as the eagle flieth; a nation whose tongue thou shalt not understand; a nation of fierce countenance, which shall not regard the person of the old, nor shew favour to the young: and he shall eat the fruit of thy cattle, and the fruit of thy land, until thou be destroyed" (vv. 49–51). This enemy will "besiege thee in all thy gates, until thy high and fenced walls come down, wherein thou trustedst, throughout all thy land" (v. 52). And while they are thus besieged, "thou shalt eat the fruit of thine own body, the flesh of thy sons and of thy daughters" because of difficulty "wherewith thine enemies shall distress thee" (v. 53). Even the most gentle of men and tenderest of women will "eat them [their children] for want of all things secretly in the siege" (vv. 54–57).

- **Deuteronomy 28:58–61 They will also be decimated by diseases.** Because of their disobedience, the Lord will bring plagues upon them and upon their posterity, "even great plagues, and of long continuance, and sore sicknesses" (v. 59). He will bring upon them "all the diseases of Egypt, which thou wast afraid of; and they shall cleave unto thee" along with "every sickness, and every plague, which is not written in the book of this law" until they all shall be destroyed (vv. 60–61).

- **Deuteronomy 28:62–67 They will be scattered among all nations, considered as a cursed people, and treated with no mercy.** Because they would not be obedient to the commandments of the Lord, He will "destroy you, and to bring you to nought; and ye shall be plucked from off the land whither thou goest to possess it" (vv. 62–63). They will then be scattered "among all people, from the one end of the earth even unto the other; and there thou shalt serve other gods, which neither thou nor thy fathers have known, even wood and stone" (v. 64). There in captivity they will find "no

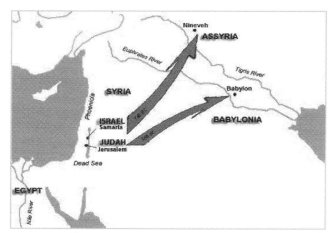

Israel went into Assyria, Judah into Babylon. From there they dispersed around the world

ease, neither shall the sole of thy foot have rest: but the Lord shall give thee there a trembling heart, and failing of eyes, and sorrow of mind: and thy life shall hang in doubt before thee; and thou shalt fear day and night, and shalt have none assurance of thy life" (vv. 65–66).

● **Deuteronomy 29:22–23 The land of Israel will lie desolate until the time of their return.**
Those who visit the land will find only "brimstone, and salt, and burning"—a land "that it is not sown, nor beareth, nor any grass groweth therein, like the overthrow of Sodom, and Gomorrah."

The Eventual Gathering of Israel

● **Deuteronomy 30:1–10 Israel will eventually return to the land possessed by their fathers, and upon their return, both they and their lands will be blessed.** While Israel remains captive among the nations, she will recall both the blessings and the curses pronounced upon them by Moses (v. 1). And thus humbled, they will "return unto the Lord thy God, and shalt obey his voice according to all that I command thee this day, thou and thy children, with all thine heart, and with all thy soul" (v. 2). When this happens, "then the Lord thy God will turn thy captivity, and have compassion upon thee, and will return and gather thee from all the nations, whither the Lord thy God hath scattered thee" (v. 3). They will be brought back into "the land which thy fathers possessed, and thou shalt possess it; and he [God] will do thee good, and multiply thee above thy fathers" (vv. 4–5).

The Lord will then "put all these curses upon thine enemies, and on them that hate thee, which persecuted thee" (v. 7). The Israelites will become "plenteous in every work of thine hand, in the fruit of thy body, and in the fruit of thy cattle, and in the fruit of thy land" (v. 9) because they will have chosen to "hearken unto the voice of the Lord thy God, to keep his commandments and his statutes which are written in this book of the law … with all thine heart, and with all thy soul" (v. 10).

● **Deuteronomy 30:15–20 Moses set before them their choices and exhorted them to love God.** Their choice was clear—either "life and good" or "death and evil" (v. 15). If they chose the good they would "live and multiply: and the Lord thy God shall bless thee in the land whither thou goest to possess it" (v. 16). But if they chose evil, "if thine heart turn away, so that thou wilt not hear, but shalt be drawn away, and worship other gods, and serve them" then Moses declared "I denounce unto you this day, that ye shall surely perish, and that ye shall not prolong your days upon the land, whither thou passest over Jordan to go to possess it" (v. 18). Moses called upon "heaven and earth to record this day" the choices he had placed before them (v. 19). And he urged them to choose the good—to "love the Lord thy God, and … obey his voice, and … cleave unto him: for he is thy life, and the length of thy days" (v. 20). If they did these things, they would be permitted to "dwell in the land which the Lord sware unto thy fathers, to Abraham, to Isaac, and to Jacob, to give them" (v. 20).

THE LAST DAYS OF MOSES

(Deuteronomy 31–34)

Moses' Farewell and Blessings on Israel

These chapters are essentially an appendix to the book, including exhortations to Joshua and a final celebration before the departure of Moses.

Moses and Joshua

- **Deuteronomy 31:1–8 Moses gives Joshua charge of Israel and urges him and the people to be courageous and strong.** Moses declared himself to be 120 years old and no more able to "go out and come in" as he used to do (v. 2). Also, the Lord had already told him "Thou shalt not go over this Jordan" (v. 2). But Moses said, "The Lord thy God, he will go over before thee, and he will destroy these nations from before thee, and thou shalt possess them: and Joshua, he shall go over before thee, as the Lord hath said" (v. 3). He urged the Israelites to "be strong and of a good courage, fear not, nor be afraid of [their enemies]: for the Lord thy God, he it is that doth go with thee; he will not fail thee, nor forsake thee" (vv. 5–6).

Moses then said to Joshua in the sight of all Israel, "be strong and of a good courage: for thou must go with this people unto the land which the Lord hath sworn unto their fathers to give them; and thou shalt cause them to inherit it. And the Lord, he it is that doth go before thee; he will be with thee, he will not fail thee, neither forsake thee: fear not, neither be dismayed" (vv. 7–8).

The Midianite War

- **Numbers 31 Israelite warriors failed to carry out orders.** The Lord commanded Moses to "avenge the children of Israel of the Midianites," and "afterward shalt thou be gathered unto thy people" (v. 2). In doing so, Israelite soldiers were under orders from the Lord to cleanse the land of this society. Only female children and young virgins were to be spared because they could be integrated into the culture of Israel without corrupting it. The soldiers violated this commandment and brought back large numbers of captives who should have been destroyed. They destroyed the males (v. 7), and burned their cities (v. 10). But then they took for spoil all the women of Midian along with their children" in addition to "all their flocks, and all their goods" (v. 9).

Moses was under the revolting necessity of requiring them to fulfill their orders by killing all the male children and all the women, leaving alive only the young virgins and girls (vv. 17–18). They then had to remain outside the camp for 7 days, purifying themselves against all the blood they had shed (vv. 19–24).

When the Midianite war was over, Israel made an accounting of their losses and their spoils (vv. 25–48). To their astonishment they discovered that this terrible conflict had been fought without the loss of a single Israelite man (v. 49). On the other hand, the spoils of the Midianite war were extensive:

— 675,000 sheep

— 72,000 head of beef

— 61,000 donkeys

— 32,000 prisoners (female children and young virgins).

The end of the Midianite war marked the last major project of the prophet Moses. The Lord had said that when the affairs of this war were completed Moses would be "gathered to his people." Moses therefore gave his final instructions and blessings to the tribes of Israel in anticipation of his departure.

The Final Acts of Moses

● **Deuteronomy 31:9–13 Moses delivers the law to the priests and commands that it be read to all Israel every seven years.** He wrote down all the laws and his explanations of them and "delivered it unto the priests the sons of Levi, which bare the ark of the covenant of the Lord, and unto all the elders of Israel" (v. 9). He then commanded them to read it aloud to all Israel "every seven years, in the solemnity of the year of release [the jubilee year]" at the feast of tabernacles (vv. 10–11). By this means, they would be reminded, and their children and visitors would "hear … that they may learn, and fear the Lord … and observe to do all the words of this law" (v. 12).

● **Deuteronomy 31:14–15 Moses presents Joshua at the tabernacle, where the Lord gives him his charge.** The Lord told Moses, "Behold, thy days approach that thou must die," and directed him to bring Joshua to the tabernacle "that I may give him a charge" (v. 14). They did so, and "the Lord appeared in the tabernacle in a pillar of a cloud" that "stood over the door of the tabernacle" (v. 15).

Moses and Joshua at the tabernacle

- **Deuteronomy 31:16–18 The Lord tells Moses and Joshua that the people will "go a whoring after the gods of … the land."** The Lord warned them, saying, "Moses, Behold, thou shalt sleep with thy fathers; and this people will rise up, and go a whoring after the gods of the strangers of the land, whither they go to be among them, and will forsake me, and break my covenant which I have made with them" (v. 16). This could not have been encouraging to either of them, but the Lord wanted Joshua to understand clearly what lay ahead of him. When they apostatized, the Lord's "anger shall be kindled against them … and I will forsake them, and I will hide my face from them, and they shall be devoured, and many evils and troubles shall befall them; so that they will say in that day, Are not these evils come upon us, because our God is not among us?" (v. 17).

- **Deuteronomy 31:19–22 The Lord gives Moses a song about their eventual apostasy, which Moses taught to Israel to be a witness against them when they would rebel against God (v. 19).** The Lord affirmed again that "when I shall have brought them into the land which I sware unto their fathers, that floweth with milk and honey; and they shall have eaten and filled themselves, and waxen fat; then will they turn unto other gods, and serve them, and provoke me, and break my covenant" (v. 20). When that day came, this song would "testify against them as a witness; for it shall not be forgotten out of the mouths of their seed" (v. 21). "Moses therefore wrote this song the same day, and taught it [to] the children of Israel" (v. 22).

Ten Commandments on parchment

- **Deuteronomy 31:24–26 Moses commands that the book of the law be placed in the Ark of the Covenant.** Moses had previously commanded the priests to read the law to all Israel every seven years. Now, having completed the writing of it into a "book," he "commanded the Levites, which bare the ark of the covenant of the Lord, saying, Take this book of the law, and put it in the side of the ark of the covenant of the Lord your God" (vv. 25–26).

- **Deuteronomy 31:26–30 The book of the law will stand as a witness against them (v. 26)** in the day when they eventually rebelled. Moses observed, "while I am yet alive with you this day, ye have been rebellious against the Lord; and how much more after my death?" (v. 27). He gave this warning to "all the elders of [the] tribes, and [the] officers, that I may … call heaven and earth to record against them" (v. 28). "For I know that after my death ye will utterly corrupt yourselves, and turn aside from the way which I have commanded you; and evil will befall you in the latter days; because ye will do evil in the sight of the Lord, to provoke him to anger through the work of your hands" (v. 29). He then "spake in the ears of all the congregation of Israel the words of [the] song" he had received from the Lord (v. 30).

Moses' Song Testifies of Christ

● **Deuteronomy 32:1–47 Moses' song testifies concerning the Rock of their salvation.** The opening words are a stirring witness of Jehovah's role as Savior:

1. GIVE ear, O ye heavens, and I will speak; and hear, O earth, the words of my mouth.

2. My doctrine shall drop as the rain, my speech shall distil as the dew, as the small rain upon the tender herb, and as the showers upon the grass:

3. Because I will publish the name of the Lord: ascribe ye greatness unto our God.

4. He is the Rock, his work is perfect: for all his ways are judgment: a God of truth and without iniquity, just and right is he.

● **Deuteronomy 32:4 Israel's Rock is Jehovah—who is Jesus Christ.** The Apostle Paul said of Israel during their wanderings: "For they drank of that spiritual Rock that followed them: and that Rock was Christ" (1 Cor. 10:4).

Elder Bruce R. McConkie said: "Christ is the Stone of Israel (Gen. 49:24). [He said] 'I am the good shepherd, and the stone of Israel. He that buildeth upon this rock shall never fall.' (D&C 50:44) Christ is thus the stone or foundation upon which all men must build. Of him the psalmist prophesied: 'The stone which the builders refused is become the head stone of the corner.' (Ps. 118:22; Matt. 21:42; Mark 12:10–11; Luke 20:17–18) Peter [taught] that the Saints 'as lively stones' should build 'a spiritual house,' with Christ, the Stone of Israel, as the foundation. (1 Pet. 2:1–9)"[4].

● **Deuteronomy 32:8–9 The children of Israel were chosen in the premortal existence.** We are told that "the most High divided to the nations their inheritance, when he separated the sons of Adam, [and] he set the bounds of the people according to the number of the children of Israel" (v. 8). And his chosen people—the "Lord's portion"—is Jacob (the children of Israel) (v. 9).

● **Deuteronomy 32:15–18 Jeshurun (the "upright") have rejected the Rock for other gods.** The prediction is that the children of Israel (the "upright") will "wax fat" temporally and then forsake their God who made them—lightly esteeming the "Rock of [their] salvation" (v. 15). They will provoke the Lord by their worship of strange gods and their participation in abominations (v. 16). They will sacrifice to devils rather than to God—gods whom they have never met and do not know, gods that are new and were unknown to their forefathers (v. 17). Meanwhile, they will be unmindful of the only true God who "begat [them]" and "formed [them]" (v. 18).

● **Deuteronomy 32:31–33 The rock (false gods) of the wicked "is not as our Rock" (Christ).** Even their enemies know that their frivolous and false gods are "not as our Rock" (v. 31). The fruits of worshiping these false idols are like "the vine of Sodom, and of the fields of Gomorrah: their grapes are grapes of gall, their clusters are bitter: Their wine is the poison of dragons, and the cruel venom of asps" (vv. 32–33). In other words, their false worship leads only to destruction and death; it never truly benefits them.

● **Deuteronomy 32:39–40 Jehovah (Christ) is the God of life and He lives forever.** The fact is, there is NO other God of this earth. Idols do not live, and they do not give life. But our God is the God of life—He gives life and He takes it away as He sees fit (v. 39). He wounds and He heals. And there is nobody who can counter what He declares because He is all-powerful—even the elements obey Him. And He will live forever (v. 40).

- **Deuteronomy 32:45–47 Israel is urged to build upon the Rock and be preserved in the promised land (Matt.** 7:24–27; D&C 50:44). When Moses had finished reading the words of this song to the children of Israel, he said to them, "Set your hearts unto all the words which I testify among you this day, which [also] ye shall command your children to observe to do" (vv. 45–46). He reminded them that the words of the law are not trivial—"it is your life: and through this thing ye shall prolong your days in the land, whither ye go over Jordan to possess it" (v. 47). It was a matter of life and death.

Moses Gives His Last Blessing to the Tribes of Israel

We will not attempt to read and explain all of these blessings. They are very similar to the blessings which Jacob (Israel) gave to his sons just before his death (Genesis 49:1–28). We will pay particular attention to Moses' prophecy concerning the descendants of Joseph, through Ephraim and Manasseh, because they are the blessings we have inherited today.

- **Deuteronomy 33:13–17 The blessing upon the tribes of Joseph.** This blessing begins with a blessing upon the land that Joseph's descendants will inherit. It will be a land possessing "precious things of heaven, …dew, and … the deep [water] that coucheth beneath" (v. 13). "Precious fruits" will be "brought forth by the sun," and other beauties will be "put forth by the moon" (v. 14). It will be a land possessing "ancient mountains," which contain "precious things" and will be "lasting" (v. 15). Jacob called these mountains "everlasting hills" (Genesis 49:26), meaning that they go on and on forever—just as the Rocky Mountains do from Alaska to the southern tip of Chile.

These "precious things of the earth" will be provided by "the good will of him that dwelt in the bush [Jehovah]" (v. 16). They will be conferred "upon the head of Joseph, … him that was separated from his brethren" (v. 16). We know, of course, that Joseph himself was separated from his father and brothers and then was the means by which they were gathered and saved. This will also be true of Joseph's posterity—they will be separated from the other tribes, become mighty in their land, and then be the means of gathering and saving all of Israel. They will literally "push the people together to the ends of the earth," these descendants of Ephraim and Manasseh (v. 17).

Instructions Concerning Inheritances

- **Numbers 32:1–33 Two and one-half tribes receive their lands of inheritance east of the Jordan River, after promising to send warriors to help Israel conquer the land of Canaan.** Reuben and Gad and half the tribe of Manasseh received their inheritances in the lands they had most recently conquered east of Jordan—the land of Bashon and the land of the Amorites.

- **Numbers 33:50—34:29 Moses gives instructions about inheritances.** They were first commanded, "When ye are passed over Jordan into the land of Canaan; Then ye shall drive out all the inhabitants of the land from before you, and destroy all their pictures, and destroy all their molten images, and quite pluck down all their high places: And ye shall dispossess the inhabitants of the land, and dwell therein: for I have given you the land to possess it" (33:51–53). They were warned that if they failed to do this, "then it shall come to pass, that those which ye let remain of them shall be pricks in your eyes, and thorns in your sides, and shall vex you in the land wherein ye dwell" (33:55). And perhaps even more ominous a warning was this: "Moreover it shall come to pass, that I shall do unto you, as I thought to do unto them" (33:56).

  After doing this, they were to divide the land of Canaan according to the size of each tribe—larger tribes getting more land and smaller tribes getting less (33:54). He then specified the borders of Israel's inheritance in Canaan, and named princes of tribes who were to divide the land (34:1–29).

- **Numbers 35: 1–5, 7–8 Levites are to possess their own cities inside the tribal boundaries of all the other tribes.** Since the Levites had the specific assignment to function as priests for all the people, they did not receive a tribal homeland. Instead, Moses commanded all the other tribes to "give unto the Levites of the inheritance of their possession cities to dwell in" as well as "suburbs for the cities round about them" (v. 2). The Levites would then live in their cities and have "suburbs" around them "from the wall of the city and outward a thousand cubits round about" (vv. 4–5), which they could use "for their cattle, and for their goods, and for all their beasts" (v. 3). They were to establish 48 such Levite cities in the promised land (v. 7). Those tribes that had more land and cities would provide more cities to the Levites than those tribes that had fewer land and cities, but every tribe was required to "give of his cities unto the Levites according to his inheritance which he inheriteth" (v. 8).

- **Numbers 35:6, 9–15, 22–28 Cities of refuge are established for those guilty of manslaughter.** Among the 48 Levite cities, there were to be 6 cities designated for refuge, "which ye shall appoint for the manslayer, that he may flee thither" (vv. 6, 13). Three of these were to be located east of the Jordan River and three of them west of the river (v. 14). A "manslayer" was defined as a person "which killeth any person … unawares" (v. 11). Such persons, who had killed someone unintentionally, could flee to one of these cities "that [he] die not, until he stand before the congregation in judgment" (v. 12). Anyone—an Israelite, a "stranger", or a "sojourner"—"every one that killeth any person unawares may flee thither" (v. 15). Moses then listed circumstances that might be considered manslaughter:

  — If he "thrust him suddenly without enmity" (v. 22).

  — If he "cast upon him any thing without laying of wait" (v. 22).

  — If he killed him "with any stone, wherewith a man may die, seeing him not, … and was not his enemy, neither sought his harm" (v. 23).

In any such cases, "the congregation shall judge between the slayer and the revenger of blood according to these judgments" (v. 24). If the man was found guilty of manslaughter he was to be "restore[d] … to the city of his refuge, whither he was fled: and he shall abide in it unto the death of the [current] high priest" (v. 25). If the man were ever to be found outside the border of the city of his refuge, "and the revenger of blood find him without the borders of the city of his refuge, and the revenger of blood kill the slayer; he shall not be guilty of [murder]" (vv. 26–27) because "he should have remained in the city of his refuge until the death of the high priest" (v. 28). Finally, "after the death of the high priest the [man]slayer shall return into the land of his possession" as a free man (v. 28).

● **Numbers 35:16–21, 29–34 Murderers shall be executed by the revenger of blood.** To fully understand the above procedures we should know that murderers were not to be protected in this manner. "The murderer shall surely be put to death" (vv. 16, 18). Murder was defined as the *intentional* killing of another—out of hatred or with malicious intent (v. 21)—no matter what the murder weapon (vv. 17–18, 21).

Under Israelite law, "the revenger of blood himself shall slay the murderer: when he meeteth him, he shall slay him" (v. 19). But this was not to be done without the testimony of witnesses to the murder (v. 30). And "one witness shall not testify against any person to cause him to die" (v. 30); it requires two or three witnesses.

They were to "take no satisfaction for [pity] the life of a murderer," because under Israelite law he "is guilty of death [and] "shall be surely put to death" (v. 31). The same would be true of a man guilty of manslaughter who left the city of refuge before the death of the high priest (v. 32). By this law they would ensure that they did not "pollute the land wherein ye are: for blood … defileth the land: and the land cannot be cleansed of the blood that is shed therein, but by the blood of him that shed it" (v. 33). "Defile not therefore the land which ye shall inhabit, wherein I dwell: for I the Lord dwell among the children of Israel" (v. 34).

● **Numbers 36 Rules of inheritance for daughters are also given (See Numbers 27:1–11 above for details).** Daughters in Israel were directed to marry within their own tribe, and could not receive an inheritance otherwise because inheritances could not move from tribe to tribe.

Moses Is Translated on Mt. Nebo

The time finally arrived when Moses had to depart from the people. It was a very sad moment, given the many years that he had led them and the great miracles he had performed on their behalf. They had never had any other prophet-leader, and they did not want him to leave them. But Moses, obedient to the Lord's command, took his departure.

Josephus wrote concerning this departure of Moses:

> When Moses had spoken thus at the end of his life, and had foretold what would befall to every one of their tribes afterward, with the addition of a blessing to them, the multitude fell into tears, insomuch that even the women, by beating their breasts, made manifest the deep concern they had when he was about to die. The children also lamented still more, as not able to contain their grief; and thereby declared, that even at their age they were sensible of his virtue and mighty deeds …

The old grieved, because they knew what a careful protector they were to be deprived of, and so lamented their future state; but the young grieved, not only for that, but also because it so happened that they were to be left by him before they had well tasted of his virtue …

[And] although he was always persuaded that he ought not to be cast down at the approach of death, since the undergoing it was agreeable to the will of God … yet what the people did so overbore him that he wept himself. Now as he went thence to the place where he was to vanish out of their sight, they all followed after him weeping; but Moses beckoned with his hand to those that were remote from him, and bade them stay behind in quiet, while he exhorted those that were near to him that they would not render his departure so lamentable.[5]

● **Deuteronomy 32:48–50 God commands Moses to climb Mount Nebo.** Mt. Nebo was a high peak on the Avarim range, which is part of the mountain divide (Hebrew, "pisgah") east of the north end of the Dead Sea. The Lord commanded Moses, "Get thee up into this mountain Abarim, unto mount Nebo, which is in the land of Moab, … and behold the land of Canaan, which I give unto the children of Israel for a possession" (v. 49). There Moses would "die" and "be gathered unto thy people; as Aaron thy brother died in mount Hor, and was gathered unto his people" (v. 50).

● **Deuteronomy 32:51–52 Moses was not permitted to enter the land of promise.** He was not be permitted to enter the land of promise because of his disobedience at Meribah-Kadesh, in the wilderness of Zin, where he struck the rock to bring forth water and, in his anger toward the disobedience of the people, took credit for it himself rather than giving credit to the Lord (v. 51, see Numbers 20:12–13 and 24; 27:14).

There were other reasons for his not going into the land. Joshua was an experienced warrior, and could provide excellent leadership of their military conquests. And the Lord did not want Moses to "die" in any such conquests. He had other work for him to do while still in the flesh. See the discussion below about whether Moses actually "died" as we understand the word today. Moses was permitted to "see the land before thee; but thou shalt not go thither unto the land which I give the children of Israel" (v. 52).

● **Deuteronomy 34 Joshua was the author of this last chapter of Deuteronomy.** The reader will notice a change in voice in this final chapter of Deuteronomy. Obviously, with Moses' departure he could not have been the author of this chapter. The author was Joshua, who paid tribute to Moses in the final verses.

● **Deuteronomy 34:1–4 Moses sees all of the promised land.** Moses went up onto Mt. Nebo, where "the Lord shewed him all the land of Gilead, unto Dan, and all Naphtali, and the land of Ephraim, and Manasseh, and all the land of Judah, unto the utmost sea, and the south, and the plain of the valley of Jericho, the city of palm trees, unto Zoar" (vv. 1–3). This is defined by the Lord as "the land which I sware unto Abraham, unto Isaac, and unto Jacob, saying, I will give it unto thy seed" (v. 4). Eventually, before or during the Millennial reign, Israel will re-inhabit all of it.

● **Deuteronomy 34:5–6 Moses "died" there but has no sepulcher.** Joshua tell us that "according to the word of the Lord," "Moses the servant of the Lord died there in the land of Moab" (v. 5). He says that the Lord "buried him in a valley in the land of Moab, over against Beth-peor" (v. 6). But he adds that "no man knoweth of his sepulchre unto this day" (v. 6). No doubt, they went in search of his burial place, but they did not find one. So the only thing that the writer who finished the book of Deuteronomy (probably Joshua) knew for sure was that Moses was gone from the earth (he "died").

Moses was translated on Mt. Nebo

- **Deuteronomy 34:7 Moses was 120 years old but not near death.** He was not a man who was suffering from old age. His "eye was not dimmed nor his natural force abated" when he left the children of Israel.

Josephus said: "Now as soon as they were come to the mountain called Abarim, (which is a very high mountain, situate over against Jericho, and one that affords, to such as are upon it, a prospect of the greatest part of the excellent land of Canaan), he dismissed the senate; and as he was going to embrace Eleazar and Joshua, and was still discoursing with them, a cloud stood over him on the sudden, and he disappeared in a certain valley, although he wrote in the holy books that he died, which was done out of fear, lest they should venture to say that, because of his extraordinary virtue, he went to God"[6].

Elder Bruce R. McConkie said: "The Old Testament account that Moses died and was buried by the hand of the Lord in an unknown grave is an error … It is true that he may have been 'buried by the hand of the Lord,' if that expression is a figure of speech which means that he was translated. But the Book of Mormon account, in recording that Alma 'was taken up by the Spirit,' says, 'the scriptures saith the Lord took Moses unto himself; and we suppose that he has also received Alma in the spirit, unto himself.' (Alma 45:18–19). It should be remembered that the Nephites had the Brass plates, and that they were the 'scriptures' which gave the account of Moses being taken by way of translation"[7].

President Joseph Fielding Smith said: "Elijah and Moses were preserved from death: because they had a mission to perform, and it had to be performed before the crucifixion of the Son of God, and it could not be done in the spirit. They had to have tangible bodies. Christ is the first fruits of the resurrection; therefore if any former prophets had a work to perform preparatory to the mission of the Son of God, or to the dispensation of the meridian of times, it was essential that they be preserved to fulfill that mission in the flesh. For that reason Moses disappeared from among the people and was taken up into the mountain, and the people thought he was buried by the Lord. The Lord preserved him, so that he could come at the proper time and restore his keys, on the heads of Peter, James, and John, who stood at the head of the dispensation of the meridian of time"8.

- **Jude 1:9** This account of Satan and Michael disputing over the "body" of Moses is not fully understood, but perhaps had to do with Satan's anger that Moses did note taste of death.

The Greatness of the Prophet Moses

● **Deuteronomy 34:8–9 Joshua was "full of the spirit of wisdom"** because Moses had laid his hands upon him before he left, "and the children of Israel hearkened unto him."

● **Deuteronomy 34:10–12 Joshua says, "there arose not a prophet since in Israel like unto Moses, whom the Lord knew face to face."** He performed dozens of spectacular miracles as he led them out of Egypt, through the wilderness, and right up to the borders of Canaan (v. 11). With the possible exception of Enoch (who Moses greatly admired), no other prophet had shown such things to so many with a "mighty hand" as did Moses (v. 12).

Josephus said: "Now Moses lived in all one hundred and twenty years; a third part of which time, abating one month, he was the people's ruler; and he died on the last month of the year, which is called by the Macedonians Dystrus, but by us Adar, on the first day of the month. He was one that exceeded all men that ever were in understanding, and made the best use of what that understanding suggested to him. He had a very graceful way of speaking and addressing himself to the multitude; and as to his other qualifications, he had such a full command of his passions, as if he had hardly any such in his soul, and only knew them by their names, as rather perceiving them in other men than in himself. He was also such a general of an army as is seldom seen, as well as such a prophet as was never known, and this to such a degree, that whatsoever he pronounced, you would think you heard the voice of God himself"[9].

Notes

1. *Teachings of the Prophet Joseph Smith*, 198–199.
2. *Mormon Doctrine*, 2nd ed. [1966], 438.
3. *Mormon Doctrine*, 175.
4. *Mormon Doctrine*, 768.
5. *Antiquities of the Jews*, Book IV, Chapter 8, Paragraph 48.
6. *Antiquities of the Jews*, Book IV, Chapter 8, Paragraph 48.
7. *Mormon Doctrine*, 805.
8. *Doctrines of Salvation*, 2:110–111.
9. *Antiquities of the Jews*, Book IV, Chapter 8, paragraph 49.

CHAPTER 18

Joshua Leads Israel
Into the Promised Land

(Joshua; 1 Chronicles 2–8)

‿◦◦◦‿

INTRODUCTION

The Book of Joshua

● **Author:** Joshua is generally assumed to be the author with the exception of the concluding section (Joshua 24:29–33), which was added by another writer.

● **Position:** Historical sequel to Deuteronomy. The Pentateuch (Genesis, Exodus, Leviticus, Numbers, and Deuteronomy) constitutes the "Law" in Jewish tradition. The book of Joshua is the first of the "Prophets" in that same tradition.

● **Purpose:** To show the fulfillment of the Lord's promises to Israel in the Promised Land. The historical account also includes the teachings and exhortations of Joshua to the Israelites. The most famous of these is the declaration, "Choose you this day whom ye will serve … but as for me and my house, we will serve the Lord" (Joshua 24:15).

● **Time Span:** From the translation of Moses until the death of Joshua (ca. 1427 BC).

● **Length:** 24 chapters

● **Key Sections:**
— Chapters 1–12   History of the conquest of Canaan.
— Chapters 13–21 Allotment of the land to the various tribes of Israel.
— Chapters 22–24 Joshua's farewell address and an account of his death

Who Was Joshua?

● **Numbers 13:8, 16** Joshua was the son of Nun, of the tribe of Ephraim.

● **Numbers 11:28** Joshua was a servant of Moses, as a young man.

● **Numbers 13:16** He was originally called Oshea or Hoshea, which means "savior" or "salvation".

- **Deut. 32:44**   Moses changed his name to Joshua, meaning "he shall save" or "salvation of Jehovah".

- **Septuagint**   In the Septuagint version of the scriptures, he is called "Jesus".

- **Acts 7:45**   In the New Testament he is also specifically called "Jesus".

- **Hebrews 4:8**   In the original Hebrew, Jesus and Joshua are the same name. He therefore had the same name as our Savior, Jesus Christ.

The Greatness of Joshua

- **Exodus 17**   Joshua first distinguished himself as a general in the battle against the Amalekites while the Israelites were on their way to Mt. Sinai.

- **Exodus 24:9–13**   Joshua was among 70 elders who saw the Lord at the foot of Mt. Sinai.

- **Exodus 24:12–18**   Joshua accompanied Moses into the higher reaches of Mount Sinai, patiently waiting until Moses returned from talking with the Lord.

- **Numbers 13:1–2**   Joshua was one of 12 spies sent by Moses into Canaan to search it out.

- **Numbers 14:6–10**   Only Joshua and Caleb showed faith in God in reporting their findings.

- **Deut. 1:37–38**   Joshua was divinely designated as Moses' successor.

- **Numbers 27:18–23**   Joshua was solemnly consecrated by Moses to be his successor.

W. Cleon Skousen said:

> Moses sent 12 spies into Canaan to search out the land (Numbers 13:1–2). Joshua was one of them, being designated to represent the entire tribe of Ephraim (Numbers 13:8). When the tribes returned, only Joshua and Caleb of Judah had the faith to believe that with God's help Israel could conquer Canaan (Numbers 13:31 plus 14:6–9). In fact, Joshua and Caleb almost lost their lives trying to get the people to support Moses and the Lord (Numbers 14:10). It will be recalled that as a result of this mutiny the Lord condemned Israel to wander in the wilderness for an additional 38 years. The Lord said that out of that entire generation of adults only Joshua and Caleb would live to enter the promised land (Numbers 14:27–38). …

> It will be further recalled that when Israel had finally raised up a new generation and Moses led them toward Trans-Jordan, the armies of Israel were amazingly successful in overcoming any tribes who tried to destroy or subvert them. All of these victories were under the military direction of Joshua which added tremendous stature to his image as Israel's commander in chief.

> Finally, when Moses was told that it was time that he be "gathered to his people," he ordained Joshua to be his successor by the laying on of hands (Numbers 27:18–23), and gave Joshua the Lord's charge to him, "Be strong and of a good courage: for thou shalt bring the children of

> Israel into the land which I sware unto them: and I will be with thee" (Deuteronomy 31:23). . . Joshua knew that from this moment through to the end of his days, Israel would be his personal responsibility.[1]

THE ISRAELITES ENTER CANAAN

The Lord's Charge and Israel's Covenant

● **Joshua 1:1–4 The extent of the promised land.** He begins with a description of the extent of the promised land, which can be seen in the satellite photo at right (v. 4).

● **Joshua 1:1–9 The Lord charges Joshua to serve with courage and faithfulness.** Joshua had the same priesthood power and authority that Moses had (v. 5). He was to make the law the basis of all he did. He was not to vary from it, and it was not to depart out of his mouth—that is, all that he spoke was to conform to it, and he was to meditate upon it constantly (vv. 7–8).

● **Joshua 1:10–18** The tribes with inheritances east of the Jordan River were Reuben, Gad, and Manasseh— providing that they covenanted to assist the others in conquering Canaan.

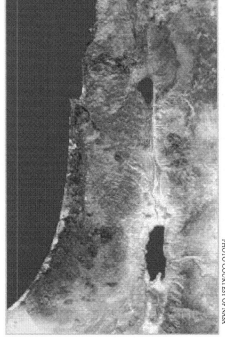

PHOTO COURTESY OF NASA

Satellite view of promised land

Rahab Assists Israelite Spies

● **Joshua 2:1–7 Israelite spies are aided by Rahab in Jericho.** Before entering the promised land, Joshua sent two men to spy on the conditions in the land, and specifically Jericho, which would be their first target of conquest (v. 1). After they entered the city, they found lodging at the house of Rahab, who the scriptures call a "harlot" (v. 1).

The King of Jericho became aware of their entry into the city and demanded that Rahab surrender the men to him (vv. 2–3). Rahab hid the two men in stalks of flax on her roof (vv. 4, 6). Then she told the king that the two men had indeed come but she did not know they were Israelites. She told them that the men had only recently left her home and if they hurried they might catch them (vv. 4–5). The king's men then searched for them all the way to the Jordan river, shutting the gates of the city behind them (v. 7).

● **Joshua 2:8–16 Rahab extracts an oath that they will not harm her or her family, and she lets them down over the wall.** Rahab retrieved the spies from her roof and said that she knew the Lord had given the Israelites the land and that the inhabitants of Jericho were terrified of them (vv. 8–9). They were all very much acquainted with the miracle Moses performed in parting the Red Sea, and they also knew what they had done to the Amorites on the other side of the Jordan River (v. 10). These things caused the people of Jericho's "hearts [to] melt, neither did there remain any more courage in any man, because of you: for the Lord your God, he is God in heaven above, and in earth beneath" (v. 11).

Rahab asked them to make an oath with her, since she had showed them kindness, that would not harm her or her family, and "give me a true token" of this oath (vv. 12–13). The men did so, saying "Our life for yours, if ye utter not this our business. And it shall be, when the LORD hath given us the land, that we will deal kindly and truly with thee" (v. 14). Then "she let them down by a cord through the window: for her house was upon the town wall, and she dwelt upon the wall" (v. 15). She advised them to go into the mountains, "lest the pursuers meet you; and hide yourselves there three days, until the pursuers be returned: and afterward may ye go your way" (v. 16).

Rahab lets spies down outside the wall

The men again assured her that they would keep their oath, and gave her the token that she had requested—a line of scarlet thread in the window by which she had let them down outside the wall (vv. 17–18). If she revealed their purpose to anyone then the oath would be void (v. 20), but otherwise they would see that nobody did her or her family any harm (v. 19). Satisfied with this, she let them go and put the scarlet line in her window (v. 21).

- **The value placed on an oath or promise by men of ancient times.** We can see by this story the very high regard men of that culture had for their solemn oaths. We see a similar thing in the oath that Nephi made to Laban's servant, and the confidence Zoram had in Nephi's promise after he made that oath (1 Nephi 4:30–35). Unfortunately, men of that day were more faithful to their covenants with other men than they were to the covenants they made with God.

- **Was Rahab a harlot?** This is much dispute among scholars about this question. The Hebrew word *rahab* is translated "harlot," and that is what the Hebrew texts contain. It certainly would have attracted no attention if strangers stayed in her home, even those who were of other nationalities. But Adam Clarke contends that the scripture in this case is mistranslated: "I am fully satisfied that the term zonah in the text, which we translate harlot, should be rendered tavern or inn-keeper or hostess"[2].

Both James and Paul cite Rahab as an Old Testament example of true faith (Hebrews 11:31). After the destruction of Jericho she dwelt in Israel for the remainder of her life. (Joshua 6:22–25.) A Rahab is mentioned in the genealogy of the Savior. (Matthew 1:5.) Since no other woman of that name is mentioned in the scriptures, most scholars assume it is the same woman.

W. Cleon Skousen said: "It would … seem apparent that Rahab was not a Canaanite even though she was living in a Canaanite city. This seems clear from the fact that she subsequently married a prince of Judah (Matthew 1:5. The New Testament spelling is "Rachab"), which marriage would have been unlawful had she been of Hamitic lineage (Genesis 24:3). This conclusion is further supported by the fact that she was the direct lineage through which the Savior was born"[3].

- **Joshua 2:22–24 The spies return and report to Joshua.** As recommended by Rahab, they went into the mountains for three days until their pursuers had given up and gone back to Jericho

(v. 22). Then they crossed the Jordan River and reported to Joshua all that had happened to them (v. 23). They could see that the whole land would be theirs because its inhabitants "do faint because of us" (v. 24).

Crossing the Jordan River

● **Joshua 3:1–7 Joshua instructs the Israelites on how to cross the Jordan.** He moved the camp of Israel from Shittim down to the banks of the Jordan River (v. 1). After three days of preparation, he sent instructions through the camp that the people were to follow the ark of the covenant into the water (vv. 2–3). They were not to get too close, remaining "about two thousand cubits" away from it (v. 4) while following it "that ye may know the way by which ye must go: for ye have not passed this way heretofore" (v. 4). He instructed the priests to lead the way, which would make them the first to step into the waters of the river (v. 6).

The Israelites cross the Jordan River

Joshua then said to the people, "Sanctify yourselves: for to morrow the Lord will do wonders among you" (v. 5). They were about to witness a miracle every bit as impressive as Moses' parting of the Red Sea.

● **Joshua 3:7; 4:14 The significance of this event in the eyes of the people.** The Lord said to Joshua, "This day will I begin to magnify thee in the sight of all Israel, that they may know that, as I was with Moses, so I will be with thee" (Josh. 3:7). The miracle that he performed on that day caused the Israelites to "fear" [respect] Joshua just as they had "feared Moses, all the days of his life" (Josh. 4:14).

● **Joshua 3:8, 10, 12–13, 15–17 The waters of the Jordan River parted before them.** Joshua had commanded the priests, when they entered into the river bearing the ark of the covenant, that they were to "stand still in Jordan" (v. 8). He told the people, "Hereby ye shall know that the living God is among you, and that he will without fail drive out from before you the Canaanites, and the Hittites, and the Hivites, and the Perizzites, and the Girgashites, and the Amorites, and the Jebusites" (v. 10). They were to select twelve priests from among them—one from each tribe (v. 12). Then he promised them that as soon as the feet of the priests bearing the ark went into that water "the waters of Jordan shall be cut off from the waters that come down from above; and they shall stand upon an heap" (v. 13).

This miracle at the Jordan River was perhaps even more impressive than when Moses parted the waters of the Red Sea. The Red Sea was a stationary body of water, while the Jordan River was a flowing stream. To part the Jordan River's waters they would have had to stop flowing and stand up on one side. The other side would have become dry from a lack of flowing water. And all of this was done at the season of the year when "Jordan overfloweth all his banks all the time of harvest" (v. 15). This was no trickling stream; it was a river overflowing its banks.

But so it was. Just as soon as "they that bare the ark were come unto Jordan, and the feet of the priests that bare the ark were dipped in the brim of the water, ... the waters which came down from above stood and rose up upon an heap," while the waters below that flowed down toward the Dead Seas "were cut off: and the people passed over right against [very near to] Jericho" (vv. 15–16). Thus, "the priests that bare the ark of the covenant of the Lord stood firm on dry ground in the midst of Jordan, and all the Israelites passed over on dry ground, until all the people were passed clean over Jordan" (v. 17).

- **Joshua 4:19 The date of this miracle and Israel's entrance into the promised land.** Israel passed over the River Jordan on the tenth day of the first month, which would mean 10 days after the spring equinox (March 21st + 10 days = March 31st).

- **1 Corinthians 10:1–4 The significance of Israel's passing through water as they entered the promised land.** Paul taught that the passage of the Israelites through the Red Sea was a symbol of their baptism as a people. The same could be said for this parting of waters on the Jordan River. It is appropriate that the Israelites, as a people, should be symbolically "baptized" as they entered their land of promise. After all, it is through the ordinance of baptism that we all gain entrance into the kingdom of heaven.

- **Joshua 3:16 The significance of the location.** We are told that the Israelites crossed very near to Jericho, which would put the point of their crossing in a specific place as indicated on the map at right. This place on the river is rich with symbolism in its location and history. Consider the following facts:

  — **Jesus descended below all things here.** The Rift Valley, through which the Jordan flows, is the lowest depression on earth. From the river's headwaters in the foothills of Mt. Hermon, it descends nearly 1,600 feet to where it ends at the mouth of the Dead Sea. That place is the lowest spot on the planet earth. Since baptism symbolizes the death and burial—and then resurrection—of our Lord, His being baptized at this spot is rich in symbolism. Both literally and figuratively, as He was baptized He descended below all things.

  — **Israel passed through these waters.** At this same place, the waters of the Jordan were parted to allow the children of Israel to pass through on dry ground as as they entered the promised land. Note the symbolism of the children of Israel passing through the waters (baptism) in order to receive their promised inheritance. Note also that the place where they passed through was exactly the same place where Jesus would later be baptized.

Site where Israel entered Canaan

— **Elijah parting the waters with his mantle.** According to 2 Kings 2:6-8, the prophet Elijah miraculously divided the Jordan River's waters by smiting them with his mantle. This also appears to have taken place near where the Savior was later baptized. Elijah held the keys of sealing by which the dead could receive the same blessings as the living. His parting of the waters seems to symbolize his priesthood power, by which millions of our Father's children will receive the blessings of baptism and the temple

— **Elisha did the same thing after inheriting Elijah's mantle.** According to 2 Kings 2:13-14, Elisha had the same power after receiving Elijah's mantle. In like manner, the prophets today exercise priesthood keys in administering the saving ordinances of the gospel, each one inheriting the mantle of his predecessor.

● **Joshua 4:7 Twelve memorial standing stones are set up to commemorate the miracle.** Once all the people had passed through the riverbed and were on the Canaan side, Joshua commanded them to select twelve men—one from each tribe—to carry memorial stones out of the riverbed and set them up next to the river (vv. 2–5).

The stones were taken from the riverbed and placed where all the people could see them and be reminded of God's miracle there (vv. 6–7). This they did, and the Bible record says, "they are there unto this day" (vv. 8–9). The name of the place where they erected these stones is Gilgal, which in Hebrew means "circle of standing stones."

A standing stone

● **Joshua 5:1 Canaan's inhabitants were in the Israelites' hands,** so long as they kept their covenants with the Lord. The inhabitants of the land were also fearful of the Israelites because of the miracles of Moses and their utter destruction of the Amorites on the other side of the river. Now, when they "heard that the Lord had dried up the waters of Jordan from before the children of Israel, until we [they] passed over, ... their heart melted, neither was there spirit in them any more, because of the children of Israel."

Circumcision Is Renewed and Manna Ceases

● **Joshua 5:2–9 The covenant of circumcision was renewed.** Israel had wandered forty years in the wilderness because they were not faithful in their covenant with God. It is not surprising, then, that during that period they had failed to continue the practice of circumcision, which was the symbol of their covenant. The Lord required them to re- institute this physical token at this time, saying "Make thee sharp knives, and circumcise again the children of Israel" (v. 2). The men who came out of Egypt 40 years earlier had all been circumcised, but they were now dead. Their male children that were born in the wilderness had not been circumcised, so now they needed to do it as a symbol of their covenants (vv. 3–5). Joshua performed the surgery and they remained at their camp near Jericho "till they were whole" (v. 8). All this was done at Gilgal (v. 9).

- **Joshua 5:10–12 Manna ends after 40 years.** The Israelites had been tenderly fed with manna for 40 years—more than 12,000 times—but now they were to eat the bread of the land obtained from their own labor. They observed the Passover at their camp in Gilgal (v. 10). Then, the next day they ate unleavened bread along with "old corn" (wheat) and parched "corn" (v. 11). The next day, after eating their first meal of food in the promised land, manna ceased (v. 12).

THE CONQUEST OF CANAAN BEGINS

The Lord Is Israel's Captain

- **Joshua 5:13–15 Joshua receives a visit from the captain of the Lord's host.** As the Israelites prepared to conquer the city-states of Canaan, Joshua looked up one day to see "a man over against [standing near] him with his sword drawn in his hand" (v. 13). Not knowing who he was, Joshua asked him, "Art thou for us, or for our adversaries?" (v. 13). And the man's answer was, "Nay; but as captain of the host of the Lord am I now come" (v. 14). We learn much about who this visitor was by what happened next:

  — "Joshua fell on his face to the earth, and did worship, and said unto him, What saith my lord unto his servant?" (v. 14).

  — "The captain of the LORD's host said unto Joshua, Loose thy shoe from off thy foot; for the place whereon thou standest is holy" (v. 15).

Most scholars assume either a mortal servant of God or an angel came to strengthen Joshua and Israel as they prepared for their first battle. Two things, however, suggest that Joshua may actually have seen Jehovah:

  — First, when Joshua fell down to worship him, no attempt was made to stop him. Yet the mortal servants of God and even angels are quick to prevent others from worshiping them, even when they have demonstrated great power (Acts 10:25–26; 14:8–18; Alma 18:15–17; Revelation 22:9; 19:10; Judges 13:16).

  — Second, the personage commanded Joshua to remove his shoes because he was standing on holy ground—the same instructions Jehovah gave to Moses on Mount Sinai (Exodus 3:5).

The Battle of Jericho

"Ancient Jericho is located at Tell es-Sultan, next to a copious spring on the western edge of the Jordan Valley, just north of the Dead Sea. The site's excellent water supply and favorable climate (especially in winter) have made it a desirable place to live from the very beginning of settled habitation. A Neolithic settlement at the site goes back to about 8000 BC, thus giving Jericho the distinction of being the world's oldest city. At 670 feet below sea level, it is also the lowest city in the world.

"The site is strategically located. From Jericho one has access to the heartland of Canaan. Any military force attempting to penetrate the central hill country from the east would, by necessity, first have to capture Jericho. And that is exactly what the Bible (Joshua 3:16) says the Israelites did"[4].

● **Joshua 6:4–27 Jericho and its inhabitants are utterly destroyed.** The inhabitants of Jericho knew of the powerful destruction that Israel had directed against the kingdom of the Amorites east of Jordan. Therefore, it is no surprise that they shut up their walled city against Israel. According to recent archaeological finds, these walls were substantial—a 15-foot high stone revetment wall, on top of which was built a mudbrick parapet wall another 8-feet high—which extended all the way around the city" (Wood, "Did the Israelites Conquer Jericho? A New Look at the Archaeological Evidence.")

W. Cleon Skousen described the battle vividly as follows:

Having received … instructions [from the Lord], Joshua … organized the military might of Israel In a very special way and then ordered them to march directly toward Jericho. First came the army of Israel, then seven priests followed them blowing their trumpets of rams' horns. Behind the trumpeters came the Ark of the Covenant carried on the shoulders of several priests. Last of all came the special guard bringing up the rear (Joshua 6:7-9).

GUSTAVE DORÉ, 1896

Joshua attacks Jericho after walls collapse

The sight of this great throng must have caused the people of Jericho to rush to their battle stations in expectation of an immediate attack, but they were in for a surprise. Instead of attacking, the Israelites made one complete circle around Jericho and then marched directly back to their camp site. They did not so much as unlimber their weapons. Another peculiar thing about this meaningless maneuver was its solemnity. Not a sound was uttered by the multitude as they marched around Jericho (Joshua 6:10). Only the mournful sound of the rams' horn trumpets and the muffled plodding of the thousands of marching feet ascended to the ears of Jericho's defenders mounted on her high walls. As they watched the hosts of Israel march back to their camp they were left with a feeling of puzzled anxiety. What were the Israelites up to?

The same thing happened the next day and the next. For six consecutive days this strange military exercise was repeated. Since the Israelites made no gesture of hostility it should have occurred to the king of Jericho that an overture of peace could be made to these people. … [But instead] he would lock his people behind [Jericho's walls] and defy Israel.

This was the state of things when Israel came out to march around Jericho on the seventh day. By this time the people of the city had no doubt become bored with this idle parade-ground maneuver and may have assumed that it would continue indefinitely. But on this seventh day something unusual happened. After completing their encirclement of Jericho the hosts of Israel did not march back to camp. They began circling again. Even after the second encirclement they did not return to camp. Nor after the third, fourth, fifth or sixth. These Hebrews were maddening. Nothing could have drawn the manpower of Jericho's forces to the top of her high walls faster than this continuous circling of the city. Had the king known the mind of the Lord he would have realized that the worst place in the city for his soldiers was on top of this wall. It was a death trap.

As the armies of Israel started their seventh encirclement of Jericho every man in the ranks knew the hour for battle had come. As the Ark completed the final procession around the city the priests who carried it suddenly stopped and the long military line shuffled to a halt. Every man then turned toward that portion of the wall directly in front of him and drew his sword. A moment later the seven priests who stood before the Ark raised their trumpets of rams' horns and sounded a long clarion signal. Immediately a great shout went up from the hosts of Israel.

The roar which came from the dust-parched throats of the Hebrew soldiers seemed to reverberate back from the walls before them. Suddenly the great stacks of stone, mortar and dried mud which had been the pride of Jericho's defense, began to tremble and quake like teetering piles of collapsing building blocks. In one great thunderous debacle they came tumbling down upon themselves with soldiers, stones, mortar and bricks all grinding and crashing together in one mammoth avalanche of devastating destruction (Joshua 6:20). It was the miracle the Lord had promised. ...

Joshua ... sent in his two spies to locate Rahab and her family ... and bring her out together with all of her kindred and their various possessions ... [which they did] (Joshua 6:22–23).

Then the hosts of Israel performed their terrible task of destruction required of them: "And they utterly destroyed all that was in the city...." (Joshua 6:21). Nothing was left alive, neither of man nor beast. It was total extinction for Jericho. "And they burnt the city with fire, and all that was therein: only the silver, and the gold, and the vessels of brass and of iron, they put into the treasury of the house of the Lord" (Joshua 6:24). Even the ruins of Jericho were execrated. Joshua said, "Cursed be the man before the Lord that riseth up and buildeth this city Jericho ... . (Joshua 6:26)."[5]

- **The prevalence of the number seven in the Lord's dealing with Jericho's defense is significant.** Throughout the law of Moses, seven was used numerous times to signify the covenant. Its association with the covenant probably stems from the idea that "seven...is associated with completion, fulfilment, and perfection"[6]. By patterning the conquest of Jericho in sevens, the Lord taught Israel that their success lay in the covenant with Jehovah; his perfect power brought conquest, not their own.

- **The Hebrew shofar, or ram's horn (vv. 4–6)** was the oldest musical instrument in Israel. After being flattened by heat, the horn of a ram was forced to turn up at the ends. This shape thus created a most unusual and easily recognizable sound. In early times the horn was used to warn of approaching armies, to give the signal for attack, or to dismiss troops from the field.

- **The ark of the covenant symbolized the presence of God** in the tabernacle's Holy of Holies, so it symbolized his leadership of the armies of Israel as they carried it before them while they marched around the city. This was not a mere mortal conflict: Canaan was to be destroyed by the very God of Israel. This truth was impressively taught to Israel by the presence of the ark (vv. 4, 6–8).

Joshua 6:20 What caused the walls of Jericho to fall? Bible naysayers do not believe that Joshua's shofar horns caused the walls of Jericho to fall. In fact, they do not believe that Jericho was brought down at all, by anyone, during this period. But the evidence is increasing with time that the walls did collapse and the city was burned, just as the Bible tells us in the book of Joshua. More recent archaeological finds support the Bible account. Consider the following article published by archaeologist Bryant G. Wood in *Biblical Archaeological Review* magazine[7]:

Blowing a shofar horn

The pottery, stratigraphic considerations, scarab data and a Carbon-14 date all point to a destruction of the city around the end of Late Bronze I, about 1400 B.C.E. ...

Was this destruction at the hands of the Israelites? The correlation between the archaeological evidence and the Biblical narrative is substantial:

— The city was strongly fortified (Joshua 2:5, 7, 15, 6:5, 20).

— The attack occurred just after harvest time in the spring (Joshua 2:6; 3:15; 5:10).

— The inhabitants had no opportunity to flee with their foodstuffs (Joshua 6:1).

— The siege was short (Joshua 6:15).

— The walls were leveled, possibly by an earthquake (Joshua 6:20).

— The city was not plundered (Joshua 6:17–18).

— The city was burned (Joshua 6:24).[8]

Elder James E. Talmage said:

May we not believe that when Israel encompassed Jericho, the captain of the Lord's host and his heavenly train were there, and that before their super-mortal agency, sustained by the faith and obedience of the human army, the walls were leveled?

Some of the latest and highest achievements of man in the utilization of natural forces approach the conditions of spiritual operations. To count the ticking of a watch thousands of miles away; to speak in but an ordinary tone and be heard across the continent; to signal from one hemisphere and be understood on the other though oceans roll and roar between; to bring the lightning into our homes and make it serve as fire and torch; to navigate the air and to travel beneath the ocean surface; to make chemical and atomic energies obey our will—are not these miracles? The possibility of such would not have been received with credence before their actual accomplishment. Nevertheless, these and all other miracles are accomplished through the operation of the laws of nature, which are the laws of God.[9]

- **Joshua 7:1–13 Defeat at the City of Ai.** After conquering Jericho, Joshua turned his attention to the city of Ai, very near Bethel to the northwest (see map). He first sent spies to ascertain the challenge, and they returned with the recommendation that Joshua send "about two or three thousand men go up and smite Ai; and make not all the people to labour thither; for they are but few" (vv. 2–3).

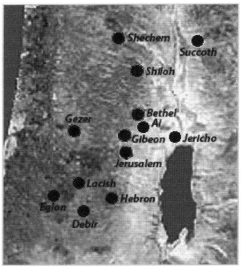

Joshua did this, but his men suffered a humiliating defeat, with 36 men losing their lives in the battle (vv. 4–5). The hearts of the Israelites "melted" at this news "and became as water" (v. 5).

Joshua was devastated. He "rent his clothes, and fell to the earth upon his face before the ark of the Lord until the eventide, he and the elders of Israel, and put dust upon their heads (v. 6). The act of placing dust on the head had the same symbolic meaning as dressing in sackcloth and sitting in ashes. It was a token of great remorse, true humility, and deep repentance. It also symbolized the unworthiness of a man when compared to God (Genesis 37:34; Job 2:12; Lamentations 2:10).

Joshua asked the Lord, "wherefore hast thou at all brought this people over Jordan, to deliver us into the hand of the Amorites, to destroy us? would to God we had been content, and dwelt on the other side Jordan!" (v. 7). He feared that the Israelites would now "turn their backs" on their enemies [flee from them], and would be surrounded by the Canaanites and destroyed (vv. 8–9).

The Lord's answer was firm: "Joshua, Get thee up; wherefore liest thou thus upon thy face?" (v. 10). "Israel hath sinned, and they have also transgressed my covenant which I commanded them: for they have even taken of the accursed thing, and have also stolen, and dissembled also, and they have put it even among their own stuff" (v. 11). That was why they had been defeated, and the Lord said Israel would be "accursed" and He would not be with them anymore "except ye destroy the accursed from among you" (v. 12). He told Joshua to get up and "sanctify the people" by telling them what had happened and cleansing the camp of the unclean idol that had been brought into it (vv. 1, 13).

Elder James E. Talmage said: "Consider the defeat of Israel by the men of Ai; a law of righteousness had been violated, and things that were accursed had been introduced into the camp of the covenant people; this transgression interposed resistance to the current of divine help, and until the people had sanctified themselves the power was not renewed unto them" (Joshua 7:10–13)"[10].

- **Joshua 7:16–23 Achan confesses that he stole things from the city of Jericho.** Joshua was directed by the Lord to the family of the tribe of Judah where Achan lived. He inter- viewed

Achan and asked him what he had done to dishonor Israel (vv. 18–19).

Achan told the truth. "When I saw among the spoils a goodly Babylonish garment, and two hundred shekels of silver, and a wedge of gold of fifty shekels weight, then I coveted them, and took them; and, behold, they are hid in the earth in the midst of my tent, and the silver under it" (v. 21). Joshua sent men to retrieve it. They did so and "laid them out before the Lord" (23).

● **Joshua 7:17–26 Achan is executed for his crime.** He was taken outside the city, where his family watched as he was stoned to death and then his body was burned. They buried his remains there under a pile of rocks (vv. 25-26).

THE STORY OF THE BIBLE, #74, p.187, 1873, 1877, 1884

Achan's stolen loot is discovered

We might well ask, "Was this punishment too harsh?" Achan's disobedience cost the lives of 36 men (v. 5). Equally important, Israel's spiritual death could have resulted from the infestation of idols, clothes, and riches from people whose lives had been lived in such retched and wanton lewdness and cruelty. These are the same people who offered up their babies to the fiery arms of Molech and engaged in public acts of sexual intercourse in groves of trees. The Lord wanted <u>none</u> of their beliefs or practices to be introduced among the Israelites. He had commanded them to utterly destroy both the people and their possessions for this reason. For Israel to fail to obey the Lord in this thing would have been tantamount to accepting the abominations of their predecessors. And it is apparent from his voluntary confession that Achan understood this (v. 20–21).

The City of Ai Is Now Taken and Destroyed

● **Joshua 8:1–29 The Lord commands them to utterly destroy Ai's inhabitants.** With evil expunged from the camp, the Lord said to Joshua, "Fear not, neither be thou dismayed: take all the people of war with thee, and arise, go up to Ai. … I have given into thy hand the king of Ai, and his people, and his city, and his land" (v. 1). They were to utterly destroy the people of Ai, just as they had the people of Jericho. But in this case, the Lord permitted them to take spoils— "the cattle thereof, shall ye take for a prey unto yourselves" (v. 2).

The Lord—who was the captain of the host and therefore their commanding general— instructed Joshua to "lay thee an ambush for the city behind it" (v. 2). Joshua sent 30 thousand men to lie in wait behind the city, ready to attack at any moment (vv. 3–4). Joshua then took the remainder of the army and approached the city of Ai from the front. When the army of Ai came out to meet them they pretended to flee in order to "draw. . . them from the city" (v. 6). At that moment, the men behind the city were to "rise up from the ambush, and seize upon the city: for the LORD your God will deliver it into your hand" (v. 7). They were then to "set the city on fire" as the Lord commanded (v. 8).

The strategy worked perfectly (vv. 9–16). In fact, "there was not a man left in Ai or Beth-el, that went not out after Israel: and they left the city open, and pursued after Israel" (v. 17). The ambush army entered the city and set it on fire, which, when the men of Ai saw behind them, they realized they were trapped. Joshua's army fell on them and destroyed them (vv. 18–21). Ultimately, they let none of the men of Ai escape; they were all killed in the battle, along with some women—12,000 in all (v. 25).

Joshua's army took the spoil of the city for themselves, as permitted in this case by the Lord (vv. 26–27). Then Joshua "burnt Ai, and made it an heap for ever, even a desolation unto this day" (v. 28). "And the king of Ai he hanged on a tree until eventide: and as soon as the sun was down, Joshua commanded that they should take his carcase down from the tree, and cast it at the entering of the gate of the city, and raise thereon a great heap of stones, that remaineth unto this day" (v. 29).

The Conference at Mount Ebal

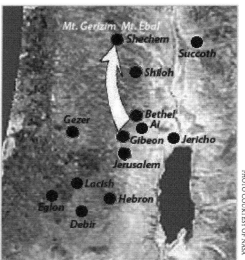

● **Joshua 8 Once Ai was taken, Joshua moved Israel to Mount Ebal and Mount Gerizim** and fulfilled the instructions of Moses to build an altar there and pronounce the blessings and cursings of the Lord from those peaks (Deut. 27).

● **Joshua 8:30–35 Joshua built an altar and read the words of the law before the congregation.** As instructed by Moses and Lord, Joshua built "an altar of whole stones, over which no man hath lift up any iron: and they offered thereon burnt offerings unto the Lord, and sacrificed peace offerings" (v. 31). Then, as instructed, half the people gathered on Mt. Gerizim and the other half on Mt. Ebal—the first group to curse Israel if they broke their covenants, and the second group to bless Israel if they kept their covenants (vv. 32–33). Then afterward, Joshua "read all the words of the law, the blessings and cursings, according to all that is written in the book of the law" (v. 34), making sure that "there was not a word of all that Moses commanded, which Joshua read not before all the congregation of Israel, with the women, and the little ones, and the strangers that were conversant among them" (vv. 34–35).

The Lord Commands the Utter Destruction of the Canaanites

● **Joshua 23:4–5 Eventually, 31 Canaanite city-states are designated to be destroyed.** The Lord intended to give the Israelites all of the land he covenanted to give to Abraham and his seed. Their inheritance would stretch from the Jordan River all the way to the Mediterranean Sea (v. 4). The Lord promised to "expel [the inhabitants] from before you, and drive them from out of your sight; and ye shall possess their land, as the Lord your God hath promised unto you" (v. 5). The complete destruction of all Canaanite cities and near-extermination of the Canaanite inhabitants may seem unduly harsh, but it should be remembered that the Canaanites were utterly corrupt. Since men tend to adopt the values or habits of those with whom they associate, it was imperative that all idolatrous nations in Canaan be destroyed.

— **1 Nephi 17:32–35 The Lord destroys a people when they become "ripe in iniquity."** Commenting on the destruction of the Canaanites, the prophet Nephi in the Book of Mormon asked, "And now, do ye suppose that the children of this land, who were in the land of promise, who were driven out by our fathers, do ye suppose that they were righteous? Behold, I say unto you, Nay. Do ye suppose that our fathers would have been more choice than they if they had been righteous? I say unto you, Nay" (vv. 33–34). The only favoritism the Lord shows is toward the righteous.

As Nephi said, "the Lord esteemeth all flesh in one; he that is righteous is favored of God. But behold, this people had rejected every word of God, and they were ripe in iniquity; and the fulness of the wrath of God was upon them; and the Lord did curse the land against them, and bless it unto our fathers; yea, he did curse it against them unto their destruction, and he did bless it unto our fathers unto their obtaining power over it" (v. 35). And of course, when the Israelites became ripe in iniquity, he drove them from the land just as he had the Canaanites before them.

— **Genesis 15:13–16 The iniquity of the inhabitants of Canaan had become "full."** The Lord told Abraham more than 400 years earlier that his posterity would go into Egypt, be enslaved, and come out "with great substance" before they would inherit the land of Canaan (vv. 13–14). Abraham himself would live a long life and die and be buried before that would happen (v. 15). Not until "the fourth generation" would the Israelites return, because "the iniquity of the Amorites [the inhabitants of Canaan] is not yet full" (v. 16).

— **Moses 8:20–22, 28–30 The people in Noah's day had become ripe in iniquity.** Noah preached repentance for many years to the people of his day, "but they hearkened not unto his words"(v. 20). They were full of pride and self-sufficiency, believing they were "mighty" and "of great renown" (v. 21). Wickedness was everywhere, with every man "being only evil continually" (v. 22). The earth was completely corrupt and full of violence (v. 28). Agency was not possible for any child born into that society because they would never know anything but evil. They had become ripe in iniquity. Therefore the Lord declared, "The end of all flesh is come before me, for the earth is filled with violence, and behold I will destroy all flesh from off the earth" (v. 30).

— **2 Peter 2:6 Peter says Sodom and Gomorrah had become thoroughly "ungodly."** There was nothing left to do but "turn. . .the cities of Sodom and Gomorrha into ashes … making them an ensample unto those that [ever] after should live ungodly."

— **Jude 1:7 Jude also noted their utter depravity.** He said that the citizens of "Sodom and Gomorrha, and the cities about them in like manner, [gave] themselves over to fornication, and going after strange flesh," and were therefore designated to suffer "the vengeance of eternal fire."

— **Leviticus 18:3, 20–25 The Lord demanded uncompromising opposition to the Canaanites and their depravity.** There was no other way for them to survive spiritually. The allure of their abominable and public sexual behaviors and their willingness to shed the innocent blood of children made them ripe in iniquity. The annihilation of the Canaanites was necessary to put an end to these practices and to ensure they did not pollute the Israelites (Deuteronomy 7:16; 9:4–6; 18:9–12; 20:16–18).

JOSHUA THE GENERAL

Conquering Southern Canaan

● **Joshua 9–10 The Israelites conquer the southern cities of Canaan.** Having conquered Ai, and having returned from their conference at Mt. Ebal, they turned their attention to the rest of the major cities of southern Canaan.

● **Joshua 9:3–27 The people of Gibeon know they are next and devise a deception to save their lives.** Some of their men dressed up as "ambassadors" [travelers] from a foreign land with "old sacks upon their asses, and wine bottles, old, and rent, and bound up; And old shoes and clouted upon their feet, and old garments upon them; and all the bread of their provision was dry and mouldy" (vv. 1–6).

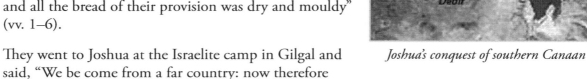

Joshua's conquest of southern Canaan

They went to Joshua at the Israelite camp in Gilgal and said, "We be come from a far country: now therefore make ye a league with us" (v. 6). Joshua was slightly suspicious of them and said, "Who are ye? and from whence come ye?" (v. 8). They answered, "From a very far country thy servants are come because of the name of the Lord thy God: for we have heard the fame of him, and all that he did in Egypt, ... to the two kings of the Amorites, ... to Sihon king of Heshbon, and to Og king of Bashan" (vv. 9–10). They said that "our elders and all the inhabitants of our country spake to us, saying, Take victuals with you for the journey, and go to meet them, and say unto them, We are your servants: therefore now make ye a league with us" (v. 11).

The Gibeonites showed Joshua their old and moldy bread, their torn wine bottles, and their old clothes and shoes, and Joshua believed them without "ask[ing] ... counsel at the mouth of the LORD" (vv. 12–14). He "made peace with them, and made a league with them,

The Gibeonites deceive Joshua

to let them live: and the princes of the congregation sware unto them" (v. 15). Three days later, as they moved into the territory of Gibeon to conquer it, the Israelites learned that the Gibeonites "were their neighbours, and that they dwelt among them" (v. 16). They had been deceived.

The Israelites did not destroy them upon learning of their deception "because the princes of the congregation had sworn unto them by the Lord God of Israel" to do them no harm. This caused "all the congregation" of the Israelites to "murmur … against the princes" (v. 18), but they said to them, "We have sworn unto them by the Lord God of Israel: now therefore we may not touch them" (v. 19). If they were now to destroy them then "wrath [would] be upon us, because of the oath which we sware unto them" (v. 20). But what they could do is turn them into slaves— "hewers of wood and drawers of water unto all the congregation" (v. 21). They had promised to be the Israelite's servants, and now they would be held to their promises as well.

Joshua was very upset at their deception because Moses had warned Israel not to make any covenants with the Canaanites (Deuteronomy 7:2). Joshua was determined to be obedient. "As the LORD commanded Moses his servant, so did Moses command Joshua, and so did Joshua; he left nothing undone of all that the LORD commanded Moses (Joshua 11:15). Nevertheless, since the oath had been made he honored it. But he said unto them, "Now therefore ye are cursed, and there shall none of you be freed from being bondmen, and hewers of wood and drawers of water for the house of my God" (v. 23). They answered that they had heard that the Israelites were commanded to destroy all of the inhabitants of the land and they had deceived them to save their lives (v. 24). Their dishonesty saved their lives, but they became perpetual slaves to the Israelites.

- **Joshua 10:1–11 Adoni-zedek, king of Jerusalem, forms a confederacy of five kings to make war against Gibeon for allying themselves with the Israelites.** He had heard what the Israelites had done to Jericho and to Ai, and that the Gibeonites had made peace with them (v. 1). This was frightening because "Gibeon was a great city … one of the royal cities, and … it was greater than Ai, and all the men thereof were mighty" (v. 2). He therefore formed a confederacy with the kings of Hebron, Jarmuth, Lachish, and Eglon, for the purpose of attacking Gibeon (vv. 3–4).

When they camped around Gibeon and started attacking them, the Gibeonites sent word to Joshua in Gilgal, saying, "Slack not thy hand from thy servants; come up to us quickly, and save us, and help us: for all the kings of the Amorites that dwell in the mountains are gathered together against us" (v. 6). The Lord assured Joshua that He would deliver their entire army into his hands and "there shall not a man of them stand before thee" (v. 8). So he took his army and traveled all night from Gilgal to Gibeon (v. 9), where "the Lord discomfited them before Israel, and slew them with a great slaughter at Gibeon" (v. 10). Joshua's army chased them south toward their homelands, through the settlements of Beth-horon, and Azekah, and Makkedah. And as these armies came near to Beth-horon, "the LORD cast down great [hail]stones from heaven upon them [all the way to] Azekah, and they died" (v. 11). In fact, there were more of them killed by the hailstones than by the swords of the Israelite army (v. 11).

Miracles in the Heavens

- **Joshua 10:12–14 Joshua commands the sun and the moon to stand still.** It was during this war with the five Amorite kings that Joshua performed one of his greatest miracles. He said, in the sight and hearing of the armies of Israel, "Sun, stand thou still upon Gibeon; and thou, Moon, in the valley of Ajalon. And the sun stood still, and the moon stayed, until the people had avenged themselves upon their enemies" (vv. 12–13). The sun stood still and did not go down "about a whole day" (v. 13). There had never been a day "before it or after it, that the Lord hearkened unto the voice of a man" in this manner (v. 14).

Joshua commands the sun and moon

- **Joshua 10:13 The book of Jasher.** In speaking of this miracle, the scripture asks, "Is not this written in the book of Jasher?" The book of Jasher is one of those books that appears in the Apocrypha—books not included in the King James Bible but which do appear in the Catholic bible.

John Pratt said:

> The Book of Jasher includes details about antediluvian [before the flood] patriarchs which are confirmed by modern revelation. The question arises of how the author of Jasher could have known specific facts from before the Great Flood, such as Cainan becoming very wise when he was forty years old. These correlations attest that it was composed from exceedingly ancient reliable sources.

> The Book of Jasher has been popular among members of the LDS Church as a supplement to their study of the Old Testament ever since its publication was announced in the *Times and Seasons* in June, 1840[11]. ...

> The book is a history of the world from the creation until the period of the Judges in Israel. It contains much more information than is found in Genesis for that same period, which makes very interesting reading and clears up many confusing issues in the Bible. It is written mostly as a secular history, but it does contain many references to what God was doing. It is similar to the Books of Joshua through Chronicles in the Bible which describe many historical events such as battles and wars, but which also point out the hand of God in the affairs of men.

> Perhaps the closest approach to an official acknowledgment of the Book of Jasher among the Latter-day Saints was when the Prophet Joseph Smith quoted from it as a source which had "not been disproved as a bad author"[12]. ... The LDS Church has never taken an official stand on the authenticity of the Book of Jasher, but when apostles make lists of "lost books" from the Bible, Jasher is generally included. One article in the "I Have a Question" column of *The Ensign* responded to the question of its authenticity[13]. ... The article concluded with ... the Lord's advice on how to study the Apocrypha:

> *"There are many things contained therein that are true, and it is mostly translated correctly; There are many things contained therein that are not true, which are interpolations by the hands of men. ... Therefore,*

whoso readeth it, let him understand, for the Spirit manifesteth truth; And whoso is enlightened by the Spirit shall obtain benefit … And whoso receiveth not by the Spirit, cannot be benefitted. …" (D&C 91:1–6).

Anyone who has read the Book of Jasher will agree that it certainly contains much truth (many stories from the Bible), and it certainly appears to contain some later interpolations of men, so reading by the Spirit seems like an excellent way to discern which is which."[14]

● **Helaman 12:13–15 Mormon's explanation of Joshua's miracle.** In speaking of the mighty power of God, Mormon said, "if he say unto the earth—Move—it is moved. Yea, if he say unto the earth—Thou shalt go back, that it lengthen out the day for many hours—it is done" (vv. 13–14). Then, in apparent reference to the miracle performed by Joshua he explained, "according to his word the earth goeth back, and it appeareth unto man that the sun standeth still; yea, and behold, this is so; for surely it is the earth that moveth and not the sun" (v. 15). The sun never moves relative to the earth. If it appears to stand still, then the miracle has to do with the earth's movements and not the sun's.

● **Similar prophecies in our day:**

— **D&C 29:14** Before the second coming of the Savior, the "sun shall be darkened," the moon "turned into blood," and stars will "fall from heaven." The first two may have to do with pollution in the air which will make it "appear" that these things have happened. The reference to stars falling from heaven probably speaks of asteroids hitting the earth, since "shooting stars" would be nothing new or particularly unusual.

— **D&C 45:40–42** Speaks of "blood, and fire, and vapors of smoke." These signs, both "in the heavens above, and in the earth beneath" seem to reference war, though the scripture ends with a repeat of the predictions of D&C 29:14 (above).

— **D&C 88:87** "The earth shall tremble and reel to and fro as a drunken man." This scripture repeats the prophecy contained in D&C 29:14 (above), but elaborates on the stars falling from heaven: "the stars shall become exceedingly angry, and shall cast themselves down as a fig that falleth from off a fig–tree."

— **D&C 133:49** All of these things will accompany the appearance of Jesus Christ.

● **Joshua 10:24 Israel's army put their feet on the necks of the five kings they defeated.** To place one's foot upon the neck of a fallen enemy was symbolic—an act that demonstrated complete subjugation. It demonstrated that a defeated enemy had been literally trodden underfoot. This fact is often represented in Egyptian and Assyrian sculptures and wall paintings (1 Kings 5:3; Isaiah 51:23).

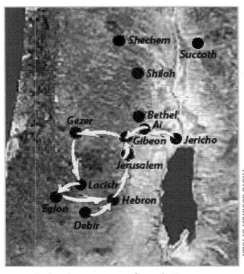

Joshua's conquest of south Canaan

● **Joshua 10:28–43 The destruction of the five nations of southern Canaan was total—utterly**

destroying "all the breathed." Joshua's army went from Makkedah to Libnah to Lachish, defeating and annihilating all their enemies as they went (vv. 28–2). When the armies of Gezer came up to help Lachish they were defeated also "until he had left him none remaining" (v. 33). From there, they moved on to Eglon and to Hebron and to Debir—destroying the cities and every soul within them (vv. 36–39).

Thus, when this southern campaign was finished, they had cleansed the land—"all the country of the hills, … and of the vale, and of the springs, and all their kings: he left none remaining, but utterly destroyed all that breathed, as the Lord God of Israel commanded" (v. 40).

They were now in possession of the land from Gaza on the west to Goshen, Hebron, and then north through Jerusalem to Gibeon. "And all these kings and their land did Joshua take at one time, because the Lord God of Israel fought for Israel" (v. 42).

Conquering Northern Canaan

● **Joshua 11 The Israelites then gained control of northern Canaan.** With south Canaan now secured, the Israelites turned their attention toward the north. This was a larger area and would require more time to conquer (v. 18).

● **Joshua 11:6, 9 Their tactics included the "houghing" of horses.** To hough (pronounced "huff") a horse is to cut the leg tendons above and behind the tarsal joint or ankle, thus rendering the horse useless. This tactic was commanded by the Lord in order to disable their enemies' captured horses. The Israelites were foot soldiers rather than charioteers. The concern was that if the Israelites used the captured horses and chariots as vehicles of war, they might turn from faith in God and trust in the arm of flesh (2 Samuel 8:4; Isaiah 31:1). Houghing the horses would prevent this from happening.

Joshua's conquest of north Canaan

● **Joshua 11:18–20 The kings of northern Canaan fought back fiercely but were also utterly destroyed.** It took a "long time" to defeat them (v. 18). None of the cities "made peace with the children of Israel" like the Hivites (the inhabitants of Gibeon) had done. All of the other cities (south and north) "they took in battle" (v. 19). When they hardened their hearts and came against the army of Israel, it only facilitated their utter destruction (v. 20).

● **Joshua 11:22 The Anakim are called a race of "giants" (Numbers 13:32–33).** But as we learned while studying the book of Numbers this word is probably mistranslated. The original word meant something like "vicious and destructive" rather than "big and scary." They utterly destroyed the Anakim who lived in the land of Israel, but a few still lived outside Israel in Gaza,

Gath, and Ashdod. In this particular case, these "giants" may indeed have been large in stature, because Goliath came from Gath (1 Samuel 17:4).

● **Joshua 12 The Israelites' victories are summarized in this chapter.** These included cities "in the mountains, and in the valleys, and in the plains, and in the springs, and in the wilderness, and in the south country; the Hittites, the Amorites, and the Canaanites, the Perizzites, the Hivites, and the Jebusites" (v. 8). In all, two kings on the east of Jordan, and thirty-one on the west, were conquered by Israel. But this did not include all of the land given to the Israelites by the Lord. Joshua was now "old and stricken in years," and there still remained "very much land to be possessed" (Joshua 13:1).

The Tabernacle Is Established at Shiloh

● **Joshua 18:1 The Israelites gather together at Shiloh and set up the Tabernacle.** This beloved portable temple had served them for more than 40 years—never with a permanent place to rest. Now it had a home, and Shiloh would remain the site of temple worship for the Israelites until the day when Solomon built his temple at Jerusalem.

ISRAEL IN JOSHUA'S DAY

Inheritances Assigned in the Promised Land

● **Joshua 18:2–4 Seven tribes had not yet received their inheritances (v. 2).** Joshua said unto them, "How long are ye slack to go to possess the land, which the LORD God of your fathers hath given you?" (v. 3). He asked for three men from each tribe, to "go through the land, and describe it according to the inheritance of them; and they shall come again to me" (v. 4).

● **Joshua 18:5 Judah will be in the south and Joseph in the north.** This designation was the foundation of what would eventually become two competing kingdoms: the Kingdom of Judah and the Kingdom of Israel.

● **Joshua 18:7–9 Israel is divided into seven more tribal areas.** The Levites would have no tribal inheritance, and Gad, and Reuben, and half the tribe of Manasseh had already received their inheritances on the east side of the Jordan River (v. 7). Joshua had now declared the homelands for Judah and Joseph (v. 5). That left seven tribes in need of a homeland. The designated men from each tribe passed through the land, and recorded in a book the cities within each of the seven areas (v. 9). Then they returned to Joshua at Shiloh.

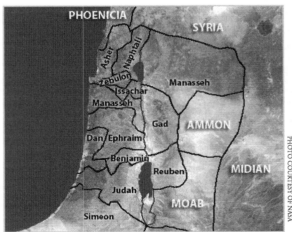

Designated tribal inheritances for Israel

- **Joshua 18–19 Joshua cast lots to determine which tribe would inherit which land.** At the command of the Lord, Joshua now gave the remaining tribes their inheritances. He began by drawing lots for Benjamin, as described in chapter 18. Then he drew lots for Simeon, Zebulun, Issachar, Asher, Naphtali, and Dan, as described in chapter 19.

The original area promised to the children of Israel was much larger than present-day Israel. The Lord told Joshua that all of the original land promised to Abraham would be given to Israel (Genesis 15:18; Joshua 1:4).

The extent of that land is generally the region south and southwest of the Lebanon mountains, north and east of Egypt, east of the Mediterranean coastal plain, and west of the Arabian desert. But today, Palestine is only roughly 150 miles from Dan to Beersheba, and at its greatest width is about 75 miles across.

Although the Israelites who went into the promised land with Joshua were generally faithful and obedient, as a nation Israel soon returned to their old ways and lost the blessings promised to them of winning the whole land.

It was not until the time of David and Solomon (about two hundred years later) that Israel controlled all the land given in the original covenant, and then only for a short while, for they soon lost the outermost parts of it again.

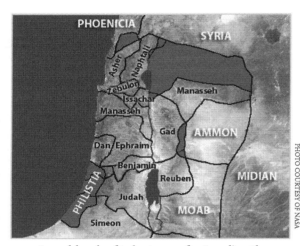

Actual lands of inheritance for Israel's tribes

- **Not all intended areas were inherited.** The description of Israel's lands of inheritance in Joshua 13–19 were the intended boundaries, and the ones which will apply in the Millennium when these tribes will re-inherit their homelands. Sad to say, Israel never did completely inherit all of these territories because they allowed some of the previous inhabitants to remain on the land. This was contrary to the instructions of the Lord, and eventually they paid a heavy price for intermixing with the Canaanites and their abominable religious practices.

Cities of Refuge

- **Joshua 20 Lists the six cities of refuge and their purpose.** These six were among the 48 cities given to the Levites by the Lord through Moses. Some were east of the Jordan River and some were west of it.

- **Joshua 21 Forty-eight cities are appointed all over the land for the Levites.** The tribe of Levi had no designated land to inherit like the other tribes. Instead, they were to function as the priests and judges of the people, living in designated cities throughout the land of Israel. This chapter lists those cities.

- **Joshua 21:43–45 With all of Israel's enemies eliminated, they lived in peace.** The promise made to Abraham was now fulfilled. The Israelites now inhabited "all the land which he sware to give unto their fathers; and they possessed it, and dwelt therein" (v. 43). They could now rest because "there stood not a man of all their enemies before them" (v. 44). Every good thing that had been promised to them through Moses was now given to them in rich abundance (v. 45).

Controversy over an Altar

- **Joshua 22:1–9 Two and one-half tribes are dismissed with a blessing and return to the east side of the Jordan River where their inheritances are located.** This included the tribes of Reuben, Gad, and half the tribe of Manasseh (v. 1).

- **Joshua 22:10–20 They build an altar to the Lord on the Jordan River, nearly causing a civil war.** This was a very large altar of testimony to show that they were the Lord's people (v. 10). This caused a lot of controversy in Israel because the only authorized place for offering sacrifices was at the tabernacle in Shiloh. This rule helped the Israelites avoid idolatry of any kind by offering unauthorized sacrifices to strange gods. In fact, the other tribes were so angry that they gathered together at Shiloh, preparing to go to war (v. 12). Cooler heads prevailed, and they sent an emissary of ten men from all the other tribes to ask them why they had built an altar (vv. 14–16). They feared that the Lord would turn away from all of Israel because of it (vv. 17–20). The tragedy in all of this is that in a short time Israel would no longer react strongly against idolatry, and would, in fact, build altars all over the land.

- **Joshua 22:26–34 The tribes who built the altar show that it will be used for legitimate worship and not idolatry.** They had built the altar, "not for burnt offering, nor for sacrifice: But that it may be a witness between us, and you, and our generations after us" that they were people of the Lord (vv. 27–28). "It is a witness between us and you," they said (v. 28). "God forbid that we should rebel against the Lord" (v. 29). This explanation pleased Phinehas, the high priest, and all the princes of the other tribes (v. 30). They returned to Shiloh and told the other tribes what they had learned, "and the thing pleased the children of Israel; and the children of Israel blessed God, and did not intend to go up against them in battle, to destroy [them]" (v. 33). "And the children of Reuben and the children of Gad called the altar Ed [Hebrew for "witness"]: for it shall be a witness between us that the Lord is God" (v. 34).

JOSHUA'S FAREWELL SPEECHES

- **Joshua 23:1–2 Joshua was now "old and stricken in age" (v.** 1). He desired to speak to his people one last time so he "called for all Israel, and for their elders, and for their heads, and for their judges, and for their officers" (v. 2) to come together to hear two addresses that he had prepared for them.

Joshua's First Address: Separation from the World

(Joshua 23)

- **Joshua 23:2–12 Advice on how to keep themselves unspotted from the world.** Joshua warned Israel of four things they must do to guard against evil influences from the heathen nations that surrounded them:

  — **Joshua 23:6** Be courageously obedient. Do "all that is written in the book of the law of Moses" and "turn not aside therefrom to the right hand or to the left."

  — **Joshua 23:7** Beware of social intercourse with surrounding nations. They were not to "come … among these nations … that remain among you" lest they become poisoned by their unholy cultures.

  — **Joshua 23:7–11** Refrain from worshiping their false gods. They were not to "make mention of the name of their gods, nor cause to swear by them, neither serve them, nor bow yourselves unto them." They were to "cleave unto the Lord your God," who had driven out these abominable practices by making one Israelite more mighty than a thousand of their enemies (vv. 9–10). "Take good heed therefore unto yourselves, that ye love the Lord your God" (v. 11).

  — **Joshua 23:12** Avoid intermarriages with them. This could lead to "go[ing] back" to the former wickedness of Israel.

- **Joshua 23:13 Otherwise, "snares and traps," "scourges," and "thorns" awaited Israel.** Joshua declared flatly that "the Lord your God will no more drive out any of these nations from before you; but they shall be snares and traps unto you, and scourges in your sides, and thorns in your eyes, until ye perish from off this good land which the Lord your God hath given you" (v. 13).

- **Joshua 23:14 The Lord has kept His promises to them.** They should "know in all your hearts and in all your souls, that not one thing hath failed of all the good things which the Lord your God spake concerning you; all are come to pass unto you, and not one thing hath failed thereof."

- **Joshua 23:15–16 When they turn away from the Lord, He will destroy them.** Just as surely as He had kept His word in blessing them, He will "bring upon you all evil things, until he have destroyed you from off this good land" if they forget Him and stop keeping His commandments (v. 15). If they violate the covenant of righteousness they made with the Lord and go and serve other gods, "then shall the anger of the Lord be kindled against you, and ye shall perish quickly from off the good land which he hath given unto you" (v. 16).

Joshua's Second Address: Agency and Consequences

(Joshua 24:1–27)

Joshua's second farewell address caused the people to renew their covenants with God.

● **Joshua 24:1–13 A reminder of all that the Lord had done for them.** Starting with the story of Abraham, and continuing with Isaac and Jacob, their captivity in Egypt, and their liberation by Moses, Joshua rehearsed the history of their forebearers (vv. 1–10). He reminded them that after they crossed the Jordan River into the promised land, the Lord had given them victory over "Jericho …, the Amorites, and the Perizzites, and the Canaanites, and the Hittites, and the Girgashites, the Hivites, and the Jebusites," all of whom he had "delivered … into your hand" (v. 11). He had given them "a land for which ye did not labour, and cities which ye built not, and ye dwell in them; of the vineyards and oliveyards which ye planted not do ye eat" (v. 13).

● **Joshua 24:14–15 "Choose you this day whom ye will serve."** These immortal words of Joshua speak for themselves and need no explanation: "Now therefore fear the Lord, and serve him in sincerity and in truth: and put away the gods which your fathers served on the other side of the flood, and in Egypt; and serve ye the Lord" (v. 14). "And if it seem evil unto you to serve the Lord, choose you this day whom ye will serve … but as for me and my house, we will serve the Lord" (v. 15).

President Joseph Fielding Smith said:

Now, my brethren and sisters, in this time of peace—I do not know how long it will last—in this day of prosperity let us be humble and remember the Lord and keep his command- ments and feel that the dangers before us are far greater than they are in the days of trial and tribulation. Do not think for a moment that the days of trial are over. They are not. If we keep the commandments of the Lord, we shall prosper, we shall be blessed; the plagues, the calamities that have been promised will be poured out upon the peoples of the earth, and we shall escape them, yea, they shall pass us by.

But remember the Lord says if we fail to keep his word, if we walk in the ways of the world, they will not pass us by, but we shall be visited with floods and with fire, with sword and with plague and destruction. We may escape these things through faithfulness. Israel of old might have escaped through faithfulness, but they refused to keep the commandments of the Lord and they were not saved.

Therefore I plead with you: Pay your tithing, keep the Word of Wisdom, pray unto the Lord, honor him in all things by keeping his commandments, that his blessings may be poured out and that we may receive them in abundance, and in humility we may walk before him and be entitled not only to the blessings that come to us in this mortal life, but to the blessings of eternal life, the greatest gift of God.

We have the means of escape through obedience to the gospel of Jesus Christ. Will we escape? When I see, even among the Latter-day Saints the violation of the laws of the Lord, I fear and I tremble. I have been crying repentance among the stakes of Zion for 30 years, calling upon the people to turn to the Lord, keep his commandments, observe the Sabbath day, pay their honest tithing, do everything the Lord has commanded them to do, to live by every word that proceedeth forth from the mouth of God. By doing this we shall escape the calamities.

I am going to repeat what I have said before, for which I have been severely criticized from certain quarters, that even in this country we have no grounds by which we may escape, no sure foundation upon which we can stand, and by which we may escape from the calamities and destruction and the plagues and the pestilences, and even the devouring fire by sword and by war, unless we repent and we keep the commandments of the Lord, for it is written here in these revelations.

So I cry repentance to the Latter-day Saints, and I cry repentance to the people of the United States, as well as to the people of all the earth.[15]

● **2 Nephi 2:27 We are free to choose.** We have moral agency as a gift—with consequences or blessings according to our choices. As Nephi said, "And they are free to choose liberty and eternal life, through the great Mediator of all men, or to choose captivity and death, according to the captivity and power of the devil; for he seeketh that all men might be miserable like unto himself."

● **2 Nephi 28:7–9 Satan seeks to take away our agency by making us think that our decisions have no consequences.** He does his insidious work through subtlety, lies, and half-truths (Moses 4:4; 3 Nephi 2:2; Alma 12:4). He wants us to think that we can "eat, drink, and be merry" without consequence because "tomorrow [when] we die … it shall be well with us" (v. 7). True, what we are doing may be a "little bit" wrong, but Satan whispers in our ears that "God … will justify in committing a little sin; yea, lie a little, take the advantage of one because of his words, dig a pit for thy neighbor; there is no harm in this; and do all these things, for tomorrow we die; and if it so be that we are guilty, God will beat us with a few stripes, and at last we shall be saved in the kingdom of God" (v. 8). These are the actual teachings of many churches and philosophies today—"false and vain and foolish doctrines" taught by people who are "puffed up in their hearts, and … seek deep to hide their counsels from the Lord; and their works [are] in the dark" (v. 9).

Elder Gordon B. Hinckley said: "I should like to suggest three standards by which to judge each of the decisions that determine the behavior patterns of your lives. These standards are so simple as to appear elementary, but I believe their faithful observance will provide a set of moral imperatives by which to govern without argument or equivocation each of our actions and which will bring unmatched rewards. They are: 1. Does it enrich the mind? 2. Does it discipline and strengthen the body? 3. Does it nourish the spirit?"[16].

THE END OF AN ERA

Joshua and Eleazar Die

● **Joshua 24:26–27 Joshua sets up another memorial.** He wrote down the words of counsel he had given to Israel "in the book of the law of God," and also "took a great stone, and set it up there under an oak … by the sanctuary of the Lord" in Shiloh (v. 26). He told the Israelites, "Behold, this stone shall be a witness unto us; for it hath heard all the words of the Lord which he spake unto us: it shall be therefore a witness unto you, lest ye deny your God" (v. 27).

● **Joshua 24:28 The people depart to their inheritances.** The conference was over. It was the last time they would hear their prophet-leader Joshua speak to them. They left for their homelands, "every man unto his inheritance."

● **Joshua 24:29–31 Joshua dies at age 110 and is buried in Ephraim.** Among all the impressive things we might say about Joshua, this one stands out: "Israel served the Lord all the days of Joshua"—something that not even Moses could say. What's more, they remained faithful "all the days of the elders that overlived Joshua, and which had known all the works of the Lord, that he had done for Israel" (v. 31).

● **Joshua 24:33 The high priest Eleazar dies also.** Not long afterward, "Eleazar the son of Aaron died; and they buried him in a hill that pertained to Phinehas his son, which was given him in mount Ephraim."

The Bones of Joseph

● **Joshua 24:32 An ancient promise to Joseph is kept.** When Joseph, Jacob's son, was dying, he extracted a promise from the children of Israel that they would take his body with them when they left Egypt (Genesis 50:25). Most likely his body had been embalmed in the Egyptian manner. Upon Israel's departure from Egypt, Moses honored the promise and "took the bones of Joseph with him" (Exodus 13:19). This verse records that Joseph's remains were interred in the promised land, just as he had wished. They were buried "in a parcel of ground which Jacob bought of the sons of Hamor the father of Shechem for an hundred pieces of silver: and it became the inheritance of the children of Joseph."

Notes

1. Adapted from Chapter 21, "Joshua, The Great Ephraimite General, Takes Command," *The Third Thousand Years*, (1964), 473.
2. *Bible Commentary*, 6 vols. [n.d.], 2:11.
3. *The Third Thousand Years* [1964], 475.
4. Bryant G. Wood, "Did the Israelites Conquer Jericho? A New Look at the Archaeological Evidence." Revised and updated version of a paper presented to the Near East Archaeological Society, Gordon-Conwell Theological Seminary, South Hamilton, MA, December 4, 1987.
5. *The Third Thousand Years*, (1964), 483-485.
6. Douglas, *New Bible Dictionary*, s.v. "number," 898.
7. *16*(2) (March/April 1990): 44-58.
8. "Did the Israelites Conquer Jericho? A New Look at the Archaeological Evidence." Revised and updated version of a paper presented to the Near East Archaeological Society, Gordon- Conwell Theological Seminary, South Hamilton, MA, December 4, 1987.
9. *Articles of Faith*, 12th ed. [1924], 222–223.
10. *The Articles of Faith*, 12th ed. [1924], 105.
11. Vol.1, No. 8 (June 1840), 1271.
12. *Times and Seasons* (1 Sep 1842), 3:902.

13.   See Edward J. Brandt, *Ensign* (June 1981) 36–37.

14.   "How Did the Book of Jasher Know?" *Meridian Magazine* (Jan. 7, 2002). An article published online: http://www.johnpratt.com/items/docs/lds/meridian/2002/jasher.html

15.   *Doctrines of Salvation*, comp. Elder Bruce R. McConkie, 3 vols. (1954–56), 3:34–35.

16.   "Caesar, Circus, or Christ?" *BYU Speeches of the Year*, October 26, 1965, 4.

Chapter 19

Apostasy and the Judge–Heroes of Israel

(Judges)

℘℃℞

INTRODUCTION

The Book of Judges

- **Author:** Anonymous author(s). The prophet Samuel might have participated in its compilation, and may even have written some (but not all) of it.

- **Position:** The books of Judges and Ruth contain the only available Jewish history during the turbulent period of general apostasy that occurred from sometime after the death of Joshua to the birth of the prophet Samuel.

- **Purpose:** Judges relates a continuous cycle of apostasy and repentance—a pattern of sin and bondage followed by humility and repentance. Each period of decline is marked by a statement such as: "Then the sons of Israel again did evil in the sight of the Lord" (Judg. 2:11; 3:7, 12; 4:1; 6:1; 10:6; 13:1).

- **Time Span:** Death of Joshua (ca. 1427 BC) to the birth of Samuel (shortly before 1095 BC).

- **Length:** 21 chapters

- **Key Sections:** — Chapters 1–3   Introduction.

  — Chapters 3–16   History of the judges.

  — Chapters 17–21 Stories about Israelite idolatry and disobedience.

Why Judges Ruled Israel

- **A repeating cycle:** The reign of the judges is similar in many ways to the history of the Nephites prior to the coming of Christ. It is a story of one continuous cycle of apostasy and repentance. When the Israelites turned away from the Lord, their enemies began to prevail (Judges 2:14–15). Suffering under oppression and war, the people would cry unto God and he would raise up a Deborah or a Gideon to deliver them. But once peace and security were reestablished, the people turned again to their former ways (Judges 2:16–19).

The story of the time of the judges is thus primarily a sad and tragic one, although in this period lived some of the most remarkable men and women of the Old Testament. In their lives of courage, faith, and personal greatness, as well as in the lives of those who forsook the Lord and pursued selfish ends, are many lessons of importance for Saints today.

Josephus, the noted Jewish historian, usually spoke highly of his people. Yet, his commentary on the condition of the Israelites during the period of the judges was anything but praise: "After this, the Israelites grew effeminate as to fighting any more against their enemies, but applied themselves to the cultivation of the land, which producing them great plenty and riches, they neglected the regular disposition of their settlement, and indulged themselves in luxury and pleasures; nor were they any longer careful to hear the laws that belonged to their political government: whereupon God was provoked to anger, and put them in mind, first, how, contrary to his directions, they had spared the Canaanites; and, after that, how those Canaanites, as opportunity served, used them very barbarously"[1].

- **Judges 1 Israel continued its conquest of Canaan.** Judah, Simeon, and Joseph continued to attempt to conquer the remnants of the Canaanites who remained in the lands of Judah, Manasseh, Ephraim, Zebulun, Asher, Naphtali, and Dan.

- **Judges 1:1–7 The Israelites inquire of the Lord, who tells them that Judah should be the first to attempt to conquer remaining Canaanites (v. 2).** Judah sought the help of Simeon, and together they were victorious over the Canaanites and Perizzites (vv. 3–4). They captured a leader named Adoni-bezek in Bezek and cut off his thumbs and his great toes (vv. 5–6). This was a form of justice, since he had done the same to "threescore and ten kings" before him (v. 7). Mutilating captives was a common practice among the heathen. He admitted, "God hath requited me," was taken to Jerusalem, and died there (v. 7).

- **Judges 1:27–36 Other tribes failed to complete the task of conquering Canaan.** Manasseh failed to conquer Beth-shean, Taanach, Dor, Ibleam, or Megiddo (v. 27). Rather than drive them out as they had been commanded, they put these town under tribute and allowed them continue to live in the land (v. 28).

Ephraim failed to drive out the Canaanites in Gezer (v. 29). Zebulun failed to drive out the inhabitants of Kitron and Nahalol, putting them under tribute instead (v. 30). Asher failed to drive out the

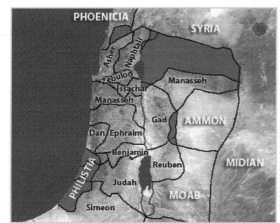

Some areas (in gray) were never conquered

inhabitants of Accho, Zidon, Ahlab, Achzib, Helbah, Aphik, and Rehob, living among them instead (v. 31). Asher also chose to live among the Canaanites (v. 32). Naphtali failed to drive out the inhabitants of Beth-shemesh and Beth-anath, allowing them also to remain upon the land by paying a tribute to them (v. 33). The tribe of Dan, which had originally been assigned lands in the north of Israel were not able to conquer them because "the Amorites forced the children of Dan into the mountain" and "would not suffer them to come down to the valley" (v. 34). These were eventually overpowered by "Joseph" (Manasseh and Ephraim), but were allowed to remain "in mount Heres in Aijalon, and in Shaalbim … And the coast … from the going up to Akrabbim, from the rock, and upward" (vv. 35–36).

● **Judges 2:1–5 An angel rebukes Israel for disobedience.** The angel reminded them that they had been given the land by the Lord who always keeps His words of covenant (v. 1). But He had told them to "make no league with the inhabitants of this land; ye shall throw down their altars" (v. 2; Exodus 34:12; Deuteronomy 20:16–18; Joshua 9:7). But they had not kept this covenant with the Lord (v. 2).

— **Deuteronomy 20:16–18** Through Moses, they had been commanded to "save alive nothing that breatheth," and to "utterly destroy them" (vv. 16–17). This was so that the Canaanites could not "teach you … to do after all their abominations, which they have done unto their gods" (v. 18).

● **Judges 2:3–5 The Lord refuses to remove their enemies.** Having broken the covenant He made with them, the Israelites would now have to live with their enemies, and "they shall be as thorns in your sides, and their gods shall be a snare unto you" (v. 3). This caused great sorrow in Israel, and they repented with sacrifices (vv. 4–5).

● **Judges 2:10–13 A new generation rejects the Lord and chooses to worship Baal and Ashtaroth.** The new generation—the one born to those who entered the land of promise— "knew not the Lord, nor yet the works which he had done for Israel" (v. 10). Whether that was because their parents failed to teach them (as Moses had counseled) or because the children simply chose to rebel, we do not know. But we know that they "did evil in the sight of the Lord, and served Baalim … and … forsook the Lord God of their fathers" (vv. 11–12), bowing down to the pagan gods of Baal and Ashtaroth (vv. 12–13).

● **Judges 3:5–7 Israel could not resist their influence and culture.** These practices had a profound influence on Israelite children and youth, who found the worship of Jehovah restrictive and boring by comparison to the sensuous religious practices of the Canaanites. They intermarried with them and agreed to serve their gods in the groves that had been constructed for their fertility rites (vv. 6–7).

Sidney B. Sperry said:

The Book of Judges makes clear that Israel did not conquer all of Canaan when first she entered it. … For a long time during the days of the Judges many of the Israelites were essentially 'hillbillies' [Judges 6:2], hemmed in by their enemies on every side. After the generations of Israelites who had been acquainted with Joshua passed away, the effects of Canaanite morals and religion began to be apparent upon the younger generation. For long periods of time the Canaanites conquered Israel and this fact alone would tend to disrupt her settled religious life and practice. Times were rough and banditry was rampant. As the record itself states: 'In those days there was no king in Israel; every man did that which was right in his own eyes' [Judges 17:6].

All of this seems to have taken place because Israel did not drive the Canaanites completely out. The Lord said to the Israelites: 'Ye have not hearkened to My voice; what is this ye have done? Wherefore I also said: I will not drive them out before you; but they shall be unto you as snares, and their gods shall be a trap unto you.' [Judges 2:2–3.] … Israel's conduct during this period had a lasting effect upon her religion and morals. For centuries Israel's prophets and wise men referred to it and denounced her allegiance to old Canaanite practices. It is plain that Israel, during the period of the Judges, compromised her relatively high religious ideals with Canaanite practices and certain elements in her population must have apostatized completely.[2]

Israel's Enemies

Israel was literally surrounded by enemies, not to mention those that they allowed to live within their borders. Throughout the book of Judges we see these enemies rising up and conquering all or part of Israel for a time. Time and again, when they found themselves oppressed and humbled themselves, the Lord provided a deliverer (judge) to set them free. But then, after a few years, the cycle would repeat itself as another enemy attacked them.

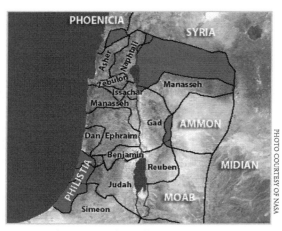

Israel's enemies literally surrounded them

— **Canaanites** These were the nations inside of Israel who were allowed to remain when Israel conquered Canaan.

— **Mesopotamia** This included the heathen nations in Syria and in the area of Ur—homeland of Abraham—which were to the north of Israel.

— **Ammonites** These were the heathen descendants of Abraham through Lot, who lived to the east of Israel.

— **Midianites** These were the heathen descendants of Abraham through Keturah, who occupied the wilderness to the east of Israel on the other side of Ammon and Moab.

— **Moabites** These were the heathen descendants of Abraham through Lot who lived on the southeastern border of Israel.

— **Edomites** These were the heathen descendants of Esau, who lived south of Moab (not shown on the map above) and southeast of the Dead Sea.

— **Philistines** These were the heathen people who dwelt along the southwest Canaan seacoast.

— **Phoenicians** These were the heathen people who dwelt along the seacoast to the northwest of Israel.

Israel's Judge-Heroes

● **Judges 2:16–19 The Lord raises up "judges" for Israel.** These so-called judges, according to the record, appear to be more military heroes rather than officers of the judiciary. "The English word 'judge' doesn't well describe these leaders. Though the root of the Hebrew word used means primarily 'to judge,' it is used secondarily also in the extended meaning 'to govern.' Most of the 'judging' done in this period was a matter of giving advice and rendering decisions. Regular court procedures are nowhere described for the times of the Judges in Israel. In fact, the most common function they are seen to perform is that of military leadership."[3].

In this chapter we will touch on all of the following judge-heroes of Israel:

Hero:	Noted as:	Tribe or City:	Enemy:	Ruled:
Othniel	Caleb's nephew.......	Judah.............	Mesopotamia.....	8 yrs
Ehud	The "fat king"........	Benjamin........	Moabites.........	18 yrs
Shamgar	600 by himself.......	(not known).....	Philistines........	(unknown)
Deborah	Prophetess.	Ephraim.........	Canaanites.	20 yrs
Gideon	....	Manasseh........	Midian	7 yrs
Abimalech	....			3 yrs
Tola	....	Issachar.	}	Total of
Jair	....	City of Gilead.	}	45 yrs
Jephthah	Jair's daughter.......	City of Gilead.	Ammonites.......	(unknown)
Ibzan	....	Bethlehem....................	}	
Elon	....	Zebulun.	}	More than
Abdon	....	Ephraim......................	}	17 yrs
Samson	....	Dan.............	Philistines........	40 yrs

The judges did not rescue or govern all of unified Israel during their periods of leadership. The chronicler of these stories likely took the most impressive of the heroes from each of the tribes during this generally apostate period and combined their stories into one book containing their achievements and their moral lessons for Israel.

● **Judges 3:1–7 Intermarriage with the heathen nations was a natural result of serving "Baalim and the groves."** The nations which remained after Israel took possession of their lands were "the Canaanites, Hittites, and Amorites, and Perizzites, and Hivites, and Jebusites" (v. 5). The Lord used these nations to "prove Israel ... to know whether they would hearken unto the commandments of the Lord" (v. 4). Contrary to what the Lord had commanded them, they intermarried with these peoples, and as a result, "served their gods" (v. 6). We are told that "the children of Israel did evil in the sight of the Lord, and forgat the LORD their God, and served Baalim and the groves" (v. 7). The groves were local worship centers for heathen gods and included a tree or pole and altars, often among groves of trees.

OTHNIEL

● **Judges 3:8–11 Othniel was a judge-hero during a time when Mesopotamia had over-powered Israel.** This oppression lasted 8 years.

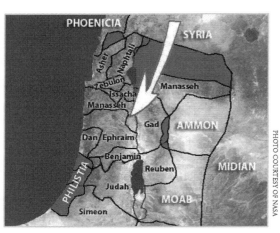

Mesopotamia came from the north

Because of their gross behavior in serving other gods, "the anger of the LORD was hot against Israel, and he sold them into the hand of Chushan-rishathaim king of Mesopotamia: and the children of Israel served Chushan-rishathaim eight years" (v. 8). Finding themselves oppressed, "the children of Israel cried unto the Lord, [and] the Lord raised up a deliverer" named Othniel (v. 9). Othniel was a newphew of Caleb—who had been a spiritual (but not a military) leader in Israel. Remember that Caleb was one of only two men (Joshua and Caleb) of the original Israelites who left Egypt who were permitted to enter the promised land. He was a good and righteous man. Now "the Spirit of the Lord came upon" his nephew Othniel, who "went out to war: and the Lord delivered Chushan-rishathaim king of Mesopotamia into his hand" and he defeated him (v. 10).

After Othniel delivered Israel, there were 40 years of peace, and then Israel returned to abominations.

EHUD

● **Judges 3:12–31 Ehud was a judge-hero in Israel during a time when Moab had overpowered the tribe of Benjamin.** This oppression lasted 18 years.

Because of Israel's return to abominations, "the Lord strengthened Eglon the king of Moab against Israel" (v. 12). Along with the Ammonites and the Amalekites, the king of Moab "went and smote Israel, and possessed the city of palm trees" (v. 13). "So the children of Israel served Eglon the king of Moab eighteen years" (v. 14). Finding themselves again oppressed, "the children of Israel cried unto the Lord, the Lord raised them up a deliverer, Ehud the son of Gera, a Benjamite" who was left-handed (v. 15). Ehud determined to send "a present" to the king of Moab (v. 15). He made "a dagger which had two edges, of a cubit length; and he did gird it under

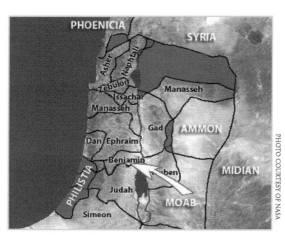

The Moabites overpowered Benjamin

his raiment upon his right thigh" (v. 16).

He brought the present personally to the king, who was a grossly fat man (v. 17). The king sent away the others around him as he sat in his summer parlor (vv. 18–19). Ehud said to him, "I have a message from God unto thee" and the king stood up (v. 20). As he held forth the gift with his right hand, the left-handed Ehud then stabbed him to death with his left hand (v. 21). As the dagger went into his belly, the king's fat closed around the knife, making it impossible to pull it out (v. 22). "Then Ehud went forth through the porch, and shut the doors of the parlour upon him, and locked them" (v. 23). Suspecting that the king was sleeping, his servants did not disturb him for a good long time, but eventually obtained a key and opened the door, finding their king "dead on the earth" (vv. 24–25).

Meanwhile, Ehud escaped while the king's servants were waiting outside his locked door (v. 26). Returning to his people, "he blew a trumpet in the mountain of Ephraim," rallying Israelite forces to attack and destroy the surprised Moabites (vv. 27–28). The victory was total. All ten thousand of the Moabite soldiers—"lusty, and all men of valour"—were killed, and the Israelites were delivered from Moabite bondage (vv. 29–30).

After Ehud delivered Israel, there were 80 years of relative peace, and then Israel returned to abominations.

SHAMGAR

● **Judges 3:31 Shamgar was a judge-hero in Israel during a period when the Philistines had overpowered Israel.** This was apparently during the 80 years of relative peace that followed Ehud's defeat of the Moabites. Because they had begun to return to their abominations, the Lord allowed the Philistines to oppress Israel. This oppression lasted an unknown length of time. It was perhaps brief, because we have only one verse in the scriptures concerning this oppression. The one detail we have about this story is that Shamgar killed 600 Philistines with an ox goad—a long, spiked pole used to prod animals.

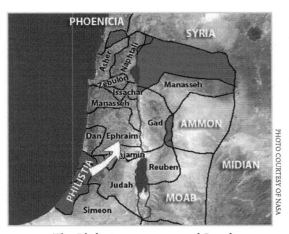

The Philistines overpowered Israel

BARAK AND DEBORAH

● **Judges 4 Barak and Deborah were judge-heroes in Israel during a time when King Jabin of the Canaanites oppressed Ephraim.** This oppression lasted 20 years.

The real deliverer in this case was Deborah, not Barak. Deborah was a prophetess ("shophet"—lawgiver or governor) in Israel. She was much respected for her wisdom and judgment (vv. 4–5).

After 80 years of peace and Ehud's death, the Israelites had returned again to their abominations. Therefore the Lord allowed Jabin, king of Canaan, and his military general Sisera to conquer and oppress the Ephraimites with 900 chariots of iron (vv. 2–3). Desiring Israel's deliverance, Deborah wisely called upon Barak to accomplish it (v. 6). Barak refused to go unless Deborah went with him (v. 8). This she consented to do, though he prophesied that it would "not be for thine honour; for the Lord shall sell Sisera into the hand of a woman. And Deborah arose, and went with Barak to Kedesh" (v. 9). They took 10,000 men from the tribes of Zebulun and Naphtali to face Sisera and his 900 iron chariots (v. 10).

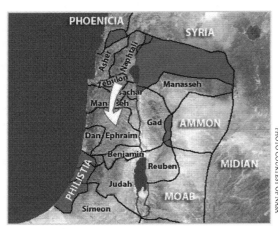

Jabin the Canaanite overpowered Ephraim

President Joseph F. Smith said:

> One of the highest qualities of all true leadership is a high standard of courage. When we speak of courage and leadership we are using terms that stand for the quality of life by which men determine consciously the proper course to pursue and stand with fidelity to their convictions. There has never been a time in the Church when its leaders were not required to be courageous men; not alone courageous in the sense that they were able to meet physical dangers, but also in the sense that they were steadfast and true to a clear and upright conviction.

> Leaders of the Church, then, should be men not easily discouraged, not without hope, and not given to forebodings of all sorts of evils to come. Above all things the leaders of the people should never disseminate a spirit of gloom in the hearts of the people. If men standing in high places sometimes feel the weight and anxiety of momentous times, they should be all the firmer and all the more resolute in those convictions which come from a God-fearing conscience and pure lives. Men in their private lives should feel the necessity of extending encouragement to the people by their own hopeful and cheerful intercourse with them, as they do by their utterances in public places. It is a matter of the greatest importance that the people be educated to appreciate and cultivate the bright side of life rather than to permit its darkness and shadows to hover over them.

> In order to successfully overcome anxieties in reference to questions that require time for their solution, an absolute faith and confidence in God and in the triumph of his work are essential.

> The most momentous questions and the greatest dangers to personal happiness are not always met and solved within oneself, and if men cannot courageously meet the difficulties, and obstacles of their own individual lives and natures, how are they to meet successfully those public questions in which the welfare and happiness of the public are concerned?[4]

After Deborah and Barak delivered Israel, there were 40 years of peace, and then Israel returned to abominations.

When the day of battle arrived, Deborah said to Barak, "Up; for this is the day in which the Lord hath delivered Sisera into thine hand" and "the Lord [is] gone out before thee" (v. 14). With confidence in Deborah's inspiration, "Barak went down from mount Tabor, and ten thousand men after him. And the Lord discomfited Sisera, and all his chariots, and all his host, with the edge of the sword before Barak" (vv. 14–15). Barak pursued after Sisera's men and chariots, who became mired in the mud and were destroyed such that "there was not a man left" (v. 16).

In the midst of this battle, "Sisera lighted down off his chariot, and fled away on his feet" (v. 15), coming eventually "to the tent of Jael the wife of Heber the Kenite" (a friendly Israelite) for protection (v. 17). Jael, Heber's wife, gave him milk to drink, then put him to bed for rest (vv. 18–19). He asked her to protect him from anyone who might come and inquire after him (v. 20).

Instead, after he had fallen asleep, she took a hammer and drove a long nail through his temples, nailing him to the floor and killing him (v. 21). When Barak arrived, she showed him the dead general (v. 22). Deborah's prophecy about Sisera being "sold into the hand of a woman" had been fulfilled.

● **Judges 5 Deborah composed a song to commemorate the victory,** which contains a key for overcoming every adversary: "Praise ye the Lord for the avenging of Israel, when the people willingly offered themselves" (Judges 5:2).

GIDEON

● **Judges 6:1–6 Gideon was a judge-hero in Israel during a time when the Midianites overpowered and persecuted Manasseh.** This oppression lasted 7 years.

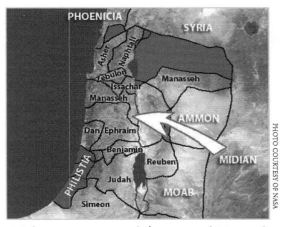

Midianites overpowered & persecuted Manasseh

The Midianites would attack Israel at harvest time in hordes like locusts and take all their crops. The Israelites were forced to flee to caves for protection. They cried unto the Lord for help, and He sent a prophet (unnamed) to call them to repentance (vv. 7–10). Then He sent an angel to Gideon, calling him to deliver the Israelites (vv. 11–12). Gideon protested, "if the Lord be with us, why then is all this befallen us? and where be all his miracles which our fathers told us of ...? but now the Lord hath forsaken us, and delivered us into the hands of the Midianites" (v. 13). The angel retorted, "Go in this thy might, and thou shalt save Israel from the hand of the Midianites"(v. 14).

Gideon Feels Inadequate

● **Judges 6:15–24 Gideon seeks a sign of God's support for him, and receives one.** He could not believe that he might be able to deliver Israel, because "my family is poor in Manasseh, and I am the least in my father's house" (v. 15). The angel reassured him that the Lord would be with him, "and thou shalt smite the Midianites as one man" (v. 16). Gideon then asked for a sign to reassure him that this would be so (v. 17).

An angel gives Gideon a miraculous sign

"When Gideon asked for a 'sign' he seemed only to want a sign that the messenger was a bona fide emissary of the Lord (v. 17). On this point, note that messengers may sometimes be from the wrong source and discernment is important. (D&C 129; 2 Cor. 11:13–15; 1 Corinthians 12:10; 1 John 4:1–2). Also, signs may be given, based upon man's faith and the will of God (D&C 63:10).[5]

Gideon retreated to his home and made a meal of lamb soup and unleavened bread (vv. 18–19). The angel instructed him to place the meat and bread upon a rock and pour out the broth over them, which he did (v. 20). Then the angel touched the food with his staff and "there rose up fire out of the rock, and consumed the flesh and the unleavened cakes. Then the angel of the Lord departed out of his sight" (v. 21). Convinced now that the angel was from the Lord, Gideon cried out, "Alas, O Lord God! ... because I have seen an angel of the Lord face to face," fearing that he might now die (v. 22). But the Lord spoke to him saying, "Peace be unto thee; fear not: thou shalt not die" (v. 23).

● **Judges 6:25–32 He throws down his father's altar to Baal and destroys the nearby grove.** This he did at the instruction of the Lord, and offered a sacrifice in its place, using the wood of the torn-down grove for the fire (vv. 25–27). For doing this, the men of the city sought to kill him but his father defended him, and named him "Jerubbaal" in honor of what he had done (vv. 28–32). The name means "let the shameful thing contend for itself."

● **Judges 6:33–35 Gideon is filled with the Spirit and with courage—32,000 volunteers join him.** The combined armies of the Midianites and Amalekites gathered together for battle (v. 33). Like the Book of Mormon general Captain Moroni, Gideon went through the lands of Manasseh, Asher, Zebulun, and Naphtali, blowing a trumpet and rallying 32,000 Israelites to his cause.

● **Judges 6:36–40 Gideon uses a fleece to obtain two more signs of support from the Lord.** Despite his 32,000 soldiers, he was still outnumbered 4–to-1 by the Midianites' 120,000 men. He sought a sign to know that the Lord will indeed be with him. He put a fleece of wool on the floor, and said "if the dew be on the fleece only, and it be dry upon all the earth beside, then shall

I know that thou wilt save Israel by mine hand, as thou hast said" (v. 37). When he rose up the next morning, it was so, and he "wringed the dew out of the fleece, a bowl full of water" (v. 38).

After this sign was given, he asked for another to be sure that the manifestation was from the Lord. He said, "let it now be dry only upon the fleece, and upon all the ground let there be dew" (v. 39). And when he arose in the morning, it was so (v. 40).

Gideon wrings the fleece

- **Judges 7:1–3 The Lord says Gideon has too many soldiers.** He told Gideon to invite anybody who is afraid to depart. 22,000 did so, leaving only 10,000 men.

- **Judges 7:4–8 The Lord says there are still too many soldiers and provides a way to test them.** Gideon watched as the men drank water. Those who lay face-down and lapped the water like a dog were excused; those who drank from cupped-hands stayed. This eliminated another 9,700 men—leaving only 300. This is astonishing, since the army of the Midianites was "like grasshoppers for multitude; and their camels were without number, as the sand by the sea side for multitude" (v. 12).

- **Judges 7:9–14 Gideon sneaks into the Midianite camp and hears their fears of his army.** He overheard a man telling his dream to a friend, who interpreted it as their impending destruction by the armies of Gideon, "a man of Israel: for into his hand hath God delivered Midian, and all the host" (v. 14).

- **Judges 7:15—8:21 Gideon rallies his troops and prepares to frighten the Midianites with noise and lights.** In the middle of the night, Gideon's men surrounded the Midianites, and upon his signal they blew their trumpets and flashed their lights and shouted, "The sword of the Lord, and of Gideon (v. 18). The Midianites "ran, and cried, and fled" in terror (v. 21).

Gideon rallied other Israelites to join the cause, pursued the Midianite army, and utterly destroyed it (Judges 7:22—8:21).

Gideon's army surprises the Midianites

- **Judges 8:22–23 The people want to make Gideon their king—but he refuses, saying, "The Lord shall rule over you."**

Elder Thomas S. Monson said:

> We can take strength from the example of Gideon. You will remember how Gideon and his army faced the overwhelming strength of forces vastly superior in equipment and in number. ... The outcome of that mighty battle is recorded in one short sentence: 'And they stood every man in his place ... ' (Judges 7:21), and the victory was won.
>
> Today, we are encamped against the greatest array of sin, vice, and evil ever assembled before our eyes. Such formidable enemies may cause lesser hearts to shrink or shun the fight. But the battle plan whereby we fight to save the souls of men is not our own. It was provided ... by the inspiration and revelation of the Lord. Yes, I speak of that plan which will bring us victory. ... And as we do battle against him who would thwart the purposes of God and degrade and destroy mankind, I pray that each of us will stand in his or her appointed place, that the battle for the souls of men will indeed be won.[6]

- **Judges 8:24–27 Gideon makes a golden robe from the spoils of his battles.** This was a common practice among the heathen—making golden robes for their gods. As a cultural gesture, it would have seemed appropriate to his people. But it became a snare to his family who worshiped the robe instead of worshiping God. "When the text says the Israelites 'went a whoring after it,' the idiom means they looked upon it as if it were an idol, and idol worship is often condemned in these terms as infidelity to God."[7]

- **Judges 8:29–31 Gideon has 70 sons by many different wives—including Abimelech by one of his concubines.** This troublesome son would prove to be a deadly scourge upon Israel.

- **Judges 8:28, 32–35 Gideon dies and Israel returns to its abominations.** Israel enjoyed 40 years of peace under Gideon's leadership (v. 28). But he had no sooner died than they returned to their abominations (v. 33). They did not remember the Lord, nor even show any kindness to Gideon's family (vv. 34–35).

JOTHAM—A PROPHET, NOT A JUDGE

- **Judges 9:1–6 Jotham was not a judge-hero in Israel.** But he prophesied in Israel during a time when Abimelech oppressed Manasseh. Abimelech, one of Gideon's sons, whose name means "my father is king" was insane for power. He demanded that Manasseh make him their king or be divided by the 70 sons of Gideon. He raised an army of Israelites and raided the Baal temple treasury. He then attacked and captured all of his brothers except for Jotham, who managed to escape. He dragged all 68 of the others to a single stone where he killed them with his own hands.

- **Judges 9:7–54 Jotham prophesies the destruction of Abimelech and his followers.** Abimelech attacked and utterly wasted one rebellious city—sewing it with salt. He set another city on fire, burning alive its inhabitants. He then attacked Thebez, but was mortally wounded by a millstone thrown by a woman. He had one of his soldiers slay him so he would not be known as one whom "a woman slew."

TOLA AND JAIR—TWO RIGHTEOUS RULERS

- **Judges 10:1–5 Tola, from Isaachar, ruled in Israel for 23 years and Jair, from Gilead (Gad), ruled in Israel for 22 years, during which time Israel enjoyed peace.** Jair had 30 sons and gave each of them a city in Gilead. But after Jair died Israel returned to its abominations.

JEPHTHAH

- **Judges 10:6–14 Jephthah was a judge- hero in Israel for during a time when the Ammonites were oppressing Israel.** This oppression lasted 23 years.

The Ammonites oppressed Israel for 23 years

Israel "did evil again in the sight of the Lord, and served Baalim, and Ashtaroth, and the gods of Syria, and the gods of Zidon, and the gods of Moab, and the gods of the children of Ammon, and ... of the Philistines, and forsook the Lord" (v. 6).

Because of these abominations, "the anger of the Lord was hot against Israel, and he sold them into the hands of the Philistines, and into the hands of the children of Ammon" for 18 years (vv. 7–8). The Ammonites distressed the tribes of Israel on the east side of the Jordan River and also the tribes of Judah, Benjamin, and Ephraim west of the river in Israel proper (v. 9). Thus humbled, the Israelites prayed for relief (v. 10).

- **Judges 11:1–28 Jephthah was a social outcast— the son of an innkeeper (harlot) whom nobody respected.** His father's other sons threw him out of the household saying, "Thou shalt not inherit in our father's house; for thou art the son of a strange woman" (v. 2) But when Israel found itself oppressed, they turned to him for his help because he was "a mighty man of valor" (v. 1). Jephthah agreed, but only if they would make him their ruler if he was victorious (v. 9). He proceeded, after a series of letters protesting their treatment of Israel, to defeat the armies of the Ammonites (vv. 10–29).

- **Judges 11:30–31 Jephthah's famous vow to offer a child to God if he is victorious.** Just before going into battle, Jephthah vowed and vow to the Lord. The Bible records it this way: "If thou shalt without fail deliver the children of Ammon into mine hands, Then it shall be, that whatsoever cometh forth of

Jephthah's daughter celebrates

the doors of my house to meet me, when I return in peace from the children of Ammon, shall surely be the Lord's, and I will offer it up for a burnt offering" (vv. 30–31). But this passage is mis-translated in our Bible. He was not offering to sacrifice one of his children on an altar. He was offering to make the first child to come out to greet him upon his return into a Nazarite—dedicated to God's service—which service was always initiated by offering an appropriate sacrifice.

- **Judges 11:32–40 Jephthah's daughter is the first to come out upon Jephthah's return.** Jephthah was victorious in battle and returned home. The first person to come out the door when he returned was his daughter. He was distressed that she would be the one to become a Nazarite. She would remain a virgin (which was the custom in Israel) because of her vows. But she accepted the responsibility willingly, fully supporting her father's vow and showing herself to be a righteous woman. She was not offered on an altar as so many Bible commentators seem to think.

- **Judges 12:1–3 Civil war with Ephraim breaks out and is put down by Jephthah.** Once the war against the Midianites was won, the Ephraimites complained because they were not allowed to help, just as they did after Gideon's victory (Judges 8:1–3). Perhaps this was typical of Ephraim—to hang back until the victory was won and then pretend they wanted to be part of it all along.

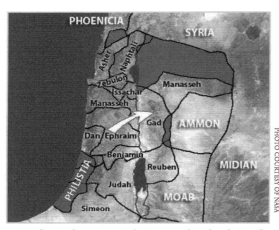

Civil war between Ephraim and Gilead (Gad)

- **Judges 12:4–7 Cultural differences lead to 42,000 deaths.** The Ephraimites did not accept the people of Gad as Israelites. They said, "Ye Gileadites are fugitives of Ephraim among the Ephraimites, and among the Manassites" (v. 4).

When war broke out, the Gileadites took control of the passages over the Jordan River to prevent the men of Ephraim from retreating over it into their homeland. But it was hard to tell the difference between a man from Gad and a man from Ephraim. So the Gileadites devised a clever way to tell the difference. If a man asked to cross they would ask him if he was an Ephraimite. If he said "No," then they asked him to say the word "Shibboleth" (vv. 5–6). Apparently, an Ephraimite could not say the word correctly and would be thus exposed as an enemy and slain (v. 7). This brief civil war was bloody. We are told that 42,000 Ephraimites were killed in the conflict.

Six years of peace followed—until the death of Jephthah, who was buried in Gilead.

IBZAN, ELON, AND ABDON

● **Judges 12:8–15 Ibzan, Elon, and Abdon presided during 37 years of additional peace.**

— **Ibzan** presided for 7 years. From Bethlehem, he had 60 children (vv. 8–10).

— **Elon** presided for 10 years. He was a Zebulonite (vv. 11–12).

— **Abdon** presided for about 8 years. He was from Ephraim (vv. 13–15).

SAMSON

The story of Samson is told with prejudice. His sins are excused as being God's will for him in order to make the story sound more favorable. But Samson's story is really one of opportunities lost. He acted as a deliverer of Israel from the Philistines for 20 years. He might have been one of the greatest prophets and deliverers Israel had ever known. But unfortunately, he was also a headstrong and disobedient rebel.

Zorah, the city where Samson's home was located, was in an area that had originally been assigned to the tribe of Judah (Joshua 15:33). It was later inhabited by the tribe of Dan, which had been unable to take over the land it was assigned in northern Israel (see map at the end of this chapter).

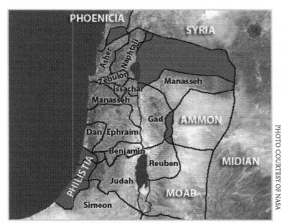

Zorah was a city in the tribal land of Dan

The Annunciation of Samson's Birth

● **Judges 13:2–14 Manoah's barren wife receives a vision.** She was the wife of a man named Manoah (v. 2). The scriptures record that "the angel of the LORD appeared unto the woman, and said unto her, Behold now, thou art barren, and bearest not: but thou shalt conceive, and bear a son" (v. 3). She was counseled to avoid wine, strong drink, and any kind of unclean food, because her newborn son would be a Nazarite: "no razor shall come on his head: for the child shall be a Nazarite unto God from the womb: and he shall begin to deliver Israel out of the hand of the Philistines" (vv. 4–5).

She reported the vision to her husband Manoah, who prayed for an explanatory vision from the angel (vv. 6–8). The angel came again and repeated the same instructions: The mother should not "drink wine or strong drink, nor eat any unclean thing" (vv. 13–14).

● **Judges 13:15–23 The angel declines to eat Manoah's bread or tell him his name, performs a miracle, and then departs.** Hoping to keep the angel with them a little longer, Manoah offered to prepare a meal. But the angel, apparently being a spirit being, said, "I will not eat of thy bread" (v. 16). Furthermore, if Manoah wanted to offer a burnt offering of a lamb, he should "offer it unto the Lord" (v. 16). Realizing now that the person was "an angel of the Lord," Manoah asked the angel what his name was, so that they could hold him in honorable remembrance (v. 17). But the angel declined to tell him, saying, "Why askest thou thus after my name, seeing it is secret?" (v. 18).

Manoah then took the meat offering he had prepared of a lamb, and "offered it upon a rock unto the Lord" (v. 19). We are told that "the angel did wondrously" while Manoah and his wife watched—apparently consuming the offering in flames, because "when the flame went up toward heaven from off the altar, … the angel of the Lord ascended in the flame of the altar" (v. 20). Manoah and his wife "fell on their faces to the ground" (v. 20), and Manoah feared for his life because, he said, "we have seen God" (vv. 21–22). But his wife reasoned with him that this was not so (v. 23).

● **Judges 13:24–25 Samson is born and is greatly blessed.** The name "Samson" means "wonderful." "The angel does not say that it [his name] was secret, but … *hu peli*, "wonderful"— one of the names given to Jesus Christ [Isaiah 9]. In fact there are a number of impressive parallels to the birth of the Savior:

— He was announced by an angel.

— He was born of a previously barren woman

— He was blessed with tremendous gifts.

Samson Is Indulgent, Immoral, Selfish, and Revengeful

● **Judges 14:1–4 He demands a woman of Timnath (a Philistine) for a wife.** We get a glimpse of his self-centeredness as he demands of his parents, "Get her for me to wife" (v. 2). His parents did not approve, saying, "Is there never a woman among the daughters of thy brethren, or among all my people, that thou goest to take a wife of the uncircumcised Philistines?" (v. 3). But Samson cared nothing about violating his covenants by marrying outside of Israel. "Get her for me," he demanded again, "for she pleaseth me well" (v. 3).

Excuses for Samson's behavior. Whoever wrote this account seeks to justify Samson's disobedience by now saying, "his father and his mother knew not that it was of the Lord, that he sought an occasion against the Philistines: for at that time the Philistines had dominion over Israel" (v. 4). This is not true. God is never the source of sinful choices.

President Spencer W. Kimball said: "Few men have ever knowingly and deliberately chosen to reject God and his blessings. Rather, we learn from the scriptures that

Samson slays a lion with his bare hands

because the exercise of faith has always appeared to be more difficult than relying on things more immediately at hand, carnal man has tended to transfer his trust in God to material things. Therefore, in all ages when men have fallen under the power of Satan and lost the faith, they have put in its place a hope in the 'arm of flesh' and in 'gods of silver, and gold, of brass, iron, wood, and stone, which see not, nor hear, nor know' (Dan. 5:23)—that is, in idols. This I find to be a dominant theme in the Old Testament. Whatever thing a man sets his heart and his trust in most is his god; and if his god doesn't also happen to be the true and living God of Israel, [he] is laboring in idolatry"[8].

Samson's Incredible Strength

● **Judges 14:5–9 Samson slays a lion with his bare hands.** As he traveled to Timnath to find the woman he wanted, "behold, a young lion roared against him" (v. 5). The Spirit of the Lord came upon him, manifesting for the first time the gift of strength that God had given him so that he might deliver Israel from the oppression of the Philistines. Empowered by the Spirit, "he rent [the lion] as he would have rent a kid" with "nothing in his hand" (v. 6). He then traveled on to visit with the woman, "who pleased Samson well" (v. 7).

Later, when Samson returned to marry the woman, "he turned aside to see the carcase of the lion: and, behold, there was a swarm of bees and honey in the carcase of the lion" (v. 8). He grabbed some of the honey and continued on while eating of it. He also gave some to his parents, not telling them "that he had taken the honey out of the carcase of the lion" (v. 9).

Samson's Pride and Violent Temper

● **Judges 14:10–14 At the wedding feast Samson boasts with a riddle and bets they cannot solve it.** The customs of the time called for a wedding feast. Samson provided one, and invited "thirty companions to be with him" (vv. 10–11). As part of the festivities, he put forth a riddle about his slaying of the lion. He promised, if they could solve the riddle within 7 days, he would give them "thirty sheets and thirty change of garments" (v. 12). If they could not, then they would have to give him the same (v. 13). Then he put forth the riddle: "Out of the eater came forth meat, and out of the strong came forth sweetness" (v. 14). It was a tough one to figure out, and they could not do it.

Samson puts forth his riddle

● **Judges 14:15–17 Samson's wife betrays his trust.** With time running out, they went to Samson's wife and said, "Entice thy husband, that he may declare unto us the riddle, lest we burn thee and thy father's house with fire," justifying the threat by accusing her of seeking to "take that we have" (v. 15).

Samson's wife "wept before him, and said, Thou dost but hate me, and lovest me not: thou hast put forth a riddle unto the children of my people, and hast not told it me" (v. 16). He reminded her that he had not even told his father or mother, so why should he tell it to her? But she persisted in her crying and pleading for seven days, and he finally relented. "He told her, because she lay sore upon him: and she told the riddle to the children of her people" (v. 17).

- **Judges 14:18–20 Samson slays 30 men in a murderous rage.** The men of the city to whom he had put the riddle returned and gave him their answer before the sun went down on the seventh day: "What is sweeter than honey? and what is stronger than a lion?" (v. 18). Samson was furious, realizing his wife had betrayed him. He raged at them, "If ye had not plowed with my heifer, ye had not found out my riddle" (v. 18).

  Samson then "went down to Ashkelon, and slew thirty men … and took their spoil, and gave change of garments unto them which expounded the riddle" then returned home to his father's house (v. 19). His wife, whom he left behind, was then "given to his companion, whom he had used as his friend" (v. 20).

- **Judges 15:1–5 Samson returns and burns their fields.** Not knowing that she had remarried, Samson returned to Ashkelon with a gift for his wife. But when he attempted to enter her chamber, her father stopped him, saying, "I verily thought that thou hadst utterly hated her; therefore I gave her to thy companion: is not her younger sister fairer than she? take her, I pray thee, instead of her" (vv. 1–2). In another violent rage, he "went and caught three hundred foxes, and took firebrands, and turned tail to tail, and put a firebrand in the midst between two tails" (v. 4). Then, "when he had set the brands on fire, he let them go into the standing corn of the Philistines, and burnt up both the shocks, and also the standing corn, with the vineyards and olives" (v. 5).

- **Judges 15:6–8 Samson's wife and her father are killed, and Samson takes revenge "with a great slaughter."** When they realized that Samson was the one who had burned their fields, and learned why he had done it, the men of the city burned his wife and her father to death (v. 6). Samson swore to "be avenged of you," and "smote them hip and thigh with a great slaughter" (vv. 7–8).

- **Judges 15:9–17 Samson kills 1,000 with the jawbone of an ass.** After the slaughter at Ashkelon, Samson fled to the mountains of Judea, followed by those seeking revenge. When the men of Judah realized what was happening, 3,000 of them demanded of Samson, "Knowest thou not that the Philistines are rulers over us? what is this that thou hast done unto us? And he said unto them, As they did unto me, so have I done unto them" (v. 11). He allowed them to bind him "with two new cords" and deliver him to the Philistines (vv. 12–13).

  As the Philistines shouted angrily at him upon his delivery to them, "the Spirit of the Lord came mightily upon [Samson], and the cords that were upon his arms became as flax that was burnt with fire, and his bands loosed from off his hands"

Samson with the jawbone of an ass

(v. 14). He picked up "a new jawbone of an ass, and put forth his hand, and took it, and slew a thousand men therewith" (v. 15). Boasting of what he had done, "he cast away the jawbone out of his hand, and called that place Ramath-lehi" (which means "the casting away of the jawbone") (vv. 16–17).

● **Judges 15:18–20 The place named "Lehi" is in Judah.** The area of Judah where Samson sought refuge was called Lehi, which means "jawbone." This is the homeland after which the Nephite prophet Lehi, who lived in Judah, was named. While living there, and after slaying 1,000 Philistines with the jawbone of an ass, Samson became extremely thirsty, fearing he might die (v. 18). Miraculously, the Lord provided water in the hollowed-out jaw, which revived him. He therefore called the place En-hakkore (which means "spring of him that calleth") and it "is in Lehi unto this day" (v. 19).

● **Judges 16:1–2 Samson goes to Gaza, sleeps with a harlot, and is locked in by his pursuers.** Traveling down to Gaza, which is in the land of the Philistines, Samson slept with a harlot (v. 1). Becoming aware of his presence in their city, the Gazites locked the gate of the city, surrounded him, and lay in waiting all night, seeking to kill him (v. 2).

● **Judges 16:3 Samson removes the gate of Gaza, and takes it with him.** Unfortunately for his intended captors, Samson "arose at midnight, and took the doors of the gate of the city, and the two posts, and went away with them, bar and all, … upon his shoulders, and carried them up to the top of [a] hill … [in] Hebron.

THE STORY OF THE BIBLE #84, p214, 1873, 1877, 1884

Samson carries the gates of Gaza

Samson Pursues a New Wife—Delilah

● **Judges 16:4–5 Samson goes to the valley of Sorek to pursue Delilah, another Philistine woman.** He knew from the beginning that she would betray him, but didn't care. He childishly gambled with his life. It was almost a death wish. Her name was Delilah (v. 4). The rulers of the city conspired with her to discover the secret of Samson's strength by offering her 1,100 pieces of silver from each and every one of them (v. 5). It was a sizable amount of money.

● **Judges 16:6–14 Delilah seeks to know the secret of his strength.** Delilah went to Samson and asked him, "Tell me, I pray thee, wherein thy great strength lieth" (v. 6). She made no pretense about why she wanted to know. It was that "thou mightest be bound to afflict thee" (v. 6). Though he knew this, in order to continue to receive her feminine favors, he played

GUSTAVE DORÉ, 1896

Samson and Delilah

along with the charade. "If they bind me with seven green withs that were never dried, then shall I be weak," he said (v. 7). Soon thereafter, they brought the green withs and "she bound him with them" (v. 8). While men hid themselves in her chamber, she woke Samson with a warning, "The Philistines be upon thee, Samson," whereupon "he brake the withs, as a thread of tow is broken when it toucheth the fire" (v. 9).

Samson easily breaks Philistine bands

Accusing Samson of mocking her, Delilah said, "now tell me, I pray thee, wherewith thou mightest be bound" (v. 10). Samson said, "If they bind me fast with new ropes that never were occupied, then shall I be weak, and be as another man" (v. 11). The ropes were provided by men who again secreted themselves in her chamber (v. 12). Delilah bound him with them, then cried out, "The Philistines be upon thee, Samson." But again, "he brake them from off his arms like a thread" (v. 12).

Delilah protested again that Samson was mocking her, and asked for a third time, "wherewith thou mightest be bound." He answered that the secret was to "[weave] the seven locks of my head with [a] web" (v. 13). This she did, "fasten[ing] it with [a] pin," then calling out again, "The Philistines be upon thee, Samson." Samson woke out of his sleep and simply "went away with the pin of the beam, and with the web" (v. 14).

- **Judges 16:15–20 The famous haircut—Samson loses his strength.** Delilah asked in frustration, "How canst thou say, I love thee, when thine heart is not with me? thou hast mocked me these three times, and hast not told me wherein thy great strength lieth" (v. 15). She continued to "press … him daily with her words, and urged him, so that his soul was vexed unto death (v. 16). Finally, he told the truth. "There hath not come a razor upon mine head; for I have been a Nazarite unto God from my mother's womb: if I be shaven, then my strength will go from me, and I shall become weak, and be like any other man" (v. 17). The answer reveals the shallowness of his understanding. It was not his hair but the Nazarite vow that was the source of his strength. The hair was only a symbol of his covenant. But removing it would signal his utter abandonment of his covenant vows.

Seeing that he was completely sincere in his answer, Delilah told the Philistines to bring their money because "he hath shewed me all his heart" (v. 18). She then caused Samson to sleep on her lap while a servant "shave[d] off the seven locks of his head" (v. 19). Samson's strength left him, and when she cried out again, "The Philistines be upon thee, Samson," he was unaware that "the Lord was departed from him," and he could not escape (v. 20).

Delilah cuts Samson's hair

- **Judges 16:21–22 Samson is blinded, shackled, imprisoned, and forced to grind grain like an ox.** "The Philistines took him, and put out his eyes, and brought him down to Gaza, and bound him with fetters of brass; and he did grind in the prison house." There he remained for many days while "the hair of his head began to grow again after he was shaven" (v. 22).

Samson grinds grain like an ox

Destroying the Temple of Dagon

- **Judges 16:23–25 A day of Philistine celebration.** Eventually, "the lords of the Philistines gathered them together for to offer a great sacrifice unto Dagon their god, and to rejoice: for they said, Our god hath delivered Samson our enemy into our hand" (v. 23). They loved to gawk at this once mighty man, "the destroyer of our country, which slew many of us" (v. 24). On this day of national celebration, "they called for Samson out of the prison house [to make] them sport: and they set him between the pillars" (v. 25). They had no idea that this now-humbled man had repented and sought the Lord's help in delivering Israel from these arrogant Philistine pagans.

- **Judges 16:26–31 Samson destroys the coliseum and all in attendance.** As he was brought forth from the prison he asked "the lad that held him by the hand" to take him to the spot where he could "feel the pillars whereupon the house standeth, that I may lean upon them" (v. 26). He was familiar with this coliseum, having been in Philistia many times during his days of youthful rebellion. The place was packed with "men and women; and all the lords of the Philistines"—about 3,000 people in all (v. 27). Samson then "bowed himself with all his might," causing the pillars to topple and bringing down the house "upon the lords, and upon all the people that were therein. So the dead which he slew at his death were more than they which he slew in his life" (v. 30). His people retrieved his body and buried it in the "buryingplace of Manoah his father" (v. 31).

Samson topples temple of Dagon

MICAH—A RULER, NOT A JUDGE

In the closing chapters of Judges the writer relates incidents that illustrate the perverse state of religion and morality in Israel in those days, when every man "did that which was right in his own eyes" (Judges 17:6; 21:25). The stories of Micah the Levite and the Danite migration (Judges 17–18), and the near destruction of the Benjamites after the rape of the concubine at Gibeah

(Judges 19–21), are examples of Israel's advanced state of apostasy. The Israelites were guilty of the abominations of Sodom. They became embroiled in another major civil war, and as a result, the tribe of Benjamin was very nearly wiped out.

The Danite Migration

- **Judges 17 Micah was of the tribe of Dan.** He was not a righteous man. His house was full of idols and he consecrated his own Levite priest.

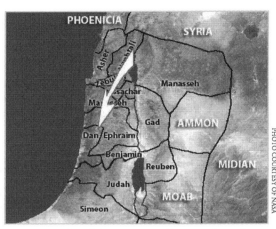

- **Judges 18:1–13 The tribe of Dan was seeking for an inheritance because they had not obtained one since entering Canaan (Judges 18:1).** They originally settled at the headwaters of the Jordan River. Since that area was the northernmost tribal inheritance, it became a common saying to speak of the domain of Israel as being "from Dan even to Beersheba" (Judges 20:1). The Danites re-located to an area west of Ephraim and Benjamin and north of Judah.

The tribe of Dan eventually moved south

- **Judges 18:14–31 The Danites take Micah's idols and set them up for their own worship.** This shows their utter hypocrisy, since they had sought the Lord's advice through Micah's Levite priest in re-locating their people (Judges 18:3–6). And yet, after obtaining the land, they immediately began to worship idols.

The Near-Destruction of Benjamin

- **Judges 19:1–12 A Levite concubine (secondary wife) becomes a harlot, then returns to her father.** Her Levite husband traveled to her father's house and retrieved her, staying several days there before leaving for home, taking the woman and his servant with him. Along the way, they passed by Jerusalem without stopping to rest there because the Levite did not want to stay the night among Jebusites, who were "not of the children of Israel" (v. 12).

- **Judges 19:10–12 The city of Jerusalem was inhabited by the Jebusites during the time of the judges.** Jerusalem did not become a holy city and a capital for the Israelites until David conquered the Jebusites.

- **Judges 19: 13–27 The sins of Sodom are manifested in Gibeah.** They decided to stay the night in Gibeah, a city of

The Levite's wife found dead

the tribe of Benjamin. The Levite, his concubine, and his servant at first camped in the streets of Gibeah because no one would take them in for the night. An elderly man returning home from his day's work noticed them and gave them lodging at his home for the night. Later that night, the men of the city surrounded the house and de- manded that the Levite come out "that we may know him" (v. 22). The old man offered instead his daughter and the Levite's concubine. "But the men would not hearken to [the old man]: so the [Levite] took his concubine, and brought her forth unto them; and they knew her, and abused her all the night until the morning: and [then] let her go" (v. 25). She fell down dead on the old man's door- step "and her hands were upon the threshold" (v. 27).

● **Judges 19:28–30 The concubine's body is divided into twelve pieces.** The Levite took his concubine's body home, cut it into twelve pieces and sent them, one to each tribe of Israel.

"There is no doubt that with the pieces he sent to each tribe a circumstantial account of the barbarity of the men of Gibeah; and it is very likely that they considered each of the pieces as expressing an execration, 'If ye will not come and avenge my wrongs, may ye be hewn in pieces like this abused and murdered woman!' They were all struck with the enormity of the crime, and considered it a sovereign disgrace to all the tribes of Israel"⁹.

● **Judges 20 The smallest tribe becomes much smaller.**
The tribes of Israel were outraged at the manifestation of homosexuality in Benjamin. They rose up and attacked what was already one of the smallest tribes and nearly annihilated them in a vengeful civil war. Altogether, according to the account, a total of 25,100 Benjamites were slain, leaving only 600 alive (Judges 20:46–47).

GUSTAVE DORÉ, 1896

These 600 were allowed by the princes of Israel to take wives, although not in a righteous manner, so that the tribal identity could be perpetuated. The inhabitants of Jagbesh-gilead were destroyed for not engaging in the war with Benjamin, and afterwards 400 virgins from among them were taken captive to become wives of the surviving Benjamites. Nevertheless, the tribe of Benjamin remained small thereafter.

Working with unmuzzled oxen

Notes

1. *Antiquities*, bk. 5, chap. 2, par. 7.
2. Sperry, *Spirit of the Old Testament* (1940), 51–52.
3. Rasmussen, *Introduction to the Old Testament*, 2 vols. [1972], 1:149.
4. *Gospel Doctrine*, 155.
5. Rasmussen, *Introduction to the Old Testament*, 2 vols. [1972], 1:150.
6. "Correlation Brings Blessings," *Relief Society Magazine*, Apr. 1967, 246–247.
7. Rasmussen, *Introduction to the Old Testament*, 1:151.
8. "The False Gods We Worship," *Ensign*, June 1976, 4.
9. Clarke, *Bible Commentary*, 6 vols. [n.d.], 2:182.

Ruth and Hannah's Examples of Righteousness

(Ruth; 1 Samuel)

ℬℭ

THE STORY OF RUTH

The Book of Ruth

● **Author:** Anonymous.

● **Position:** Judges and Ruth are the only available Jewish histories during the turbulent period of general apostasy that occurred from sometime after the death of Joshua to the birth of the prophet Samuel. Ruth is one of 11 books of the Old Testament that are considered "Hagiographa" (sacred writings) to the Jews. The others are the books of Chronicles (counted as one book), Ezra-Nehemiah (also counted as one book), Esther, Job, Psalms, Proverbs, Ecclesiastes, Song of Solomon, Lamentations, and Daniel.

Ruth, the Moabite

● **Purpose:** Ruth's story is unsurpassed in beauty and tenderness. It illustrates the principles of loyalty and devotion within the family. It also illustrates the integration of a righteous non-Israelite into the fold of Israel. It teaches us about "nobility" in God's eyes. It is not about race—it is about faithfulness and virtue. The story provides a serene contrast to the wickedness, turbulence, and disorder that prevailed in Israel during the time of the judges. Perhaps most importantly, Ruth and Boaz were righteous progenitors of the Lord, Jesus Christ (Ruth 4:13–18; Matthew 1:5–17).

● **Time Span:** The middle of the twelfth-century BC, during the time of the judges.

- **Length:** 4 chapters

- **Key Sections:** — Chapter 1 The family of Elimelech moves to Moab; marriages and deaths; return to Bethlehem.

  — Chapters 2–3 Courtship of Boaz and Ruth.

  — Chapter 4 Ruth and Boaz's marriage.

Events in Moab

- **Ruth 1:1–2 Elimelech's family moves to Moab.** In the time of the judges, a famine came upon the land of Judah, causing a man name Elimelech, his wife Naomi, and their two sons to move to the land of Moab.

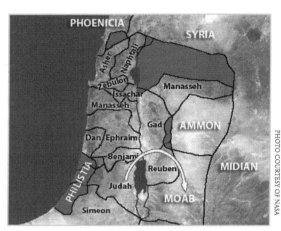

Elimelech moved from Jerusalem to Moab

- **Ruth 1:3–5 Elimelech and both his sons die, leaving Naomi and Ruth as widows.** While there, Elimelech died, leaving Naomi a widow with her two sons (v. 3). These sons married two Moabite women, Orpah and Ruth, and they all continued to live there for another ten years (v. 4). Then, tragically, both of the sons died, leaving Naomi bereft of both her husband and her sons (v. 5).

- **Ruth 1:6–13 Naomi prepares to return to Judah where her kinsfolk could take care of her and where the famine had now abated (vv. 6–7).** She invited her two daughters- in-law to return to their families also, saying, "the Lord deal kindly with you, as ye have dealt with the dead, and with me" (v. 8). She also asked the Lord to bless them, "that ye may find rest, each of you in the house of her husband. Then she kissed them; and they lifted up their voice, and wept" (v. 9). At first, they protested, saying, "Surely we will return with thee unto thy people" (v. 10). Naomi insisted, "Turn again, my daughters: why will ye go with me? are there yet any more sons in my womb, that they may be your husbands? … go your way; for I am too old to have an husband" (vv. 11–12). She felt sorrow that they were caught up in the troubles that had come to her (v. 13).

Her comments about having no more sons are associated with the customs of the time. If a woman were left widow- ed, she would be married to the oldest living brother of the dead man, and he would care for her as his own wife. Ruth was explaining that she had no more sons, and if they returned with her to Judah they might be left as widows without support.

Ruth clings to Naomi

● **Ruth 1:14–18 Ruth's inspiring loyalty to Naomi.** Orpah took Naomi's advice and kissed her goodbye, "but Ruth clave unto her" (v. 14). Naomi urged her to return "back unto her people, and unto her gods" as her sister had done (v. 15), but Ruth would not, saying, "Intreat me not to leave thee, or to return from following after thee: for whither thou goest, I will go; and where thou lodgest, I will lodge: thy people shall be my people, and thy God my God" (v. 16).

President John Taylor said to those Saints who had forsaken their homeland to come to Zion: "'Thanks be to the God of Israel who has counted us worthy to receive the principles of truth.' These were the feelings you had and enjoyed in your far distant homes. And your obedience to those principles tore you from your homes, firesides and associations and brought you here, for you felt like one of old, when she said, 'Whither thou goest I will go; thy God shall be my God, thy people shall be my people, and where thou diest there will I be buried.' And you have gathered to Zion that you might be taught and instructed in the laws of life and listen to the words which emanate from God, become one people and one nation, partake of one spirit, and prepare yourselves, your progenitors and posterity for an everlasting inheritance in the celestial kingdom of God"[1].

● **Ruth 1:19–22 They return to Bethlehem—Naomi's homeland.** Returning to Bethlehem caused a stir among the people, who marveled, "Is this Naomi?" (v. 19). But Naomi said, "Call me not Naomi, call me Mara: for the Almighty hath dealt very bitterly with me. I went out full, and the Lord hath brought me home again empty" (vv. 20–21). The name Naomi means "sweet" or "pleasant," while the name Mara means "sea of bitterness." Naomi was using a play on words to express her sorrowful condition. This was not an accusation, only Naomi's way of saying she endured much tragedy in Moab.

Ruth Meets Boaz in Bethlehem

● **Ruth 2:1–3 Ruth supports them by gleaning in the fields of Boaz.** Naomi and Ruth had returned to Jerusalem at the time of the barley harvest (Ruth 1:22). This offered a means of survival, since the poor were able to glean the corners of fields for their sustenance. Ruth proposed that she "go to the field, and glean ears of corn [wheat]" and Naomi agreed (v. 2). She did so, and as it happened, she found herself "on a part of the field belonging unto Boaz," who was "a mighty man of wealth" and "of the family of Elimelech" (vv. 1, 3).

GUSTAV DORÉ (1865)

Ruth gleaning in the field

"Harvesting was difficult work and demanded long hours. Young men moved through the fields grasping handfuls of the grain and cutting through the stalks with sickles.

These small bunches of grain were then bound into bundles called sheaves. As the men worked rapidly, a number of stalks fell to the ground. If the men were careful and took the time, these too could be gathered up. However, any stalks that dropped were allowed to remain where they fell. Poor people, following the reapers, were permitted to 'glean,' or gather, the random stalks—possibly all that stood between them and starvation. In addition, the edges of the field, where the sickle was not as easily wielded, were left unharvested. The poor were welcome to that portion, as well. The destitute of Bethlehem now included Ruth and Naomi and Ruth offered to go into the fields and glean"[2].

● **Ruth 2:4–12 Boaz likes and respects Ruth.**
Boaz came from Bethlehem to visit his field (v. 4). When he did, he noticed Ruth and asked his reapers, "Whose damsel is this?" (v. 5). They told him that she was a Moabite who had come back to Jerusalem with Naomi (v. 6). She had asked for permission to glean in the fields and had been working at it all day long (v. 7). Impressed, Boaz told Ruth she could glean in the fields with his own laborers and told her that he had "charged the young men that they shall not touch thee." Also, when she was thirsty she could "go unto the vessels, and drink of that which the young men have drawn" (v. 9). Obviously, he liked and respected her.

Boaz meets Ruth for the first time

At this invitation, Ruth "fell on her face, and bowed herself to the ground, and said unto him, Why have I found grace in thine eyes, that thou shouldest take knowledge of me, seeing I am a stranger?" (v. 10). And Boaz replied that he had heard "all that thou hast done unto thy mother in law since the death of thine husband: and how thou hast left thy father and thy mother, and the land of thy nativity, and art come unto a people which thou knewest not heretofore" (v. 11). He blessed her, saying, "The Lord recompense thy work, and a full reward be given thee of the Lord God of Israel, under whose wings thou art come to trust" (v. 12).

● **Ruth 2:17–20 Ruth learns that Boaz is a kinsman.** She gleaned in the field until evening, then took an ephah (50 pounds) of barley back to Naomi (vv. 17–18). This was a bountiful harvest, and Naomi asked her, "Where hast thou gleaned to day?" (v. 19). Ruth told her that the man's name was Boaz, whereupon Naomi exclaimed, "Blessed be he of the Lord, who hath not left off his kindness to the living and to the dead. And Naomi said unto her, The man is near of kin unto us, one of our next kinsmen" (v. 20).

● **Ruth 3:1–11 Naomi encourages Ruth to pursue Boaz as a husband.** Boaz was more than a generous relative. He was a kinsman, who by law could marry Ruth. Realizing this, Naomi determined to "seek rest for thee, that it may be well with thee" (v. 1).

Naomi knew that Boaz would be winnowing barley that night on the threshingfloor of the field (v. 2), and would likely sleep there as well. She advised her daughter-in-law to "Wash thyself therefore, and anoint thee, and put thy raiment upon thee, and get thee down to the floor: but make not thyself known unto the man, until he shall have done eating and drinking" (v. 3). She was to carefully note the place where Boaz slept, and "go in, and uncover his feet, and lay thee down; and he will tell thee what thou shalt do" (v. 4). Ruth was obedient, saying, "All that thou sayest unto me I will do" (v. 5).

Ruth went to the field, waited until Boaz had retired to bed, and then "came softly, and uncovered his feet, and laid her down" (v. 7). There is nothing inappropriate here; she sleeps at his feet. She uncovers his feet—probably to wake him up. Boaz knew of her righteousness and virtue. And Naomi knew of Boaz's virtue also. Sure enough, when Boaz stirred in the night, he awoke and found Ruth sleeping at his feet (v. 8). She boldly asked him to "spread … thy skirt over thine handmaid," which is an idiom that means "protect me," or, in other words, "be my protector or husband" (v. 9).

"When Boaz awoke from his sleep by the pile of grain, which he was guarding as was the custom during harvest time, he was startled by Ruth's presence. She was direct in her proposal. The word rendered 'skirt' also means 'wing,' and her request is not unlike our idiom 'take me under your wing.' Gesenius, the famous Hebraist, says it was a proper proposal of marriage—even though the girl was doing the proposing!"[3].

He was impressed that she was not interested in chasing after "young men, whether poor or rich" (v. 10), and said he would "do to thee all that thou requirest: for all the city of my people doth know that thou art a virtuous woman" (v. 11).

"Boaz, who was an honourable man, and, according to [Ruth 3:10], no doubt somewhat advanced in years, praised Ruth for having taken refuge with him, and promised to fulfil her wishes when he had satisfied himself that the nearer [kin] would renounce his right and duty. … He acknowledged by this … declaration—that … it would [then] be his duty … to marry Ruth [and] he took no offence at the manner in which she had approached him and proposed to become his wife. On the contrary, he regarded it as a proof of feminine virtue and modesty, that she had not gone after young men, but offered herself as a wife to an old man like him. This conduct on the part of Boaz is a sufficient proof that women might have confidence in him that he would do nothing unseemly. And he justified such confidence."[4].

- **Ruth 3:12–18 Rules regarding "next of kin" in Israel would permit Boaz to marry her so long as the "next of kin" refused to do so.** Boaz told Ruth that "it is true that I am thy near kinsman: howbeit there is a kinsman nearer than I" (v. 12). Boaz advised her to stay the rest of the night, and in the morning he would ask the nearer kinsman if he intended to do his duty (v. 13). This she did, departing in the morning before anyone would notice (v. 14). Boaz filled her veil with six measures of barley and sent her home (v. 15). She returned and reported to her mother-in-law all that had happened.

- **Ruth 4:1–12 Boaz obtains the right to marry Ruth.** He found the nearer kinsman at the gate and sat down with him along with ten elders of the city as witnesses (vv. 1–2). Then he said to the nearer kinsman, "Naomi, that is come again out of the country of Moab, selleth a parcel of land, which was our brother Elimelech's" (v. 3). He knew that the man would want the land, and he did, saying, "I will redeem it" (v. 4). Boaz then told him that if he took the land he would also have to take Ruth to wife "to raise up the name of the dead upon his inheritance" (v. 5). This he did not want to do, and he said to Boaz, "redeem thou my right to thyself; for I cannot redeem it" (v. 6).

In was the custom in Israel, when confirming a deal of any kind, for a man to "pluck … off his shoe, and [give] it to his neighbour" as a witness of the deed (v. 7). This the man did, and Boaz called upon the men who were there to witnesses that he had "bought all that was Elimelech's … of the hand of Naomi" (vv. 8–9), including "Ruth the Moabitess, the wife of Mahlon, … to be my wife, to raise up the name of the dead upon his inheritance" (v. 10). Of this they agreed to be witnesses, also wishing Boaz and Ruth a large and prosperous posterity (vv. 11–12).

● **Ruth 4:13–22 Boaz and Ruth produce a noble heritage.** Obed was born to them (v. 13–17), who was the father of Jesse and the grandfather of King David. Therefore, Christ, a descendant of David, was also one of their descendants. The birth of Obed was a great joy to them, and the women of Jerusalem said to Naomi that the child was "a restorer of thy life, and a nourisher of thine old age: for thy daughter in law, which loveth thee, which is better to thee than seven sons, hath born him" (v. 15). Naomi became a nurse-grandmother to the child (v. 16).

Elder Thomas S. Monson said: "In our selection of heroes, let us nominate also heroines. First, that noble example of fidelity—even Ruth. Sensing the grief-stricken heart of her mother-in-law, who suffered the loss of each of her two fine sons, and feeling perhaps the pangs of despair and loneliness which plagued the very soul of Naomi, Ruth uttered what has become that classic statement of loyalty: 'Intreat me not to leave thee, or to return from following after thee: for whither thou goest, I will go; and where thou lodgest, I will lodge: thy people shall be my people, and thy God my God.' (Ruth 1:16). Ruth's actions demonstrated the sincerity of her words. There is place for her name in the Hall of Fame"[5].

THE STORY OF HANNAH

The Tabernacle at Shiloh

The tabernacle housing the ark of the covenant was located at Shiloh, (Joshua 18:1), where the people of that day came to worship and sacrifice to the Lord before the great temple of Solomon was built in Jerusalem. Eli was the high priest, and his two rebellious sons, Hophni and Phinehas, were priests.

Hannah at the Tabernacle

● **1 Samuel 1:4–5 Elkanah took his wives and their families to Shiloh to make peace offerings.** After the fat, kidneys, and other parts were burned, part of the sacrificial animal was given back to the offerer to be eaten in a special feast. Elkanah gave this meat to his wives and children. Hannah received a more choice portion because of Elkanah's special love for her.

● **1 Samuel 1:6–7 Hannah's adversary was Peninnah, the other wife who "was constantly striving to irritate and vex her, to make her fret—to make her discontented with her lot, because the Lord had denied her children.** "She was greatly distressed, because it was a great reproach to a woman among the Jews to be barren; because, say some, every one hoped that the Messiah should spring from her line" (Clarke, *Bible Commentary*, 6 vols. [n.d.], 2:207).

● **1 Samuel 1:9 Eli sat upon a seat by a post of the temple.** In those days, it was customary for priests to sit on a stool or some other seat in the temple courtyard, near the gate of the city, where they would hear cases or complaints and render judgment concerning them.

● **1 Samuel 1:10–18 Hannah was a faithful woman who went to the temple to plead with the Lord for a son.** Hannah "was in bitterness of soul, and prayed unto the Lord, and wept sore" (v. 10). To be childless in ancient Israel was considered an unbearable curse for a woman. She made a vow, dedicating her future son to the Lord, to serve Him as a Nazarite all his life (v. 11). This kind of "separation" was permitted under the law (Numbers 6:5). It was the same vow that the mother of Samson had made concerning him. (Judges 13:5).

Shiloh in the center of Israel

As she prayed there on the tabernacle grounds, she "spake in her heart only" with no audible voice; only her lips moved (v. 13). Taking notice of her, and seeing her mouth moving without making a sound, "Eli thought she had been drunken" (vv. 12–13). He judged her harshly, saying, "How long wilt thou be drunken? put away thy wine from thee" (v. 14). Hannah protested, "No, my lord, I am a woman of a sorrowful spirit: I have drunk neither wine nor strong drink, but have poured out my soul before the Lord. Count not thine handmaid for a daughter of Belial [meaning a "worthless or profane person"]: for out of the abundance of my complaint and grief have I have spoken" (vv. 15–16).

With that explanation, Eli's harsh criticism turned to kindness. As one holding the priesthood and authorized to bless her, he said, "Go in peace: and the God of Israel grant thee thy petition that thou hast asked of him" (v. 17). This was a promise that her prayer would be answered. Gratefully, she thanked him, went her way, and "her countenance was no more sad" (v. 18).

● **1 Samuel 1:20 Sometime later Hannah conceived and bore a son and named him Samuel, which means "heard of God" or "name of God".** It was a lifelong reminder to both Hannah and Samuel of the special circumstances and commitments of his birth.

Eli sat at the tabernacle gate

- **1 Samuel 1:21–28 Samuel returned to begin his ser- vice at age 3.** "Weaning took place very late among the Israelites … Hebrew mothers were in the habit of suck- ling their children for three years … Samuel was to be presented to the Lord immediately after his weaning had taken place, and to remain at the sanctuary forever … [where] he was to receive his training at the sanctuary." (Keil and Delitzsch, *Commentary on the Old Testament*, 10 vols. [1996], 2:2:26). Though giving him up for the rest of his life must have been hard, Hannah was faithful to her covenant concerning Samuel. And the Lord then bless- ed her with three more sons and two daughters (1 Sam. 2:21).

Hannah prays for a son

- **1 Samuel 2:1–11 Hannah's prayer shows her to be a woman with great faith and love for God.** Among other things, she said, "My heart rejoiceth in the Lord, mine horn ["power" or "strength"] is exalted in the Lord: my mouth is enlarged over mine enemies; because I rejoice in thy salvation. There is none holy as the Lord: for there is none beside thee: neither is there any rock like our God" (vv. 1–2). The rock was a representation of Jesus Christ.

Hannah presents Samuel to Eli

Notes

1. In *Journal of Discourses*, 14:189.
2. Readers Digest, *Great People of the Bible and How They Lived* [1974], 129.
3. Rasmussen, *Introduction to the Old Testament*, 1:157.
4. Keil and Delitzsch, *Commentary on the Old Testament*, 10 vols. [1996], 2:1:483.
5. "My Personal Hall of Fame," *Ensign*, Nov. 1974, 108.

CHAPTER 21

Samuel and Saul

(1 Samuel 2–8; 1 Chronicles 9–16)

ℰℭℛ

INTRODUCTION

Concurrent Scriptures

This period of Israel's history is covered by two different books:

- **1 & 2 Samuel**   Written by the prophet Samuel.

- **1 Chronicles**   Also written by the prophet Samuel (and possibly others), but focusing on kings, wars, and other temporal events of that period.

Keeping two histories—one religious, the other temporal—is similar to what happened with the large and small plates of Nephi.

The Book of First Samuel

- **Author:**   Probably the prophet Samuel himself.

- **Position:**   First and Second Samuel are combined in the Hebrew scriptures but are separated in the Greek Bible. They are the beginning of the historical record of the kings of Israel (like the large plates of Nephi).

- **Purpose:**   To set forth the commencement of the history of Israel under King Saul and his successor, King David.

- **Time Span:**   The birth of Samuel (ca. 1125 BC) until the death of Saul and his sons.

- **Length:**   31 chapters

- **Key Sections:**   — Chapters 1–8   The rise of Samuel as a great prophet of the Lord

      — Chapters 9–15   The reign of Saul as the first king in Israel

      — Chapters 16–31 The rise of David as the succeeding king in Israel

The Book of First Chronicles

- **Author:**   Unknown.

- **Position:**   First and Second Chronicles are combined in the Hebrew scriptures. They relate Israelite history in broad strokes, being more of a religious history (like the small plates of Nephi).

- **Purpose:**   Along with Second Chronicles, provides a concise history of the Lord's people from Adam down to the return of the Jews to Palestine. The emphasis is on religious events and themes, especially temple worship. First and Second Chronicles (counted as one book) are also one of the 11 books of the Old Testament that belong to the Hagiographa ("sacred writings") of the Jewish canon, along with the books of Ruth, Ezra-Nehemiah (also counted as one book), Esther, Job, Psalms, Proverbs, Ecclesiastes, Song of Solomon, Lamentations, and Daniel.

- **Time Span:**   From Adam to the death of David, and Solomon's assumption of the throne (ca. 1015 BC).

- **Length:**   29 chapters

- **Key Sections:**
  - — Chapters 1–9   Genealogies of leading families from the beginning
  - — Chapter 10   Defeat of Israel by Philistines & end of Saul's reign
  - — Chapters 11–22 The reign of David
  - — Chapters 23–29 The beginning of Solomon's reign

ELI AND HIS SONS

- **1 Samuel 2:12–35 Eli's sons—Hophni and Phineas— were extremely wicked priests.** They emulated the behavior of priests at the temples of Baal and other false gods, using priestly power to obtain worldly wealth and satisfy their lusts.

They took for themselves the flesh of sacrificial animals, before the fat portions had been burned on the altar, when Israelites came to offer sacrifices at the tabernacle. They also took some of the flesh belonging to the offerer for his sacrificial meal (vv. 12–17). These were serious transgressions of God's laws, equivalent to robbing God. They also seduced women who assembled at the door of the tabernacle (v. 22). We can imagine the scandal their behavior created among the people, being the sons of the High Priest.

Eli's sons defrauded people at the gate

THEBIBLEREVIVAL.COM, #6

- **1 Samuel 2:22–29 Eli, who was very old, rebuked his sons, but took no action.** He did not stop them nor remove them from their priestly duties (1 Samuel 3:10–14, 19–20). This brought the whole ordinance of making sacrifices into contempt among the people (vv. 17, 24). As a result, "a man of God" (some unnamed prophet) came to Eli and condemned Eli because he honored his sons more than God (vv. 27–29). All of this was happening at the tail-end of the period of the judges, when apostasy was rampant among the Israelites. Even the priests were corrupt.

- **1 Samuel 2:30 The Lord honors only those who honor him.** The Lord said to Eli, "them that honour me I will honour, and they that despise me shall be lightly esteemed" (v. 30). This is similar to the complaint the Lord had against the Saints who lived in Missouri during the time of Joseph Smith: "They were slow to hearken unto the voice of the Lord their God; therefore, the Lord their God is slow to hearken unto their prayers, to answer them in the day of their trouble. In the day of their peace they esteemed lightly my counsel; but, in the day of their trouble, of necessity they feel after me" (D&C 101:7–8).

- **1 Samuel 2:31–34 The Lord curses Eli and his posterity.** He cursed Eli and his posterity, saying, "there shall not be an old man in thine house for ever" (v. 32). Those who do live for awhile will "grieve thine heart," and "all the increase of thine house shall die in the flower of their age" (v. 33). Moreover, "thy two sons … Hophni and Phinehas; in one day they shall die both of them" (v. 34).

- **1 Samuel 2:35; 3:1 A prophecy concerning Samuel.** The Lord told Eli that after he and his sons had been removed from their priestly offices, "I will raise me up a faithful priest, that shall do according to that which is in mine heart and in my mind: and I will build him a sure house; and he shall walk before mine anointed for ever" (v. 35). This was a reference to "the child Samuel [who] ministered unto the Lord before Eli" (v. 1).

- **1 Samuel 3:1 Revelation had ceased in Israel as a result of their corruption and apostasy.** "The word of the Lord was precious [rare] in those days; there was no open vision."

- **1 Samuel 3:12–13 The responsibility of parents to restrain their children.** Eli was cursed, not because of his own evil behavior, but because he failed to teach his children to live righteously. As we know from modern revelation, if parents have children in Zion and "teach them not to understand the doctrine of repentance, faith in Christ the Son of the living God, and of baptism and the gift of the Holy Ghost by the laying on of the hands, when eight years old, the sin be upon the heads of the parents" (D&C 68:25). In Eli's case the Lord "told him that I will judge his house for ever for the iniquity which he knoweth; because his sons made themselves vile, and he restrained them not" (v. 13). His boys were cursed for their vile behavior. Eli was cursed for not teaching or "restraining" them properly.

President Spencer W. Kimball said: "The Lord punished the temple worker Eli, charging him with the serious sins of his sons … because his sons made themselves vile, and he restrained them not.' (1 Samuel 3:12–13). In modern times the Lord said, 'Now, I, the Lord, am not well pleased with the inhabitants of Zion, for there are idlers among them; and their children are also growing up in wickedness.' (D&C 68:31) … How sad if the Lord should charge any of us parents with having failed to teach our children. Truly a tremendous responsibility falls upon a couple when they bring children into the world.

Not only food, clothes, shelter are required for them, but loving, kindly disciplining and teaching"[1].

President Joseph F. Smith said: "There should [not] be any of us so unwisely indulgent, so thoughtless and so shallow in our affection for our children that we dare not check them in a wayward course, in wrong-doing and in their foolish love for the things of the world more than for the things of righteousness, for fear of offending them"[2].

SAMUEL BECOMES A PROPHET

● **1 Samuel 3:2–10 The Lord calls Samuel to be a prophet—at about age 12.** Eli was getting older and his vision was nearly gone (v. 2). And Samuel had never yet received revelation from the Lord (v. 7). But late one night, after both had gone to bed, Samuel was awakened by the voice of the Lord (vv. 3–4). He awoke and called out, "here am I," thinking it was Eli calling him (v. 4). Hearing no reply, he ran to Eli's beside and said, "Here am I; for thou calledst me." And Eli said, "I called not; lie down again" (v. 5).

The Lord spoke to Samuel again, and he ran to Eli's side again, thinking he was calling to him. Eli told him to go back to bed (v. 6). Then, the Lord called out to Samuel a third time, and when he ran to Eli's side "Eli perceived that the LORD had called the child" (vv. 7–8).

The aged priest instructed Samuel to "Go, lie down: and it shall be, if he call thee, that thou shalt say, Speak, LORD; for thy servant heareth. So Samuel went and lay down in his place" (v. 9). The Lord called out "Samuel, Samuel" again, but this time He "came, and stood" in Samuel's presence. The boy responded this time, "Speak; for thy servant heareth" (v. 10).

We should note that Eli did not hear the Lord's voice. The Lord communicates sometimes through the whisperings of the Holy Ghost, or with a "still, small voice." In this case, only Samuel could hear the still, small voice of the Lord.

● **1 Samuel 3:11–14 The Lord's words to Samuel.** He told Samuel, "Behold, I will do a thing in Israel, at which both the ears of every one that heareth it shall tingle" (v. 11). It had been hundreds of years since a seer had been called among the people of Israel. The Lord said he would "perform against Eli all things which I have spoken concerning his house ... because his sons made themselves vile, and he

Samuel to Eli: "Here am I"

restrained them not" (vv. 12–13). Because of this, "the iniquity of Eli's house shall not be purged with sacrifice [be forgiven] … for ever" (v. 14).

● **1 Samuel 3:15–18 Samuel tells Eli the vision.** The next day, Samuel "opened the doors of the house of the Lord" as usual. He was afraid to tell Eli the vision because of what the Lord had said concerning Eli and his family (v. 15). But Eli pressed him by asking, "What is the thing that the Lord hath said unto thee? I pray thee hide it not from me: God do so to thee, and more also, if thou hide any thing from me of all the things that he said unto thee" (v. 17). So "Samuel told him every whit, and hid nothing from him," and Eli responded by saying, "It is the Lord: let him do what seemeth him good" (v. 18).

Samuel the prophet and seer

● **1 Samuel 3:19–21 The Lord honors the prophecies of Samuel.** As Samuel continued to grow and mature, "the Lord was with him, and did let none of his words fall to the ground" (v. 19). "And all Israel from Dan even to Beer-sheba knew that Samuel was established to be a prophet of the Lord" (v. 20). Thus, for the first time in centuries, "the Lord appeared again in Shiloh [at the tabernacle]" and "revealed himself to Samuel in Shiloh" providing him with "the word of the Lord" (v. 21).

President Heber J. Grant said: "You need have no fear that when one of the Apostles of the Lord Jesus Christ delivers a prophecy in the name of Jesus Christ, because he is inspired to do that, that it will fall by the wayside. I know of more than one prophecy, which, looking at it naturally, seemed as though it would fall to the ground as year after year passed. But lo and behold, in the providences of the Lord, that prophecy was fulfilled"[3].

LOSING AND REGAINING THE ARK

● **1 Samuel 4:1–9 The Israelites took the ark of the covenant to the battlefield.** They believed that its presence would protect them from their enemies. This belief grew out of a defeat they suffered at the hands of the Philistines, wherein they lost about 4,000 men (vv. 1–2). They could not understand why the Lord had permitted them to fail, and decided to "fetch the ark of the covenant of the Lord out of Shiloh unto us, that … it may save us out of the hand of our enemies" (v. 3).

This they did, bringing the ark, along with the priests Eli, Hophni and Phinehas to their camp (v. 4). When this most sacred of all Israelite objects came into camp "all Israel shouted with a great shout, so that the earth rang again" (v. 5).

When the Philistines heard the noise of the shout and understood that the ark of the covenant had come into the Israelite camp, they were afraid, saying, "God is come into the camp … Woe unto us! for there hath not been such a thing heretofore" (vv. 6–7). They knew that "these are the Gods that smote the Egyptians with all the plagues in the wilderness" (v. 8). The Philistines resolved to fight "like men" that they might not end up as servants to the Hebrews (v. 9).

● **1 Samuel 4:10–11 The Philistines capture the ark at Eben-ezer and kill Eli's sons.** Despite the presence of the ark of the covenant, the Philistines defeated the Israelites with "a very great slaughter; for there fell of Israel thirty thousand footmen" (v. 10). And among the slain were "the two sons of Eli, Hophni and Phinehas" (v. 11). This fulfilled the Lord's prophecy that Eli's two sons would die on the same day (1 Samuel 2:34).

"The Lord is come into the camp!"

● **1 Samuel 4:12–18 When these events are reported to Eli, he falls, breaks his neck, and dies.** The loss of the ark to a pagan enemy was unthinkable to the Israelites. And to lose the two sons of the high priest as well was cause for great mourning. A soldier who escaped back to Shiloh came running into the city "the same day with his clothes rent, and with earth upon his head" [as sign of deep sorrow and mourning] (v. 12). Eli, who had permitted the ark to be taken from its place within the tabernacle, had been greatly worried concerning it (v. 13). When the news arrived that it had been lost "all the city cried out" (v. 13). The soldier "came in hastily, and told Eli" who was at that time 98 years old and blind (vv. 14–15). He reported that "Israel is fled before the Philistines, and there hath been also a great slaughter among the people, and thy two sons also, Hophni and Phinehas, are dead, and the ark of God is taken" (vv. 16–17). For Eli, this was a triple tragedy—the loss of his sons, the defeat of Israel, and the loss of the ark of the covenant into enemy hands. The shock was so great that "he fell from off the seat backward by the side of the gate, and his neck brake, and he died: for he was an old man, and heavy" (v. 18). Israel was now bereft of its high priest also, who had "judged Israel forty years: (v. 18).

● **1 Samuel 4:19–22 Eli's daughter-in-law also dies in childbirth.** The wife of Phinehas was "with child, near to be delivered" when she received the news "that the ark of God was taken, and that her father in law and her husband were dead" (v. 19).

● **1 Samuel 5:1–5 The Philistine god Dagon falls down before the ark.** The triumphant Philistines brought the ark of the covenant back to their city of Ashdod and placed it into the "house" [temple] of Dagon, placing it beside their idol-god (vv. 1–2). But when they rose up the following morning they found that "Dagon was fallen upon his face to the earth before the ark of the Lord. And they took Dagon, and set him in his place again" (v. 3). The next morning, they found Dagon again "fallen upon his face to the ground before the ark of the Lord; and the head of Dagon and both the palms of his hands were cut off upon the threshold; only

The Philistine fish-god Dagon

the stump of Dagon was left to him" (v. 4). Fearful, "neither the priests of Dagon, nor any that [came] into Dagon's house, tread on the threshold of Dagon" thereafter (v. 5).

● **1 Samuel 5:6–9 The Philistines are plagued by the Lord for taking the ark.** The citizens of Ashdod broke out in "emerods." Aren Maeir believes, based on Hebrew meanings and archaeological evidence, that these were either hemorrhoids or some kind of penile malady (syhpillis?)[4]. Others argue that it was the plague, spread by the mice that overran their cities. Whatever it was, it afflicted not only those of the city but also "the coasts thereof" (v. 6). This men of Ashdod now wanted to send the ark away, because of this outbreak and also what had happened to the idol of Dagon (v. 7). Calling together "all the lords of the Philistines," they asked, "What shall we do with the ark of the God of Israel? And they answered, Let the ark of the God of Israel be carried … unto Gath," which they did (v. 8). But while doing this, the plague of "emerods" became very destructive, smiting "the men of the city, both small and great … [who all developed] emerods in their secret parts" (v. 9).

● **1 Samuel 5:10–12 The Philistines send the ark to Ekron.** First, they sent it to Ekron, but the people of Ekron were not happy with this decision, accusing them of sending it "to slay us and our people"(v. 10). And indeed, there came a "deadly destruction throughout all the city" because "the hand of God was very heavy there" (v. 11). Even those who did not die were "smitten with … emerods," causing "the cry of the city [to reach] up to heaven" (v. 12).

● **1 Samuel 6:1–9, 17–18 The Philistines determine to send the ark away.** The ark was in Philistine hands for a total of 7 months (v. 1). They desperately wanted to get rid of it because of the trouble that descended upon any city to which it came. They consulted their "priests and the diviners, saying, What shall we do to the ark of the LORD? tell us wherewith we shall send it to his place" (v. 2). The answer illustrated the depth of their idolatry and superstition: "If ye send away the ark of the God of Israel, send it not empty; but … return [to the God of Israel] a trespass offering: then ye shall be healed, and it shall be known to you why his hand is not removed from you" (v. 3).

The trespass offering they decided to send with the ark was "five golden emerods, and five golden mice, according to the number of the lords of the Philistines" (v. 4). They made images of their the emerods and also of the mice that were devastating their land, in hopes that the God of Israel "will lighten his hand from off you, and from off your gods, and from off your land" (v. 5). The five golden emerods represented the cities of Ashdod, Gaza, Askelon, Gath, and Ekron (v. 17). The seven golden mice represented all the cities of the Philistines (v. 18).

The Philistines remembered how the Egyptians had rid themselves of their ten plagues—by sending the Israelites away (v. 6). They therefore determined to "make a new cart" and put two "milch kine [milk cattle], on which there hath come no yoke, and tie the kine to the cart" (v. 7). Then, they would put the ark on the cart, along with all their golden images "in a coffer by the side thereof" and send the cart away without a driver (v. 8). If the cart headed toward Beth-shemesh, then they would conclude that the God of Israel had done all the evil against them; but otherwise, they would know that these things happened only by chance (v. 9).

- **1 Samuel 6:10–14 Riding on a cart without human involvement, the Ark miraculously finds its way back into Israelite hands.** The Philistines did exactly as they had planned (vv. 10–11), and sent the cart away without a driver. The cattle immediately headed toward Beth-shemesh, "along the highway, lowing as they went, and turned not aside to the right hand or to the left" (v. 12). When it arrive at Beth- shemesh, the Israelites were "reaping their wheat harvest in the valley: and they lifted up their eyes, and saw the ark, and rejoiced to see it" (v. 13). The cart "came into the field of Joshua, a Beth-shemite, and stood there [by] a great stone" (v. 14). They made a fire upon the stone with the wood of the cart, and offered the cattle as "a burnt offering unto the Lord" (v. 14).

GUSTAVE DORÉ, 1865

The Philistines send the ark away on a cart

- **1 Samuel 6:15–19 The Lord smites the Beth-shemites for looking into the ark of the covenant without proper authority.** They placed both the ark of the covenant and the coffer that contained the golden objects onto the "stone of Abel" that stood there in the field of Joshua (v. 18), and then "offered burnt offerings and sacrificed sacrifices the same day unto the Lord" (v. 15). Unfortunately, "the men of Beth-shemesh … looked into the ark of the Lord" at that time—a privilege that was restricted to the high priest, and then only on one day a year—the Day of Atonement. For this affront, the Lord smote 50,070 men, causing great lamentation in Beth-shemesh (v. 19).

- **1 Samuel 6:20–21; 7:1–2 The Beth-shemites send the ark to Kirjath-jearim, where it remains for 20 years.** Now fearing the presence of the ark in their city, the Beth-shemites wondered if anybody was worthy to stand before this holy object that represented the Lord, and they wondered to whom they might send it away from them (v. 20). They called upon the inhabitants of Kirjath-jearim [a Levite city] to "come ye down, and fetch [the ark] up to you" (v. 21). This they did, taking it to "the house of Abinadab in the hill, and sanctified Eleazar his son to keep the ark of the Lord" (v. 1). There it remained for 20 years while Israel lamented in general unrighteousness.

- **1 Samuel 14:18 While the ark remains in Kirjath-jearim, it is not used by Saul's administration.** Its only mention during Saul's reign comes when Saul called for the ark and then chose not to utilize it in an anticipated battle.

- **1 Chronicles 13:3 Saul apparently has little or no esteem for the ark.** We know this because David later said: "Let us bring again the ark of our God to us: for we enquired not at it in the days of Saul."

- **1 Chronicles 16:39–40 During its 20 years at Kirjath-jearim, the ark is separated from the tabernacle, which remains at Gibeon.** Sacrifices continued on the great altar at the tabernacle

(vv. 39–40), along with the keeping of the "law of the Lord" there (v. 40). But the ark of the covenant was not in the holy of holies. It was by itself at Kirjath-jearim.

● **2 Samuel 6 The ark is not heard of again until David moves it from Kirjath-jearim to his city, Zion.** Note that there is no mention of the tabernacle being moved there at this time. The ark's presence was a symbol of God's presence in David's city [Jerusalem] after he made it the capitol of his kingdom. It did not return to the holy of holies until David's son Solomon built his temple there, which replaced the tabernacle.

SAMUEL'S RIGHTEOUS LEADERSHIP

● **1 Samuel 7 The Lord protects Israel under a righteous prophet.** Samuel exhorted Israel to forsake their pagan worship of Ashtaroth and Baalim and to serve only the Lord (v. 3). Recognizing Samuel as a prophet and seer, they responded to his teachings and agreed to put away their idols (v. 4). He gathered them together at Mizpeh, and there instructed them to fast and seek the Lord while he prayed for them (v. 5). This they did, and Samuel "judged" (delivered) them there at Mizpeh (v. 6).

Samuel obtains the Lord's help

Hearing that the Israelites were gathered together at Mizpeh, the Philistines conspired to attack and destroy them there, causing great fear among the Israelites (v. 7). They asked Samuel to petition the Lord to protect them, and he offered sacrifice in their behalf (v. 9). As he was doing so, the Philistines approached, ready to attack, but the Lord "thundered with a great thunder on that day upon the Philistines, and discomfited them; and they were smitten before Israel" who pursued them all the way back to Beth-car (vv. 10–11).

During the period of the judges, Israel never could re-main righteous for any lengthy period of time. But under Samuel they prospered, "and the hand of the Lord was against the Philistines all the days of Samuel" (v. 13). They reclaimed all the cities that the Philistines had taken from them, and "there was peace between Israel and the Amorites" (v. 14). Samuel led them "all the days of his life" (v. 15), making a circuit each year from Beth-el to Gilgal to Mizpeh, "judg[ing] Israel in all those places" (v. 16). Then he would return to his home in Ramah, where he built an altar and judged Israel as their prophet and seer (v. 17).

KING SAUL

"Make Us a King ... Like All the Nations"

● **1 Samuel 8:1–5 The children of Israel reject Samuel's unrighteous sons as judges and demand a king.** As Samuel grew older, "he made his sons judges over Israel" (v. 1). These two sons, named Joel and Abiah, became judges in Beer-sheba (v. 2). But they were not righteous judges. They "walked not in his ways, but turned aside after lucre, and took bribes, and perverted judgment" (v. 3). We may recall that Eli's sons were also wicked, but he made no attempt to correct them. In Samuel's case we have a righteous father whose sons simply chose to reject the God for whom their father served. The elders of Israel came to Samuel and said, "Behold, thou art old, and thy sons walk not in thy ways: now make us a king to judge us like all the nations" (v. 5).

● **1 Samuel 8:6–18 Samuel warns Israel about kings.** The idea of having a king over Israel displeased Samuel, and he took the matter to the Lord in prayer (v. 6). The Lord instructed him to "Hearken unto the voice of the people in all that they say unto thee: for they have not rejected thee, but they have rejected me, that I should not reign over them" (v. 7). This had been the tendency of Israel ever since they left Egypt—to forsake the Lord and serve other gods (v. 8). The Lord said to Samuel, "hearken unto their voice: howbeit yet protest solemnly unto them, and shew them the manner of the king that shall reign over them" (v. 9). Samuel did so, listing the evils that kings would do to them:

— "He will take your sons, and appoint them for himself, for his chariots, and to be his horsemen; and some shall run before his chariots" (v. 11).

— "He will appoint him captains over thousands, and captains over fifties; and will set them to ear his ground, and to reap his harvest, and to make his instruments of war, and instruments of his chariots" (v. 12).

— "He will take your daughters to be confectionaries, and to be cooks, and to be bakers" (v. 13).

— "He will take your fields, and your vineyards, and your oliveyards, even the best of them, and give them to his servants" (v. 14).

— "He will take the tenth of your seed, and of your vineyards, and give to his officers, and to his servants" (v. 15).

— "He will take your menservants, and your maidservants, and your goodliest young men, and your asses, and put them to his work" (v. 16).

— "He will take the tenth of your sheep: and ye shall be his servants" (v. 17).

— "Ye shall cry out in that day because of your king which ye shall have chosen you; and the Lord will not hear you in that day" (v. 18).

President Spencer W. Kimball said:

> "Give us a king" cried the children of Israel when they had seen the glory of the surrounding kingdoms. From Moses and Joshua through about three centuries they had been led by the less colorful judges. There was an absence of glory and pageantry, and then the people led by their elders demanded, "Now make us a king to judge us like all the nations" (1 Samuel 8:5). …
>
> And Samuel called the people together and explained to them that the people of the Lord should be different with higher standards. "We want to be like other peoples" they demanded. "We do not want to be different" … (1 Samuel 8:11–18)
>
> Not so different are we today! We want the glamor and frothiness of the world, not always realizing the penalties of our folly. … We cannot stand to be different! … The Lord says he will have a peculiar people but we do not wish to be peculiar. …
>
> When, oh when, will our Latter-day Saints stand firm on their own feet, establish their own standards, follow proper patterns and live their own glorious lives in accordance with Gospel inspired patterns, aping no one who has not a better program! Certainly good times and happy lives and clean fun are not dependent upon the glamorous, the pompous, the extremes.[5]

● **1 Samuel 8:19–22 Nevertheless, the Israelites still demand a king, and the Lord instructs Samuel to appoint one for them.** The Israelites rejected all the warnings Samuel gave them, saying, "Nay; but we will have a king over us; That we also may be like all the nations; and that our king may judge us, and go out before us, and fight our battles" (vv. 19–20). After reporting back to the Lord on their reaction, Samuel was instructed to "Hearken unto their voice, and make them a king" (vv. 21–22).

Notes

1. Sweden Area Conference, Aug. 1974, 47–48.
2. *Gospel Doctrine*, 5th ed. [1939], 286.
3. *Gospel Standards*, comp. G. Homer Durham [1941], 68.
4. "Did captured ark afflict Philistines with E.D.?" *Biblical Archaeology Review*, 34:03, May/June 2008.
5. *Church News*, 15 Oct. 1960, 14.

CHAPTER 22

King Saul and the Rise of David

(1 Samuel 9–17)

☙ℭ

SAUL IS ANOINTED KING

● **1 Samuel 9:3–6 Saul seeks help from the prophet Samuel.** He had lost his father's asses and was seeking for them (v. 3). Though he sought them diligently over a wide area, he could not find them anywhere (v. 4). They were about to return home when he realized that they were in the city where "a man of God … an honourable man" dwelled, who was also a prophet. "All that he saith cometh surely to pass," Saul said. "Now let us go thither; peradventure he can shew us our way that we should go" (vv. 5–6).

● **1 Samuel 9:9–14 Samuel calls Saul a "seer."** This might suggest that he had access to the Urim and Thummim as the presiding prophet in Israel. Saul and his servant went into the city where Samuel, "the man of God" resided to ask him to help them find their lost asses (vv. 9–10). They found young women there who had come to draw water, and asked, "Is the seer here?" (v. 11). And they answered, "He is; behold, he is before you: make haste now, for he came to day to the city; … Now therefore get you up; for about this time ye shall find him" (vv. 12–13). And indeed, when they went into the city "Samuel came out … to go up to the high place" (v. 14).

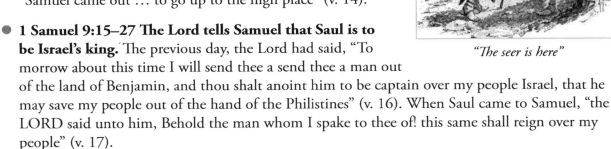

"The seer is here"

● **1 Samuel 9:15–27 The Lord tells Samuel that Saul is to be Israel's king.** The previous day, the Lord had said, "To morrow about this time I will send thee a send thee a man out of the land of Benjamin, and thou shalt anoint him to be captain over my people Israel, that he may save my people out of the hand of the Philistines" (v. 16). When Saul came to Samuel, "the LORD said unto him, Behold the man whom I spake to thee of! this same shall reign over my people" (v. 17).

Not knowing that Samuel was the prophet he was seeking, Saul asked, "Tell me, I pray thee, where the seer's house is" (v. 18). "And Samuel answered Saul, and said, I am the seer … ye shall eat with me to day" (v. 19). He told Saul not to worry about his lost asses because "they are found" (v. 20).

More importantly, Samuel asked Saul, "And on whom is all the desire of Israel? Is it not on thee, and on all thy father's house?" (v. 20). Saul could not believe it. He said, "Am not I a Benjamite, of the smallest of the tribes of Israel? and my family the least of all the families of the tribe of Benjamin? wherefore then speakest thou so to me?" (v. 21). Samuel sat him down to eat and ordered the best portion of the meat to be laid before him (vv. 22–24). He commanded him to eat it because it had been specially prepared for him beforehand as an honored guest (v. 24). They communed awhile before Samuel sent him away, then Samuel asked Saul's servant go on alone so he could "shew [Saul] the word of God" (vv. 25–27).

- **1 Samuel 9:2 Saul was "a choice young man, … and there was not among the children of Israel a goodlier person than he."** His good qualities included:

  — **1 Samuel 9:3–4**   He was diligent in his search for his father's donkeys.

  — **1 Samuel 9:5–10**   He was willing to listen to and follow the wise counsel of his father's servant.

  — **1 Samuel 9:18–25**   He trusted and communed with the prophet Samuel.

  — **1 Samuel 9:20–21**   He was humble.

  — **1 Samuel 10:6–10**   He was spiritually reborn, and he prophesied.

  — **1 Samuel 11:11–13**   He forgave his critics.

  — **1 Samuel 11:13**   He recognized the help of the Lord in Israel's victory over the Ammonites.

- **1 Samuel 10:1 Samuel anoints Saul to be Israel's "captain."** While they were alone, "Samuel took a vial of oil, and poured it upon his head, and kissed him, and said, "the Lord hath anointed thee to be captain over his inheritance" (v. 1). The title "captain" was chosen as a reminder that the Lord was still Israel's king.

"Anointing with oil was a symbol of endowment with the Spirit of God; as the oil itself, by virtue of the strength which it gives to the vital spirits, was a symbol of the Spirit of God … and spiritual power [Leviticus 8:12]. Hitherto there had been no other anointing among the people of God than that of the priests and [the] sanctuary … When Saul, therefore, was consecrated as king by anointing, the monarchy was inaugurated as a divine institution…and the king was set apartfrom the rest of the nation as 'anointed of the Lord.'"[1].

Samuel anoints Saul Israel's first king

● **1 Samuel 10:21–23 On the day of his presentation to the people, Saul hid himself and could not be found.** Samuel called the tribe of Benjamin to come forward "by their families," then selected out the family of Matri (v. 21). But when Saul the son of Kish was called forward, "when they sought him, he could not be found" (v. 21). The Lord revealed to Samuel that Saul "hath hid himself among the stuff" (v. 22). They ran and "fetched him thence," to present him to the people. And "when he stood among the people, he was higher than any of the people from his shoulders and upward" (v. 23).

Saul is presented to the people

● **1 Samuel 11 Saul rescues Israel from the attacking Ammonites and is confirmed again as king.** The arrogant Ammonites had only agreed to make peace if they could "thrust out all your right eyes, and lay it for a reproach upon all Israel" (v. 2), and gave them only seven days to decide (v. 3). Hearing of this danger, Saul came out of the fields and led Israel in a devastating attack on the Ammonites, driving them back into their own country (vv. 4–11). This made the people very sure they wanted Saul as their king, and his kingship was renewed again in a solemn ceremony at Gilgal (vv. 12–15).

● **1 Samuel 12 Samuel's testimony of how the Lord had blessed Israel.** The Israelites were in a humble frame of mind, having been delivered from the attacking Ammonites. In a sermon very similar to the one King Benjamin delivered to the Nephites, Samuel reminded them that he had never taken anything from them, nor defrauded them, nor oppressed them, nor took bribes from them (vv. 2–3). He then took the occasion to remind them of all the times when Israel forgot the Lord and experienced great calamity. He urged them to serve the Lord lest an even greater calamity overtake them (vv. 4–21). He told them that "it hath pleased the Lord to make you his people" (v. 22), and that as the Lord's servant he would "pray for you … [and] teach you the good and the right way" (v. 23).

Saul's Weaknesses Begin to Show

● **1 Samuel 13:1–8 Two years after Saul was anointed king, the Philistines gathered a mighty army to attack Israel.** Saul and his son Jonathan had had some success against the Philistines, but this army was an overpowering threat, consisting of 30,000 chariots and 6,000 horsemen (v. 5). Saul's men were so afraid that many of them hid and scattered (v. 6). Saul gathered his people at Gilgal and asked Samuel to come there and offer sacrifices to the Lord in behalf of the people. But when Samuel did not arrive in 7 days as expected, some of the Israelites began to scatter in fear (v. 8).

● **1 Samuel 13:9 When Samuel does not arrive on time, Saul offers the sacrifices himself.** This he was not authorized to do because he did not have the proper priesthood authority to sacrifice on behalf of all Israel; only the high priest could do so. This act demonstrated both his impatience and his arrogance—thinking that, because he was king, he could do whatever he wanted to do.

- **1 Samuel 13:10–14 Samuel rebuked Saul for his presumptuous act.** Saul had no sooner made the sacrificial offering than Samuel arrived "and Saul went out to meet him, that he might salute him" (v. 10). Knowing prophetically that he had erred, Samuel asked him, "What hast thou done? And Saul said, Because I saw that the people were scattered from me, and that thou camest not within the days appointed, and that the Philistines gathered themselves together at Michmash; Therefore said I, The Philistines will come down now upon me to Gilgal, and I have not made supplication unto the LORD: I forced myself therefore, and offered a burnt offering" (vv. 11–12).

  Samuel chastised him for doing "foolishly" and not keeping the Lord's commandments (v. 13). Then, saying he was not "a man after [the Lord's] own heart," he declared that whereas the Lord might have conferred the kingdom upon him and his posterity forever, "now thy kingdom shall not continue" (v. 14). This meant that his kingship would not pass to his son Jonathan but would end with his death.

- **1 Samuel 13:19–21 The Israelites do not know how to work with iron.** To say that there was "no smith" in Israel means that the iron age had not yet arrived in Israel. The Philistines guarded the secret carefully to maintain superiority in weapons over the softer brass weapons of the Israelites. And even these brass weapons—the share, coulter, axe, mattock, and goad—had to be taken to the Philistines for sharpening.

- **1 Samuel 14:15 The "spoilers" among the Philistines are assigned to go out and destroy crops, homes, barns, cattle, and so forth.** Their prime purpose was not to take human life, but to make living difficult for the civilian population, thus subduing them with fear—the classic motivation of a terrorist.

Saul Is Rejected by the Lord as Israel's King

- **1 Samuel 14:43–45 Saul arrogantly decrees the death of his own son.** When he was rebuked by Samuel, he sought to justify himself. Nor did he repent later. He saw himself, rather than God, as the source of Israel's law. The extent of this arrogance is illustrated by his reaction when his son accidentally disobeyed a decree he had made to all Israel. Saul commanded the people to fast until evening for the Lord's help in their battle with the Philistines (v. 24). His son Jonathan, who was unaware of the decree, ate a little bit of honey (v. 43). Saul then declared that his son must die for his disobedience (v. 44). This, despite the military victories Jonathan had won for Israel over the Philistines. The people utterly refused to let it happen, saying, "God forbid: as the Lord liveth, there shall not one hair of his head fall to the ground; for he hath wrought with God this day. So the people rescued Jonathan, that he died not" (v. 45).

- **1 Samuel 15:1–11 Saul disobeys the Lord's commandments regarding the Amalekites.** This incident revealed how completely unrepentant Saul was for his earlier disobedience in offering sacrifice. Through Samuel, the Lord had commanded Saul to utterly destroy the Amalekites and to take no spoils for themselves (vv. 1–3). The Amalekites are the ones who cruelly attacked the most helpless among the Israelites when they first came out of Egypt. Saul gathered together an army of 200,000 footmen—10,000 of them from Judah—and prepared to attack the Amalekites. After allowing the Kenites to depart from among them, Saul's army "utterly destroyed all the people with the edge of the sword" (v. 8).

Yet, contrary to the Lord's instructions, he allowed Agag, king of the Amalekites, to live and took him captive. He also kept spoils—"the best of the sheep, and of the oxen, and of the fatlings, and the lambs, and all that was good, and would not utterly destroy them: but every thing that was vile and refuse, that they destroyed utterly" (v. 9). For this act of disobedience the Lord said, "It repenteth me that I have set up Saul to be king: for he is turned back from following me, and hath not performed my command- ments. And it grieved Samuel; and he cried unto the LORD all night" (vv. 10–11).

● **1 Samuel 15:13–24 "Obedience is better than sacrifice."**
When Samuel came to Saul after his victory of the Amalekites, Saul greeted him by saying, "Blessed be thou of the Lord: I have performed the commandment of the Lord" (v. 13). Samuel's response was cutting and direct: "What meaneth then this bleating of the sheep in mine ears, and the lowing of the oxen which I hear?" (v. 14). Samuel then weakly blamed the people, saying, "the people spared the best of the sheep and of the oxen, to sacrifice unto the Lord thy God; and the rest we have utterly destroyed" (v. 15).

Samuel confronts Saul's disobedience

This was the last straw for Saul. Samuel reminded him that "when thou wast little in thine own sight, wast thou not made the head of the tribes of Israel, and the Lord anointed thee king over Israel?" (v. 17). But now, being mighty in his own estimation, Saul had kept the spoils of the battle and "didst evil in the sight of the Lord" (v. 19). Saul arrogantly argued with the prophet, saying, "I have obeyed the voice of the Lord, and have gone the way which the Lord sent me, and have brought Agag the king of Amalek, and have utterly destroyed the Amalekites" (v. 20). It was the people, he said, who disobeyed, not him, and they had done so in order to sacrifice unto the Lord (v. 21).

Samuel's response was again direct and has become timeless: "Hath the LORD as great delight in burnt offerings and sacrifices, as in obeying the voice of the Lord? Behold, to obey is better than sacrifice, and to hearken than the fat of rams" (v. 22). From this we learn two very important principles concerning obedience:

— v. 22   Obedience is the first law of heaven, and is greater than sacrifice

— v. 23   "Stubbornness is as … idolatry." Anything we put before the Lord becomes our substitute "god."

● **1 Samuel 15:23–28 Saul repents, but it is too little and too late.** Saul had become puffed up with pride and was disobedient, rebellious, and stubborn. Honor from people was more important to him than honor from God. The Lord declared that "because thou hast rejected the word of the LORD, he hath also rejected thee from being king" (v. 23).

Only then, realizing he would lose his honored position among the people, did Saul attempt to repent. He said to Samuel, "I have sinned: for I have transgressed the commandment of the

Lord, and thy words: because I feared the people, and obeyed their voice. Now therefore, I pray thee, pardon my sin, and turn again with me, that I may worship the Lord" (vv. 24–25). This request was rejected by Samuel, and he turned to go away (v. 26). Saul reached out and "laid hold upon the skirt of his mantle, and it rent" (v. 27). Using the symbolism of his rent mantle, Samuel proclaimed, "The Lord hath rent the king- dom of Israel from thee this day, and hath given it to a neighbour of thine, that is better than thou" (v. 28).

● **1 Samuel 15:32–35 Samuel executes Agag.** Saul had failed to keep the Lord's commands with exactness regarding the Amalekites. But Samuel would not fail to do so. He commanded, "Bring ye hither to me Agag the king of the Amalekites" (v. 32). Sensing he was in deep trouble, Agag "came unto him delicately" and plead for his life by saying, "Surely the bitterness of death is past" (v. 32). But Samuel was not fooled by this blood- thirsty man's sudden conversion to charity.

GUSTAVE DORÉ, 1865

Samuel confronts and executes Agag

Samuel said to Agag, "As thy sword hath made women childless, so shall thy mother be childless among women. And Samuel hewed Agag in pieces before the Lord in Gilgal" (v. 33).

This was the final encounter between Samuel and Saul. Samuel traveled to Ramah, and Saul returned to his house in Gibeah. Saul would continue to reign, suffering from a grief-stricken conscience and bouts of anger and depression.

Whereas Saul might have been a mighty hero in Israel and established a righteous dynasty that would have lasted for many generations, he died without a successor. But not before he committed multiple grievous acts of violence against David, his anointed successor.

THE RISE OF DAVID

David Is Anointed to Become King

● **1 Samuel 16:1–13 David is anointed while Saul is still upon the throne.** The failure of Saul, Israel's first king, caused Samuel great distress. The Lord said to him, "How long wilt thou mourn for Saul, seeing I have rejected him from reigning over Israel? fill thine horn with oil, and go, I will send thee to Jesse the Beth-lehemite: for I have provided me a king among his sons" (v. 1). Samuel was afraid. "How can I go?" he said, "if Saul hear it, he will kill me" (v. 2). Nevertheless, the Lord commanded him to take a heifer with him and invite Jesse to join him. While doing so, the Lord promised to show him who the next king should be (v. 3).

Jesee lived in Bethlehem. And the coming of Samuel to this little town made the elders nervous. "Comest thou peaceably?" they asked Samuel (v. 4). And he answered them, "Peaceably: I am come to sacrifice unto the Lord: sanctify yourselves, and come with me to the sacrifice" (v. 5). In particular, he "sanctified Jesse and his sons, and called them to the sacrifice" as the Lord had instructed him (v. 5).

One by one, the sons of Jesse passed before him as he sought the Lord's confirmation of His choice. When Eliab passed by first, Samuel said to himself "Surely the Lord's anointed is before [me]" (v. 6). But the Lord gave him an important principle: "Look not on his countenance, or on the height of his stature … for the Lord seeth not as man seeth; for man looketh on the outward appearance, but the Lord looketh on the heart" (v. 7).

David—a simple shepherd boy

Elder Marvin J. Ashton said: "We … tend to evaluate others on the basis of physical, outward appearance: their 'good looks,' their social status, their family pedigrees, their degrees, or their economic situations. The Lord, however, has a different standard by which he measures a person. … He does not take a tape measure around the person's head to determine his mental capacity, nor his chest to determine his manliness, but He measures the heart as an indicator of the person's capacity and potential to bless others"[2].

The parade of potential kings continued as Abinadab and then Shammah passed by, each without the Lord's confirmation to Samuel (vv. 8–9). Jesse caused all the remaining five of his sons who were present to pass before the prophet, but none of them were chosen either (v. 10).

Elder N. Eldon Tanner said:

> By referring to Samuel's experience while choosing a king, we may get a better understanding of the fact that man is not qualified to judge. The Lord had rejected Saul as king of Israel and instructed the prophet Samuel to choose a new king. He told him to go to the house of Jesse, who had eight sons, and that while there the anointed one would pass before him and Samuel would know who was to be chosen.

> When the first son, Eliab, came before him, Samuel thought he was the chosen one, but the Lord refused him and then gave the prophet Samuel the key as to how to judge: 'Look not on his countenance, or on the height of his stature; because I have refused him: for the Lord seeth not as man seeth; for man looketh on the outward appearance, but the Lord looketh on the heart.' (1 Sam. 16:7). Each of the seven sons then passed before Samuel and was rejected. Then David, the youngest, was sent for and was approved by the Lord. The reason, therefore, that we cannot judge is obvious. We cannot see what is in the heart. We do not know motives, although we impute motives to every action we see. They may be pure while we think they are improper.

It is not possible to judge another fairly unless you know his desires, his faith, and his goals ... At best, man can judge only what he sees; he cannot judge the heart or the intention, or begin to judge the potential of his neighbor."[3]

There was nothing particularly wrong with these sons of Jesse. They were simply not the one the Lord had chosen to be king. Samuel asked Jesse, "Are here all thy children? And he said, There remaineth yet the youngest, and, behold, he keepeth the sheep. And Samuel said unto Jesse, Send and fetch him: for we will not sit down till he come hither" (v. 11), and "he sent, and brought him in" (v. 12). David was "ruddy, and ... of a beautiful countenance, and goodly to look to" (v. 12). But more importantly, he was the Lord's chosen servant. The Lord said to Samuel, "Arise, anoint him: for this is he. Then Samuel took the horn of oil, and anointed him in the midst of his brethren: and the Spirit of the Lord came upon David from that day forward" (vv. 12–13).

David is anointed by the prophet Samuel

David Serves King Saul

● **1 Samuel 16:14–23 Because Saul had been disobedient, the Spirit of the Lord departed from him.** Increasingly, having been rejected of the Lord, Saul failed to find peace with himself. He became a miserable, guilt-ridden man, and he sought a musician to soothe his depression. Once again, the anonymous writer of this book of the Bible imputes Saul's depression to God. He quotes Saul's servants as saying, "Behold now, an evil spirit from God troubleth thee" (v. 15). There is no such thing as "an evil spirit from God." Satan was working upon Saul, making him resentful, angry, and feeling deprived of what was rightfully his—the same attitudes that Satan has toward God and Christ. The JST corrects this passage to say, "An evil spirit which was not of the Lord troubled him" (JST 1 Samuel 16:14).

Saul's servants suggested that they be allowed to "seek out a man, who is a cunning player on an harp: and it shall come to pass, when the evil spirit from God is upon thee, that he shall play with his hand, and thou shalt be well" (v. 16). Saul agreed (v. 17). And immediately, one of Saul's servants recalled, "I have seen a son of Jesse the Beth- lehemite, that is cunning in playing, and a mighty valiant man, and a man of war, and prudent in matters, and a comely person, and the Lord is with him" (v. 18). It sounded like an excellent choice. So Saul sent a message to Jesse, saying, "Send me David thy

David soothed Saul with his music

son, which is with the sheep" (v. 19). Saul had no idea that this was the man who had already been anointed to be his replacement on the throne.

Jesse sent his son to Saul with gifts—bread, and a bottle of wine, and a kid (v. 20). And when David stood before Saul, "he loved him greatly; and he became his armourbearer" (v. 21). Saul wrote to Jesee asking, "Let David, I pray thee, stand before me; for he hath found favour in my sight" (v. 22). The request was granted. "And it came to pass, when the evil spirit from God was upon Saul, that David took an harp, and played with his hand: so Saul was refreshed, and was well, and the evil spirit departed from him" (v. 23). David's musical talents were extensive. He is the author of most of the Psalms found in our Bible today.

DAVID SLAYS GOLIATH

● **1 Samuel 17:1–3 Saul's army battles the Philistines in the valley of Elah.** Elah was one of the numerous valleys or wadis descending from the hill country of Judah toward the Mediterranean Sea. This particular battle occurred near Azekah almost directly west and a little south of Jerusalem. The two armies stood on opposite sides of the valley—"the Philistines stood on a mountain on the one side, and Israel stood on a mountain on the other side: and there was a valley between them" (v. 3).

● **1 Samuel 17:4 The Philistines send forth a "champion" to do battle.** Although it seems peculiar to us today, in ancient times it was not unusual for opposing armies, which were generally quite small, to select one representative from each side to fight a personal contest. The outcome of that contest determined the winner of the battle.

● **1 Samuel 17:4–11 The Philistines choose Goliath.** He came from Gath, an area well known in earlier days for its "Anakims"—large and violent men (Joshua 11:22). He was "six cubits and a span" tall—9 feet 9 inches (v. 4). He wore a helmet of brass and a coat [armor] of mail [brass mesh] that weighed five thousand shekels—150 pounds (v. 5). He also had "greaves of brass upon his legs, and a target [shield] of brass [that he held] between his shoulders" (v. 6). Just the staff of his spear was "like a weaver's beam" and the iron spearhead weighed "six hundred shekels"—12–26 pounds (v. 7).

As Goliah stepped forth onto the battle field, another soldier "bearing a shield went before him" (v. 7). And Goliath "stood and cried unto the armies of Israel, and said unto them, Why are ye come out to set your battle in array? am not I a Philistine, and ye servants to Saul? choose you a man for you, and let him come down to me" (v. 8). In keeping with the "battle of champions" tradition, he proposed, "If he be able to fight with me, and to kill me, then will we be your servants: but if I prevail against him, and kill him, then shall ye be our servants, and serve us" (v. 9). He defied the armies of Israel to send someone out to fight him, and the Israelites "were dismayed, and greatly afraid" (vv. 10–11). This challenge continued daily for forty days (v. 16).

● **1 Samuel 17:13–27 David is not afraid of Goliath.** David's three oldest brothers were in the army that faced the Philistines at Elah (v. 13). And because Saul was also with the army David had returned to his sheep herding duties for awhile. As the days dragged on, his father sent

David with some food for his brothers and their captain (vv. 17–18). David did so, arriving in time to hear Goliath's latest challenge (vv. 19–23). The army of Saul was "sore afraid" of him and his defiant taunts against Israel (vv. 24–25). They said that "the man who killeth him, the king will enrich him with great riches, and will give him his daughter, and make his father's house free in Israel" (vv. 25, 27). David's response was bold: "who is this uncircumcised Philistine, that he should defy the armies of the living God?" (v. 26).

- **1 Samuel 17:31–37 David, with great faith and courage, volunteers to fight Goliath.** Saul's soldiers reported David's words to Saul, who then sent for him (v. 31). David was unafraid. He said to Saul, "Let no man's heart fail because of him; thy servant will go and fight with this Philistine" (v. 32). Saul did not believe he could do it. "Thou art not able to go against this Philistine to fight with him," he said to David, "for thou art but a youth, and he a man of war from his youth" (v. 33). David insisted he was able, saying that while he was tending his father's sheep, "there came a lion, and a bear, and took a lamb out of the flock: And I went out after him, and smote him, and delivered it out of his mouth: and when he arose against me, I caught him by his beard, and smote him, and slew him" (vv. 34–35). He then boldly proclaimed, "this uncircumcised Philistine shall be as one of them, seeing he hath defied the armies of the living God" (v. 36). "The Lord that delivered me out of the paw of the lion, and out of the paw of the bear, he will deliver me out of the hand of this Philistine. And Saul said unto David, Go, and the Lord be with thee" (v. 37).

- **1 Samuel 17:38–40 David rejects armor and takes instead a sling and some stones.** For his protection, Saul attempted to cover David with his own armor—a helmet of brass and a coat of mail (v. 38). But David chose not to use them, saying, "I cannot go with these; for I have not proved them. And David put them off him" (v. 39). Instead, "he took his staff in his hand, and chose him five smooth stones out of the brook, and put them in a shepherd's bag which he had … and his sling was in his hand: and he drew near to the Philistine" (v. 40).

David chooses 5 smooth stones

- **1 Samuel 17:41–44 Goliath mocks David.** As David went forth to meet Goliath, the giant from Gath drew near to him (v. 41). And when he saw this youth without armor— "ruddy and of a fair countenance"— "he disdained him" (v. 42). "Am I a dog, that thou comest to me with staves?" he said to David, and he "cursed David by his gods" [as a Philistine he would have worshiped Dagon] (v. 43). He challenged David, "Come to me, and I will give thy flesh unto the fowls of the air, and to the beasts of the field" (v. 44).

- **1 Samuel 17:45–47 David's absolute trust in the Lord.** David was not intimidated. "Thou comest to me with a sword, and with a spear, and with a shield," he said, "but I come to thee in the name of the Lord of hosts, the God of the armies of Israel, whom thou hast defied. This day will the Lord deliver thee into mine hand; and I will smite thee, and take thine head from thee;

and I will give the carcases of the host of the Philistines this day unto the fowls of the air, and to the wild beasts of the earth; that all the earth may know that there is a God in Israel" (vv. 45–46). David had absolute faith that God would give him victory over Goliath, no matter what his size. "The Lord saveth not with sword and spear," said David, "for the battle is the Lord's, and he will give you into our hands" (v. 47).

● **1 Samuel 17:48–54 David slays and beheads Goliath.** Goliath moved forward toward David to kill him. But David did not flinch. Rather than running away, "David hasted, and ran toward the army to meet the Philistine" (v. 48). As he did so, he "put his hand in his bag, and took thence a stone, and slang it, and smote the Philistine in his fore- ead" (v. 49). This was perhaps one of the few parts of his body that were exposed, and David's shot had to be precise. The stone struck him with such force that it "sunk into his forehead; and he fell upon his face to the earth" (v. 49).

David slays and beheads Goliath

There is much to learn from this encounter. David "prevailed over the Philistine with a sling and with a stone" and "slew him" with "no sword in [his] hand" (v. 50). He knew that his safety was in the hands of the Lord, and he trusted absolutely that he would be victorious. But we should also remember that it took skill to do what he did. David had prepared himself for this day by becoming expert with a sling. He had confidence in his own abilities, while relying on the Lord to protect him. It takes both personal effort and faith to achieve the Lord's purposes.

Having brought down this vile blasphemer, "David ran, and stood upon the Philistine, and took his sword, and drew it out of the sheath thereof, and slew him, and cut off his head therewith. And when the Philistines saw their champion was dead, they fled" (v. 51). The army of Israel pursued them all the way to their cities of Ekron and Gath (v. 52). They also took spoils of everything their tents contained (v. 53). For his trophies, David took Goliath's armor and put it in his tent, and he took the head of Goliath to Jerusalem (v. 54).

● **1 Samuel 17:52–58 Saul takes note of David's heroics.** He asked Abner, "the captain of the host, … whose son is this youth?" (v. 55). Abner did not know, but at the king's command he brought David before King Saul "with the head of the Philistine in his hand" (vv. 56–57). He asked him, "Whose son art thou, thou young man? And David answered, I am the son of thy servant Jesse the Beth-lehemite" (v. 58). It seems odd that Saul did not recognize him as the youth who had soothed him with his music, but perhaps in this setting, and with Goliath's head in his hand, he did not look the same. But there was no forgetting him now. David had become a hero to all of Israel.

Notes

1.   Keil and Delitzsch, *Commentary on the Old Testament*, 10 vols. [1996], 2:2:95

2.   In Conference Report, Oct. 1988, 17; or *Ensign*, Nov. 1988, 15.

3.   "Judge Not That Ye Be Not Judged," *Ensign*, July 1972, 35.

CHAPTER 23

King Saul's Hatred and Jonathan's Friendship for David

(1 Samuel 18–31; 2 Samuel 1)

୫୬୧୫

A STUDY IN CONTRASTS

David and Jonathan's Friendship

● **1 Samuel 18:1, 3–4 Jonathan loves David "as his own soul."** David quickly became a hero after he killed Goliath. King Saul and the entire kingdom honored him. However, none was as true to David as was Jonathan, Saul's son. The Bible tells us that "the soul of Jonathan was knit with the soul of David, and Jonathan loved him as his own soul" (v. 1). Jonathan made a covenant of friendship with David (v. 3). A covenant was absolute in their society; one would rather die than violate a covenant made with another person.

Jonathan & David's covenant friendship

As Saul's son, Jonathan was next in line to be king. However, the prophet Samuel had anointed David to become the next king, and Jonathan had Jonathan & David's covenant friendship absolutely no jealousy of him. Jonathan "strippedhimself of the robe that was upon him, and gave it to David, and his garments, even to his sword, and to his bow, and to his girdle" (v. 4).

Notice that in this case we see a wonderfully righteous son (Jonathan) coming from a terribly wicked father (Saul)—just the opposite of what happened in the case of Samuel's sons. The righteousness or wickedness of a child is not always the result of good or poor parenting. Children have agency, and they sometimes choose the opposite of what their parents have chosen.

Saul's Growing Hatred

- **1 Samuel 18:2, 5 Saul takes David into his home and sets him over his armies."** Rather than let him return to his father's house, Saul took him into his own house and made him commander of all his armies (vv. 2, 5). David showed absolute loyalty to King Saul and "behaved himself wisely" wherever Saul sent him (v. 5).

- **1 Samuel 18:6–7 David becomes a national hero.** "He was accepted in the sight of all the people, and also in the sight of Saul's servants" (v. 5). When Saul and David returned triumphant from the battle with the Philistines, "the women came out of all cities of Israel, singing and dancing, to meet king Saul, with tabrets, with joy, and with instruments of musick" (v. 6). But their praise was greater for David than it was for their king. The words to their songs included these words: "Saul hath slain his thousands, and David his ten thousands" (v. 7).

- **1 Samuel 18:8–11 Saul becomes jealous of David, and seeks to kill him.** These words enraged Saul. "They have ascribed unto David ten thousands," he complained, "and to me they have ascribed but thousands" (v. 8). With this kind of loyalty from the people, Saul feared "what can he have more but the kingdom?" (v. 8). Filled with suspicion and paranoia, "Saul eyed David from that day and forward" (v. 9).

GUSTAVE DORÉ, 1865

Saul tries to kill David with his javelin

The following day "the evil spirit from God" came upon Saul. (Notice here again the scribe's insertion of a false doctrine; evil spirits do <u>not</u> come from God.) Under the influence of this spirit, Saul "prophesied in the midst of the house" while "David played [his harp] with his hand, as at other times" (v. 10). With David in this defenseless position, Saul said to himself "I will smite David even to the wall" with the javelin that he had in his hand (vv. 10–11). He threw the javelin at David twice, but David avoided it and fled from his presence (v. 11).

President Ezra Taft Benson said:

> Saul became an enemy to David through pride. He was jealous because the crowds of Israelite women were singing that "Saul hath slain his thousands, and David his ten thousands" (1 Samuel 18:6–8).
>
> The proud stand more in fear of men's judgment than of God's judgment. ... "What will men think of me?" weighs heavier than "What will God think of me?" ... Fear of men's judgment manifests itself in competition for men's approval. The proud love "the praise of men more than the praise of God" (John 12:42–43) ... Would we not do well to have the pleasing of God as our motive rather than to try to elevate ourselves above our brother and outdo another?
>
> Some prideful people are not so concerned as to whether their wages meet their needs as they are that their wages are more than someone else's. Their reward is being a cut above the rest ... When pride has a hold on our hearts, we lose our independence of the world and deliver our freedoms to the

bondage of men's judgment. The world shouts louder than the whisperings of the Holy Ghost. The reasoning of men overrides the revelations of God, and the proud let go of the iron rod.[1]

● **1 Samuel 18:12–16 David behaves wisely and the Lord blesses him, and because of this, Saul fears him.** Saul knew that the Lord had withdrawn from him and was now with David (v. 12). Because of this, "Saul was afraid of David" and "removed him from him, and made him his captain over a thousand" (v. 13). In this capacity, David regularly "went out and came in before the people" as a national hero (v. 13). He could have become arrogant and relished his new-found celebrity, but instead "David behaved himself wisely in all his ways" (v. 14). This only made Saul fear him more, "but all Israel and Judah loved David" (vv. 15–16).

● **1 Samuel 18:17–19 Saul offers David his daughter Merab if he will fight the Philistines.** His real motive was a hope that David would be killed (v. 17). He offered David his daughter Merab if he would go and fight the Philistines (v. 17). David's humble response was, "Who am I? and what is my life, or my father's family in Israel, that I should be son in law to the king?" (v. 18). It never happened, because Merab was given instead to another (v. 19).

● **1 Samuel 18:20–25 Saul's daughter Michal loves David, providing Saul with another opportunity to get rid of him.** When Saul came to know that his daughter Michal loved David, "the thing pleased him" because he saw in it another opportunity to send him into dangerous battle (v. 20). She would be "a snare to him" to get him to go and battle the Philistines (v. 21). He therefore offered Michal to him and told his servants to encourage him to become "the king's son in law" (vv. 21–22). Again, David demurred, saying, "Seemeth it to you a light thing to be a king's son in law, seeing that I am a poor man, and lightly esteemed?" (v. 23). His family was not prominent in Israel and he had no dowry to offer the king.

When Saul heard this response, he told his servants to say, "The king desireth not any dowry, but an hundred foreskins of the Philistines, to be avenged of the king's enemies" (v. 25). The point was to "make David fall by the hand of the Philistines" (v. 25).

● **1 Samuel 18:27–30 David defeats the Philistines and earns Michal as his wife.** Contrary to what Saul had supposed, David was not killed by the Philistines, but instead "arose and went, he and his men, and slew of the Philistines two hundred men; and David brought their foreskins, and they gave them … to the king, that he might be the king's son in law. And Saul gave him Michal his daughter to wife" (v. 27).

In Saul's eyes, David had everything. The Lord was with him. His daughter Michal loved David. The Philistines retreated from him. David "behaved himself more wisely than all the servants of Saul" and "his name was much set by" among the people (v. 30). Thus, "Saul was yet the more afraid of David; and Saul became David's enemy continually" (v. 29).

Jonathan and Michal's Loyalty to David

● **1 Samuel 19:1–7 Jonathan intervenes between David and Saul.** Saul wanted David dead, and he made it known "to Jonathan his son, and to all his servants" (v. 1). Jonathan made this known to David, warning him to "take heed to thyself until the morning, and abide in a secret place, and hide thyself" (v. 2). Jonathan then went to his father and tried to reason with him. "Let not the king sin against his servant, against David; because he hath not sinned against thee, and because his works have been [toward thee] very good" (v. 4). He reminded his father that David had risked his life to slay Goliath, which resulted in a great victory for Israel over the Philistines and caused even Saul to rejoice (v. 5). "Wherefore then wilt thou sin against innocent blood," he asked, "to slay David without a cause?" (v. 5). Saul was convinced and swore an oath, "As the Lord liveth, he shall not be slain" (v. 6). At these words, Jonathan brought David to his father "and he was in his presence, as in times past" (v. 7).

- **1 Samuel 19:9–10 Despite his oath not to do so, Saul continues to seek David's life.** As he had done before (1 Samuel 18:8–11), while sitting in his home with his javelin in his hand, and with David playing music before him, Saul was filled with anger again. He "sought to smite David even to the wall with the javelin; but he slipped away out of Saul's presence" (v. 10).

- **1 Samuel 19:11–17 Michal, David's wife, helps him escape.** Saul was determined to kill David, and "sent messengers unto David's house, to watch him, and to slay him in the morning" (v. 11). Michal, Saul's daughter and David's wife, warned him that if he didn't escape that night he would be killed in the morning (v. 11). "So Michal let David down through a window: and he went, and fled, and escaped" (v. 12).

Michal helps David escape

Michal then "took an image, and laid it in the bed, and put a pillow of goats' hair for his bolster, and covered it with a cloth" (v. 13). When Saul's messengers arrived to kill him, she told them that David was sick (v. 14). Saul demanded that they bring David to him, bed and all, "that I may slay him" (v. 15). But of course, when they tried they found "an image in the bed, with a pillow of goats' hair for his bolster" (v. 16). Saul demanded to know why his daughter Michal had "deceived me so, and sent away mine enemy, that he is escaped?" and Michal answered with a claim that David had threatened to kill her unless she let him go" (v. 17).

- **1 Samuel 19:18 David flees to the prophet Samuel.** Seeking the Lord's protection, David fled to the prophet Samuel in Ramah. After telling him what had happened, both of them moved to Naioth for their safety.

- **1 Samuel 20:1–3, 12–17 Jonathan and David make a covenant of friendship.** David did not understand why Saul wanted to kill him. He fled to Jonathan in Ramah and asked, "What have I done? what is mine iniquity? and what is my sin before thy father, that he seeketh my life?" (v. 1). Jonathan assured him that "my father will do nothing either great or small, but that he will shew it me" (v. 2). David was not so sure. "Thy father certainly knoweth that I have found grace in thine eyes" and will say "Let not Jonathan know this" (v. 3). He felt that there was "but a step between me and death" (v. 3).

Jonathan pledged to David, "Whatsoever thy soul desireth, I will even do it for thee" (v. 4). With an oath, he promised that if his father was planning "to do thee evil, then I will shew it thee, and send thee away, that thou mayest go in peace" (v. 13). In return, Jonathan asked, "thou shalt not only while yet I live shew me the kindness of the Lord, that I die not: But also thou shalt not cut off thy kindness from my house for ever" even after "the Lord hath cut off the enemies of David every one from the face of the earth" (v. 15). Thus Jonathan made a covenant not just with David but with "the house of David" (v., 16). This is a covenant that David would not forget later on, nor did he forget the loving kindness he received from Jonathan, who "loved him as he loved his own soul" (v. 17).

Jonathan & David's covenant of peace

- **1 Samuel 20:5–7, 18–23 Jonathan proposes a sign: he will shoot an arrow to inform David of Saul's intentions.**
The next day was a new moon, and Jonathan was expected to be with his father at dinner on that night (v. 5). David would hide himself in a field, and wait three days for the sign (v. 5). If Saul noticed that David was missing Jonathan was to tell him that he had gone to Bethlehem for a family sacrifice (v. 6). Jonathan was to take note whether that was fine with Saul or whether it made him angry (v. 7). Agreeing to this, Jonathan proposed the following sign:

— He would shoot three arrows toward where David was hiding "as though I shot at a mark [target] (v. 20) and then send a boy to retrieve them (v. 21).

— If he tells the boy "Behold, the arrows are on this side of thee, take them" then David was to come forth "for there is peace to thee, and no hurt; as the Lord liveth" (v. 21).

— But if he tells the boy, "Behold, the arrows are beyond thee," then David should "go thy way: for the Lord hath sent thee away" (v. 22).

— And whatever the case might be, regarding the oath they had made with each other, "the Lord be between thee and me for ever.

- **1 Samuel 20:24–33 Saul tries to kill Jonathan for defending David.** Events went exactly according to plan. David hid himself in the field, and Jonathan went to dinner with his father (v. 24). Jonathan and Abner were there, but David's seat was empty (v. 25). Saul assumed David was absent because of ritual uncleanness, and let it go (v. 26). But when he was absent on the second night he asked his son Jonathan, "Wherefore cometh not the son of Jesse to meat, neither yesterday, nor to day?" (v. 27). Jonathan told him that David had gone to Bethlehem to be with his family and had asked to be excused (vv. 28–29).

Realizing that his son knew of David's whereabouts, "Saul's anger was kindled against Jonathan," and he called him a "son of [a] perverse rebellious woman" (an insult to Jonathan's mother) (v. 30). "I know that thou hast chosen the son of Jesse to thine own confusion," he said, and "as long as the son of Jesse liveth upon the ground, thou shalt not be established, nor thy kingdom" (vv. 30–31)

Saul demanded that Jonathan go and bring David unto him "for he shall surely die" (v. 31). Jonathan was bold enough to challenge his father, saying, "Wherefore shall he be slain? what hath he done?" (v. 32), whereupon Saul "cast a javelin at him to smite him" (v. 33).

Jonathan warns David with arrows

- **1 Samuel 20:35–38 Jonathan warns David to flee.** As previously agreed, Jonathan "went out into the field at the time appointed with David, and a little lad with him" (v. 35). He told the boy, "Run, find out now the arrows which I shoot. And as the lad ran, he shot an arrow beyond him" (v. 36). Then, as the boy ran to get the arrow, Jonathan cried out, "Is not the arrow beyond thee?" (v. 37). This was the signal that Saul was seeking David's life. He urged the boy to hurry and bring the arrows to him (v. 38).

- **1 Samuel 20:39–42 Jonathan and David part in sorrow.** The little boy had no idea what was going on; only "Jonathan and David knew the matter" (v. 39). Jonathan gave the boy his armor and asked him to carry it back to the city (v. 40). And when he was gone, "David arose out of a place toward the south, and fell on his face to the ground" (v. 41). Both were tearful at this parting, but David's distress exceeded Jonathan's. He "bowed himself three times: and they kissed one another, and wept one with another, until David exceeded" (v. 41). Jonathan blessed David, saying, "Go in peace, forasmuch as we have sworn both of us in the name of the Lord, saying, The Lord be between me and thee, and between my seed and thy seed for ever" (v. 42), and then they departed—Jonathan back to the city and David into the hills for safety. There David hid in the cave of Adullam for a time.

The cave of Adullam where David hid

DAVID BECOMES A FUGITIVE

- **1 Samuel 21:1–6 David eats the shewbread of the tabernacle.** He had to avoid starvation. He fled therefore to the tabernacle and asked Ahimelech the priest for food (v. 1). He wanted "five loaves of bread" or "what[ever] there is present" (v. 3). Ahimelech replied that they had no "common bread" available, only the "hallowed" shewbread in the holy place of the tabernacle (v. 4). This could be eaten by the priests each time it was replaced, but only "if the young men have kept themselves at least from women" (v. 4). David assured the priest that it had been three days since he had even seen a woman (v. 5). What's more, he argued that while "the vessels of the young men are holy," the bread itself "is in a manner common" until it is sanctified by its presence in the vessel (v. 5). The priest gave David the shewbread, because there was nothing else he could eat and the bread would be replaced anyway as a matter of course (v. 6).

- **Matthew 12:1–8 The Savior's justification of David's need.** When Jesus went through the corn (wheat) fields on a particular Sabbath day, "his disciples were an hungred, and began to pluck the ears of corn, and to eat" (v. 1). Always looking for a reason to criticize, the Pharisees said, "Behold, thy disciples do that which is not lawful to do upon the sabbath day" (v. 2). And in answer, the Savior referenced what David had done at the tabernacle. "Have ye not read what David did, when he was an hungred, and they that were with him; How he entered into the house of God, and did eat the shewbread, which was not lawful for him to eat, neither for them which were with him, but only for the priests?" (vv. 3–4). Even the Pharisees believed that David's actions were justified, and the Lord used the story of David to illustrate that "the Son of man is Lord even of the sabbath day" (v. 8).

- **1 Samuel 21:7–9 David's whereabouts becomes known.** Unfortunately, while David was at the tabernacle, "a certain man of the servants of Saul was there that day, detained before the Lord; and his name was Doeg, an Edomite, the chiefest of the herdmen that belonged to Saul" (v. 7). Thus, David's whereabouts was now known and he had to flee again for safety. He had no weapon, so he took with him the sword of Goliath, which he had captured and was now being kept in the tabernacle (vv. 8–9).

- **1 Samuel 21:8-15 David flees to Philistia.** These were Israel's fiercest enemies, the very ones he had decimated in the battle with Goliath. Knowing they would remember and fear him, he faked madness. Then, after a while, he returned to the cave of Adullam.

- **1 Samuel 22:1, 3–4 David seeks protection for his parents in Moab.** David had returned again to the cave of Adullam, "and when his brethren and all his father's house heard it, they went down thither to him" (v. 1). Knowing that Saul would slaughter them if he found them, David "went thence to Mizpeh of Moab: and he said unto the king of Moab, Let my father and my mother, I pray thee, come forth, and be with you, till I know what God will do for me" (v. 3). The king of Moab agreed, "and they dwelt with him all the while that David was in the hold [cave]" (v. 4).

- **1 Samuel 22:2; 1 Chronicles 12:22 Deserters leave Saul to join David.** Family members were not the only ones who came to David's aid. "Every one that was in distress, and every one that was in debt, and every one that was discontented, gathered themselves unto him; and he became a captain over them: and there were with him about four hundred men" (v. 2). Over time, observing the ruthlessness and wickedness of Saul, "day by day there came to David to help him … a great host, like the host of God" (1 Chronicles 12:22).

- **1 Samuel 22:5 David flees to Judah.** The prophet Gad advised him, "Abide not in the hold [cave]; depart, and get thee into the land of Judah," and David did so, hiding in the forest of Hareth.

- **1 Samuel 22:6–19 Saul kills 85 priests and their families for helping David.** Saul and his troops were, at that time, in Ramah (v. 6). He asked his soldiers, "will the son of Jesse give every one of you fields and vineyards, and make you all captains of thousands, and captains of hundreds"? (v. 7). Yet, he said, "all of you have conspired against me, and there is none that sheweth me that my son hath made a league with the son of Jesse, and there is none of you that is sorry for me, or sheweth unto me that my son hath stirred up my servant against me, to lie in wait" (v. 8). He was feeling very sorry for himself. But then Doeg the Edomite, who had seen David at the tabernacle, said, "I saw the son of Jesse coming to Nob, to Ahimelech … And he enquired of the Lord for him, and gave him victuals, and gave him the sword of Goliath the Philistine" (vv. 9–10). Saul demanded that "Ahimelech the priest, the son of Ahitub, and all his father's house, the priests that were in Nob" come to him to answer for what they had done (v. 11).

Saul demanded of Ahimelech, "Why have ye conspired against me, thou and the son of Jesse, in that thou hast given him bread, and a sword, and hast enquired of God for him, that he should rise against me, to lie in wait, as at this day?" (v. 13). The high priest responded, "who is so faithful among all thy servants as David, which is the king's son in law, and goeth at thy bidding, and is honourable in thine house?" (v. 14). David had told him that he was on the king's business and he "knew nothing of all this, less or more." And he had not enquired of the Lord for him (v. 15). Unsatisfied with this answer, Saul said, "Thou shalt surely die, Ahimelech, thou, and all thy father's house" (v. 16).

Saul commanded his soldiers to "slay the priests of the Lord; because their hand also is with David, and because they knew when he fled, and did not shew it to me" (v. 17). But his servants would not do it, fearing to "put forth their hand to fall upon the priests of the Lord" (v. 17). Saul turned to Doeg the Edomite and demanded that he do it, and "he fell upon the priests, and slew on that day fourscore and five [85] persons that did wear a linen ephod" (v. 18). His anger still unsatisfied, Saul then fell upon "Nob, the city of the priests," where he "smote … with the edge of the sword, both men and women, children and sucklings, and oxen, and asses, and sheep" (v. 19), annihilating them all.

- **1 Samuel 22:20–23 One of the sons of Ahimelech escapes and flees to David.** He reported that Saul "had slain the Lord's priests" (v. 21). And David said, "I knew it that day, when Doeg the Edomite was there, that he would surely tell Saul" (v. 22). And David felt very bad about what had happened. "I have occasioned the death of all the persons of thy father's house," he said to the priest Abiathar (v. 22). "Abide thou with me, fear not: for he that seeketh my life seeketh thy life: but with me thou shalt be in safeguard" (v. 23).

- **1 Samuel 23:1–6 Even while an exile, David defeats the Philistines and rescues an Israelite city.** Word came to him that the Philistines were attacking Keilah, robbing the Israelites' "threshingfloors" [harvested wheat]. David sought the Lord in prayer, asking if he should "go and smite these Philistines," and the Lord said, "go" (v. 2). This was a scary fight to pick with the Philistines. His men said, "we be afraid here in Judah: how much more then if we come to Keilah against the armies of the Philistines?" (v. 3). But when David asked the Lord again, "the Lord answered him and said, Arise, go down to Keilah; for I will deliver the Philistines into thine hand" (v. 4). David went, and "smote them with a great slaughter," taking their cattle as spoils and saving the inhabitants of Keilah (v. 5).

- **1 Samuel 23:7–8 Saul prepares his armies to destroy Keilah.** It mattered not that David had rescued one of his cities from the Philistines. Saul was so intent on killing David, that he was willing to destroy anybody and anything that protected him. Hearing that David was in Keilah, Saul said, "God hath delivered him into mine hand; for he is shut in, by entering into a town that hath gates and bars" (v. 7). He commanded his men to go down to the city, surround it, and besiege it (v. 8).

- **1 Samuel 23:9–13 David escapes to save the city's inhabitants from destruction.** Believing that Saul would seek to kill him, he conferred with Abiathar, who had saved the ephod [Urim and Thummim] from the massacre at Nod. David inquired through the ephod whether the men of the city would betray him if Saul came down to destroy them, and the Lord said they would (v. 12). So David took his 600 men "and departed out of Keilah, and went whithersoever they could go" (v. 13). And when Saul heard that David had escaped, they did not attack the city.

- **1 Samuel 23:14–18 While David is in hiding, Jonathan visits him and "strengthen[s] his hand in God."** David had fled into the wilderness, where he hid "in strongholds … in a mountain in the wilderness of Ziph" (v. 14). Though Saul sought him every day, he could not find him. But while he was "in a wood," Jonathan found him "and strengthened his hand in God" (v. 16). He assured David, "Saul my father shall not find thee; and thou shalt be king over Israel, and I shall be next unto thee; and that also Saul my father knoweth" (v. 17). They renewed their covenant of friendship and parted (v. 18).

DAVID'S LOYALTY TO KING SAUL

- **1 Samuel 24:1–3 During another attempt to find and kill David, Saul stops to rest in a cave.** He had heard that David was in the wilderness of En-gedi, and took 3,000 men with him to find David among "the rocks of the wild goats" (vv. 1–2). Needing rest, he went into a cave near some sheep enclosures to sleep, and it so happened that David and his men were "in the sides of the cave" (v. 3).

David spares Saul as he sleeps

- **1 Samuel 24:4–6 David's men suggest that David kill Saul, but David refuses because he is Israel's anointed king.** The Lord had promised David, "Behold, I will deliver thine enemy into thine hand, that thou mayest do to him as it shall seem good unto thee" (v. 4). His men felt this was his opportunity to rid himself of this vile and bloodthirsty king. But David refused. Instead, "David arose, and cut off the skirt of Saul's robe privily" (v. 4). Footnote 4a in our Bibles explains that David cut off the hem of Saul's robe—the portion of the robe that symbolized authority. And after he had done this, "David's heart smote him, because he had cut off Saul's skirt" (v. 5). "The Lord forbid that I should do this thing unto my master, the LORD's anointed," he said, "to stretch forth mine hand against him, seeing he is the anointed of the Lord" (v. 6).

- **1 Samuel 24:7–12 David calls unto Saul and points out that he has spared his life and will never harm him.** When Saul arose and began to leave, "David also arose afterward, and went out of the cave, and cried after Saul, saying, My lord the king. And when Saul looked behind him, David stooped with his face to the earth, and bowed himself" (v. 8). In case Saul believed the rumors that David sought to harm him, he pointed out that "the Lord had delivered thee to day into mine hand in the cave: and some bade me kill thee: but mine eye spared thee; and I said,

I will not put forth mine hand against my lord; for he is the Lord's anointed" (v. 10). He held up the skirt of Saul's robe as evidence that he could have killed him, and said, "know thou and see that there is neither evil nor transgression in mine hand, and I have not sinned against thee;yet thou huntest my soul to take it" (v. 11). "The Lord judge between me and thee, and the Lord avenge me of thee," he said, "but mine hand shall not be upon thee" (v. 12).

David shows Saul that he spared his life

- **1 Samuel 24:16–19 Saul is profoundly touched by David's loyalty and righteousness.** Saul called unto him, "Is this thy voice, my son David? And Saul lifted up his voice, and wept" (v. 16). "Thou art more righteous than I," he acknowledged, "for thou hast rewarded me good, whereas I have rewarded thee evil" (v. 17). "When the Lord … delivered me into thine hand, thou killedst me not" (v. 18), he said. "Wherefore the Lord reward thee good for that thou hast done unto me this day" (v. 19).

- **1 Samuel 24:20–22 Saul knows that David will be king.** "I know well that thou shalt surely be king," he admitted, "and that the kingdom of Israel shall be established in thine hand" (v. 20). "Swear now therefore unto me by the Lord, that thou wilt not cut off my seed after me, and that thou wilt not destroy my name out of my father's house" (v. 21). Though he did not and would not keep his own oath not to kill David, he wanted David's promise not to harm him or his family. "And David sware unto Saul" (v. 22).

David's Multiple Marriages

- **1 Samuel 25:42–44 David marries two women.** Saul had given Michal, David's first wife, to another man (v. 44). David therefore married Abigail, daughter of Nabal in Carmel, and Ahinoam of Jezreel. Although Abigail is mentioned here before Ahinoam, the latter was the mother of David's oldest son, Amnon, and is always listed first among his wives. We will discuss David's multiple marriages in a later chapter.

Saul Tries One More Time to Kill David

- **1 Samuel 26 This chapter details David's second refusal to kill King Saul, although it would have been a simple thing to do.** As proof, David took the king's spear and bottle of water, carried them to the other side of the ravine, and then chided Abner, the king's captain, for his failure to protect the king. Once again the character of David shone forth.

- **1 Samuel 27:1–3 David takes refuge in Philistia.** He despaired that he would "perish one day by the hand of Saul," and decided that he should "speedily escape into the land of the Philistines; and Saul shall despair of me, to seek me any more in any coast of Israel: so shall I escape out of his hand" (v. 1). He took his 600 men and went to "Achish, the son of Maoch, king of Gath" to seek asylum (v. 2). This was granted, so David and "his men, every man with his household, even David with his two wives" found refuge there (v. 3). They stayed there for 16 months (v. 7).

● **1 Samuel 27:4 From this time on Saul stopped seeking to kill David.** We are not told whether it was because of his earlier oath or because David was now in the territory of one of Israel's most hated enemies. But the long season of revenge was now over. Saul never again sought for David's life.

THE DEATHS OF SAMUEL AND SAUL

Samuel's Death Causes Saul to Fear

● **1 Samuel 28:3–5 Samuel dies, the Philistines attack, and Saul fears greatly.** When the prophet Samuel died, "all Israel … lamented him, and buried him in Ramah, even in his own city" (v. 3). The universally-accepted prophet of Israel was gone, and Saul had put away all false prophets—"those that had familiar spirits, and the wizards"—out of the land (v. 3). Now, when the Philistines came again to battle Saul, "he was afraid, and his heart greatly trembled" (v. 5).

● **1 Samuel 28:6–10 Saul turns to spiritualists for comfort and direction.** Saul tried taking the matter of how to deal with the Philistines to the Lord, but he received no answer, "neither by dreams nor by Urim, nor by prophets" (v. 6). So in desperation, he told his servants to "seek me a woman that hath a familiar spirit, that I may go to her, and enquire of her" (v. 7).

His servants said to him, "Behold, there is a woman that hath a familiar spirit at En-dor," so "Saul disguised himself, and put on other raiment," and took two men with him to meet with her "by night" (v. 8). He asked her to "divine unto me by the familiar spirit, and bring me him up, whom I shall name unto thee" (v. 8). She reminded him that King Saul had "cut off those that have familiar spirits, and the wizards, out of the land" and accused him of laying a snare for her "to cause [her] to die" (v. 9). But Saul swore an oath unto her that "there shall no punishment happen to thee for this thing" (v. 10).

GUSTAVE DORÉ, 1865

● **1 Samuel 28:11–15 A witch at Endor conjures up "Samuel" for Saul.** She asked Saul, "Whom shall I bring up unto thee? And he said, Bring me up Samuel" (v. 11). When a spirit appeared who claimed to be Samuel, "she cried with a loud voice: and the woman spake to Saul, saying, Why hast thou deceived me? for thou art Saul" (v. 12). Saul answered, "Be not afraid: for what sawest thou?" and she replied "I saw gods [spirits] ascending out of the earth" (v. 13). When Saul

Witch of Endor conjures up a spirit for Saul

asked what form he had, she said, "An old man cometh up; and he is covered with a mantle. And Saul perceived that it was Samuel, and he stooped with his face to the ground, and bowed himself" (v. 14). Then the spirit that was pre- tending to be Samuel said to Saul, "Why hast thou disquieted me, to bring me up? And Saul answered, I am sore distressed; for the Philis- tines make war against me, and God is departed from me, and answereth me no more, neither by prophets, nor by dreams: therefore I have called thee, that thou mayest make known unto me what I shall do" (v. 15).

Contrasting Sources of Revelation

● **1 Samuel 28:16–20 Saul's evil source of revelation.** This was not really Samuel, but a false and evil spirit pretending to be him. There is no reason to suppose that the Lord, who had refused to respond to Saul through legitimate avenues, would then send him a legitimate revelation through the witch at Endor. Saul himself did not see the "Samuel" described by the witch; he just assumed it to be the former prophet.

The spirit spoke to him, either directly or through the witch. "Wherefore ... dost thou ask of me," the spirit said, "seeing the LORD is departed from thee, and is become thine enemy?" (v. 16). He reminded Saul that "the Lord hath done to [you], as he spake by me [supposedly Samuel]"—He "hath rent the kingdom out of thine hand, and given it to thy neighbour, even to David" (v. 17). And now, the spirit said, "the Lord will also deliver Israel [and] thee into the hand of the Philistines: and to morrow shalt thou and thy sons be with me" [meaning they would die] (v. 19). At this news, "Saul fell straightway all along on the earth, and was sore afraid ... and there was no strength in him; for he had eaten no bread all the day, nor all the night" (v. 20).

● **1 Samuel 30:1–8 David's righteous source of revelation.** At about the same time, the Amalekites invaded Judah and burned the city Ziklag with fire (v. 1). They also carried away alive all the women of the city (v. 2). David and his men came to the city too late, finding it "burned with fire; and their wives, and their sons, and their daughters ... taken captives" including David's two wives (vv. 3, 5). This caused such weeping that "they had no more power to weep" (v. 4). The people spoke openly of stoning him because of their grief for their children. David was also greatly grieved, and he sought comfort from the Lord (v. 6). He asked Abiathar the priest to bring him the ephod (v. 7). The breastplate of the high priest, which held the Urim and Thummim, was attached to the ephod (Exodus 28:26–30). Thus, this revelation was sought and received through legitimate means, and David received an immediate answer. "David enquired at the Lord, saying, Shall I pursue after this troop? shall I overtake them? And he answered him, Pursue: for thou shalt surely overtake them, and without fail recover all" (v. 8).

Saul and His Sons Are Killed

● **1 Samuel 31:1–6 Saul and three sons (including Jonathan) are killed by the Philisines.** The battle against the Philistines was disasterous, with "the men of Israel [fleeing] from before the Philistines, and [falling] down slain in mount Gilboa" (v. 1). The Philistines then "followed hard upon Saul and upon his sons; and the Philistines slew Jonathan, and Abinadab, and Malchi-shua, Saul's sons" (v. 2). Saul himself was "sore wounded of the archers" (v. 3). Fearing that the

Philistines might torture him before killing him, "Saul [said] unto his armourbearer, Draw thy sword, and thrust me through therewith; lest these uncircumcised come and thrust me through." But his armourbearer "would not; for he was sore afraid," so "Saul took a sword, and fell upon it" (v. 4). Then, assuming his master was dead, "his armourbearer … fell likewise upon his sword, and died with him" (v. 5). "So Saul died, and his three sons, and his armourbearer, and all his men, that same day together" (v. 6).

GUSTAVE DORÉ, 1865

Saul and his sons die in battle

● **2 Samuel 1:1–12 David's response to Saul's and Jonathan's deaths.** David returned from his successful campaign against the Amalekites and "abode two days in Ziklag" (v. 1). On the third day, a survivor from Saul's battle with the Philistines came into camp "with his clothes rent, and earth upon his head," who went to David and "fell to the earth, and did obeisance" (v. 2). He told David that he had come from Saul's camp and that "the people are fled from the battle, and many of the people also are fallen and dead; and Saul and Jonathan his son are dead also" (v. 4). David demanded to know how he knew this, and the man told him that he had found Saul still barely alive and had killed him at Saul's request. Saul had begged him, "Stand, I pray thee, upon me, and slay me: for anguish is come upon me, because my life is yet whole in me" (v. 9). This he did, knowing that Saul could not survive his wounds anyway.

THEBIBLEREVIVAL.COM, #7

The soldier had then taken "the crown that was upon his head, and the bracelet that was on his arm, and have brought them hither unto my lord" (v. 10). At this news, "David took hold on his clothes, and rent them; and likewise all the men that were with him: And they mourned, and wept, and fasted until even, for Saul, and for Jonathan his son, and for the people of the Lord, and for the house of Israel; because they were fallen by the sword" (vv. 11–12).

David laments the death of Saul

● **2 Samuel 1:13–16 David slays the soldier for killing King Saul.** He asked him who he was, and he answered, "I am the son of a stranger, an Amalekite" (v. 13). These were the people who had so often attacked the Israelites at harvest-time, spoiling their cities and stealing their crops. They were also the people whom David had only recently destroyed for burning Ziklag and taking their women captive.

David asked him, "How wast thou not afraid to stretch forth thine hand to destroy the Lord's anointed?" (v. 14). This was something that David had steadfastly refused to do for years, despite the fact that Saul was actively seeking to kill him. He had absolute respect for the king whom the Lord had anointed through His prophet.

David then called upon one of his soldiers to "fall upon him. And he smote him that he died" (v. 15). David then said to the dead man, "Thy blood be upon thy head; for thy mouth hath testified against thee, saying, I have slain the Lord's anointed" (v. 16).

- **2 Samuel 1:17-27 David deeply laments the deaths of Saul and Jonathan with a Psalm.** He encouraged the people of Judah to teach their children how to play it with the "use of a bow" (v. 18), and it was recorded in the Book of Jasher (one of the Apocrypha) (v. 19).

To Saul, the king of Israel, David wrote, "Ye daughters of Israel, weep over Saul, who clothed you in scarlet, with other delights, who put on ornaments of gold upon your apparel" (v. 24). And to Jonathan, his dear friend, he wrote, "How are the mighty fallen in the midst of the battle! O Jonathan, thou wast slain in thine high places. I am distressed for thee, my brother Jonathan: very pleasant hast thou been unto me: thy love to me was wonderful, passing the love of women" (vv. 25–26).

Of them both, he said, "The beauty of Israel is slain upon thy high places: how are the mighty fallen!" (v. 19). "Saul and Jonathan were lovely and pleasant in their lives, and in their death they were not divided: they were swifter than eagles, they were stronger than lions" (v. 23). "How are the mighty fallen, and the weapons of war perished!" (v. 27).

Notes

1.   In Conference Report, Apr. 1989, 4–5; or *Ensign*, May 1989, 5.

Chapter 24

King David's Rule, Fall, and Remorse

(2 Samuel)

༺༈༻

INTRODUCTION

The Enigma of King David

A faithful Jew and friend of the Latter-day Saints once said concerning David: "If the Latter-day Saints ever hope to make friends with the Jewish people, they must stop talking about David as a tragic, sinful figure, for we view him as one of the great figures of our history." So we must ask ourselves, "Was David a good man?" Of course he was. In his early life he exhibited some of the most Christ-like characteristics to be found in any Old Testament figure. His faith, loyalty, charity, and devotion to the cause of Jehovah is not exceeded by anyone in the Bible or any other book of scripture.

There is no doubt that David was also a great man. Under David, Israel reached its golden age, the peak of its political and military power. For the first time, under his reign, the Israelites controlled the whole land of promise. Israel had not achieved such heights before that time, nor have they since.

David—artist, soldier, ruler, and king

So, should we emphasize the David who killed Goliath, or the David who killed Uriah? Should we view him as the servant who refused to lift his hand against the Lord's anointed, or as the Lord's anointed who lifted his hand against a faithful and loyal servant? Was his life a tragedy, or a triumph? This chapter explores all of these aspects of David's life—the good and the bad.

The Book of Second Samuel

- **Author:**   Unknown.

- **Position:**   The books of First and Second Samuel are combined in the Hebrew scriptures but are separated in the Greek Bible. They are the beginning of the historical record of the kings of Israel (like the large plates of Nephi).

Purpose:	To provide a detailed portrait of David as King of Israel—his great strengths, his leadership, his magnanimity in the face of cruel persecution from King Saul, and his weakness in succumbing to carnal temptation.
Time Span:	From the death of Saul to just prior to the death of David (ca. 1015 BC).
Length:	24 chapters
Key Sections:	— Chapters 1–10 David's ascension to the throne and early successes.
	— Chapters 11–21 David's personal sorrows and tribulations after his sin with Bathsheba and to the end of his reign.
	— Chapters 22–24 David's psalm of praise for God's mercy, inspired pronouncements, and final acts.

KING DAVID

King of Judah

● **2 Samuel 2:1–4, 11 David is anointed king at Hebron.** After Saul's death David sought the Lord's advice concerning where he should establish himself, and the answer was Hebron (v. 1). So he went there with his family and his army and they dwelt in Hebron and its surrounding cities for the next 7 ½ years (v. 11). And while he was there, "the men of Judah came, and … anointed David king over the house of Judah" (v. 4).

● **2 Samuel 2:4–10 The kingdom of Israel is divided.** Saul was buried by "the men of Jabesh-gilead," and David thanked them for "shew[ing] this kindness unto your lord, even unto Saul" (vv. 4–5). David wished them well, that "the Lord shew kindness and truth unto you," and also promised that "I also will requite you this kindness, because ye have done this thing" (v. 6). He encouraged them to "let your hands be strengthened, and be ye valiant: for your master Saul is dead, and also the house of Judah have anointed me king over them" (v. 7).

Samuel anoints David at Hebron

Ignoring David's leadership in Judah, Abner the captain of Saul's army took Ish-bosheth, one of Saul's sons, and "made him king over … all Israel" (vv. 8–9). Ish-bosheth was 40 at the time, and he reigned for 2 years (v. 10).

Thus, the tribe of Judah accepted David as king, but for more than seven years there was no unity, and two opposing kings reigned. David refused to take action against Ish-bosheth because he had covenanted with Jonathan not to retaliate against Saul's family when he (David) came to power (1 Samuel 20:14–16).

● **2 Samuel 2:12–32 Civil war breaks out.** Despite David's intentions of peaceful co-existence, a battle eventually ensued at the "pool of Gibeon"—a large well, hewn into the rock, large enough for the women to walk down into by means of stairs. Ish-bosheth came there with his general Abner and his army, and they were met by David's general Joab and his men (vv. 12–13). They engaged in "very sore battle that day," and Abner's (Ish-bosheth's) forces were beaten by Joab and the forces of David (v. 17).

Abner fled from the scene, but was pursued by Asahel, Joab's brother, who was "as light of foot as a wild roe" (vv. 18–19). Abner yelled back at Asahel that he should content himself by taking the armor of one of the younger men, but Asahel refused. Abner saw that he must either kill or be killed, and therefore turned his spear and ran it clear through the body of Asahel so that "the spear came out behind him" (vv. 20–23). Joab and his forces were momentarily stunned by Asahel's death, but then pursued Abner all the way to the hill of Ammah in the wilderness of Gibeon (v. 24).

GUSTAVE DORÉ, 1896

Civil war between David and Ishbosheth

As their forces gathered for battle at this site, Abner called out to Joab, saying, "Shall the sword devour for ever? knowest thou not that it will be bitterness in the latter end? how long shall it be then, ere thou bid the people return from following their brethren?" (v. 26). Agreeing that the bloodshed should stop, "Joab blew a trumpet, and all the people stood still, and pursued after Israel no more, neither fought they any more" (v. 28). David's forces had lost 20 men, including Asahel (v. 30), and Abner's forces had lost 360 men (v. 31) before they called off the battle and returned to their homes.

● **2 Samuel 3:1 War continues and David's forces prevail.** The battle between Abner and Joab's forces was not the end of civil war in Israel. Unfortunately, skirmishes continued as Judah and Israel fought a "long war" for supremacy. But over time, David's army slowly gained the upper hand.

● **2 Samuel 3:2–21 Abner deserts to David's side.** Eventually, Ish-bosheth wrongfully accused his general, Abner, of sleeping with Rizbah, one of Saul's concubines (vv. 7–8). Abner retaliated against Ish-bosheth by turning the hearts of the people toward

THEBIBLEREVIVAL.COM. #7

David sends Abner away

King David, then also deserted himself (vv. 17–20). David accepted Abner's offer to gather together the forces of Israel in support of him, then sent him away (v. 21).

● **2 Samuel 3:22–39 Joab avenges his brother Asahel's death by murdering Abner.** When Joab returned from battle he was angry with David for accepting Abner (vv. 21–24). He believed that Abner was deceiving David "to know all that thou doest" (v. 25). Without David's knowledge, Joab requested that Abner return (v. 26). Then, "Joab took him aside in the gate to speak with him quietly, and smote him there under the fifth rib, that he died, for the blood of Asahel his brother" (v. 27). David was shocked by this murder, and proclaimed, "I and my kingdom are guiltless before the Lord for ever from the blood of Abner" (v. 28). David mourned Abner's death greatly and proclaimed to Joab and all the people, "Know ye not that there is a prince and a great man fallen this day in Israel? And I am this day weak, though anointed king; and these men … be too hard for me: the Lord shall reward the doer of [this] evil according to his wickedness" (vv. 38–39).

● **2 Samuel 4 Ish-bosheth, king of Israel, is also slain.** The death of Abner caused great fear in Ish-bosheth and his people (v. 1). David loomed as a threat to their sovereignty, and some of Ish-bosheth's men switched their loyalty to David. Two of them, captains in Ish-bosheth's army, assassinated Ish-bosheth as he lay sleeping in his bed (vv. 5–7). Then, they beheaded him and took his head to David, saying, "Behold the head of Ish-bosheth the son of Saul thine enemy, which sought thy life; and the Lord hath avenged my lord the king this day of Saul, and of his seed" (v. 8). What they didn't know was that David had promised both Saul and Jonathan that he would do no harm to their family after he (David) came to power. (1 Samuel 20:15–16; 24:22).

Ishbosheth's head brought to David

Although he was at war with Ish-bosheth, David did not condone the treachery of these assassins. He reminded them that he had put to death the man who killed King Saul, though the man thought he would be rewarded for doing so (v. 10). How much more worthy of death were they who had "slain a righteous person in his own house upon his bed?" (v. 11). David then had them executed, cut off their hands and feet (symbolizing the nature of their crime), and hung their bodies up for all to see over the pool in Hebron (v. 12). He then gave Ish-bosheth's head a decent burial in the tomb where Abner was laid (v. 12).

David Becomes King of a United Israel

● **2 Samuel 5:1–5 All the tribes of Israel are united into one kingdom loyal to David.** With Ish-bosheth now dead, and no legitimate heir to Saul being available, the tribes of Israel who had followed him went to David and reminded him, "we are thy bone and thy flesh" (v. 1). They remembered that while Saul was king, it was David who most often "leddest out and broughtest in Israel: and the Lord said to thee, Thou shalt feed my people Israel, and thou shalt be a captain over Israel" (v. 2). So, now they wanted him to reign over all of them. David "made a league with them in Hebron before the Lord: and they anointed David king over Israel" (v. 3). David was then 30 years old, and reigned for a total of more than 40 years—7 ½ years over Judah, and 33 years over all Israel (vv. 4–5).

● **2 Samuel 5:6–10 David conquers Mt.** Zion and establishes the City of David. One of David's first uni- fying acts, after becoming king of all Israel, was to establish his capital on the border of the northern and southern tribes. He chose the Jebusite city that we know today as Jerusalem. The site of Jerusalem was already ancient and significant in David's day:

The City of David below the temple mount on the south

— This was the site of the City of Salem, whose king was Melchizedek, and whose people were translated.

— Because it was later controlled by the Jebusites, it became known as Jebu-Salem and eventually Jeru-salem.

— The temple mount was the site where Abraham nearly offered Isaac on an altar.

— On these mountains the Lord Jesus Christ was eventually crucified.

The Jebusites felt so secure behind the walls of their fortress that they taunted David and his men by suggesting that even the Jebusite blind and lame could defend their fortress. They had great confidence in their position atop a steep hill with deep valleys all around them except on the north (where the temple mount is). But David had no intention of making a frontal attack. He sent his men up through a water shaft and captured the city by that clever strategy.

David Brings the Tabernacle and the Ark to Jerusalem

● **2 Samuel 6:1–5 David retrieves the ark of the covenant.** During the reign of Saul, the ark of the covenant was little used. It was not even kept at the tabernacle, where it once resided, but in a Levite city in the home of Abinadab. David wanted to bring it to his new capitol—to Jerusalem—to signify the Lord's presence there. He gathered together 30,000 men and went to the house of Abinadab in Gibeah, where the ark had resided ever since it was recovered from the Philistines (vv. 1–3). They put the ark on a "new cart" driven by the two sons of Abinadab: Uzzah and Ahio (vv. 3–4). Then they drove the cart toward Jerusalem, with "David and all the house of Israel play[ing] before the Lord on all manner of instruments made of fir wood, even on harps, and on psalteries, and on timbrels, and on cornets, and on cymbals" (v. 5).

● **2 Samuel 6:6–11 Uzzah attempts to steady the ark and dies.** When the procession got to Nachon's threshingfloor, "Uzzah put forth his hand to the ark of God, and took hold of it; for the oxen shook it" (v. 6). Since the days of Moses, Israel had been under the strict command of the Lord that only authorized Levites, and only under certain specified conditions, could handle sacred instruments. It was a very sacred object, symbolic of the presence of the Lord Himself. Uzzah was way out of line in presuming to touch it. The Lord was displeased with his presumptuousness and "smote him there for his error; and there he died by the ark of God" (v. 7).

Uzzah died when he touched the ark

"David was displeased" because he felt that "the Lord had made a breach upon Uzzah" (v. 8), and he named the place Perez-uzzah (meaning "breach of Uzzah"). It made David very much afraid of the ark, and he did not dare bring it to Jerusalem (vv. 9–10). Instead, he left it at the home of "Obed-edom the Gittite" (v. 10), where it remained for three months. And while it was there, the Lord blessed Obed-edom's household (v. 11).

● **2 Samuel 6:12–23 David dances with joy at its arrival, embarrassing his wife Michal.** When David heard that Obed-edom's house had been blessed by the presence of the ark, he "went and brought up the ark of God from the house of Obed-edom into the city of David with gladness" (v. 12). He made sacrifices and also "danced before the Lord with all his might" while "girded with a linen ephod" (vv. 13–14). As the procession arrived in Jerusalem "with shouting, and with the sound of the trumpet, … Michal Saul's daughter looked through a window, and saw king David leaping and dancing before the Lord; and she despised him in her heart" (vv. 15–16).

● **2 Samuel 6:17–19 David officiates in sacrifices at the tabernacle.** David had built a temporary tabernacle in Jerusalem, and when the ark came to Jerusalem he "set it in his place, in the midst of the tabernacle" (v. 17). Then David "offered burnt offerings and peace offerings before the Lord" and "blessed the people in the name of the Lord of hosts" (v. 18). He gave every person "a cake of bread, and a good piece of flesh, and a flagon of wine [and then] all the people departed every one to his house" (v. 19).

David danced before the ark

Given the fact that David had dressed "girded with a linen ephod" (vv. 13–14), and that he was now making sacrifices unto the Lord, we may conclude that at some point in his life David had been given the proper priesthood authority to officiate in such ordinances. Perhaps it was at the time that Samuel anointed him to become king. King Saul had lost his kingdom for offering unauthorized sacrifices. But in those days, the prophet Samuel held the priesthood authority and Saul did not. Now, in David's time, there is no prophet there to officiate and David did so without condemnation from the Lord. We may therefore conclude that David was a prophet, a priest, and a king—the first of Israel's leaders to hold all three offices at the same time.

● **2 Samuel 6:20–23 Michal mocks David for his dancing.** David returned to his house, expecting to "bless his household." Michal, his wife and the daughter of Saul, came out to meet him and said, "How glorious was the king of Israel to day, who uncovered himself to day in the eyes of the handmaids of his servants, as one of the vain fellows shamelessly uncovereth himself!" (v. 20). She believed that a king should behave in a more dignified manner. David replied, "It was before the Lord, which chose me before [instead of] thy father. . . and … all his house, to appoint me ruler over the people of the Lord, over Israel" (v. 21).

Michal despised David's dancing

Her father may have been more "kingly," but David was reminding her that the Lord had chosen him. "Therefore will I play before the Lord," David said, "and I will yet be more vile than thus, and will be base in mine own sight: and of the maidservants which thou hast spoken of, of them shall I be had in honour" (v. 22). Because of her criticism, David thereafter ignored her, and "Michal the daughter of Saul had no child unto the day of her death (v. 23).

Dreams of a Permanent Temple

● **2 Samuel 7:1–11 David wants to build a temple at Jerusalem.** The tabernacle built by Moses was now 300 years old. And as David "sat in his house, … the Lord [having] given him rest round about from all his enemies," he said to Nathan the prophet: "See now, I dwell in an house of cedar, but the ark of God dwelleth within curtains" (v. 2). He felt that the Lord needed a beautiful home as well. And Nathan encouraged him, saying, "Go, do all that is in thine heart; for the Lord is with thee" (v. 3).

David wanted to build the Lord a house

The Lord was also pleased with David's desire, saying, "Shalt thou build me an house for me to dwell in? … I have not dwelt in any house since the time that I brought up the children of Israel out of Egypt, even to this day, but have walked in a tent and in a tabernacle" (vv. 4–6). Yet in all those years the Lord had never complained about not having "an house of cedar" (v. 7).

The Lord reminded David that he had "[taken] thee from the sheepcote, from following the sheep, to be ruler over my people, over Israel: And I was with thee whithersoever thou wentest, and have cut off all thine enemies out of thy sight, and have made thee a great name, like unto the name of the great men that are in the earth" (vv. 8–9). The day will come when the Lord will "appoint a place for my people Israel, and will plant them, that they may dwell in a place of their own, and move no more; neither shall the children of wickedness afflict them any more, as beforetime" (v. 10). In that sense, the Lord "will make thee an house" as well (v. 11).

- **1 Chronicles 22:8 The Lord does not permit David to build a temple.** David testified, "the word of the Lord came to me, saying, Thou hast shed blood abundantly, and hast made great wars: thou shalt not build an house unto my name, because thou hast shed much blood upon the earth in my sight."

- **1 Chronicles 22:9–10 Instead, a son named Solomon will build it.** The Lord promised, "Behold, a son shall be born to thee, who shall be a man of rest; and I will give him rest from all his enemies round about: for his name shall be Solomon, and I will give peace and quietness unto Israel in his days. He shall build an house for my name; and he shall be my son, and I will be his father; and I will establish the throne of his kingdom over Israel for ever."

- **2 Samuel 7:12–15 Another version of the same promise.** The book of 2 Samuel quotes the Lord as saying, "When thy days be fulfilled, and thou shalt sleep with thy fathers, I will set up thy seed after thee, which shall proceed out of thy bowels, and ... he shall build an house for my name, and I will stablish the throne of his kingdom for ever. I will be his father, and he shall be my son. If he commit iniquity, I will chasten him with the rod of men, and with the stripes of the children of men: But my mercy shall not depart away from him, as I took it from Saul, whom I put away before thee."

The Davidic Covenant:
God's Promises to David and His Posterity

- **2 Samuel 7:16–17 The Davidic covenant: David's throne will be established forever.** The Lord promised David through the prophet Nathan that "thine house and thy kingdom shall be established for ever before thee: thy throne shall be established for ever." This is referred to as the "Davidic covenant," and it was fulfilled with the birth of the Lord Jesus Christ. While speaking to the apostle John on the Isle of Patmos, the Lord said, "I Jesus have sent mine angel to testify unto you these things ... . I am the root and the offspring of David, and the bright and morning star" (Revelation 22:16). And when Jesus entered Jerusalem during the last week of his earthly life, the people cried out "Hosanna to the Son of David: Blessed is he that cometh in the name of the Lord; Hosanna in the highest" (Matthew 21:9). They recognized in Jesus the fulfillment of the Davidic covenant—the King of Kings and the promised Messiah.

- **2 Samuel 7:18–29 David is amazed, but humbly accepts the Lord's will.** He had asked the question before to the prophet Samuel (1 Samuel 18:18). Now, hearing this eternal promise concerning his throne, he asked again, "Who am I, O Lord God? and what is my house, that thou hast brought me hitherto?" (v. 18). He knew that the Lord knew his mortal weaknesses (v. 20). And he recognized that the Lord would do these things "for thy word's sake, and according to thine own heart" (v. 21). He praised the Lord, saying, "there is none like thee, neither is there any God beside thee" (v. 22). He praised the Lord's people also: "What one nation in the earth is like thy people, even like Israel, whom God went to redeem for a people to himself, and to make him a name, and to do for you great things and terrible" (v. 23). "For thou hast confirmed to thyself thy people Israel to be a people unto thee for ever: and thou, Lord, art become their God" (v. 24). "And now, O Lord God, the word that thou hast spoken concerning thy servant, and concerning his house, establish it for ever, and do as thou hast said" (v. 25).

● **Psalm 89 David writes a psalm of gratitude and covenant in response to the Lord's promises.** It was a Messianic psalm—one which gives praise to the Lord and His Messiah. David writes of the mercy, greatness, justice, and judgment of the Holy One of Israel (vv. 1–18). He acknowledges that his (David's) seed and throne (through Christ) will be established forever (vv. 19–26). And he writes that God's "firstborn" will be made higher than the kings of the earth (v. 27).

The Lord Makes David and All Israel Mighty

● **2 Samuel 8:1–8 The Lord is with David in all his military campaigns.** We read that he "smote" and "subued" the Philistines (v. 1), the Moabites (v. 2), the Mesopotamians (vv. 3–4), and the Syrians (vv. 5–8). In all these campaigns the Lord was with him, and as a result he accomplished great things for Israel:

— David secured for Israel the undisputed possession of all of the land of Canaan.

— He ruled over the entire land of Israel that had been promised to Abraham.

— He established the kingdom of Israel as a model where the will of God was followed in all things.

● **2 Samuel 8:15–18 David reigned over all of Israel with justice and judgment (v. 15).** Not only was David wise, but he also appointed strong men to surround him. He made Joab his military commander and Jehoshaphat his recorder (v. 16). Zadok and Ahimelech were the priests; and Seraiah was the scribe (v. 17). And he appointed Benaiah the son of Jehoiada over both the Cherethites and the Pelethites, and his sons as chief rulers (v. 18).

● **2 Samuel 9 David restores the property of Saul to Mephibosheth, son of Jonathan, and cares for him as a son.** Remembering his promises to both Saul and Jonathan, David then asked, "Is there yet any that is left of the house of Saul, that I may shew him kindness for Jonathan's sake?" (v. 1). He was informed that there was a son of Jonathan still alive "which is lame on [both] feet" (vv. 2–3, 13). David sent immediately for him (v. 4).

David's kindness to Jonathan's lame son

When Mephibosheth, the son of Jonathan and grand-son of Saul, "was come unto David, he fell on his face, and did reverence. And David said, Mephibosheth. And he answered, Behold thy servant! And David said unto him, Fear not: for I will surely shew thee kindness for Jonathan thy father's sake, and will re-store thee all the land of Saul thy father; and thou shalt eat bread at my table continually" (vv. 5–7).

Mephilbosheth was stunned; "he bowed himself, and said, What is thy servant, that thou shouldest look upon such a dead dog as I am?" (v. 8).

David then "called to Ziba, Saul's servant, and said unto him, I have given unto thy master's son all that pertained to Saul and to all his house. Thou therefore, and thy sons, and thy servants [he had 15 sons and 20 servants], shall till the land for him, and thou shalt bring in the fruits, that thy master's son may have food to eat: but Mephibosheth thy master's son shall eat bread alway at my table" (vv. 9–10). This was an honor usually reserved for the king's sons (v. 11), but it was granted unto Mephibosheth, the son of Jonathan, and unto his son Micha (v. 12).

- **2 Samuel 10 David's army smites the Syrians and Ammonites for their offenses against Israel.** David was one who did not forget kindnesses. He had once been a fugitive among the Ammonites, and when their king died and his son Hanun reigned in his stead, David sent servants to show kindness unto him (vv. 1–2). But the new king's servants convinced him that David was not showing kindness but was instead sending servants "to search the city, and to spy it out, and to overthrow it" (v. 3). So Hanun "took David's servants, and shaved off the one half of their beards, and cut off their garments in the middle, even to their buttocks, and sent them away" (v. 4). Both of these actions were extremely insulting to a Hebrew, and "the men were greatly ashamed: and the king [David] said, Tarry at Jericho until your beards be grown, and then return" (v. 5).

David punishes the Ammonites

The Ammonites knew that their actions would "stink" before David, so they hired thousands of Syrians to help them defend themselves (v. 6). David "sent Joab, and all the host of the mighty men" against them to battle (v. 7). Joab split his forces, sending part of them to battle the Ammonites and keeping part of them to battle the Syrians (vv. 8–10). In a manner similar to the Book of Mormon's captain Moroni, Joab challenged his soldiers to "play [fight like] men for our people, and for the cities of our God" and then to let the Lord "do that which seemeth him good" (vv. 11–12).

As Joab's forces drew near them, the Syrians fled before them (v. 13). And when the Ammonites "saw that the Syrians were fled, then fled they also" into their own city (v. 14). Joab took his forces and returned to Jerusalem (v. 14). Humiliated, the Syrians "gathered themselves together" on the east side of the Jordan river to attack Israel again (vv. 15–16). So David "gathered all Israel together, and passed over Jordan, and came to Helam" to fight them (v. 17). Once again, "the Syrians fled before Israel; and David slew the men of seven hundred chariots of the Syrians, and forty thousand horsemen, and smote Shobach the captain of their host, who died there" (v. 18). All those kings who had served the Syrian king Hadarezer "saw that they were smitten before Israel, [and] they made peace with Israel, and served them. So the Syrians feared to help the children of Ammon any more" (v. 19).

THE FALL OF KING DAVID

David and Bathseba

Continual success can lead to complacency. Under David, Israel's forces always prevailed, and they enjoyed unparalleled safety within their borders as a result. David, who had always led his forces into battle personally, stopped going to war, letting Joab do the fighting while he remained in Jerusalem. "Things were getting too easy for David; he had leisure to stay at home while Joab and his men were out fighting Ammonites and Syrians. In his leisure he looked from his rooftop at his neighbor's wife. Leisure and lust led to adultery and then to murder, which sins had eternal repercussions, as well as tragic earthly results"[1].

- **2 Samuel 11:1–5 David commits adultery with Bathsheba.** David was walking on his roof (v. 2). Many homes in Palestine have flat roofs. People often walk or sit on their roofs in the refreshing cool of evening or to catch a daytime breeze in the heat of the day. The roof of David's palace was high enough that he could look down into the inner courts of a number homes below his palace. While on the roof, he saw Bathsheba bathing, was attracted to her, and then acted upon his lustful thoughts (vv. 3–4).

David watches Bathsheba bathe from his porch

- **He could have avoided his tragedy by simply turning away and casting the thought out of his mind.** Instead, he asked who she was and was told "Bathsheba, the daughter of Eliam, the wife of Uriah the Hittite" (v. 3).

- **He sent for her, took her into his chambers, and "lay with her" (v.** 4). She returned home, but the story had only begun. As a result of this act, "the woman conceived, and sent and told David, and said, I am with child" (v. 5).

- **President Spencer W.** Kimball said:

  The thought that stirred the look that provoked the lust was evil in its beginning. To want, to desire, to crave—that is to lust. So when the thought is born which starts a chain reaction, a sin has already been committed. If the thought is sown, then develops into lust, it is almost certain to bring eventually the full harvest of the act of the heinous sin, adultery…

Murder is generally thought of as premeditated killing, and certainly no such act was ever completed unless the thought had preceded the action. No one ever robbed a bank until he had "cased" it, planned the robbery and considered the "getaway." Likewise adultery is not the result of a single thought. There first is a deterioration of thinking. Many sinful chain- thoughts have been coursing through the offender's mind before the physical sin is committed.

Yes, as a man thinketh, so *does* he. If he thinks it long enough he is likely to do it, whether it be theft, moral sin, or suicide. Thus the time to protect against the calamity is when the thought begins to shape itself. Destroy the seed and the plant will never grow. Man alone, of all creatures of earth, can change his thought pattern and become the architect of his destiny.[2]

President David O. McKay said: "What a man continually thinks about determines his actions in times of opportunity and stress. A man's reaction to his appetites and impulses when they are aroused gives the measure of that man's character. In these reactions are revealed the man's power to govern or his forced servility to yield"[3].

President McKay also said, "Many years ago a young man came to me while I was president of the European Mission and made a confession of a wrong and sinful act. He justified himself by saying that he happened to be in a bookstore at the closing hour, and when the door was locked he yielded to temptation. He rather blamed the circumstances for his fall. But I said, 'It wasn't the circumstances; it wasn't the locked door, nor the enticement. You had thought of that before you went to that bookstore. If you had never thought of that act, there would have been no circumstance strong enough to entice or to tempt you, a missionary, to fall. The thought always precedes the act.'"[4].

- **2 Samuel 11:6–13 David tries unsuccessfully to cover his sin.** He brought Uriah home from the war to be with his wife so that Uriah and any others would assume the child already conceived was Uriah's (v. 6). But his plan failed when Uriah would not return home; he slept instead "at the door of the king's house" (v. 8–9). David was frustrated and asked why he did not go home (v. 10). And Uriah answered, "The ark, and Israel, and Judah, abide in tents; and my lord Joab, and the servants of my lord, are encamped in the open fields; shall I then go into mine house, to eat and to drink, and to lie with my wife? as thou livest, and as thy soul liveth, I will not do this thing" (v. 11). Uriah had integrity and a sense of duty. And David's plan was falling apart.

David told Uriah to remain in Jerusalem for two days, and made him drunk at a feast, hoping he would go home to sleep it off. But he didn't. He "went out to lie on his bed with the servants of his lord, but went not down to his house" (vv. 12–13).

- **2 Samuel 11:14–17 David commits the greater sin of murder while trying to cover his sin.** Being unable to get Uriah to sleep with his own wife, David concluded that he would have to arrange for Uriah's death. That way, he could marry the widow and all would appear to be legitimate. David "wrote a letter to Joab, and sent it by the hand of Uriah" (v. 14). The letter commanded, "Set ye Uriah in the forefront of the hottest battle, and retire ye from him, that he may be smitten, and die" (v. 15). Joab placed him against the enemy's most valiant fighters, and when the battle commenced "there fell some of the people of the servants of David; and Uriah the Hittite died also" (vv. 16–17). The deed was done. David probably felt relieved. But he was personally responsible for this pre-medi- tated death, having commanded his general to put him in danger. That was murder. And David had now committed it.

THEBIBLEREVIVAL.COM, #7

David caused Uriah to die in battle

Elder Richard G. Scott said: "Do not take comfort in the fact that your transgressions are not known by others. That is like an ostrich with his head buried in the sand. He sees only darkness and feels comfortably hidden. In reality he is ridiculously conpicuous. Likewise our every act is seen by our Father in Heaven and His Beloved Son. They know everything about us. … If you have seriously transgressed, you will not find any lasting satisfaction or comfort in what you have done. Excusing transgression with a cover-up may appear to fix the problem, but it does not. The tempter is intent on making public your most embarrassing acts at the most harmful time. Lies weave a pattern that is ever more confining and becomes a trap that Satan will spring to your detriment"[5].

● **2 Samuel 12:1–8 Nathan the prophet confronts David with his sin.** Nathan told a parable to illustrate the Lord's displeasure with David. "There were two men in one city; the one rich, and the other poor. The rich man had exceeding many flocks and herds: But the poor man had nothing, save one little ewe lamb, which he had bought and nourished up: and it grew together with him, and with his children; it did eat of his own meat, and drank of his own cup, and lay in his bosom, and was unto him as a daughter. And there came a traveller unto the rich man, and he spared to take of his own flock and of his own herd, to dress for the wayfaring man that was come unto him; but took the poor man's lamb, and dressed it for the man that was come to him" (vv. 1–4).

David was outraged at the rich man's actions against the poor man. "And he said to Nathan, As the Lord liveth, the man that hath done this thing shall surely die: And he shall restore the lamb fourfold, because he did this thing, and because he had no pity" (vv. 5–6).

Then Nathan declared forcefully: "Thou art the man" (v. 7). "Nathan's allegory was skillfully drawn, and his climatic '*Attah ha ish!*' ('Thou art the man') must have crashed in upon the conscience of David like the harbingers of doom's day"[6].

JAMES J. TISSOT, 1904

Nathan confronts David

"Thus saith the Lord God of Israel, I anointed thee king over Israel, and I delivered thee out of the hand of Saul; And I gave thee thy master's house, and thy master's wives into thy bosom, and gave thee the house of Israel and of Judah; and if that had been too little, I would moreover have given unto thee [more]. [Why] hast thou despised the commandment of the Lord, to do evil in his sight? thou hast killed Uriah the Hittite with the sword, and hast taken his wife to be thy wife, and hast slain him with the sword of the children of Ammon" (vv. 7–9).

● **2 Samuel 12:10–14 Nathan pronounces the Lord's punishment for David.** Because David had suffered Uriah to die by the sword, "Now therefore the sword shall never depart from thine house" (v. 10). "I will raise up evil against thee out of thine own house, and I will take thy wives before thine eyes, and give them unto thy neighbour, and he shall lie with thy wives in the sight of this sun" (v. 11). David had committed his sin secretly, but the Lord would exact His punishment upon David "before all Israel, and before the sun" (v. 12).

David did not attempt to deny his sin. He confessed to Nathan, "I have sinned against the Lord" (v. 13). Perhaps because of this, the Lord promised him "thou shalt not die," which was the usual punishment for unrepented adultery. Nevertheless, "because by this deed thou hast given great occasion to the enemies of the LORD to blaspheme, the child also that is born unto thee shall surely die" (v. 14).

● **Psalm 51 David's deep repentance for his sin is expressed .** "His repentant feelings were no doubt sincere, but he could not repent enough to restore the life of his friend, Uriah, nor the virtue of his wife. Though he later hoped and prayed that his soul would not be left forever in hell (the spirit prison), yet the eternal destiny of doers of such twin sins does not look good"[7].

— vv. 1–3	David acknowledges God and his mercy, as well as his own sins. He notes that our sins are "ever before us" until we are forgiven.
— vv. 2,7,10	Note his pleas to be made clean. Anyone who has committed sin and felt "dirty" for doing so will understand this plea.
— v. 11	Note also his plea for the Holy Spirit not to be taken away.
— vv. 9–14	The results of true repentance are described as a "cleansing", a "restoration" and a "deliverance".
— vv. 16–17	The principles of repentance are stated very clearly here.

David sought forgiveness with many tears

The Seriousness of Deliberately Committed Sins

● **Ezekiel 18:24 It is possible to negate a lifetime of good deeds with acts of wickedness.** This scripture highlights two very important principles:

1. Any one sin, however small, deliberately committed and un-repented, is sufficient to keep us out of the celestial kingdom.

2. Our good deeds do not 'outweigh' our sins. We will not be judged by comparing the good that we do with the sins we commit. All sins must be forsaken, repented, and atoned, no matter how much good we have otherwise done in our lives.

● **D&C 1:31–33 God cannot look upon any sin with the least degree of allowance.** The suffering of our Savior ought to impress on our minds that the penalty for sins is very grievous indeed. Sin <u>never</u> goes unpunished, and must be paid for <u>in full</u>. If it were otherwise, God would not be equally just to all His children. Nevertheless, because of the atonement of His Son Jesus Christ, "he that repents and does the commandments of the Lord shall be forgiven" (v. 32). But "he that repents not, from him shall be taken even the light which he has received; for my Spirit shall not always strive with man, saith the Lord of Hosts" (v. 33).

● **The Hierarchy of the Most Serious Sins.** To understand this hierarchy we must understand the difference between forgiveness and pardon:

— <u>Forgiveness</u> means to escape some or all of the punishment associated with the sin through the Atonement of Jesus Christ. We are forgiven when we fully repent.

— <u>Pardon</u> occurs after we have fully suffered ourselves for our sins. When the punishment has been fully served, we are released from suffering.

With these definitions in mind, we can understand more clearly the penalties for murder and for the unpardonable sin.

— <u>Murder is unforgivable but pardonable</u>—Murder cannot be atoned for by another. The murderer must pay the full price of his sin, after which he is pardoned and released from suffering. This was the promise made to David by the Lord.

— <u>The sin against the Holy Ghost is unpardonable</u>—There is neither any forgiveness for it, nor any pardon. There is no end to the suffering; the suffering goes on forever.

The Prophet Joseph Smith said: "All sins shall be forgiven, except the sin against the Holy Ghost; for Jesus will save all except the sons of perdition. What must a man do to commit the unpardonable sin? He must receive the Holy Ghost, have the heavens opened unto him, and know God, and then sin against Him. After a man has sinned against the Holy Ghost, there is no repentance for him. He has got to say that the sun does not shine while he sees it; he has got to deny Jesus Christ when the heavens have been opened unto him, and to deny the plan of salvation with his eyes opened to the truth of it; and from that time he begins to be an enemy. This is the case with many apostates of the Church of Jesus Christ of Latter-day Saints"[8].

The Seriousness of Adultery

- **Alma 39:5 Alma explains the seriousness of adultery.** To his son who had committed adultery he said, "these things are an abomination in the sight of the Lord; yea, most abominable above all sins save it be the shedding of innocent blood or denying the Holy Ghost."

President Spencer W. Kimball said:

> The enormity of this sin is underlined by numerous scriptures, and particularly by Alma's words to his immoral son [Alma 39:5] … To a young man seeking help who had allowed himself to indulge heavily in fornication but was not quite yet repentant, I wrote:
>
> 'Your sin is the most serious thing you could have done in your youth this side of murder. Your last experience in immorality was far more obnoxious than the first. You had been to the temple and had made solemn vows of chastity before God and holy angels. You made covenant that you would never have such ungodly relations. You had already done it and then did it again with that solemn promise on your lips.'
>
> The grievousness of the sin enhances the difficulty of repenting. Sometimes offenders reach the point of no return and cannot repent, for the Spirit of the Lord will not always strive with man. Esau sold his birthright for "one morsel of meat." Many young people sell their birthrights or put them in serious jeopardy for one hour in dark places, one unwarranted thrill, one exciting experience in a car or in a harlot's bed. One sad experience may not totally destroy, for repentance is in order, but one experience of fornication can break down the bars, blast and scar a life, and start a soul on a lifetime of regret and anguish"[9].

- **Adultery is forgivable, though it is very near to murder (which is not forgivable) in its seriousness.** Elder Boyd K. Packer said: "The discouraging idea that a mistake (or even a series of them) makes it everlastingly too late, does not come from the Lord. He has said that *if* we will repent, not only will He forgive us our transgressions, but He will forget them and remember our sins no more. … Repentance is like soap; it can wash sin away. Ground-in dirt may take the strong detergent of discipline to get the stains out, but out they will come"[10].

- **Had David immediately confessed and repented of his adultery, he would have been forgiven.** But because he did not repent, but sought to cover his sins, they were compounded by an even worse sin: murder.

- **D&C 10:24–27 This is the process that Satan uses to entrap us—in a snare of our own making.** Sometimes he makes us angry toward what is right (v. 24). Other times he encourages us to deceive others, thinking "this is no harm" (v. 25). And by these processes he "flatters" us into thinking that what we have done is not serious and it is also not sinful to lie about it (v. 25). "And thus he flattereth them, and leadeth them along until he draggeth their souls down to hell; and thus he causeth them to catch themselves in their own snare" (v. 26). That is what happened to David. And Satan seeks by this process to destroy the souls of all men (v. 27).

The Seriousness of Murder

● **2 Samuel 12:13 Another Bible error.** Because David would not die for his sin, the scribe who wrote 2 Samuel wrote this verse to say, "The Lord also hath put away thy sin; thou shalt not die." But this is false doctrine. God does not "put away" our sins as if they had not happened. The Joseph Smith Translation reads, "The Lord also hath NOT put away thy sin" (JST 2 Samuel 12:13). It is true that David would not be required to die for his sin. But it would not be forgotten or unpunished. That should be obvious from the pronouncements of woes that Nathan gave him after this verse in the Bible.

Elder Bruce R. McConkie said: "Murderers are forgiven eventually but only in the sense that all sins are forgiven except the sin against the Holy Ghost; they are not forgiven in the sense that celestial salvation is made available to them.[11]. After they have paid the full penalty for their crime, they shall go on to a telestial inheritance. (Rev. 22:15)"[12].

President Spencer W. Kimball said:

> As to crimes for which no adequate restoration is possible, I have suggested … that perhaps the reason murder is an unforgivable sin is that, once having taken a life—whether that life be innocent or reprobate—the life-taker cannot restore it. He may give his own life as payment, but this does not wholly undo the injury done by his crime. He might support the widow and children; he might do many other noble things; but a life is gone and the restitution of it in full is impossible. Repentance in the ordinary sense seems futile.

> Murder is so treacherous and so far-reaching! Those who lose their possessions may be able to recover their wealth. Those defamed may still be able to prove themselves above reproach. Even the loss of chastity leaves the soul in mortality with opportunity to recover and repent and to make amends to some degree. But to take a life, whether someone else's or one's own, cuts off the victim's experiences of mortality and thus his opportunity to repent, to keep God's commandments in this earth life. It interferes with his potential of having 'glory added upon [his head] for ever and ever.' (Abraham 3:26)"[13].

The Prophet Joseph Smith said: "A murderer, for instance, one that sheds innocent blood, cannot have forgiveness. David sought repentance at the hand of God carefully with tears, for the murder of Uriah; but he could only get it through hell: he got a promise that his soul should not be left in hell. Although David was a king, he never did obtain the spirit and power of Elijah and the fullness of the priesthood; and the priesthood that he received, and the throne and kingdom of David is to be taken from him and given to another by the name of David in the last days, raised up out of his lineage"[14].

The Results in David's Life

The price of David's sin of murder and adultery was high. He spent the rest of his life regretting it. Many of his psalms express the feelings of his heart during this period.

— **Psalm 38** David sorrows for his sins and begs the Lord not to forsake him.

— **Psalm 51** David pleads for divine forgiveness and mercy and desires a broken heart and a contrite spirit—"Create in me a clean heart, O God" (v. 10).

— **Psalm 16:10** David is promised eventual pardon. After seeking forgiveness all the rest of his life, God promised him that his soul would not remain in hell forever.

— **Psalm 86:12–13** David is promised eventual pardon. He receives assurance that his soul would eventually be "delivered ... from the lowest hell."

David wrote many psalms of sorrow for sin

- ● **D&C 132:38–39 David cannot inherit eternal exaltation.** His assurances of eventual pardon could not relieve him of the penalties of murder nor restore the blessings he had lost. They were gone forever. In this scripture the Lord tells us that David was accepted of Him in all things (including his multiple wives). The only exception to this was "in the case of Uriah and his wife; and, therefore he hath fallen from his exaltation, and received his portion; and he shall not inherit them out of the world, for I gave them unto another, saith the Lord" (v. 39).

- ● **Acts 2:29–34 David had not yet been released from hell at the time of the Savior's mortal ministry.** He will eventually be released from hell after he has paid the full price for his murder of Uriah. But Peter made it clear in his discourse on the day of Pentecost that "David ... is both dead and buried, and his sepulchre is with us unto this day" (v. 29). Since all righteous prophets from before the Savior's day were resurrected with Him, the fact that David remained in his tomb tells us something important about his status. Furthermore, Peter says, "David is not ascended into the heavens" with the Lord who will sit on the right hand of the Father (v. 34).

Elder Marion G. Romney said: "David, ... though highly favored of the Lord (he was, in fact, referred to as a man after God's own heart), yielded to temptation. His unchastity led to murder, and as a consequence, he lost his families and his exaltation"[15].

President Joseph F. Smith said: "For the crime of adultery with Bathsheba, and for ordering Uriah to be put in the front of battle in a time of war, where he was slain by the enemy, the priesthood, and the kingdom were taken from David, the man after God's own heart, and his soul was thrust into hell ... But even David, though guilty of adultery and murder of Uriah, obtained the promise that his soul should not be left in hell, which means, as I understand it, that even he shall escape the second death"[16].

President Joseph Fielding Smith said: "David committed a dreadful crime, and all his life afterwards sought for forgiveness. Some of the Psalms portray the anguish of his soul; yet David is still paying for his sin. He did not receive the resurrection at the time of the resurrection of Jesus Christ. Peter declared that his body was still in the tomb, and the Prophet Joseph Smith has said, 'David sought repentance at the hand of God carefully with tears, for the murder of Uriah;

but he could only get it through hell: he got a promise that his soul should not be left in hell.' Again we ask: Who wishes to spend a term in hell with the devil before being cleansed from sin?"[17].

● **2 Samuel 12:15–19 David and Bathsheba's child dies soon after birth.** When David and Bathsheba's child was born "the Lord struck the child … and it was very sick" (v. 15). "David therefore besought God for the child; and David fasted, and went in, and lay all night upon the earth" (v. 16). His servants and friends tried to raise him up "but he would not, neither did he eat bread with them" (v. 17). And after seven days the child died (v. 18). His friends did not dare tell him since he was so grief-stricken while the child was sick (v. 18), but when David saw them whispering, he asked, "Is the child dead? And they said, He is dead" (v. 19).

David fasted and prayed for his sick child

● **2 Samuel 12:20–23 David accepts the will of the Lord.** When he realized that the Lord had taken his child (as Nathan had prophesied He would), "then David arose from the earth, and washed, and anointed himself, and changed his apparel, and came into the house of the Lord, and worshipped: then he came to his own house; and when he required, they set bread before him, and he did eat" (v. 20). His servants were confused at his sudden change in mood and behavior—weeping and fasting while the child was sick and then rising and eating when the child was dead (v. 21). David's answer is very instructive of how we should react when the Lord's will is done. He said, "While the child was yet alive, I fasted and wept: for I said, Who can tell whether God will be gracious to me, that the child may live? But now he is dead, wherefore should I fast? can I bring him back again? I shall go to him, but he shall not return to me" (vv. 22–23). I doubt seriously whether I could accept the loss of my child so quickly. But David's words are very true, and the best we can do in such a situation is to live our lives so that "we can go to them" in the celestial worlds where they have gone.

● **2 Samuel 12:24 A second son, Solomon, is born to David and Bathsheba.** The Lord was gracious to David and Bathsheba by giving them a second son soon after the first. And as the Lord had prophesied to David in the matter of building the temple, they called the child Solomon, "and the Lord loved him."

TRAGEDY IN THE HOUSE OF DAVID

The Fruits of David's Sins in His Family

Nathan had prophesied to David that sin and death would be part of his own family: "Now therefore the sword shall never depart from thine house. … I will raise up evil against thee out of thine own house, and I will take thy wives before thine eyes, and give them unto thy neighbour, and he shall lie with thy wives in the sight of this sun" (2 Samuel 12:10–12). As we move into the 13th chapter of 2 Samuel, we see the beginning of those tragedies.

- **2 Samuel 13:1–22 The tragedy of Tamar.** Tamar was the lovely daughter of David by his wife Maacah. She was the half-sister of Amnon, who, as David's eldest son through Ahinoam, was crown prince and heir to David's throne. Amnon felt a consuming lust for his sister Tamar, and like his father had done with Bathsheba, he gave in to his passions. Then, once he had gratified his lust, Amnon despised Tamar (v. 15) and she mourned (v. 19–20). David was furious with Amnon, but because of his own sins he did not act to correct this sin.

Amnon raped his sister Tamar

- **2 Samuel 13:23–39 Absalom sought revenge for the wrong done to his sister.** He concealed his rage for two years, then invited King David and all his sons to a feast. David declined the invitation, fearing the entire court would be a burden on his son, but he sent his eldest son, Amnon, the apparent heir to the throne (vv. 25–27). As the feast progressed, Amnon became "merry with wine" (v. 28). Absalom gave the signal, and his servants swept down and killed Amnon. Absalom then escaped to his grandfather's home in Geshur.

The Rebellion and Death of Absalom

Absalom was David's handsome, talented, but rebellious third son, by his wife Maacah, the daughter of Talmai, king of Geshur (2 Samuel 3:3). After having his brother Amnon killed, Absalom fled to Geshur, where his grandfather was king. He lived there three years. (2 Samuel 13:38). Eventually he returned, but David refused to meet him for two years. (2 Samuel 14:24, 28, 33).

- **2 Samuel 15:1–6 Absalom flatters David's people and "steals their hearts."** As the king's son, "Absalom prepared him chariots and horses, and fifty men to run before him" (v. 1). He would also stand beside the gate of the city and stop people who were coming to counsel with his father

David. He would tell them that "there is no man deputed of the king to hear thee" (v. 3), and that if he "were made judge in the land, that every man which hath any suit or cause might come unto me, and I would do him justice!" (v. 4). If anybody came before him to "do obeisance," he would take them by the hand and kiss them (as if he cared very deeply for them) (v. 5). Through all these flattering actions, "Absalom stole the hearts of the men of Israel" (v. 6).

● **2 Samuel 15:7–11 Absalom raises an army and captures Hebron.** After 40 years of such flattery, Absalom decided it was time to act. He went to his father and said, "I pray thee, let me go and pay my vow, which I have vowed unto the Lord, in Hebron" (v. 7). He claimed to have made a vow while he was in hiding in Syria that "If the Lord shall bring me again indeed to Jerusalem, then I will serve the Lord" (v. 8). His father, of course, bid him to "go in peace," and "he arose, and went to Hebron" (v. 9). But what he really had in mind was deposing his father the king. He "sent spies throughout all the tribes of Israel, saying, As soon as ye hear the sound of the trumpet, then ye shall say, Absalom reigneth in Hebron" (v. 10). He took 200 of his father's troops with him, though they had no idea what he had in mind (v. 11).

● **2 Samuel 15:12–37 Absalom then captured Jerusalem and usurped his father's throne.** The conspiracy of Absalom was strong and serious because "the people increased continually" that were following him (v. 12). Among those he recruited was Ahithophel, one of David's military counselors, and when David heard it he hoped and prayed that his counsel would not help the conspiracy (v. 31).

● **2 Samuel 15:32–37 David recruits Hushai to spy on Absalom.** Hushai had intended to defect to David's side, but was convinced by David to "return to the city, and say unto Absalom, I will be thy servant, O king; as I have been thy father's servant hitherto, so will I now also be thy servant" (v. 34). By this means, David hoped to "defeat the counsel of Ahithophel" (v. 34). Whatever Hushai heard he was to tell to the priests Zadok and Abiathar, and have their sons come and report it to David (vv. 35–36).

● **Psalm 55 A psalm of David, expressing his feelings over Absalom's revolt.** Note especially the following verses:

> "For it was not an enemy that reproached me; then I could have borne it: neither was it he that hated me that did magnify himself against me; then I would have hid myself from him: But it was thou, a man mine equal, my guide, and mine acquaintance. We took sweet counsel together, and walked unto the house of God in company (vv. 12–14).

> "He hath put forth his hands against such as be at peace with him: he hath broken his covenant. The words of his mouth were smoother than butter, but war was in his heart: his words were softer than oil, yet were they drawn swords" (vv. 20–21).

● **2 Samuel 15:14–30 David flees Jerusalem to avoid a massacre.** He took with him all his servants and his household, leaving only ten women (concubines) there to maintain the house (vv. 14–16). All these "went forth … and tarried in a place that was far off" (v. 17). More than 600 men from Gath went with him, as well as some "strangers" that were not Israelites (vv. 18–19). Among these was Ittai the Gittite, whom David encouraged to go back. But in Ruth-like fashion he chose to stay at David's side, saying, "As the Lord liveth, and as my lord the king liveth, surely in what place my lord the king shall be, whether in death or life, even there also will thy servant be" (v. 21). They all passed over the Kidron brook (river) and headed toward the wilderness (v. 23). Having crossed the brook in the bottom of the Kidron valley, they then climbed up the slopes of the Mt. of Olives (v. 30). David covered his head and went barefoot as a sign of mourning, as did many of the people. "And they went up, weeping as they went" (v. 30).

Zadok the priest and "all the Levites" carried with them "the ark of the covenant of God" but David told them to take it back to the city (v. 24). David said, "if I shall find favour in the eyes of the Lord he will bring me again, and shew me both it, and his habitation: But if he thus say, I have no delight in thee; behold, here am I, let him do to me as seemeth good unto him" (vv. 25–26). David was always willing to accept the will of the Lord.

David flees Jerusalem thru Kidron Valley

He said to Zadok, "Art not thou a seer? return into the city in peace, and your two sons with you, Ahimaaz thy son, and Jonathan the son of Abiathar. … I will tarry in the plain of the wilderness, until there come word from you to certify me" (vv. 27–28). So both Zadok and Abiathar returned, carrying the ark of God back to Jerusalem, "and they tarried there" (v. 29).

- **2 Samuel 16 Traitors and critics arise.** The sons of Saul were still bitter about their father's loss of the kingdom. Mephibosheth—Saul's son by the concubine Rizpah— apparently believed that with David gone from Jerusalem the kingdom might be given to him. And Shimei, of the house of Saul, cursed David when he and his followers arrived in Bahurim, calling him a "man of Belial," a "bloody man," and saying that God had allowed Absalom to take the kingdom from him because of the way he treated Saul (vv. 5–13). He continued this rant, throwing rocks and dust as they traveled along the road. But David refused to stop him, saying, "It may be that the Lord will look on mine affliction, and that the Lord will requite me good for his cursing this day" (v. 12). Meanwhile, in Jerusalem, Ahithophel continued to counsel Absalom, and Absalom took his father's concubines as wives.

- **2 Samuel 17 Ahithophel's counsel is overthrown by Hushai's.** Ahithophel counseled Absalom to pursue after David while his force was weary and weak and promised to slay "the king only" and bring back his men to join Absalom's army. But when the matter was taken to Hushai, David's spy, he counseled against this. He reminded them that David's men were "mighty men" and lived in the holes of rocks, not with the people. They would be difficult to defeat. Meanwhile, he said, nearly all of Israel already supported Absalom, so he had no need to worry about David. Hushai's counsel was taken, David was warned, and he fled over the Jordan River. When he saw that his advice was not followed, Ahithophel hanged himself.

- **2 Samuel 18:1–8 Civil war breaks out between David and Absalom.** David divided his forces into thirds and volunteered to go at the head of the battle, but his troops refused, saying, "Thou shalt not go forth: for if we flee away, they will not care for us; neither if half of us die, will they care for us: but now thou art worth ten thousand of us: therefore now it is better that thou [support] us out of the city" (v. 3). David's army went forth "by hundreds and by thousands" (v. 4) and met Absalom's forces "in the wood of Ephraim" (v. 6). This was the kind of fighting that David's "mighty men" were best suited for—hand to hand combat in rough terrain. It was difficult fighting because the battle was spread out "over the face of all the country" and "the wood devoured more people … than the sword devoured" (v. 8). They slew that day 20,000 of Absalom's men (v. 7).

● **2 Samuel 18:5, 9–15 Absalom accidentally catches himself in a tree and is killed by Joab and ten others.** In sending his army forth against Absalom, David instructed that Absalom be spared, but Joab ignored his request (v. 5). While riding through the thick woods on his mule, Absalom "went under the thick boughs of a great oak, and his head caught hold of the oak, and he was taken up between the heaven and the earth; and the mule that was under him went away" (v. 9).

One of David's warriors saw it and reported it to Joab (v. 10). Joab wondered why he had not slain Absalom on the spot, for which he would have been richly rewarded. The man responded, "Though I should receive a thousand shekels of silver in mine hand, yet would I not put forth mine hand against the king's son: for in our hearing the king charged thee and Abishai and Ittai, saying, Beware that none touch the young man Absalom" (v. 12). He knew that David would have killed him for doing so, and that Joab "wouldest have set thyself against me" (v. 13).

Absalom's head was caught in an oak

Joab resolved to do the deed himself, taking "three darts [arrows]" with him and "thrust[ing] them through the heart of Absalom, while he was yet alive in the midst of the oak" (v. 14). Then "ten young men that bare Joab's armour compassed about and smote Absalom, and slew him" (v. 15).

● **2 Samuel 18:19–32 Both Ahimaaz and Cushi run to bring David the news of their victory over Absalom.** Ahimaaz, son of the priest Zadok, asked first (v. 19), but Cushi was sent before him. When they arrived with their good tidings, David had just one question, "Is the young man Absalom safe?" (v. 29). Cushi answered that he had suffered the same fate as "all that rise against thee" (v. 32).

● **2 Samuel 18:33—19:1–4 David bitterly laments the death of his son, and cannot be consoled.** "The king was

David lamented greatly over Absalom's death

much moved, and went up to the chamber over the gate, and wept: and as he went, thus he said, O my son Absalom, my son, my son Absalom! would God I had died for thee, O Absalom, my son, my son!" (v. 33). When Joab heard that "the king weepeth and mourneth for Absalom," and that instead of joy for their victory, the day had turned into one of "mourning unto all the people: for the people heard … how the 2king was grieved for his son" (v. 2). They came into the city not as great victors, but stole quietly in like "people being ashamed steal away when they flee in battle" (v. 3). And all the while, "the king covered his face, and the king cried with a loud voice, O my son Absalom, O Absalom, my son, my son!" (v. 4).

David Faces Unrest and Civil War

- **2 Samuel 19:5–16 David bore the tragedy so bitterly that he nearly lost the kingdom by insulting those who had defended him.** Joab said to him, "Thou hast shamed this day the faces of all thy servants, which this day have saved thy life, and the lives of thy sons and of thy daughters, and the lives of thy wives, and the lives of thy concubines" (v. 5). He accused him of loving his enemies more than his friends, "for this day I perceive, that if Absalom had lived, and all we had died this day, then it had pleased thee well" (v. 6). He demanded that David "go forth, and speak comfortably unto thy servants" lest they all abandon him (v. 7). David did arise and "sit in the gate" of the city where he had been hiding, so that his people could come and speak to him (v. 8). But all up and down the land of Israel the rumor spread that "the king saved us out of the hand of our enemies, and he delivered us out of the hand of the Philistines; and now he is fled out of the land for Absalom" (v. 9). Now that Absalom was dead, they wanted to bring the king back to Jerusalem (v. 10).

  David wrote to Zadok and to Abiathar the priests, asking them to "bring the king back to his house" (v. 11). He told Amasa that he would be "captain of the host before me continually in [place] of Joab" (v. 13). And thus he changed their hearts and they said, as if with one voice, "Return thou, and all thy servants" (v. 14). They met David at the Jordan River and conducted him home (vv. 15–16).

- **2 Samuel 19:41–43 A rift develops between the ten northern tribes and the tribe of Judah.** When they saw that David had been conducted over the Jordan by the men of Judah, they asked David, "Why have our brethren the men of Judah stolen thee away, and have brought the king, and his household, and all David's men with him, over Jordan?" (v. 41). The obvious answer was because David was from Judah—"near of kin to us: wherefore then be ye angry for this matter?" (v. 42). The ten northern tribes retorted that "we have ten parts in the king, and we have also more right in David than ye" (v. 43). It bothered them that the men of Judah had taken action without consulting with them, since they were in the majority in Israel.

- **2 Samuel 20:1–7 Sheba leads a revolt of Israelites against David.** Sheba, the son of Bichri, a Benjamite, was a trouble-maker—"a man of Belial." Seeing an opportunity in rift between Israel and Judah, "he blew a trumpet, and said, We have no part in David, neither have we inheritance in the son of Jesse: every man to his tents, O Israel" (v. 1). And the men of Israel responded, leaving David and following after Sheba (v. 2).

David turned to Amasa, his new captain of the host, and commanded, "Assemble me the men of Judah within three days, and be thou here present" (v. 4). Amasa immediately left to do so, but "tarried longer than the set time which he had appointed him" (v. 5). So David turned to Abishai, Joab's brother, saying, "take thou thy lord's servants, and pursue after him, lest he get him fenced cities, and escape us" (v. 6). This he did, taking Joab's men "and all the mighty men" of David, "to pursue after Sheba the son of Bichri" (v. 7).

- **2 Samuel 20:8–13 Joab assassinates Amasa.** By this time Joab must have been seething. David had replaced him with Amasa after he, Joab, had led the effort to restore David to his throne—against Amasa and others who had supported Absalom. Then David had appeared unthankful when he mourned so much for Absalom rather than celebrating their military victory. Now, as they assembled "at the great stone which is in Gibeon," with Amasa at their head, Joab fastened a sheathed sword to his girdle underneath his outer garment (v. 8).

As Joab approached Amasa, he said, "Art thou in health, my brother?" and "took Amasa by the beard with the right hand to kiss him" (v. 9). Amasa did not see the sword in Joab's left hand. Joab thrust it forcefully under his fifth rib, "and shed out his bowels to the ground" (v. 10). Joab and Abishai his brother then pursued after Sheba, leaving Amasa "wallow[ing] in blood in the midst of the highway" (v. 12). One of Joab's men encouraged the others to follow Joab, but they "stood still" with shock over what had happened. So he "removed Amasa out of the highway into the field, and cast a cloth upon him" (v. 12). Only then did "all the people [go] on after Joab, to pursue after Sheba the son of Bichri" (v. 13).

- **2 Samuel 20:14–26 Israelites behead Sheba and end the war.** Joab and his forces returned to Jerusalem, where David made him again the captain of the host of Israel.

- **2 Samuel 20:3 David rejects his unfaithful concubines.** When he had abandoned the city to flee from his son Absalom, David had left his ten concubines "to keep the house." But while he was away, they gave themselves to Absalom to become his concubines. So now David, "put them in ward, and fed them, but went not in unto them. So they were shut up unto the day of their death, living in widowhood."

Abishai rescues the aging David

- **2 Samuel 21:1–14 Some of Saul's sons are hanged to alleviate a famine in the land.** As the famine set in, David believed that it had come upon them "because Saul smote the Gibeonites, contrary to the oath of Israel." So, according to the Biblical record, David delivered up seven sons of Saul to be hanged by the Gibeonites. "If this is true, it was done in [the] days of David's spiritual deterioration. The law would have not permitted sons to be put to death for the guilt of a father or a forefather (Deut. 24:16; Num. 35:33). It cannot have been a revelation from the Lord that either required or approved this deed done 'to avenge the Gibeonites' … This is apostate theology"[18]. David more likely gave them up to the Gibeonites for crimes that they themselves had committed.

● **2 Samuel 21:15–17 David grew old and unable to go to war anymore.** Once again, the Philistines attacked Israel, so "David went down, and his servants with him, and fought against the Philistines: and David waxed faint" (v. 15). He was no longer the vibrant and healthy youth who had slain Goliath. And now, "Ishbi-benob, which was of the sons of the giant, the weight of whose spear weighed three hundred shekels of brass in weight, he being girded with a new sword, thought to have slain David" (v. 16). But Abishai the son of Zeruiah helped David by smiting the Philistine and killing him. "Then the men of David sware unto him, saying, Thou shalt go no more out with us to battle, that thou quench not the light of Israel [meaning himself]" (v. 17).

● **2 Samuel 21:18–22 David's men slay three more "sons of Goliath."** Battles with Goliath's sons continued. There was a battle with the Philistines at Gob, where one of David's men "slew Saph, which was of the sons of the giant" (v. 18). In a second battle at Gob, another of David's men "slew the brother of Goliath … , the staff of whose spear was like a weaver's beam" (v. 19). Then, in a battle in Gath, there was "a man of great stature, that had on every hand six fingers, and on every foot six toes, four and twenty in number; and he also was born to the giant" (v. 20). When he defied Israel, as his father had done before him, "Jonathan the son of Shimea [David's brother] slew him" (v. 21). Thus, in these four battles, "these four … born to the giant in Gath … fell by the hand of David, and by the hand of his servants" (v. 22).

Concluding Events in the Reign of King David

● **2 Samuel 22:1–23:7 David wrote a psalm of gratitude to God for his goodness to him.** David praises the Lord in a psalm of thanksgiving—The Lord is his fortress and savior; he is mighty and powerful in deliverance; he rewards men according to their righteousness; he showeth mercy to the merciful; his way is perfect; he liveth, and blessed be he. (2 Samuel 22:Heading)

● **Psalm 18 may have been written about this same time.** Notice the similarity of David's praises to the psalm written in 2 Samuel 22–23. He closes this psalm with a beautiful testimony of the Lord: "The Lord liveth; and blessed be my rock; and let the God of my salvation be exalted. It is God that avengeth me, and subdueth the people under me. He delivereth me from mine enemies: yea, thou liftest me up above those that rise up against me: thou hast delivered me from the violent man. Therefore will I give thanks unto thee, O Lord, among the heathen, and sing praises unto thy name. Great deliverance giveth he to his king; and sheweth mercy to his anointed, to David, and to his seed for evermore" (vv. 46–50)

● **2 Samuel 23:3–4 The famous "last words of David"** concerning righteous leadership are found within David's 2 Samuel psalm. He quotes the Lord as telling him:

"He that ruleth over men must be just, ruling in the fear of God.

"And he shall be as the light of the morning, when the sun riseth, even a morning without clouds; as the tender grass springing out of the earth by clear shining after rain."

- **2 Samuel 23:8–39 The names of 37 great men who served David during his lifetime are listed here.** Some of the most interesting ones were:

— Adino the Eznite, chief among the captains, "who lift[ed] up his spear against eight hundred" and "slew at one time" (v. 8).

— Eleazar, son of Dodo the Ahohite, one of the three mighty men who fought the Philistines with David. "He arose, and smote the Philistines until his hand was weary, and his hand clave unto the sword: and the Lord wrought a great victory that day" (vv. 9–10).

Tissot's rendition of David's "mighty men" of battle

— Shammah the son of Agee the Hararite. When the Philistines threatened a field full of lentils and the Israelites ran, "he stood in the midst of the ground, and defended it, and slew the Philistines: and the Lord wrought a great victory" (vv. 11–12).

— Three of his mighty men who visited David when he was hiding out in the cave of Abdullam at harvest time. The Philistines were at Bethlehem, making it too dangerous to go to Jerusalem. "And David longed, and said, Oh that one would give me drink of the water of the well of Bethlehem, which is by the gate!" (v. 15). So these three men "brake through the host of the Philistines, and drew water out of the well of Bethlehem, that was by the gate, and took it, and brought it to David" (v. 16). But he would not drink it. Instead, he "poured it out unto the Lord [as an offering of thanks], saying, "O Lord … is not this the blood of the men that went in jeopardy of their lives? therefore he would not drink it" (vv. 13–17).

— Abishai, the brother of Joab, the son of Zeruiah, who "lifted up his spear against three hundred, and slew them" (v. 18).

— Benaiah the son of Jehoiada, the son of a valiant man, of Kabzeel, who did many things, including slaying "two lionlike men of Moab." He also "went down … and slew a lion in the midst of a pit in time of snow" (v. 20). He "slew an Egyptian, a goodly man: and the Egyptian had a spear in his hand; but he went down to him with a staff, and plucked the spear out of the Egyptian's hand, and slew him with his own spear" (v. 21). He became a personal guard to David (v. 23).

- **2 Samuel 24:1–9; 1 Chronicles 21:1 Satan inspires David to number the people of Israel.** This was done purely to satisfy David's own vain ambition. First Chronicles tells us that "Satan stood up … and provoked [tempted] David to number Israel" (21:1). Second Samuel says he numbered both "Israel and Judah" (v. 1). He sent Joab, the captain of the host, on this mission "that I may know the number of the people" (v. 2). Joab wished David well—that the number of his people might increase "an hundredfold"—but he wondered, "why doth my lord the king delight in this thing?" (v. 3). It was contrary to the Lord's will, and both Joab and "the captains of the host" resisted it; nevertheless, "Joab and the captains of the host went out from the presence of the king, to number the people of Israel" (v. 4). The census took 9 months and 20 days (v. 8). "And Joab gave up the sum of the number of the people unto the king: and there were in Israel eight hundred thousand valiant men that drew the sword; and the men of Judah were five hundred thousand men" (v. 9).

● **2 Samuel 24:10–17 The Lord is angry with David for numbering the people.** After finishing the census, "David's heart smote him," and he said unto the Lord, "I have sinned greatly in that I have done: and now, I beseech thee, O Lord, take away the iniquity of thy servant; for I have done very foolishly" (v. 10). This was a national sin, not just a personal one for David. All Israel had participated in it. The prophet in Israel at that time was Gad ("David's seer"), and the Lord sent him with three options (vv. 11–12). None of them were pleasant.

— Seven years of famine.

— Three months fleeing before his enemies, "while they pursue thee."

— Three days' pestilence in thy land.

David felt "in a straight" over these choices (v. 14). Seven years of famine would cause great suffering. He did not want to personally flee before his enemies for three months. So he ultimately selected three days' pestilence (v. 15), perhaps not fully under- standing the depth of suffering his people would experience. It was non-stop for three days, "and there died of the people from Dan even to Beer-sheba seventy thousand men" (v. 15).

When the pestilence reached Jerusalem, "the Lord repented him of the evil" he was doing to all Israel (v. 16). Here again, we see the interpolation of an apostate scribe, to whom anything evil done to Israel was unjustified. So he "blames God" for it. We remind ourselves again that God has no need to repent. David and his people needed to repent, "if it musts needs be, by the things which they suffer" (D&C 105:6).

David pleads for Jerusalem's plague to be lifted

The angel who had been sent forth to destroy the people was standing "by the threshing place of Araunah the Jebusite" (the top of Mount Moriah). "And David spake unto the Lord when he saw the angel that smote the people, and said, Lo, I have sinned, and I have done wickedly: but these sheep, what have they done? let thine hand, I pray thee, be against me, and against my father's house" (v. 17).

● **2 Samuel 24:18–25 David purchases the threshing floor of Araunah.** In an attempt to appease the Lord and stay the plague that was smiting Israel, David purchased Araunah's threshing floor as a place to make a sacrifice. Out of respect for King David, Araunah offered to give the spot to David as a gift, but David refused, saying that he would not make an offering to God with something that had "cost [him] nothing" (vv. 22–24). This is an important principle of sacrifice. If it doesn't cost us something, then it is not a sacrifice. Making offerings is easy when things are going well. But when we have to "pay a price" of struggle and faith in order to do so, then we might expect a blessing equal to our faith. David understood this as he sacrificed on Mount Moriah.

● **The threshing floor of Araunah on Mt.** Moriah was considered a sacred spot by three world religions—Jews, Christians, and Muslims. This rock is carefully protected today.

It is the rock upon which Abraham nearly sacrificed his son Isaac, located at the summit of Mt. Moriah above Jerusalem.

On this same spot Melchizedek built a temple above the city of Salem (peace).

On this same spot Solomon built his temple also. This rock was located inside the Holy of Holies. Upon this stone was placed the Ark of the Covenant, symbolizing the presence of Jehovah. The temple that was present in the days of our Savior's mortal life was also built on the same spot over this same rock.

Upon these same mountains the Son of God—the Only Begotten Son of our Father In Heaven—was also sacrificed. This makes the symbolism of Abraham's near-sacrifice of Isaac quite clear and dramatic.

Today, this rock is located in the center of the Dome of the Rock, which the Muslims built on this spot on the Temple Mount of Jerusalem. They believe that Mohammed ascended into heaven from this rock, making it the second most holy shrine in all the world for their religion, second only to their holy city of Mecca.

The sacred rock on Mt. Moriah, called es-Sakhara today, sits at the summit of Mt. Moriah. The temple of Solomon, and later the Dome of the Rock, were built over it (see below). Over time, the Israelites built several walls around the rock, then filled the resulting cavities in with earth to form platforms upon which the temple and other buildings could be constructed (see bottom right).

Notes

1. Rasmussen, *Introduction to the Old Testament*, 1:185.
2. *The Miracle of Forgiveness* [1969], 113–114.
3. In Conference Report, Oct. 1951, 8.
4. "Cleanliness Is Next to Godliness," *Instructor*, Mar. 1965, 86.
5. In Conference Report, Apr. 1995, 103; or *Ensign*, May 1995, 77.
6. Rasmussen, *Introduction to the Old Testament*, 1:185.
7. Rasmussen, *Introduction to the Old Testament*, 1:185.
8. *Teachings of the Prophet Joseph Smith*, sel. Elder Joseph Fielding Smith [1976], 358.
9. *The Miracle of Forgiveness* [1969], 62–63.
10. In Conference Report, Apr. 1989, 72; or *Ensign*, May 1989, 59.
11. Matt. 12:31–32; *Teachings of the Prophet Joseph Smith*, 356–357.
12. *Mormon Doctrine*, 2nd ed. [1966], 520.
13. *Miracle of Forgiveness*, 195–196.
14. *Teachings of the Prophet Joseph Smith*, 339.
15. In Conference Report, Apr. 1979, 60; or *Ensign*, May 1979, 42.
16. *Gospel Doctrine*, 5th ed. [1939], 434.
17. *Answers to Gospel Questions*, comp. Joseph Fielding Smith Jr., 5 vols. [1957–66], 1:74.
18. Rasmussen, *Introduction to the Old Testament*, 2:40.

CHAPTER 25

King David's Artistic Legacy

(Psalms)

ଚୀଙ୍କ

INTRODUCTION

The Book of Psalms

● **Title:**
The Hebrew name for Psalms was Tehillim, or songs of praise. Our title comes from the Greek psalterion, which is formed from the root pasllo, meaning "to sing".

● **Authors:**
73 of the Psalms in the collection are ascribed to David personally. Superscriptions on some of the other Psalms attribute them to various other authors.

● **Position:**
Psalms is one of 11 books of the Old Testament that belong to the Hagiographa ("sacred writings") of the Jewish canon, along with Ruth, Chronicles, Ezra-Nehemiah, Esther, Job, Proverbs, Ecclesiastes, Song of Solomon, Lamentations, and Daniel.

● **Time Span:**
Written during the reign of King David (his tenure in Jerusalem was generally the third quarter of the eleventh century B.C)..

● **Purpose:**
To express in poetry and song the essence of the gospel and its enduring truths.

● **Length:**
150 chapters (or psalms).

● **Key Sections:**
Anciently the Hebrews divided the 150 psalms into 5 separate books:

— Psalms 1–41, Psalms 42–72, Psalms 73–89, Psalms 90–106, Psalms 107–150.

— At the end of each division, the break was marked with a doxology, or formal declaration of God's power and glory (Psalms 41:13; 72:19; 89:52; 106:48).

— Psalm 150 is itself a doxology, using the Hebrew Hallelujah, "praise ye the Lord," at its beginning and end, as well as the word praise eleven other times. It is a fitting conclusion to the Tehillim, "songs of praise."

WHO WROTE THE PSALMS?

There is some dispute about the authorship of the Psalms. Some believe it was intended to be a collection of psalms without regard to authorship. They point out that David did not author all the psalms with his name attached; they were part of the collection of words and music that he used. The superscriptions on the psalms themselves indicate the following:

Psalms with David's name prefixed 70
Psalms with no superscription. 18
Psalms attributed to Solomon. 2
Psalms attributed to Asaph (a musician in David's court). 12
Psalms attributed to the sons of Korah (Levites). 10
Psalms attributed to Heman (a leader of the temple music). 1
Psalms attributed to Ethan (a leader of the temple music). 1
Psalms attributed to Moses 1
Psalms with song titles 4
Hallelujah ("Praise Ye Jehovah") Psalms. 18
Psalms of Degree. 13

Total: 150

"Seventy-three of the psalms are ascribed to David, and so it was natural that the whole collection would be referred to as his, and that this convenient way of speaking should give rise in time to the popular belief that 'the sweet psalmist of Israel' himself wrote all the so- called Psalms of David. Sacred psalmody is ascribed to him in general terms in 1 and 2 Chronicles, the accompanying instruments also being called 'instruments of David,' as in Nehemiah 12:36 and Amos 6:5. In some cases in which a psalm is ascribed to David in the Hebrew, it is certain that he could not have written it, and it has been concluded that the Hebrew titles are sometimes inaccurate"[1].

The internal evidence in the psalms attributed to him does seem to indicate Davidic authorship. Some reflect some period of his life, such as Psalms 23, 51, and 57. In addition, some psalms are attributed to David elsewhere in scripture:

— Compare Psalm 2   to Acts 4:25–26
— Compare Psalm 16   to Acts 2:25; 13:34–36
— Compare Psalm 32   to Romans 4:6–8
— Compare Psalm 69   to Acts 1:16–20
— Compare Psalm 95   to Hebrews 4:7
— Compare Psalm 109   to Acts 1:20
— Compare Psalm 110   to Matt. 22:44; Mark 12:36, 37; Luke 20:42–44; Acts 2:34

WHY THE PSALMS WERE WRITTEN

David was an artist of deep sensitivity. He danced with joy before the ark of the covenant when it was brought into Jerusalem (2 Samuel 6:14–16). He showed his deep emotions on multiple occasions, including his parting from Jonathan (1 Samuel 20:41), the death of King Saul (2 Samuel 1:11–12), and the death of his son Absalom (2 Samuel 18:33; 19:4). On none of these occasions did he seek to hide his feelings, but expressed them openly and vocally, sometimes to the dismay of the strong men around him. On many of these occasions, David composed psalms—both poetry and music—to fit the occasion.

David composed psalms to fit occasions

David's music and poetry are legendary. He is called 'the sweet psalmist of Israel' (2 Sam. 23:1). He was a skilled performer on the lyre (1 Sam. 16:16–18). He wrote the masterful tribute to Saul and Jonathan upon their deaths (2 Sam. 1:19–27). And he is referred to as a model poet and musician by the prophet Amos (Amos 6:5).

David had many reasons for writing his psalms, but there are some general and repeating themes:

Prophecies of the Messiah

● **Luke 24:44 Prophesies in the psalms will be fulfilled.** The resurrected Savior declared, "All things must be fulfilled, which were written in the law of Moses, and in the prophets, and in the psalms, concerning me."

Prophecy:	Fulfillment:
Psalm 2:6–8.	Jesus will be the Only Begotten of God in the flesh.
Psalm 89:27.	Jesus is "my firstborn, higher than the kings of the earth."
Psalm 91.	Jesus will have the protection of his Father's power. Psalm
107:23–30.	Jesus will calm the winds and the waves (Matt. 8:23–27).
Psalm 69:8–9, 20–21. . .	Jesus will not be received by his own people (John 1:11; 7:5).
Psalm 69:20.	Jesus will suffer alone in Gethsemane (Mark 14:32–41).
Psalm 41:9; 55:12–14. . .	Jesus will be betrayed by a friend (John 13:18, 21).
Psalm 22:7–8.	Jesus will be mocked (Matthew 27:39–43).
Psalm 22:16.	Jesus will be crucified (Mark 15:25).
Psalm 22:18.	The soldiers will cast lots for his clothes (Matthew 27:35).
Psalm 22:1.	Jesus: "My God, why hast thou forsaken me?" (Matt. 27:46).
Psalm 69:21.	Jesus will be given vinegar for his thirst (John 19:28–30).
Psalm 34:20.	None of his bones will be broken (John 19:33–36).
Psalm 31:5.	Jesus: "Into thy hands I commend my spirit" (Luke 23:46).
Psalm 16:9–10.	The Savior's flesh will not see corruption, and will be raised up in the Resurrection (Acts 2:31–32; 13:34–35).
Psalm 68:18.	He will ascend on high and "lead captivity captive."

Psalm 110:4. . . . . Christ is "a priest forever after the order of Melchizedek."

Psalm 118:22. . . . . "The stone which the builders refused is become the head stone of the corner."

A Summary of Other Subjects in the Psalms

● **Praise:** Many psalms speak of praising God by "making a joyful noise unto the Lord" (Psalm 66:1; Psalm 98:4; Psalm 95:1–2; Psalm 100:1)

— Psalm 7:17   David says, "I will praise the Lord according to his righteousness: and will sing praise to the name of the Lord most high." This was his motivation for many of the psalms—to praise God in times of sorrow and in times of rejoicing.

— Psalm 8:4–5   Praises God for his creations and the noble position he gave to man.

— Psalm 82:6   "Ye are gods; and all of you are children of the most High."

— Psalm 23   A psalm of praise for God's protecting care and our eventual exaltation.

— Psalm 24   Is a hymn of praise in honor of God as the Creator and as King of glory.

— Psalm 100   Reminds us that God is good and worthy and deserving of all praise.

— Psalm 121   God is the source of our strength & help in all we do & wherever we go.

— Psalms 145–150   Extol the greatness and the majesty of God.

● **Thanks:** David Asks, "What shall I render unto the Lord for all his benefits toward me?" (Psalm 116:12) His answer includes:

— "I will take the cup of salvation"   (v. 13)

— "I will … call upon the name of the Lord"   (v. 13)

— "O Lord, truly I am thy servant"   (v. 16)

— "I will offer to thee the sacrifice of thanksgiving"   (v. 17)

— "I will pay my vows unto the Lord now in the presence of all his people, in the courts of the Lord's house"   (vv. 18–19)

● **Trust:** "Trust in the Lord" is one of the most common admonitions in the book of Psalms (Psalm 4:5; Psalm 5:11; Psalm 9:10; Psalm 18:2; Psalm 56:11; Psalm 62:8; Psalm 118:8–9)

● **History:**

— Psalm 78:1–8   Israel is reminded of their obligation to instruct their children in the ways of truth.

— Psalm 78:9–72   The doings of the Lord and the children of Israel in the wilderness.

— Psalm 105:1–22   Israel is reminded that they are a covenant people and that God kept the covenant in every way during Israel's early history.

— Psalm 105:23–45 In Egypt and during Israel's wanderings, God was true to his covenant.

— Psalm 106   Israel repeatedly provoked the Lord with wickedness, but God was merciful still.

● **Protection from Enemies:**

— Psalm 7   David prayed for defense against those that persecuted him.

— Psalm 16:1   "Preserve me, O God: for in thee do I put my trust."

— Psalm 18:2   "The Lord is my rock, and my fortress, and my deliverer; my God, my strength in whom I will trust."

— Psalm 31   David expressed confidence in God and pleaded for deliverance from enemies.

— Psalm 59:16   Praises God for his protection in times of trouble.

— Psalm 69   David sought relief from afflictions and asked for judgments upon his enemies.

● **Forgiveness and Redemption:**

— Psalm 24:3–4   "Who shall ascend into the hill of the Lord? or who shall stand in his holy place? He that hath clean hands, and a pure heart."

— Psalm 38   David sorrowed because of his sins and begged the Lord not to forsake him.

— Psalm 51   David pleads for divine forgiveness and mercy and gave to God a broken heart and a contrite spirit—"Create in me a clean heart, O God" (v. 10).

— Psalm 86:5, 13   Praise to God for delivering him from the "lowest hell" despite his sins.

— Psalm 100:4–5   "The Lord is good, and his mercy unto his children is everlasting."

— Psalm 103:2–4,   "The Lord is merciful and gracious, slow to anger, plenteous in mercy."
   8–11, 17–18

● **The Creation of Heaven and Earth:**

— Psalm 19:1; Psalm 104:5–7,14,24; Psalm 136:3–9

● **The Scriptures:**

— Psalm 19:7–11   David's poetic description of the scriptures:

Synonyms include law, testimony, statutes, commandment, and judgments.
Adjectives include perfect, sure, right, pure, true, and righteous.

The scriptures are more desirable than gold and sweeter than honey.

They convert our souls	(v. 7)
They make the simple wise	(v. 7)
They cause our hearts to rejoice	(v. 8)
They enlighten our eyes	(v. 8)
They give us warning	(v. 11)

— Psalm 119 David exclaims, "O how love I thy law! It is my meditation all the day."

We make the scriptures our own & become wise by studying them (vv. 97–100).
They are "a lamp unto [our] feet, and a light unto [our] path" (vv. 105–106).
It is not enough merely to know what is in the scriptures (vv. 111–112).

● **The Temple:**

— Psalm 5:7; Psalm 15:1–3; Psalm 24; Psalm 27:4; Psalm 65:4; Psalm 84:1–2, 4, 10–12; Psalm 122; Psalm 134

— In addition, most of the other psalms are associated with acts of worship in the temple. Some may be classified as hymns, laments, songs of trust or thanksgiving, royal psalms, and wisdom psalms. Quite often a single psalm will include expressions from more than one of these types.

THE MUSIC OF THE PSALMS

David's music was both soothing and exhilarating. King Saul selected him to play the harp for him when the dark spirit of depression overcame him (1 Samuel 16:23). Yet many of his psalms were written to stirring musical arrangements with full choruses. Many psalms provide specific instructions for the music and vocal arrangements to be used. When providing these instructions, David speaks "to the chief musician" who may play them.

● **How the psalms were to be accompanied:**

— In the bass range on stringed instruments ("Neginoth upon Sheminith") (Psalm 6)

— Stringed instruments ("Neginah," "Neginoth")

— Wind instruments ("Nehiloth")

— Female voices ("Set to Alamoth") (Psalm 46)

— Singing in parts ("Set to the Sheminith") (Psalms 6, 12)

— Other titles are probably names of tunes, well known at the time, to which the psalms were to be sung.

JAMES J. TISSOT, 1904

David's music soothed Saul

- **The character of the Psalms:**

  — Maschil means "giving instruction" (Ps. 32, 42, 44–45, 52–55, 74, 78, 88–89, 112).

  — Shiggaion (Ps. 7) with Shigionoth (Hab. 3:1) may refer to an irregular erratic style.

  — Gittith "belonging to Gath" (Ps. 8, 81, 84) may relate either to the melody or to the instrument used in the performance.

THE WORDS OF THE PSALMS

The words to his music were equally profound. His prophecies of Christ are accurate and beautiful. Psalms is quoted in the New Testament more than any other book: 116 of 283 direct citations of the Old Testament in the New Testament are from Psalms.

Poetic Parallelism in the Psalms

David and other Hebrew poets used parallelism—the repetition of a thought in different words. Four kinds of parallelism are used in Hebrew poetry, in which an idea in the first line is related to another line or lines. Such repetition expands or intensifies the meaning of the original idea.

Psalm 78 written in Hebrew

- **Repeating the same idea as line 1 in different words:**

  — Psalm 19:1   "The heavens declare the glory of God; and the firmament sheweth his handywork."

  — Psalm 102:1–2   The same thought is expressed in different words five times:

    • "hear my prayer"

    • "let my cry come unto thee"

    • "hide not thy face from me"

    • "incline thine ear unto me"

    • "in the day when I call answer me speedily"

- **Contrasting an opposing idea to line 1:**

  — Psalm 1:6   "For the LORD knoweth the way of the righteous: but the way of the ungodly shall perish."

- **Completing the idea first presented in line 1:**

  — Psalm 23:4   "Yea, though I walk through the valley of the shadow of death, I will fear no evil: for thou art with me; thy rod and thy staff they comfort me."

- **Repeating the ideas of previous lines, but in reverse order.** This is called chiasmus.

  — Psalm 124:7   Our soul is escaped
  as a bird out of the snare of the fowlers:
  the snare is broken,
  and we are escaped.

Figures of Speech

Figures of speech are also used by Hebrew poets—both metaphors and similes—where comparisons are made between two ideas (e.g., "he is like a pillar"). These can be difficult to interpret since we are not always familiar with the objects used in these comparisons in Old Testament times (e.g., "they shall be as frontlets between thine eyes").

The Antiquity of Hebrew Poetry

Adam Clarke said:

> The Hebrew Psalter is the most ancient collection of poems in the world; and was composed long before those in which ancient Greece and Rome have gloried.
>
> Among all the heathen nations Greece had the honour of producing not only the first, but also the most sublime, of poets: but the subjects on which they employed their talents had, in general, but little tendency to meliorate the moral condition of men. Their subjects were either a fabulous theology, a false and ridiculous religion, chimerical wars, absurd heroism, impure love, agriculture, national sports, or hymns in honour of gods more corrupt than the most profligate of men. Their writings served only to render vice amiable, to honour superstition, to favour the most dangerous and most degrading passions of men, such as impure love, ambition, pride, and impiety. What is said of the Greek poets may be spoken with equal truth of their successors and imitators, the Latin poets; out of the whole of whose writings it would be difficult to extract even the common maxims of a decent morality. …
>
> The Hebrew poets, on the contrary, justly boast the highest antiquity: they were men inspired of God, holy in their lives, pure in their hearts, labouring for the good of mankind; proclaiming by their incomparable compositions the infinite perfections, attributes, and unity of the Divine nature; laying down and illustrating the purest rules of the most refined morality, and the most exalted piety. God, his attributes, his works, and the religion which he has given to man, were the grand subjects of their Divinely inspired muse.
>
> By their wonderful art, they not only embellished the history of their own people, because [it was] connected intimately with the history of God's providence, but they also, by the light of the Spirit of God that was within them, foretold future events of the most unlikely occurrence, at the distance of many hundreds of years, with such exact circumstantiality as has been the wonder and

astonishment of considerate minds in all succeeding generations; a fact which, taken in its connection with the holiness and sublimity of their doctrine; the grandeur, boldness, and truth of their imagery; demonstrates minds under the immediate inspiration of that God whose nature is ineffable, who exists in all points of time, and whose wisdom is infinite.[2]

THE EXTENT OF DAVID'S "TABERNACLE ORCHESTRA AND CHOIR"

Cleon Skousen noted that David established 4,000 Levite musicians among the assigned courses of … Levites" who served in the tabernacle (1 Chronicles 23:5). But his orchestra and choir also included women (1 Chronicles 25:5–6). He notes that Heman's three daughters are specifically identified as being among those who provided "song in the house of the Lord,

Levite choristers who participated in tabernacle rites

with cymbals, psalteries, harps, for the service of the house of God. … " and one of the Psalms also talks about "the damsels playing with timbrels" (Psalms 68:25).

Some of the instruments were made by David himself (1 Chronicles 23:5). Among the instruments used by the musicians were: harps, timbrels, flutes, cymbals and small drums, which, when combined together, made "an extremely impressive orchestral effect which gained great fame in ancient times"[3]. The choral groups, sometimes referred to as "singing men and singing women," joined with the instrumentalists to present the musical part of the temple service. They also combined for festive occasions and provided martial music in times of war. David considered this part of Israel's culture so important that he assigned 268 skilled musicians to train the 4,000 Levites who had been designated as musicians and singers (1 Chronicles 25:6–7).[4]

PSALMS ELSEWHERE IN SCRIPTURE

David's psalms are not the only ones found in scripture. A number of other psalms are found in other ancient and modern holy writ:

— Isaiah 38:10–20   The psalm of Hezekiah.

— Jonah 2:2–9   The prayer of Jonah.

— Exodus 15:1–21   Songs of Moses after the deliverance of Israel from Egypt.

— Judges 5:2–31	The Song of Deborah and Barak.
— Luke 1:46–55	Mary's song.
— 1 Samuel 2:1–10	The song-like prayer of Samuel's mother, Hannah.
— 2 Nephi 4:16–35	Nephi's magnificent hymn.
— D&C 121:16	The Prophet Joseph Smith's moving prayer of lamentation.
— D&C 128:19–23	The Prophet Joseph Smith's psalm about work for the dead.

OUR HYMNS ARE LATTER-DAY PSALMS

Our hymn book today is the latter-day equivalent of the psalms in David's day. And many of our hymns were inspired by the psalms. A few examples include:

— "The Lord Is My Shepherd" 108 Psalm 23

— "Praise to the Lord, the Almighty" 72 Psalm 23:6; Psalm 150

— "How Great Thou Art" 86 Psalm 8:3–9; 9:1–2

— "The Lord Is My Light" 89 Psalm 27:1

— "How Gentle God's Commands" 125 Psalm 55:22

— "Sweet Is the Work" 147 Psalm 92:1–5

Hymns by Modern-day Apostles and Prophets

The writing of inspirational poems and music is widespread among the apostles, prophets, other general authorities, and auxiliary leaders of our dispensation:

— Clayton, William	30, 326	"Come, Come Ye Saints"	Words
— Dunn, Loren C.	137	"Testimony"	Words
— Durham, G. Homer	135	"My Redeemer Lives"	Music
— Faust, James E.		"This Is the Christ"	Words
— Hanks, Marion D.	198	"That Easter Morn"	Words
— Hinckley, Gordon B.	135	"My Redeemer Lives"	Words
— McConkie, Bruce R.	21	"Come, Listen to a Prophet's Voice"	Words (v4)
	134	"I Believe in Christ"	Words
— Partridge, Edward	41	"Let Zion in Her Beauty Rise"	Words
— Penrose, Charles W.	34	"O Ye Mountains High"	Words
	76	"God Of Our Fathers, We Come Unto Thee"	Words
	248	"Up, Awake, Ye Defenders Of Zion"	Words
	336	"School Thy Feelings"	Words

THE BLESSINGS OF SINGING HYMNS

The Savior and the Prophet Sought Solace in Music

- **Matthew 26:30 At the Last Supper, Jesus and his Apostles sang a hymn** to bring peace to all their souls before the Atonement began.

  — Psalms 113–118 were the traditional songs sung at the Passover, and it may be one of these that was sung by Jesus and his disciples at that time.

- **Carthage Jail: At Carthage jail, music comforted the prophet and his brother** prior to their deaths with John Taylor singing of "A Poor Wayfaring Man of Grief."

Singing Hymns Also Blesses us

- **D&C 25:12 The Lord loves to hear us sing.** "For my soul delighteth in the song of the heart; yea, the song of the righteous is a prayer unto me, and it shall be answered with a blessing upon their heads."

The singing of hymns blesses us in many ways:

— Hymns lift our spirits.

— Hymns inspire us to live more righteously.

— Hymns remind us of our blessings.

— Hymns give us an opportunity to sing praises to the Lord.

— Hymns give us a way to bear testimony.

— Hymns help us recommit ourselves to the Lord.

— Hymns help us feel the Spirit.

— Hymns help us be more in tune with our Heavenly Father.

— Hymns help us learn and teach the gospel.

Elder Bruce R. McConkie said:

> Music is part of the language of the Gods. It has been given to man so he can sing praises to the Lord. It is a means of expressing, with poetic words and in melodious tunes, the deep feelings of rejoicing and thanksgiving found in the hearts of those who have testimonies of the divine Sonship and who know of the wonders and glories wrought for them by the Father, Son, and Holy Spirit. Music is both in the voice and in the heart. Every true saint finds his heart full of songs of praise to his Maker. Those whose voices can sing forth the praises found in their hearts are twice blest. 'Be filled with the Spirit,' Paul counseled, 'speaking to yourselves in psalms and hymns and spiritual songs, singing and making melody in your heart to the Lord.' (Eph. 5:18–19). Also: 'Let the word of Christ dwell in you richly in all wisdom; teaching and admonishing one another in psalms and hymns and spiritual songs, singing with grace in your hearts to the Lord.' (Col. 3:16). ... In view of all that the Lord Jesus Christ has done for us, ought we not to sing praises to his holy name forever?[5]

Brigham Young said: "There is no music in hell, for all good music belongs to heaven. Sweet harmonious sounds give exquisite joy to human beings capable of appreciating music. I delight in hearing harmonious tones made by the human voice, by musical instruments, and by both combined. Every sweet musical sound that can be made belongs to the Saints and is for the Saints. Every flower, shrub, and tree to beautify, and to gratify the taste and smell, and every sensation that gives to man joy and felicity are for the Saints who receive them from the Most High"[6].

Music Is an Essential Part of Worship

The First Presidency said: "Inspirational music is an essential part of our church meetings. The hymns invite the Spirit of the Lord, create a feeling of reverence, unify us as members, and provide a way for us to offer praises to the Lord. Some of the greatest sermons are preached by the singing of hymns. Hymns move us to repentance and good works, build testimony and faith, comfort the weary, console the mourning, and inspire us to endure to the end"[7].

Elder Dallin H. Oaks said, "I stopped at a ... ward meetinghouse and slipped unnoticed into the overflow area just as the congregation was beginning to sing. ... As we sang, ... I glanced around at members of the congregation and was stunned to observe that about a third of them were not singing. How could this be? ... What are we saying, what are we thinking, when we fail to join in singing in our worship services? I believe some of us ... are getting neglectful in our worship, including the singing of hymns"[8].

Elder Oaks also said:

> The singing of hymns is one of the best ways to put ourselves in tune with the Spirit of the Lord. I wonder if we are making enough use of this heaven-sent resource in our meetings, in our classes, and in our homes. ...
>
> Sacred music has a unique capacity to communicate our feelings of love for the Lord. This kind of communication is a wonderful aid to our worship. Many have difficulty expressing worshipful feelings in words, but all can join in communicating such feelings through the inspired words of our hymns. ...
>
> Our sacred music is a powerful preparation for prayer and gospel teaching. We need to make more use of our hymns to put us in tune with the Spirit of the Lord, to unify us, and to help us teach and learn our doctrine. We need to make better use of our hymns in missionary teaching, in gospel classes, in quorum meetings, in home evenings, and in home teaching visits. Music is an effective way to worship our Heavenly Father and his Son, Jesus Christ. We should use hymns when we need spiritual strength and inspiration.
>
> We who have "felt to sing the song of redeeming love" (Alma 5:26) need to keep singing that we may draw ever closer to him who has inspired sacred music and commanded that it be used to worship him.[9]

Music Is an Essential Part of Testimony

Heber J. Grant said: "There is a great deal lost in the homes of the people by not having the songs of Zion sung therein. Many a missionary robs himself of strength and power and ability to accomplish good, and to make friends, by not knowing how to sing. ... It is not the eloquence that you possess which will carry conviction to the hearts of the people, but it is the Spirit of Almighty

God that is burning in your hearts, and your desire for the salvation of souls. Brigham Young said that the Spirit of the Lord would do more to convert people than the eloquence of men. And I say that the singing of the songs of Zion, though imperfectly, with the inspiration of God, will touch the hearts of the honest more effectively than if sung well without the Spirit of God. Sing with the Spirit of God. Love the words that you sing. I love the songs of Zion"[10].

President Gordon B. Hinckley said, "I have spoken before of the experience I had as a twelve-year-old boy, a newly ordained deacon. With my father I went to our stake priesthood meeting. He sat on the stand as a member of the stake presidency, and I sat on the back row of the chapel. The men of that large congregation stood and sang, 'Praise to the man who communed with Jehovah! Jesus anointed that Prophet and Seer. Blessed to open the last dispensation, Kings shall extol him, and nations revere.'[11] As I heard them sing that hymn with power and conviction, there came into my heart a witness of the divine calling of the boy Joseph, and I am grateful that the Lord has sustained [it] seventy years since then"[12].

Sister Marjorie Hinckley said:

> On a beautiful Sunday morning in the Fall of 1841, my great-grandfather, William Minshall Evans, then sixteen years of age, was walking down the streets of Liverpool, England, on his way to church. Suddenly he heard singing that thrilled him beyond anything he had ever heard before. He followed the sound down an alley and up some rickety stairs into a room where a few people were holding a meeting. John Taylor, who later became president of the Church and who had a beautiful tenor voice was the singer. The song he sang was so beautiful that William remained to hear the sermon. Upon returning home, William was reprimanded by his elder brother, David, for being absent from his accustomed place in the choir. Asked to give an account of himself, William replied, `I have been where you should have been, and I shall not be satisfied until you all hear the wonderful truth I have heard this morning.' … William and David were converted to the gospel, and then helped convert other members of their family. … I never sing the hymns of the Church without remember- ing that it was the singing of a hymn that opened the door to the gospel for my family and made it possible for me to enjoy all the blessings that have followed.[13]

Notes

1. *Bible Dictionary*, LDS edition of the King James Version of the Bible, 755.
2. Clarke, *Bible Commentary*, 3:208.
3. Peloubet, *Bible Dictionary* [1947], s.v. "Music".
4. Skousen, *The Fourth Thousand Years* [1966], 181–182.
5. *The Promised Messiah: The First Coming of Christ* [1978], 553–554.
6. Speaking at the dedication of a theatre in Salt Lake City on March 6, 1862; In *Journal of Discourses*, 9:244.
7. *Hymns*, page ix.
8. "Worship through Music," *Ensign*, November 1994, 11.
9. "Worship through Music," *Ensign*, Nov. 1994, 10–12.
10. *Improvement Era* , 4:686; *Gospel Standards*, 170.
11. Hymns, 1985, no. 27.
12. *Ensign*, November 1993, 51.
13. *Ensign*, July 1981, 48.

CHAPTER 26

King Solomon's Rise and Fall

(1 Kings; 1–11)

༄༅

INTRODUCTION

The Book of First Kings

● **Author:** Unknown

● **Position:** The books of First and Second Kings are combined as one in the Hebrew Bible but are separated in the Greek Bible, a con- vention retained in the Latin and English versions.

● **Purpose:** To depict the panorama of kingly ascent and descent as a function of the degree of truth and righteousness cultivated by the sovereign. As a backdrop, the spiritual leadership of Elijah serves as a stark contrast to the unsteadiness of royal leadership by providing a standard of enduring faith, undeviating devotion, uncompromising righteousness, and the invocation and implementation of priesthood power.

Solomon was wise and wealthy

GUSTAVE DORÉ, 1896

● **Time Span:** From the time of the rebellion of Adonijah (fourth son of David—see 2 Sam. 3:4) (ca. 1015 BC) to the transition of prophetic leadership from Elijah to Elisha (ca. 851 BC).

● **Length:** 22 chapters

● **Key Sections:**

— Chapters 1–11 The rise and fall of King Solomon.

— Chapters 12–16 Turmoil, conspiracy, intrigue, and idolatry reign.

— Chapters 17–22 The ministry of the prophet Elijah and calling of Elisha.

● **Author:**	Unknown
● **Position:**	First and Second Chronicles were counted as one book in the Hebrew scriptures. These records preserve and communicate Israelite history in broad strokes, particularly religious history. First and Second Chronicles (counted as one book) are also one of the 11 books of the Old Testament that belong to the Hagiographa ("sacred writings") of the Jewish canon, along with the books of Ruth, Ezra-Nehemiah (see also counted as one book), Esther, Job, Psalms, Proverbs, Ecclesiastes, Song of Solomon, Lamentations, and Daniel.
● **Purpose:**	With First Chronicles, to provide a concise history of the Lord's peoples from Adam down to the return of the Jews to Palestine, with an emphasis on religious events and themes, especially temple worship. Second Chronicles more specifically recounts the reign of Solomon—in particular the building of the temple—and the division of the kingdom into two parts (Judah and Israel).
● **Time Span:**	The death of David and the assumption of the throne by Solomon (ca. 1015 BC) to the Babylonian conquest and subsequent decree of Cyrus authorizing the Jews to return to Palestine (537 BC).
● **Length:**	36 chapters
● **Key Sections:**	— Chapters 1–9 The reign of Solomon and the building of the temple
	— Chapters 10–28 Division of the kingdom into two parts, Judah and Israel
	— Chapters 29–32 The righteous reign of Hezekiah
	— Chapters 33–35 Decline under Manasseh and restoration under Josiah
	— Chapter 36 The Babylonian conquest of Judah and subsequent decree of Cyrus permitting Judah to return to rebuild Jerusalem and the temple.

THE RISE OF SOLOMON

The Last Days of King David

● **1 Chronicles 22:7–10 Solomon was chosen by God.** As he approached the end of his life, King David said to his son Solomon, "My son, as for me, it was in my mind to build an house unto the name of the Lord my God: But the word of the Lord came to me, saying, Thou hast shed blood abundantly, and hast made great wars: thou shalt not build an house unto my name, because thou hast shed much blood upon the earth in my sight" (vv. 7–8). Instead, the Lord promised David, "Behold, a son shall be born to thee, who shall be a man of rest; and I will give him rest from all his enemies round about: for his name shall be Solomon, and I will give peace and quietness unto Israel in his days" (v. 9). "He shall build an house for my name; and he shall be my son, and I will be his father; and I will establish the throne of his kingdom over Israel for ever" (v. 10).

- **1 Kings 1:1–4 David becomes old and cold.** As David became increasingly "stricken in years … he gat no heat" (v. 1). To solve the problem his servants sought for "a young virgin" who could "stand before the king, and … cherish him, and let her lie in thy bosom, that my lord the king may get heat" (v. 2). They sought for a "fair damsel" through all of Israel, and selected "Abishag a Shunammite" for the task (v. 3). She was "very fair" and "cherished the king, and ministered to him," but there was nothing sexual in their rela- tionship—"the king knew her not" (v. 4).

- **1 Kings 1:5–10 David's son Adonijah attempts to become king of Israel.** David had already experienced the sorrow of a son seeking power when Absalom rose up to challenge him and ended up dying in battle. Now another son, "Adonijah the son of Haggith exalted himself, saying, I will be king: and he prepared him chariots and horsemen, and fifty men to run before him" (v. 5). David did not discourage this activity, and Adonijah was "a very goodly [good-looking] man" (v. 6). He won the loyalty of Joab, who had defended David against Absalom but now sided with this other son. And so did Abiathar the priest (v. 7). But "Zadok the priest, and Benaiah the son of Jehoiada, and Nathan the prophet, and Shimei, and Rei, and the mighty men which belonged to David" all remained loyal to David (v. 8). When Adonijah offered sacrifice in symbolism of his claim to kingship, he "called all his brethren the king's sons, and all the men of Judah the king's servants" to join him (v. 9). But he did not invite "Nathan the prophet, and Benaiah, and the mighty men, and Solomon his brother" (v. 10). Adonijah's intention was to have Abiathar the priest anoint him king at this solemn ceremony.

- **1 Kings 1:10–27 Bathsheba and Nathan inform David of Adonijah's actions.** Becoming aware of what Adonijah was doing, "Nathan spake unto Bath-sheba the mother of Solomon, saying, Hast thou not heard that Adonijah the son of Haggith doth reign, and David our lord knoweth it not? Now therefore come, let me, I pray thee, give thee counsel, that thou mayest save thine own life, and the life of thy son Solomon" (v. 12). He advised her to go to David and tell him what Adonijah was doing (v. 13). This she did, concluding with the news that "he hath slain oxen and fat cattle and sheep in abundance, and hath called all the sons of the king, and Abiathar the priest, and Joab the captain of the host: but Solomon thy servant hath he not called" (vv. 14–19). She reminded her husband King David that "the eyes of all Israel are upon thee, that thou shouldest tell them who shall sit on the throne of my lord the king after him.

Otherwise it shall come to pass, when my lord the king shall sleep with his fathers, that I and my son Solomon shall be counted offenders" (vv. 20–21). The prophet Nathan then came and told David the same things (vv. 22–27).

Solomon Becomes King

● **1 Kings 1:28–40 David crowns Solomon king.** David reacted immediately, promising Bathsheba that he would "certainly do this day" what he had said he would do with his son Solomon (vv. 28–31). He called "Zadok the priest, and Nathan the prophet, and Benaiah the son of Jehoiada" to come before him (v. 32). Then he instructed them to "take with you the servants of your lord, and cause Solomon my son to ride upon mine own mule, and bring him down to Gihon [a spring in the valley below Jerusalem]" (v. 33). And there, David commanded, "let Zadok the priest and Nathan the prophet anoint him there king over Israel: and blow ye with the trumpet, and say, God save king Solomon" (v. 34). Then they were to bring him up to David's palace "that he may come and sit upon my throne; for he shall be king in my stead: and I have appointed him to be ruler over Israel and over Judah" (v. 35). By this means, Solomon would be made king even before David's death—an unusual step but a necessary one under these circumstances.

JAMES J. TISSOT, 1904

David put Solomon on the throne

These faithful servants of David did precisely as he had requested (vv. 36–38). "Zadok the priest took an horn of oil out of the tabernacle, and anointed Solomon" at the Gihon Spring. "And they blew the trumpet; and all the people said, God save king Solomon" (v. 39). Then "all the people came up after him, and the people piped with pipes, and rejoiced with great joy, so that the earth rent with the sound of them" (v. 40).

● **1 Kings 1:41–53 Adonijah, fearing for his life, abandons his claims to kingship.** Adonijah and all the guests that were with him heard the noise of celebration for Solomon while they were eating their post-sacrificial meal, and they wondered what it was all about (v. 41). Then "Jonathan the son of Abiathar the priest came" and informed them that "our lord king David hath made Solomon king" (v. 43). He also reported that Solomon had been anointed by "Zadok the priest, and Nathan the prophet," and that he was supported by "Benaiah the son of Jehoiada, and the Cherethites, and the Pelethites"—all of whom had "caused him to ride upon the king's mule" (vv. 44–45). And now, "Solomon sitteth on the throne of the kingdom" (v. 46). This was not good news for these conspirators. They could lose their lives for going contrary to their king—either David or Solomon. "And all the guests that were with Adonijah were afraid, and rose up, and went every man his way" (v. 49).

Fearing for his life, Adonijah went immediately to the tabernacle and "caught hold on the horns of the altar"—an act which would keep him from being slain so long as he was on that sacred spot (v. 50). And there he pleaded, "Let king Solomon swear unto me to day that he will not slay his servant with the sword" (v. 51). When Solomon heard of it, he responded "If he will shew himself a worthy man, there shall not an hair of him fall to the earth: but if wickedness shall be found in him, he shall die" (v. 52). Then, "Solomon sent, and they brought him down from the altar. And he came and bowed himself to king Solomon: and Solomon said unto him, Go to thine house" (v. 53).

- **1 Chronicles 29:20–25 David presents Solomon to the people as their new king.** He commanded the people to "bless the Lord your God. And all the congregation blessed the Lord God of their fathers, and bowed down their heads, and worshipped the Lord, and the king" (v. 20). They participated in the sacrifice of "a thousand bullocks, a thousand rams, and a thousand lambs," along with "drink offerings, and sacrifices in abundance for all Israel" (v. 21). Then with all the abundance of meat from these offerings, they "did eat and drink before the Lord on that day with great gladness.

Then David went through a second crowning ceremony for Solomon, this time in front of all of the people, where he caused him to be "anointed … unto the Lord to be the chief governor, and Zadok to be priest" (v. 22). "Then Solomon sat on the throne of the Lord as king instead of David his father, and prospered; and all Israel obeyed him. And all the princes, and the mighty men, and all the sons likewise of king David, submitted themselves unto Solomon the king. And the Lord magnified Solomon exceedingly in the sight of all Israel, and bestowed upon him such royal majesty as had not been on any king before him in Israel" (vv. 23–25).

David Advises Solomon

- **1 Kings 2:1–4 David counsels Solomon to reign righteously.** He knew that he would soon die, so he gave some final advice to his son (v. 1). "I go the way of all the earth: be thou strong therefore, and shew thyself a man; and keep the charge of the Lord thy God, to walk in his ways, to keep his statutes, and his commandments, and his judgments, and his testimonies, as it is written in the law of Moses, that thou mayest prosper in all that thou doest, and whithersoever thou turnest thyself: That the Lord may continue his word which he spake concerning me, saying, If thy children take heed to their way, to walk before me in truth with all their heart and with all their soul, there shall not fail thee (said he) a man on the throne of Israel" (vv. 2–4).

- **1 Kings 2:5–6 David advises Solomon to take vengeance on Joab for his traitorous and murderous behavior.** He reminded Solomon that Joab (1) had been disrespectful and disloyal to King David, (2) had slain Abner out of anger, and (3) had slain Amasa out of jealousy when David appointed him instead of Joab to lead his army (v. 5). In all of these cases, he had "shed the blood of war in peace," killing men not in battle but for his own anger and revenge (v. 5). "Do therefore according to thy wisdom," counseled David, "and let not his hoar head go down to the grave in peace" (v. 6).

- **1 Kings 2:7 David advises Solomon to show kindness to those who protected him while in exile from his son Absalom.** He specifically names "the sons of Barzillai the Gileadite," who he asks Solomon to allow to "be of those that eat at thy table: for so they came to me when I fled because of Absalom thy brother."

- **1 Kings 2:5–6 David advises Solomon to punish Shimei, who had cursed him while he was in exile from Absalom.** Shimei was of the family of Saul, and had accused David of being "a bloody man" (2 Samuel 16:8). He had thrown rocks at David, cursed him, and wished that Absalom would destroy him. Afterward, Shimei "came down to meet me [David] at Jordan, and I sware to him by the Lord, saying, I will not put thee to death with the sword" (v. 8). David had kept his promise. But now he advised Solomon to "hold him not guiltless … but his hoar head [in his old age] bring thou down to the grave with blood" (v. 9).

It may seem vengeful for David to seek punishment for his mortal enemies after he had gone. But remember that he is giving advice here to his son Solomon on how to preserve peace and stability in the kingdom. David had learned that traitors can bring much bloodshed upon the people through their selfish seeking for power. He is advising his son not to tolerate such intrigue and disloyalty. He said to him, "thou art a wise man, and knowest what thou oughtest to do" (v. 9). But like any good father, he gave him some final advice about who he could and could not trust.

- **1 Kings 2:10–11 David dies and is buried in the city of David after 40 years of rule.**

THE REIGN OF KING SOLOMON

Cleaning the Royal House

- **1 Kings 2:13–25 Adonijah is slain for seeking the throne through marrying one of David's wives.** With David now dead, Adonijah feared less for his life, thinking he could outwit Solomon and reinstate his own claim to the throne. He sought an audience with David's wife Bathsheba, the mother of Solomon (v. 13). And he said, "Thou knowest that the kingdom was mine, and that all Israel set their faces on me, that I should reign: howbeit the kingdom is turned about, and is become my brother's: for it was his from the Lord" (v. 15). Now, he had a request of her (v. 16). He wanted her to ask Solomon if he could marry one of David's widowed wives: Abishag (v. 17). And she agreed to speak to Solomon on his behalf (v. 18). When she went before her son, he treated her with great respect, seating her on his right hand as "the king's mother" (v. 19). Then she asked him to do her a favor, promising before she told him that he would not say no. And Solomon promised her that he would not say no (v. 20).

Then she said to Solomon, "Let Abishag the Shunammite be given to Adonijah thy brother to wife" (v. 21). She had not thought it through before asking. Solomon explained to her that if he allowed this he would be giving up the kingdom also, "for he is mine elder brother" (v. 22). In other words, if he, as an elder brother, married one of David's wives, then he would have more claim to the throne than Solomon, and he would then reign along with "Abiathar the priest, and … Joab the son of Zeruiah" who had all sought to steal the throne earlier. As his father David had counseled, Solomon could not tolerate intrigue if he were to establish peace during his reign. So "Solomon sware by the Lord, saying, God do so to me, and more also, if Adonijah have not spoken this word against his own life. Now therefore, as the Lord liveth, which hath established me, and set me on the throne of David my father, and who hath made me an house, as he promised, Adonijah shall be put to death this day" (v. 24). He immediately sent one of his captains to Adonijah, who "fell upon him that he died" (v. 25).

● **1 Kings 2:26–27 Solomon removes Abiathar from his priestly duties.** Knowing that he was part of Adonijah's conspiracy, Solomon said to Abiathar the priest, "Get thee to Anathoth, unto thine own fields; for thou art worthy of death: but I will not at this time put thee to death, because thou barest the ark of the Lord God before David my father, and because thou hast been afflicted in all wherein my father was afflicted" (v. 26). He then removed Abiathar from being a priest unto the Lord, fulfilling the prophecy of the Lord than none of Eli's descendants would eventually be left as priests (v. 27). Solomon then made Zadok the high priest in place of Abiathar (v. 35).

● **1 Kings 2:28–35 Solomon administers justice to Joab for the shedding of innocent blood.** Though Joab had been loyal to David during Absalom's uprising, he had not been loyal when Adonijah sought the throne. Thus, when he learned that Adonijah had been slain, he "fled unto the tabernacle of the Lord, and caught hold on the horns of the altar" just as Adonijah had done earlier. When Solomon learned of Joab's actions, he commanded his captain Benaiah to "Go, fall upon him" (v. 29). This he attempted to do, commanding Joab in the name of the king to "come forth," and being rebuffed by Joab, who said, "Nay; but I will die here" (v. 30).

When Benaiah reported back to Solomon, the king said, "Do as he hath said, and fall upon him, and bury him; that thou mayest take away the innocent blood, which Joab shed, from me, and from the house of my father" (v. 31). By this means, "the Lord shall return his blood upon his own head, who fell upon two men more righteous and better than he, and slew them with the sword, my father David not knowing thereof"—namely, "Abner the son of Ner, captain of the host of Israel" and "Amasa the son of Jether, captain of the host of Judah" (v. 32). "Their blood shall therefore return upon the head of Joab, and upon the head of his seed for ever: but upon David, and upon his seed, and upon his house, and upon his throne, shall there be peace for ever from the Lord" (v. 33). All of this was in accordance with the laws of Moses. Benaiah returned to Joab as he clung to the horns of the altar "and fell upon him, and slew him: and he was buried in his own house in the wilderness" (v. 34). Solomon then made Benaiah the captain of his military host (v. 35).

● **1 Kings 2:36–46 Solomon administers justice to Shimei.** At first, he simply sought to keep an eye on him. He commanded him, "Build thee an house in Jerusalem, and dwell there, and go not forth thence any whither" (v. 36). He warned him that "on the day thou goest out … thou shalt know for certain that thou shalt surely die: [and] thy blood shall be upon thine own head" (v. 37). Shimei agreed and "dwelt in Jerusalem many days" (v. 38). But after three years, when two of his servants fled from him to Gath, he went there to retrieve them and bring them back to Jerusalem (vv. 39–40).

When Solomon learned of it, he called for Shimei and reminded him that he had agreed, on pain of death, to remain at Jerusalem (vv. 41–43). Shimei had shown great wickedness in his disrespect to King David and could not be trusted to keep his word (v. 44). His disloyalty was grounded in his belief that King Saul had been unrighteously removed from the throne. But Solomon reminded him that the Lord had promised that "Solomon shall be blessed, and the throne of David shall be established before the Lord for ever" (v. 45). There was no room for intrigue and disloyalty. "So the king commanded Benaiah the son of Jehoiada; which went out, and fell upon him, that he died. And the kingdom was established in the hand of Solomon" (v. 46).

THE WISDOM OF SOLOMON

- **1 Kings 3:2–4 Solomon and his people offer sacrifices in "high places."** (JST 1 Kings 3:2–4). King David had built a temporary tabernacle in Jerusalem and made sacrifices there. But Solomon chose to make his sacrifices in "high places" [on mountain tops], as did his people (vv. 2–3). In particular, Solomon chose to make his sacrifices at Gibeon "for that was the great high place" in Israel (v. 4).

- **1 Kings 3:5 The Lord appears to Solomon and asks him what blessing he desires.** (JST 1 Kings 3:5). While Solomon was in Gibeon making sacrifices, "the Lord appeared to [him] in a dream by night: and God said, Ask what I shall give thee."

- **1 Kings 3:6–9 Solomon asks for wisdom (JST 1 Kings 3:6–9).** He first acknowledged the Lord's goodness to his father David, and that He had placed him (Solomon) on David's throne (v. 6). But he felt inadequate as Israel's king, calling himself "a little child" who didn't know how to behave among the Lord's people —a "people which thou hast chosen, a great people, that cannot be numbered nor counted for multitude" (vv. 7–8). "Give therefore thy servant an understanding heart to judge thy people, that I may discern between good and bad: for who is able to judge this thy so great a people?" (v. 9).

- **1 Kings 3:10–14 The Lord is pleased with Solomon's request, grants it, and adds many more blessings (JST 1 Kings 3:12, 14).** The Lord was pleased with Solomon's humble request (v. 10). He could have asked "for thyself long life" or "riches" or "the life of thine enemies" but did not (v. 11). Instead he desired "understanding to discern judgment" (v. 11). The Lord granted him his wish by bestowing on him "a wise and an understanding heart; so that there was none like thee before thee, neither after thee shall any arise like unto thee" (v. 12).

Then, the Lord also granted Solomon "that which thou hast not asked, both riches, and honour: so that there shall not be any among the kings like unto thee all thy days" (v. 13). Finally, He promised that if Solomon would "walk in my ways, to keep my statutes and my commandments, as thy father David did walk, then I will lengthen thy days" (v. 14).

— Thus, the Lord blessed Solomon with all of the following:

- Wisdom

- Riches

- Honor

- Length of days

— But all were conditioned upon his keeping of the commandments.

● **1 Kings 4:29–34 Solomon was wiser than other men.** The scriptures say that "God gave Solomon wisdom and understanding exceeding much, and largeness of heart, even as the sand that is on the sea shore" (v. 29). This suggests that he was not only wise, he was empathetic of people's problems and understanding of their needs. Indeed, "Solomon's wisdom excelled the wisdom of all the children of the east country, and all the wisdom of Egypt" (v. 30). Considering the vast knowledge that the Egyptians had of many things, this is a significant statement. And the fame of his wisdom spread throughout "all nations round about" (v. 31). "And there came of all people to hear the wisdom of Solomon, from all kings of the earth, which had heard of his wisdom" (v. 34).

Solomon captured some of his wisdom in 3,000 proverbs and 1,005 songs (v. 32). He skillfully used metaphors of trees, beasts, and other living things to make his points (v. 33). Many of those can be found in the books of Proverbs and Ecclesiastes.

● **1 Kings 3:16–28 An illustration of Solomon's wisdom.** The most famous of all the incidents involving Solomon's wisdom is the one involving two harlots, both of whom had given birth to a baby. They came before Solomon to settle a dispute (v. 16).

GUSTAVE DORÉ, 1896

Solomon wisely discerned the baby's mother

The first woman said, "O my lord, I and this woman dwell in one house; and I was delivered of a child with her in the house. And it came to pass the third day after that I was delivered, that this woman was delivered also: and we were together; there was no stranger with us in the house, save we two in the house. And this woman's child died in the night; because she overlaid it. And she arose at midnight, and took my son from beside me, while [I] slept, and laid it in her bosom, and laid her dead child in my bosom. And when I rose in the morning to give my child suck, behold, it was dead: but when I had considered it in the morning, behold, it was not my son, which I did bear" (vv. 17–21).

Then the other woman said, "Nay; but the living is my son, and the dead is thy son." And [the first woman] responded, "No; but the dead is thy son, and the living is my son" (v. 22). And this was the dispute that they brought before Solomon to be resolved.

Solomon could not discern the truth from their competing claims (v. 23). So he turned to a wise strategy. He said, "Bring me a sword. And they brought a sword before the king. And the king said, Divide the living child in two, and give half to the one, and half to the other" (vv. 24–25).

At this suggestion, the true mother of the child reacted, "for her bowels yearned upon her son, and she said, O my lord, give her the living child, and in no wise slay it." The other, whose child it was not, said, "Let it be neither mine nor thine, but divide it" (v. 26). And by this, King Solomon knew who the mother was. He declared, "Give her [the woman who wished the child to live] the living child, and in no wise slay it: she is the mother thereof" (v. 27). "And all Israel heard of the judgment which the king had judged; and they feared the king: for they saw that the wisdom of God was in him, to do judgment" (v. 28).

SOLOMON REIGNS IN SECURITY AND PEACE

- **1 Kings 3:1 He enters into a political marriage with the Pharaoh's daughter (JST 1 Kings 3:1).** Solomon made a political alliance with "Pharaoh king of Egypt" and took his daughter as a wife. This was a common practice in ancient days and even in the middle ages—to marry a daughter of a potentially rival king—making it much less likely that a military assault would ever occur. Solomon "brought her into the city of David, until he had made an end of building his own house, and the house of the Lord, and the wall of Jerusalem round about."

Solomon married Pharaoh's daughter

- **1 Kings 4:2–6 He reorganizes his government to solidify control.** He appointed the following, whom he trusted:

— Azariah son of Zadok the priest.

— Elihoreph & Ahiah, sons of Shisha, scribes.

— Jehoshaphat son of Ahilud, recorder.

— Benaiah son of Jehoiadam, captain of the host (v. 4).

— Zadok and Abiathar as priests.

— Azariah son of Nathan over officers.

— Zabud son of Nathan, principal officer, and the king's friend.

— Ahishar over the household.

— Adoniram son of Abda over tribute.

1 Kings 4:7–19, 22–23 He organizes Israel into twelve districts, which support his government with their donations. Solomon also appointed twelve officers over Israel, each with his own defined territory to govern. These "provided victuals for the king and his household: each man his month in a year made provision" (vv. 7–19). That was no easy task. "Solomon's provision for one day was thirty measures of find flour, and threescore measures of meal, ten fat oxen, and twenty oxen out of the pastures, and an hundred sheep, beside harts, and roebucks, and fallowdeer, and fatted fowl" (vv. 22–23).

1 Kings 4:20–21, 24–25 His people and his dominion are vast, and they live in peace. "Judah and Israel were many, as the sand which is by the sea in multitude, eating and drinking, and making merry" (v. 20). He "reigned over all kingdoms from the [Euphrates] river unto the land of the Philistines, and unto the border of Egypt" (v. 21). It also stretched "over all the region on this side the river, from Tiphsah even to Azzah, over all the kings on this side the river: and he had peace on all sides round about him" (v. 24).

The map at right shows Solomon's kingdom—which constituted the entire extent of the land which the Lord promised to Abraham and his righteous descendants. People from all over this vast territory "brought presents, and served Solomon all the days of his life" (v. 21). All of this vast territory of "Judah and Israel dwelt safely, every man under his vine and under his fig tree, from Dan even to Beer-sheba, all the days of Solomon" (v. 25).

1 Kings 4:26–28 He builds massive facilities for his army. He constructed 40,000 "stalls of horses for his chariots, and 12,000 horsemen" (v. 26). All these officers also participated in "provid[ing] victual for king Solomon, and for all that came unto king Solomon's table, every man in his month: they lacked nothing" (v. 27).

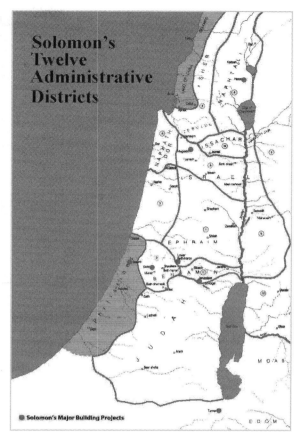

Solomon's Twelve Administrative Districts

● Solomon's Major Building Projects

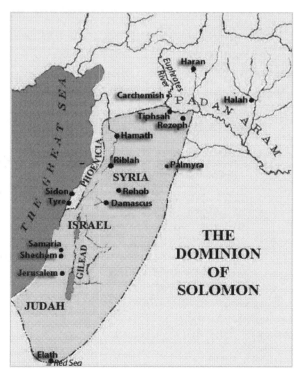

THE DOMINION OF SOLOMON

His facilities stored "barley … and straw for the horses and [camels] brought they unto the place where the officers were, every man according to his charge" (v. 28).

- **1 Kings 9:26–28 He builds an impressive navy.** His ships operated out of the Red Sea port of Ezion-geber, near Eloth, at the head of the Red sea in Edom (v. 26; see bottom of map above). He manned these ships with servants of Hiram, king of Tyre and Sidon, "shipmen that had knowledge of the sea," along with "the servants of Solomon" (v. 27). From this port they sailed to Ophir "and fetched from thence gold, four hundred and twenty talents, and brought it to king Solomon" (v. 28).

SOLOMON REIGNS IN SPLENDOR

Solomon's Great Wealth

- **1 Kings 7:1–12 Solomon builds a splendid palace.** It took 13 years to build it (v. 1) out of timbers taken from "the forest of Lebanon" (v. 2). It was 100 cubits long, 50 cubits wide, and 30 cubits high, resting upon cedar pillars that supported cedar beams (v. 2). There were 45 pillars, 15 in a row, and the cedar roof upon the beams featured windows in all three rows (vv. 3–4). It also featured "a porch of pillars," 50 cubits long and 30 cubits wide, resting upon a fourth row of pillars (v. 6).

  He also built "a porch for the throne where he might judge, even the porch of judgment: and it was covered with cedar from one side of the floor to the other" (v. 7). The residential portion of the palace featured "another court within the porch, which was of the like work," plus "an house for Pharaoh's daughter, whom he had taken to wife, like unto this porch" (v. 8).

Solomon—known for wisdom & wealth

THEBIBLEREVIVAL.COM, #29, 1896

  The palace was faced with "costly stones, … hewed stones, sawed with saws, within and without, even from the foundation unto the coping, … on the outside" (v. 9). All of this rested on a foundation of "costly stones, even great stones, stones of ten cubits, and stones of eight cubits" (v. 10). He also built a "great court round about … with three rows of hewed stones, and a row of cedar beams, both for the inner court of the house of the Lord, and for the porch of the house" (v. 12).

- **1 Kings 9:3 Solomon also builds a temple to the Lord.** His father David had wanted to build a "house of the Lord," but was told that his son would do so instead (1 Kings 8:17–19). So, when Solomon had finished building his own palace he built a splendid house for the Lord as well. And when he had finished it, "the Lord said unto him, I have heard thy prayer and thy supplication, that thou hast made before me: I have hallowed this house, which thou hast built, to put my name there for ever; and mine eyes and mine heart shall be there perpetually." We will discuss Solomon's temple in chapter 30.

● **1 Kings 9:4–9 The Lord's promises to King Solomon.** The Lord promised Solomon that the royal line of his father, David, would not fail if Solomon and his children were faithful (vv. 4–5). "But if ye shall at all turn from following me, ye or your children, and will not keep my commandments and my statutes which I have set before you, but go and serve other gods, and worship them: Then will I cut off Israel out of the land which I have given them; and this house, which I have hallowed for my name, will I cast out of my sight; and Israel shall be a proverb and a byword among all people" (vv. 6–7). When and if this happened, the Lord predicted that "every one that passeth by it shall be astonished, and shall hiss; and they shall say, Why hath the Lord done thus unto this land, and to this house? And they shall answer, Because they forsook the Lord their God, who brought forth their fathers out of the land of Egypt, and have taken hold upon other gods, and have worshipped them, and served them: therefore hath the Lord brought upon them all this evil" (vv. 8–9).

● **1 Kings 9:10–14 He pays his huge debts to Hiram of Tyre with 20 cities in Galilee.** After 20 years of building, Solomon completed his palace and the temple. They had been made out of "cedar trees and fir trees, and with gold, according to all his desire" provided to him by Hirum, king of Tyre. Now, to repay his debt, "Solomon gave Hiram twenty cities in the land of Galilee" (v. 11). But when "Hiram came out from Tyre to see the cities which Solomon had given him … they pleased him not" (v. 12). Hiram called this land "Cabul," which means "displeasing" or "dirty" (v. 13). It was a disappointment to Hiram, who had provided more than "sixscore talents of gold" to Solomon (v. 14). Since a talent is roughly 75 U.S. pounds, each talent would have been worth $840,000 at current rates of $700 per ounce for gold. Thus, "sixscore" (6 x 20 = 120) talents would be worth nearly $111 million, not to mention the value of all the wood he provided.

● **1 Kings 9:15–19 He builds other facilities and "cities in the wilderness."** These included "Millo, and the wall of Jerusalem, and Hazor, and Megiddo, and Gezer" (v. 15). Gezer had been destroyed by Pharaoh king of Egypt, who then gave it as a present to "his daughter, Solomon's wife" (v. 16). Solomon also built Beth-horon, Baalath, and Tadmor in the wilderness (vv. 17–18). These were "cities of store" for Solomon, and "cities for his chariots, and cities for his horsemen," in addition to facilities built "in Jerusalem, and in Lebanon, and in all the land of his dominion" (v. 19).

● **1 Kings 9:20–21 He makes bond servants out of non-Israelite people within the borders of his kingdom.** These included "people that were left of the Amorites, Hittites, Perizzites, Hivites, and Jebusites"—the children of those "whom the children of Israel … were not able utterly to destroy" when they took possession of the land (v. 21). These remained bond servants throughout the reign of King Solomon.

● **1 Kings 9:22–23 He makes the Israelites soldiers, servants, and princes.** They were never enslaved, but they were conscripted as soldiers, captains, rulers of his chariots, and horsemen (v. 22). He also made some into princes, "chief of the officers that were over Solomon's work, five hundred and fifty, which bare rule over the people that wrought in the work" (v. 23). Thus, one way or the other, bondservant or citizen, everyone was required to serve King Solomon.

The Visit of the Queen of Sheba

● **1 Kings 10:1–10, 13 She came to test his famous wisdom with "hard questions."** Sheba was most likely located at the bottom tip of the Arabian peninsula, in present-day Yemen. It was the source of very rare and precious spices, and, according to some ancient traditions, was ruled by a succession of 60 female rulers up to the time of Solomon.

The Queen of Sheba "came to Jerusalem with a very great train, with camels that bare spices, and very much gold, and precious stones" (v. 2). She spoke with Solomon concerning "all that was in her heart," and "Solomon told her all her questions: there was not any thing hid from the king, which he told her not" (v. 3).

Queen of Sheba visits Solomon in his palace

GUSTAVE DORÉ, 1896

When she had experienced "all Solomon's wisdom, and the house that he had built, and the meat of his table, and the sitting of his servants, and the attendance of his ministers, and their apparel, and his cupbearers, and his ascent by which he went up unto the house of the Lord; there was no more spirit [of doubt] in her" (vv. 4–5). She said to Solomon, "It was a true report that I heard in mine own land of thy acts and of thy wisdom" (v. 6). In fact, "behold, the half was not told me: thy wisdom and prosperity exceedeth the fame which I heard" (v. 7). "Happy are thy men, happy are these thy servants, which stand continually before thee, and that hear thy wisdom" (v. 8). She confessed that "the Lord thy God … delighted in thee, to set thee on the throne of Israel: because the Lord loved Israel for ever, therefore made he thee king, to do judgment and justice" (v. 9).

Then, as a present, she gave King Solomon 120 talents of gold ($111 million) along with "spices [of a] very great store, and precious stones." The gift was historic. "There came no more such abundance of spices as these which the queen of Sheba gave to king Solomon" (v. 10). In return, "king Solomon gave unto the queen of Sheba all her desire, whatsoever she asked, beside that which Solomon gave her of his royal bounty. So she turned and went to her own country, she and her servants" (v. 13).

● **1 Kings 10:11–12 Other bounties brought to King Solomon.** The Queen of Sheba's gift was not an isolated event. The "navy … of Hiram, that brought gold from Ophir, [also] brought in from Ophir great plenty of almug [sandalwood] trees, and precious stones" (v. 11). These he used in the construction of his palace and the temple, plus "harps … and psalteries for singers." There had never been, before or since, such a quantity of almug trees in Israel (v. 12).

1 Kings 10:14–29 The incredible wealth of Solomon. The amount of gold that came to Solomon in a single year was 666 talents, which equals $559,440,000 worth of gold (v. 14). This was in addition to all the goods he received from merchants, and all the spices, received from "all the kings of Arabia, and of the governors of the country" (v. 15).

From this stash of gold, he made 200 "targets" [body shields] of solid gold, each weighing 600 shekels, or about 9.3 pounds (v. 16). Since each shekel would be worth $348 at the current value of gold, then each set of body armor was worth $208,800. He also made 300 shields (the kind a soldier would carry to protect himself) out of 3 pounds of gold each, making each worth $33,600 at current values of gold. Thus, just the armor for a single soldier would cost $242,400. Solomon stored all this valuable armor "in the house of the forest of Lebanon" (v. 17).

Solomon's throne was made of ivory, overlaid with gold (v. 18). It was "round behind" with arms on each side of the seat, and two lions standing beside the arms. Six steps led up to the throne (v. 18), with a lion on each side of each step—12 lions in all; "there was not the like made in any kingdom" (vv. 19–20).

"Solomon's drinking vessels were [made] of gold, and all the vessels of the house of the forest of Lebanon were of pure gold; none were of silver." This may seem extravagant to us today, but "it was nothing accounted of in the days of Solomon" (v. 21). Every three years, the store of gold mounted as the king's navy brought to him "gold, and silver, ivory, and apes, and peacocks" (v. 22). "Solomon exceeded all the kings of the earth for riches and for wisdom" (v. 23), as "all the earth sought to Solomon, to hear his wisdom, which God had put in his heart" (v. 24).

Solid gold bowl belonging to Solomon

"And they brought every man his present, vessels of silver, and vessels of gold, and garments, and armour, and spices, horses, and mules, … year by year" (v. 25).

With all this wealth, "Solomon gathered together chariots and horsemen"—1,400 chariots and 12,000 horsemen—stationed in Jerusalem and other cities throughout his kingdom (v. 26).

For Solomon, silver was as abundant as stones, and cedar trees as common as the local sycamore trees (v. 27). Solomon imported chariots from Egypt at 600 shekels of silver ($4, 592) each.

He also imported horses for 150 shekels of silver ($1, 148) each, and "linen yarn ... at a price" (vv. 28–29). He also imported valuable goods from "the kings of the Hittites, and ... the kings of Syria" (v. 29).

SOLOMON'S DOWNFALL

The Lord's Warnings about Kings Are Fulfilled

● **Deuteronomy 17:14–20 Moses' counsel for future kings.** Moses prophesied that after they had settled in the holy land the Israelites would ask for "a king ... like as all the nations that are about" (v. 14). Although it was not a wise thing to do, nevertheless they were permitted to appoint a king if he meets the Lord's standards.

— He shall be chosen by the Lord (v. 15).

— He shall be chosen from among the Israelites, not a foreigner (v. 15).

— He shall not seek to increase his power ("horses") (v. 16). In the ancient Middle East, horses were used primarily in warfare. A king who sought to increase his military power will have forgotten the need to trust in the strength and protection of God.

— He shall not seek to return the people to Egypt (v. 16).

— He shall not multiply wives to himself (v. 17). Kings had multiple wives for political as well as personal reasons. Foreign wives risked an enticement to false gods and were forbidden, "that his heart turn not away." This situation led to Solomon's fall from God's favor (1 Kings 11:4).

— He shall not seek to multiply his wealth (v. 17), which leads to oppression and unjust taxation of the people.

— His basis for rule was to be the law of God. He must obtain a copy of the book of the law and "read therein all the days of his life: that he may learn to fear the Lord his God, to keep all the words of this law and these statutes, to do them" (v. 19).

— He shalt not become arrogant, thinking he is better than the people (v. 20).

— By doing these things he will lengthen the lives of himself and his people (v. 20).

● **1 Samuel 8:6–18 Samuel's warning about Israelite kings.** The idea of having a king over Israel displeased Samuel, and he took the matter to the Lord in prayer (v. 6). The Lord instructed him to "Hearken unto the voice of the people in all that they say unto thee: for they have not rejected thee, but they have rejected me, that I should not reign over them" (v. 7). This had been the tendency of Israel ever since they left Egypt—to forsake the Lord and serve other gods (v. 8). The Lord said to Samuel, "hearken unto their voice: howbeit yet protest solemnly unto them, and shew them the manner of the king that shall reign over them" (v. 9). Samuel did so, listing the evils that kings would do to them:

— "He will take your sons, and appoint them for himself, for his chariots, and to be his horsemen; and some shall run before his chariots" (v. 11).

— "He will appoint him captains over thousands, and captains over fifties; and will set them to ear his ground, and to reap his harvest, and to make his instruments of war, and instruments of his chariots" (v. 12).

— "He will take your daughters to be confectionaries, and to be cooks, and to be bakers" (v. 13).

— "He will take your fields, and your vineyards, and your oliveyards, even the best of them, and give them to his servants" (v. 14).

— "He will take the tenth of your seed, and of your vineyards, and give to his officers, and to his servants" (v. 15).

— "He will take your menservants, and your maidservants, and your goodliest young men, and your asses, and put them to his work" (v. 16).

— "He will take the tenth of your sheep: and ye shall be his servants" (v. 17).

— "Ye shall cry out in that day because of your king which ye shall have chosen you; and the Lord will not hear you in that day" (v. 18).

● **The fulfillment of Samuel's prophecies during the reign of Solomon:**

— 1 Kings 9:22	Israel's sons were called to be men of war.
— 1 Kings 10:26	Many horses and chariots were gathered for war.
— 1 Kings 4:21–28	The Israelites had to raise crops for Solomon and his army.
— 1 Kings 9:11	Solomon gave cities & land to those who did things for him.
— 1 Kings 4:22–23, 26–28	Food and supplies for officers and servants came from the people of Israel.

● **1 Kings 5:13–18 Solomon used conscripted labor to build elaborate buildings and the temple.** He built splendid cities, mistaking his own greed for national pride. His policies eventually left his whole nation in debt.

— He raised a levy [conscripted workers] out of all Israel of 30,000 men (v. 13).

— He rotated these workers in Lebanon, 10,000 at a time, every 3 months (v. 14).

— He also had 70,000 men who bore burdens and 80,000 men hewing stone (v. 15).

— He had 3,300 men who supervised the work (v. 16).

— They hauled "great stones, costly stones, and hewed stones" for the foundation (v. 17).

— Solomon's and Hiram's skilled workers hewed these stones and squared them (v. 18).

— They also skillfully prepared timber from Lebanon "to build the house" (v. 18).

- **1 Kings 9:20–23 Solomon also used slave labor.** Amorites, Hittites, Perizzites, Hivites, and Jebusites, who lived among the Israelites, were forced to do "bondservice" in Solomon's building program.

- **1 Kings 11:1–3 Solomon married 1,000 women outside the covenant.** He loved and married "many strange women" in addition to the daughter of Pharaoh: "women of the Moabites, Ammonites, Edomites, Zidonians, and Hittites" (v. 1).

These were women from among nations the Lord had forbidden the Israelites to marry, "for surely they will turn away your heart after their gods" (v. 2). Ignoring this commandment, Solomon married 700 wives who became his "princesses" and 300 concubines (v. 3).

Solomon had 1,000 wives & concubines

- **1 Kings 11:4–11 His foreign wives turned his heart to idolatry.** We are told that "when Solomon was old, that his wives turned away his heart after other gods"—the gods of his wives from foreign lands. Thus, "his heart was not perfect with the Lord his God, as was the heart of David his father" (v. 4).

Amoowledge and witness of the Lord was sure—the Lord had appeared unto him twice. And the Lord "had commanded him concerning this thing, that he should not go after other gods" (v. 10). Yet, in his old age, he did.

Solomon sacrificed to idol gods

Divisions and Adversaries Arise

- **1 Kings 11:11–13 Solomon's kingdom will be divided.** Because of what Solomon did in worshiping false gods, the Lord prophesied that He would "surely rend the kingdom from thee, and will give it to thy servant" (v. 11). This would not be done during Solomon's lifetime because of the promises the Lord had made to David; "but I will rend it out of the hand of thy son" (v. 12). And because of the Lord's promises to David, Solomon's kingdom would not be totally taken from his son, "but [I] will give one tribe to thy son for David my servant's sake, and for Jerusalem's sake which I have chosen" (v. 13). The rest of the tribes will be given to Solomon's servant (v. 11).

- **1 Kings 11:14–25 Adversaries arise against Solomon.** The first adversary was Hadad the Edomite, who was of royal blood in Edom (v. 14). When David and Joab had "smitten every male in Edom," this man, who was still a child, escaped into Egypt (vv. 15–17). While there he received land, a home, and "great favour in the sight of Pharaoh, so that he gave him to wife the sister of his own wife, the sister of Tahpenes the queen" (vv. 18–19). They had a son there named Genubath, who was raised "among the sons of Pharaoh" (v. 20). Now, when Hadad heard "that David slept with his fathers, and that Joab the captain of the host was dead," he asked the Pharaoh for leave to return home (vv. 21–22). He returned in time to become an adversary of Solomon.

Another adversary was Rezon the son of Eliadah. When David slew Hadadezer, king of Zobah, this man, Rezon, who was a servant of Hadadezer, "became captain over a band" and "went to Damascus, and dwelt therein, and reigned in Damascus" (vv. 23–24). Though Damascus and Syria were part of the territory of Solomon's kingdom, Rezon was "an adversary to Israel all the days of Solomon, … and he abhorred Israel, and reigned over Syria" (v. 25).

- **1 Kings 11:41–43 Solomon dies after reigning 40 years over all Israel (v. 42).** The complete record of his wisdom and his actions was recorded in "the acts of Solomon," a book which we do not have (v. 41). He died and was buried in the city of David, and his son Rehoboam "reigned in his stead" (v. 43).

CHAPTER 27

Israel Is Divided and Sinks into Apostasy and Captivity

(1 Kings 12–16; 2 Kings 1–24; 2 Chronicles 12–20)

❧❦

INTRODUCTION

The Decline and Death of Solomon

Solomon ended his life caught up in wealth and idolatry because he had broken commandments he had been given directly from the Lord (1 Kings 11:2–11). Early in his reign, Solomon married the daughter of the king of Egypt, which was probably a political marriage to protect him from invasion by the Egyptians (1 Kings 3:1). The Joseph Smith Transla- tion says "the Lord was not pleased with Solomon" because of this marriage, and thereafter blessed him "for the people's sake only" (JST 1 Kings 3:1). He went on to marry other non-Israelite women, for he "loved many [foreign] women." This may be an understatement. He had 700 wives and 300 concubines (1 Kings 11:1, 3). Eventually, he began to worship his wives' many gods and declined in righteousness (1 Kings 11:5–8).

Solomon entered into 1,000 marriages

To support the building of the temple, his palace, and his empire, Solomon imposed heavy taxation and forced labor on his people, creating great resentment (1 Kings 12:1–29). Then he died after reigning 40 years over all of Israel and left his son Rehoboam sitting on the throne.

A New King of Israel (The Northern Tribes) Is Designated

● **1 Kings 11:26–31 Jeroboam is singled out by God (through the prophet Ahijah) to rule the northern ten tribes.** Jeroboam was the son of Nebat and was an Ephrathite (resident of Ephrath, the earlier name of Bethlehem). He was also Solomon's servant (v. 26). Jeroboam was a "mighty man of valour," and Solomon could see that he was industrious; so "he made him ruler over all … the house of Joseph" (v. 28). As he made his way out of Jerusalem toward his assignment among the northern tribes, he was met by the prophet Ahijah (v. 29). Jeroboam was wearing a new garment, and the prophet took it and tore it into twelve pieces (v. 30). Then he said to Jeroboam, "Take thee ten pieces: for thus saith the Lord, the God of Israel, Behold, I will rend the kingdom out of the hand of Solomon, and will give ten tribes to thee" (v. 31).

- **1 Kings 11:40 Jeroboam flees into Egypt to escape the wrath of Solomon, who, when he heard of Ahijah's prophecy, sought to have Jeroboam killed.** Jeroboam remained in Egypt until the death of Solomon.

ISRAEL IS DIVIDED

The Northern Ten Tribes Revolt

- **1 Kings 12:1 Rehoboam becomes king of all Israel.** As the son of Solomon, this was his rightful place. All of Israel gathered together at Shechem in order to make him king.

- **1 Kings 12:2–3 Jeroboam returns from Egypt.** He was the prophetically-designated ruler of the northern ten tribes, but was willing to submit to the kingship of Jeroboam. He and all of Israel came to Shechem with a request of the new king.

- **1 Kings 12:4–5 The northern ten tribes ask Rehoboam to lighten the yoke of service Solomon had imposed on them.** They considered Solomon's conscripted service "grievous" and "heavy," and they said that if Rehoboam would make it lighter, "we will serve thee" (v. 4). He invited them to depart for three days while he considered the matter, and they disbursed (v. 5).

- **1 Kings 12:6–15 Rehoboam increases rather than decreases the burdens his father had imposed on Israel.** In doing so, he rejected counsel from his older advisers and followed the counsel of his younger advisers. The older advisers, men of experience in ruling the people, said, "If thou wilt be a servant unto this people this day, and wilt serve them, and answer them, and speak good words to them, then they will be thy servants for ever" (v. 7). This did not please him, so he sought the advice of "the young men that were grown up with him" (v. 8). These young and impetuous servants, sensing their opportunity to prosper under this young new king, said, "Thus shalt thou speak unto this people … My little finger shall be thicker than my father's loins. And now whereas my father did lade you with a heavy yoke, I will add to your yoke: my father hath chastised

Rehoboam rejected older men's counsel

you with whips, but I will chastise you with scorpions" (vv. 10–11). Rehoboam called the people back together and spoke these arrogant and unwise words to them (vv. 12–14).

The following verse again displays the "God made me do it" mentality of the writer of 1 Kings. He says, "the cause was from the Lord, that he might perform his saying, which the Lord spake by Ahijah … unto Jeroboam" (v. 15). While the Lord had indeed prophesied to Jeroboam that he would rule the northern ten tribes, he did not <u>make</u> Rehoboam respond as he did. That was Rehoboam's choice, born of arrogance and a desire for power. The Lord simply knew what he would do. He did not make him do it.

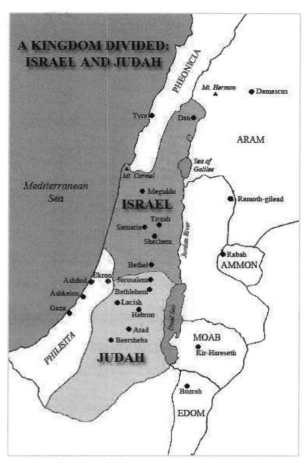

Israel and Judah became two separate nations

- **1 Kings 12:16–19 The ten tribes rebel against Rehoboam and separate themselves.** The phrase "Israel departed unto their tents" refers to the ten tribes separating themselves from Rehoboam's kingdom (v. 16). The people of Judah and Benjamin chose to remain under the rule of Rehoboam (v. 17). When Rehoboam tested their loyalty by sending Adoram to collect their tribute [tax], "all Israel stoned him with stones, that he died" (v. 18). This message was clear, and "Rehoboam made speed to get him up to his chariot, to flee to Jerusalem" (v. 18). And after that day until our own day, Israel was divided into two kingdoms. It will remain so until the Lord returns for His millennial reign as King over all Israel.

The Southern Tribes Remain with the House of David

- **1 Kings 11:43 Rehoboam continued to rule over the Southern Kingdom, called the Kingdom of Judah.** It was composed of the territory belonging to the tribes of Judah and Benjamin (1 Kings 12:20). The Bible does not mention any other sons or daughters of Solomon. Since Rehoboam's mother, Naamah, was an Ammonite (1 Kings 14:21), he was only half Israelite. But his mother's ancestry was Semitic since the Ammonites were descendants of Lot, Abraham's nephew. The house of David continued to govern the nation of Judah until the fall of Jerusalem in 587 BC.

- **1 Kings 12:21–24 Rehoboam is dissuaded by a prophet of God from waging war to reclaim the kingdom.** Determined to reclaim control over the northern ten tribes (Israel), Rehoboam assembled an army from Judah and Benjamin of 180,000 men "to fight against the house of

Israel, to bring the kingdom again to Rehoboam the son of Solomon" (v. 21). But the prophet Shemaiah received word from the Lord, saying to Rehoboam, "Thus saith the LORD, Ye shall not go up, nor fight against your brethren the children of Israel: return every man to his house" (v. 24). Believing the message was from the Lord, they returned to their homes (v. 24).

Both Kingdoms Sink into Apostasy

The remainder of the record from 1 and 2 Kings tells of a long succession of kings in both Israel and Judah. However, the record is difficult to follow since the writer jumps back and forth between kingdoms regularly in a sort of "meanwhile, back in Judah" or "meanwhile, back in Israel" fashion. We will consider each of these kingdoms separately here in the interests of clarity.

THE WICKED KINGS OF ISRAEL

(The Northern Kingdom)

● **1 Kings 12:25–33 Jeroboam sets up idol worship to keep his people from going to Jerusalem to worship.** He built up the sacred site of Shechem as his capitol, and also established Penuel. Then he sought to set up worship sites in Israel as a way of dissuading the people of Israel from feeling the need to go to Jerusalem to worship in the temple there. If they did, he feared that "the kingdom [might] return to the house of David" (v. 26). As the people went to the temple to make sacrifice, "then shall the heart of this people turn again unto their lord, even unto Rehoboam king of Judah, and they shall kill me, and go again to Rehoboam king of Judah" (v. 27).

Jeroboam set up Baal worship in Israel

Jeroboam then "made two calves of gold" [emblems of Baal worship] and said to his people, "It is too much for you to go up to Jerusalem: behold thy gods, O Israel, which brought thee up out of the land of Egypt. And he set the one in Beth-el, and the other put he in Dan" (vv. 28–29). And thus he lead his people into sin as they went to worship these idols instead of worshiping the Lord (v. 30).

Jeroboam built "an house of high places, and made priests of the lowest of the people, which were not of the sons of Levi" (v. 31). High places are altars built on hilltops. Then he "ordained a feast in the eighth month, on the fifteenth day of the month, like unto the feast that is in Judah" (v 32). Then he made sacrifices on an altar at Beth-el, "sacrificing unto the [golden] calves that he had made: and he placed in Beth-el the priests of the high places which he had made" (vv. 32–33).

● **1 Kings 13:1–6 A prophet from Judah curses Jeroboam's altar at Bethel.** The prophet arrived while "Jeroboam stood by the altar to burn incense" (v. 1). He issued a curse against the altar Jeroboam was using, saying, "O altar, altar, thus saith the Lord; Behold, a child shall be born unto the house of David, Josiah by name; and upon thee shall he offer the priests of the high places that burn incense upon thee, and men's bones shall be burnt upon thee" (v. 2). This prophecy was later literally fulfilled (2 Kings 23:15–20). Then he gave a sign to Jeroboam, saying, "the altar shall be rent, and the ashes that are upon it shall be poured out" (v. 3).

● **1 Kings 13:4–10 Jeroboam is smitten and then healed by the prophet.** Jeroboam "put forth his hand" [gestured] toward the prophet and commanded, "Lay hold on him," but when he did so, "his hand, which he put forth against him, dried up, so that he could not pull it in again to him" (v. 4). Then, in fulfillment of the sign he had given, "the altar also was rent, and the ashes poured out from the altar" (v. 5). Jeroboam begged the prophet to ask the Lord to heal him, and when "the man of God besought the Lord, … the king's hand was restored him again, and became as it was before" (v. 6). Jeroboam then invited the prophet to his home, but he refused, saying, "it [was] charged me by the word of the Lord, saying, Eat no bread, nor drink water, nor turn again by the same way that thou camest," and he left, "return[ing] not by the way that he came to Beth-el" (vv. 7–10).

● **1 Kings 13:11–19 An old Israelite prophet persuades the prophet from Judah to disobey the Lord.** "Now there dwelt an old prophet in Beth-el; and his sons came and told him all the works that the man of God had done that day" (v. 11). He asked, "What way went he?" and immediately "saddled [an] ass: and … rode thereon" until he found "the man of God … sitting under an oak" (vv. 12–14). He invited him to "come home with me, and eat bread" (v. 15), but was refused for the same reasons that the prophet had given to Jerobaom: "it was said to me by the word of the Lord, Thou shalt eat no bread nor drink water there, nor turn again to go by the way that thou camest" (vv. 16–17). Then the old prophet lied to him, saying, "I am a prophet also as thou art; and an angel spake unto me by the word of the Lord, saying, Bring him back with thee into thine house, that he may eat bread and drink water" (v. 18). And the prophet from Judah relented, "went back with him, and did eat bread in his house, and drank water" (v. 19).

GUSTAVE DORÉ, 1896

● **1 Kings 13:20–32 The prophet from Judah is slain by a lion for disobeying his instructions from the Lord.** At this point, the Bible record becomes inaccurate, perhaps to embellish the story. It says that, "as they sat at the table, … the word of the Lord came unto the prophet that brought him back," saying, "Thus saith the Lord, Forasmuch as thou hast disobeyed the mouth of the LORD, and hast not kept the commandment which the Lord thy God commanded thee, … thy carcase shall not come unto the sepulchre of thy fathers" (vv. 20–22). And when he departed, "a

The lion stayed by the prophet's carcase

lion met him by the way, and slew him: and his carcase was cast in the way, and the ass stood by it, the lion also stood by the carcase" (vv. 23–24).

"There are some problems in this story … Some help is available in the [JST] verse 18, which indicates that the old prophet said, 'Bring him back … that I may prove him; and he lied not unto him.' Also there is a change in verse 26, in which the last part reads: ' … therefore the Lord hath delivered him unto the lion, which hath torn him, and slain him, according to the word of the Lord, which he spake unto me.' These make the account more understandable and more acceptable. The young prophet should have obeyed God" (Rasmussen, *An Introduction to the Old Testament*, 2 vols. [1972], 2:4).

When word reached Bethel concerning what had happened to the prophet from Judah, the old prophet responded, "It is the man of God, who was disobedient unto the word of the Lord: therefore the Lord hath delivered him unto the lion, which hath torn him, and slain him, according to the word of the Lord" (vv. 25–26). Then he saddled his ass and went to find the body of the prophet from Judah (v. 27). He "found his carcase cast in the way, and the ass and the lion standing by the carcase: the lion had not eaten the carcase, nor torn the ass" (v. 28). He took up the body and brought it back to Bethel "to mourn and to bury him" (vv. 29–30). Then he requested, "When I am dead, then bury me in the sepulchre wherein the man of God is buried; lay my bones beside his bones," because everything the young prophet had said "against the altar in Beth-el, and against all the houses of the high places which are in the cities of Samaria, shall surely come to pass" (vv. 31–32).

● **1 Kings 14:1–6 Jeroboam's son becomes sick and he seeks the help of the prophet Ahijah.** Abijah the son of Jeroboam fell sick and he sent his wife (in disguise) to the prophet Ahijah in Shiloh to find out "what shall become of the child" (vv. 1–3). She did so, but did not need her disguise because Ahijah was blind "for his eyes were set by reason of his age" (v. 4). The Lord had forewarned Ahijah that "the wife of Jeroboam cometh to ask a thing of thee for her son; for he is sick … [and] when she cometh in … she shall feign herself to be another woman" (v. 5). When she entered Ahijah's presence he said, "Come in, thou wife of Jeroboam; why feignest thou thyself to be another? for I am sent to thee with heavy tidings" (v. 6).

● **1 Kings 14:7–13, 17–18 Ahijah curses Jeroboam's family and the child dies.** Ahijah delivered the message the Lord had given him. "Go, tell Jeroboam, Thus saith the Lord God of Israel, Forasmuch as I exalted thee from among the people, and made thee prince over my people Israel, And rent the kingdom away from the house of David, and gave it thee: and yet thou hast not been as my servant David … who followed me with all his heart, … But hast done evil above all that were before thee: for thou hast gone and made thee other gods, and molten images, to provoke me to anger, and hast cast me behind thy back: Therefore, behold, I will bring evil upon the house of Jeroboam" (vv. 7–10). The Lord said he would cut off all males from Jeroboam's family, and "him that dieth of Jeroboam in the city shall the dogs eat; and him that dieth in the field shall the fowls of the air eat" (v. 11). This was an awful curse. Among Hebrews, to be unburied is the worst thing that can happen to a dead person.

Ahijah commanded the woman to "get thee to thine own house: and when thy feet enter into the city, the child shall die" (v. 12). He would be the only one of Jeroboam's kin that would have the dignity of a grave "because in him [the child] there is found some good thing toward the Lord God of Israel in the house of Jeroboam" (v. 13). She returned, and "when she came to the threshold of the door, the child died" (v. 17). And every other thing the prophet had predicted was also fulfilled (v. 18).

- **1 Kings 14:14–16, 19 Ahijah prophesies the end of Jeroboam's reign and the captivity of Israel.** He said to Jeroboam through his wife, "the Lord shall raise him up a king over Israel, who shall cut off the house of Jeroboam that day ... even now" (v. 14). Then, speaking of the future, he said, "the Lord shall smite Israel, as a reed is shaken in the water, and he shall root up Israel out of this good land, which he gave to their fathers, and shall scatter them beyond the [Euphrates] river, because they have made their groves, provoking the Lord to anger" (v. 15). Groves are places of pagan worship on hilltops ("high places") where people engaged in immoral behavior while worshiping Baal and other pagan gods. All of this the Lord would do "because of the sins of Jeroboam, who did sin, and who made Israel to sin" (v. 16).

- **The Jeroboam Dynasty:** (975–953 BC)

  — **Jeroboam** (975 BC) continued his wickedness and was cursed by the Lord. He "made again of the lowest of the people priests of the high places: whosoever would, he consecrated him, and he became one of the priests of the high places" (1 Kings 13:33). And for this sin, the Lord swore to "cut ... off ... the house of Jeroboam [his royal descendants] ... and to destroy it from off the face of the earth" (1 Kings 13:34). Shortly thereafter, Jeroboam died and his son Nadab reigned in his stead (1 Kings 14:20).

  Jeroboam's idolatrous religion continued to curse Israel for many generations. Throughout its 200–year history, no succeeding king ever permanently reformed Israel. Each kept the sins of Jeroboam and did not repent. The chart at right shows the length of Israel's wickedness.

  — **Nadab** (954 BC), the son of Jeroboam, reigned 2 years and "did evil in the sight of the Lord, and walked in the way of his father, and in his sin wherewith he made Israel to sin" (1 Kings 15:25–26). He was assassinated by Baasha the son of Ahijah of the tribe of Issachar. Baasha then "smote all the house of Jeroboam; he left not to Jeroboam any that breathed," as commanded by the Lord to Baasha through his prophet Ahijah. (1 Kings 15:27–30).

- **The Baasha Dynasty:** (953–929 BC)

  — **Baasha** (953 BC) founded the second dynasty (ruling family) of Israel. He reigned for 24 years in wickedness, doing "evil in the sight of the Lord, and walk[ing] in the way of Jeroboam" (1 Kings 15:33–34).

The Kings of Israel

King	Age Reign
Jeroboam	22 yrs
Nadab	2 yrs
Baasha	24 yrs
Elah	2 yrs
Zimri	7 days
Omri	12 yrs
Ahab	22 yrs
Ahaziah	2 yrs
Jehoram (Joram)	12 yrs
Jehu	28 yrs
Jehoahaz	17 yrs
Joash (Jehoash)	16 yrs
Jeroboam II	41 yrs
Zachariah	6 mos
Shallum	1 mo
Menahem	10 yrs
Pekahiah	2 yrs
Pekah	20 yrs
Hoshea	9 yrs

Assyria took Israel captive during Pekah and Hoshea's reigns.

— **Elah** (930 BC), the son of Baasha, reigned 2 years in wickedness. He was slain by Zimri, the captain of his chariots, while in a drunken stupor (1 Kings 16:8–10).

— **Zimri** (929 BC) reigned only 7 days after destroying the entire house of Elah, both kin and friends, as commanded by the prophet Jehu. When the people of Israel heard about Elah's assassination, they appointed Omri, the captain of the armies of Israel, as king. He then besieged Zimri in the king's house. Zimri committed suicide by setting the palace on fire (1 Kings 16:15–18). He was the last king of the Baasha dynasty.

● **The Omri Dynasty:** (929–884 BC)

— **Omri** (929 BC) founded the third dynasty (ruling family) of Israel. He reigned for 12 years—6 in Tirzah and 6 more after defeating his rival Tibni for the throne. He established the city of Samaria as the capitol of Israel (the northern kingdom). He "wrought evil in the eyes of the Lord, and did worse than all that were before him" (1 Kings 16:23–26).

— **Ahab** (918 BC), the son of Omri, reigned for 22 years. He also "did evil in the sight of the Lord above all that were before him" (1 Kings 16:30–33). "He took to wife Jezebel the daughter of Ethbaal king of the Zidon- ians, and went and served Baal." He made Baal and Ashteroth worship the state religion by "rear[ing] up an altar for Baal in the house of Baal, which he ... built in Samaria" (1 Kings 16:32), and making a grove for the sensuous rights of Ashtoreth worship. He built an ivory palace and took Naboth's vineyard by having him killed. During his reign, Elijah sealed the heavens and predicted that, at his death, dogs would lick up his blood.

The death of King Ahab

— **Ahaziah** (898 BC), the son of Ahab, reigned 2 years and "did evil in the sight of the Lord" by following the sins of Jeroboam (1 Kings 22:51–53). He fell down through the lattice-work of his upper chamber and enquired of Baal-zebub, a god of the Philistines, whether he would live. Elijah told him he would die, then called down fire from heaven to destroy the soldiers Ahaziah sent to seize him, and then died as Elijah had said (2 Kings 1:2–18).

— **Jehoram (Joram)** (897 BC), the son of Ahab, reigned when Ahaziah died because Ahaziah had no sons. He reigned 12 years and "wrought evil in the sight of the Lord" (2 Kings 3:1–2). He put away the image of Baal that his father had made, but "cleaved unto the sins of Jeroboam" (2 Kings 3:2–3). He made an alliance with Ahaziah, king of Judah (not the same Ahaziah as above), and they attacked Syria. He was wounded, and returned to Jezreel to recover. While there, Jehu attacked and killed him, along with Ahaziah, king of Judah (2 Kings 9:14–29). He was the last king of the Omri dynasty.

- **The Jehu Dynasty:** (884–772 BC)

— **Jehu** (884 BC) reigned 28 years. He was anointed to become king by Elijah (1 Kings 19:16) and was commanded to destroy all the descendants of King Ahab and all the priests of Baal (2 Chronicles 22:7). This he did, but he did not destroy Baal worship. He "departed not from … the golden calves that were in Beth-el, and that were in Dan," and "took no heed to walk in the law of the Lord … with all his heart" (2 Kings 10:28–31). For his idolatry, the Lord told him that after four generations, the throne would be taken from his posterity (2 Kings 15:12).

Elisha tells Joash to shoot an arrow

HOLMAN BIBLE, 1890

— **Jehoahaz** (856 BC), the son of Jehu, reigned 17 years and "did that which was evil in the sight of the Lord" (2 Kings 13:1–2). He was a poor administrator, and a vassal to the king of Syria all the years of his reign (2 Kings 13:22). As a result, he brought great suffering to Israel.

— **Joash (Jehoash)** (842 BC), the son of Jehoahaz, reigned 16 years and "did that which was evil in the sight of the Lord" (2 Kings 13:10–12). Elisha died during his reign, bringing him great sorrow. Elisha had him shoot an arrow eastward out his window as a symbol of his coming victory of Syria (2 Kings 13:14–19). And he freed Israel from subjection to Syria, fulfilling this promise (2 Kings 13:25).

— **Jeroboam II** (826 BC), the son of Joash, reigned 41 years and "did that which was evil in the sight of the Lord" (2 Kings 14:23–24). Though wicked, he was a very capable leader. He reclaimed all of Israel's boundaries and dominated Syria, which brought back much of Israel's former political power (2 Kings. 14:25–27).

— **Zachariah** (773 BC), the son of Jeroboam II, reigned for only 6 months and "did that which was evil in the sight of the Lord, as his fathers had done" (2 Kings 15:8–9). He was assassinated by Shallum, who then reigned in his stead, fulfilling the prophecy made to Jehu four generations earlier (2 Kings 15:12). He was the last king in the Jehu dynasty.

- **The Last Kings of Israel:** (772–721 BC)

— **Shallum** (772 BC) reigned only 1 month, but did so wickedly. He was assassinated by Menahem, who reigned in his stead (2 Kings 15:13–14).

— **Menahem** (772 BC) reigned 10 years and "did that which was evil in the sight of the Lord" (2 Kings 15:17–18). When Pul, the king of Assyria, attacked Israel Menahem gave him "a thousand talents of silver," to allow him to stay on the throne of Israel. He obtained this money by taking it from "all the mighty men of wealth, of each man fifty shekels of silver, to give to the king of Assyria" (2 Kings 15:19–20).

— **Pekahiah** (761 BC), the son of Menahem, reigned 2 years and "did that which was evil in the sight of the Lord" (2 Kings 15:23–24). He was assassinated by his captain, Pekah, who reigned in his stead (2 Kings 15:25).

— **Pekah** (759 BC) reigned 20 years and "did that which was evil in the sight of the LORD" (2 Kings 15:27–28). During the reign of Pekah, Tiglath-pileser king of Assyria, conquered and took captive the people of Ijon, Abel-beth-maachah, Janoah, Kedesh, Hazor, Gilead, Galilee, and all the land of Naphtali. These he carried away to Assyria (2 Kings 15:29). Pekah was assassinated by Hoshea, who reigned in his stead (2 Kings 15:30).

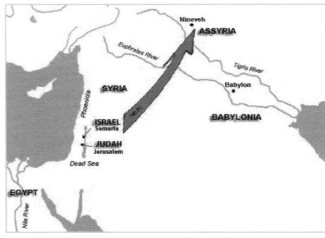

Israel was carried away captive by Assyria

— **Hoshea** (730 BC), the son of Menahem, reigned 9 years and "did that which was evil in the sight of the Lord" (2 Kings 17:1–2). He made a pact with the king of Egypt and stopped paying tribute to Assyria. As a result, "the king of Assyria shut him up, and bound him in prison," then went "throughout all the land, and went up to Samaria, and besieged it three years," finally carrying away all the rest of Israel captive into Assyria in 721 BC (2 Kings 17:4–6).

Elder James E. Talmage said, "After many minor losses in war the kingdom of Israel met an overwhelming defeat at the hands of the Assyrians, in or about the year 721 B.C. We read that Shalmaneser IV, King of Assyria, beseiged Samaria, the third and last capital of the kingdom, and that after three years the city was taken by Sargon, Shalmaneser's successor. The people of Israel were carried captive into Assyria and distributed among the cities of the Medes. Thus was the dread prediction of Ahijah to the wife of Jeroboam fulfilled. Israel was scattered beyond the river, probably the Euphrates, and from the time of this event the Ten tribes are lost to history"[1].

● **The prophets Hosea, Amos, and Micah, all warned Israel** that their sins would eventually destroy the nation.

— **Hosea** warned that the Lord would "yet [in] a little while … avenge the blood of Jezreel upon the house of Jehu, and will cause to cease the kingdom of the house of Israel. And it shall come to pass at that day, that I will break the bow of Israel in the valley of Jezreel (Hosea 1:4–5).

— **Amos** warned that "for three transgressions of Israel, and for four, [the Lord] will not turn away the punishment thereof; because they sold the righteous for silver, and the poor for a pair of shoes" (Amos 2:6).

— **Micah** pronounced curses upon Israel, saying, "I am full of power by the spirit of the LORD, and of judgment, and of might, to declare unto Jacob his transgression, and to Israel his sin" (Micha 3:8). He then rehearsed their sins (Micah 3:8–12). The "princes of the house of

Israel … abhor judgment, and pervert all equity. They build up Zion with blood" (v. 9–10). "The heads thereof judge for reward, and the priests thereof teach for hire, and the prophets thereof divine for money: yet will they lean upon the Lord, and say, Is not the Lord among us? none evil can come upon us" (v. 11).

THE KINGS OF JUDAH

(The Southern Kingdom)

While all of the above events were occurring in Israel, Judah also experienced a series of kings. In Israel, all the kings were unrighteous. But in Judah, some were righteous and others unrighteous.

● **1 Kings 14:21–24 Rehoboam also disobeys God and leads his people into idolatry.** Rehoboam, the son of Solomon, reigned in Judah for 17 years. He was 41 years old when he took the throne at his father's death (v. 21). During his reign, "Judah did evil in the sight of the Lord, and they provoked him to jealousy with their sins which they had committed, above all that their fathers had done" (v. 22). They "built them high places, and images, and groves, on every high hill, and under every green tree," which means that they were involved in the perverted sexual rites of Baalism (v. 23). "And there were also sodomites in the land: and they did according to all the abominations of the nations which the Lord cast out before the children of Israel" (v. 24). And due to all this unrighteousness, the Lord allowed Shishak, king of Egypt, to conquer them (1 Kings 14:25–28; 2 Chronicles 12:1–12).

● **1 Kings 14:25–28 Shishak, king of Egypt, attacks Jeru- salem and takes away the treasures of Solomon's temple.** His conquering forces "took away the treasures of the house of the Lord, and the treasures of the king's house," in addition to "all the shields of gold which Solomon had made" (vv. 25–26).

This was probably the "Libyan prince who founded Egypt's 22nd Dynasty … the Pharaoh Sheshong I. He reigned for 21 years (ca. 945–924 B.C.) and harbored Jeroboam as a fugitive from Solomon. Late in his reign, Shishak invaded Palestine in the fifth year of Rehoboam (925 B.C.). He subdued Judah, taking the treasures of Jerusalem as tribute, and also asserted his dominion over Israel, as is evidenced by a broken stele of his found at Megiddo. At the temple of Amun in Thebes, Shishak left a triumphal relief-scene, naming many Palestinian towns [that he conquered]"[2].

Shishak took all the king's treasures

To replace these lost treasures, "Rehoboam made in their stead brasen shields, and committed them unto the hands of the chief of the guard, which kept the door of the king's house" (v. 27).

Whenever he went to the temple of Solomon, his guards carried these new shields to protect him, then "brought them back into the guard chamber" when he returned to his house (v. 28).

- **The Dynasty of David:** (975–587 BC)

  — **Rehoboam** (975 BC). "There was war between Rehoboam and Jeroboam (Judah and Israel)" all the days of their respective reigns (1 Kings 14:30). But eventually, after 22 years of reigning in Judah, Rehoboam died and was replaced on the throne by his son, Abijam (1 Kings 14:31).

  — **Abijam** (957 BC), son of Rehoboam reigned for 3 years. He "walked in all the sins of his father, which he had done before him: and his heart was not perfect with the Lord his God, as the heart of David his father" (1 Kings 15:3). Was David "perfect" with the Lord? The JST says that David "did right in the eyes of the Lord, and turned not aside from all that he commanded him, to sin against the Lord; but repented of the evil all the days of his life, save only in the matter of Uriah the Hittite, wherein the Lord cursed him" (JST 1 Kings 15:5). David was no idolater, nor did idolatry prosper while David was king. Despite Abijam's wickedness, for the sake of promises made to David, the Lord allowed him to continue on the throne and "set up his son after him … to establish Jerusalem" in order to preserve the royal lineage through which the Messiah would come (1 Kings 15:4). But there was war between Judah and Israel "all the days of his life" (1 Kings 15:6).

  — **Asa** (955 BC), son of Abijam, reigned for 41 years. Asa was righteous, doing "that which was right in the eyes of the Lord." But he lacked faith in his later years. He brought in the things which his father had dedicated, and the things which he himself had dedicated, into the house of the Lord: silver, and gold, and vessels (1 Kings 15:9–15).

He had seen the tragic consequences of sin and had also seen his father start a reform from sinful practices in his later years. Asa launched an all-out campaign to complete the job his father had begun (2 Chronicles 14:1–16:14). He tore down idolatrous altars and images and began to eliminate the male and female prostitutes who attended the pagan temples, groves, altars, and shrines. He did not, however, remove the "high places" where Baal was worshiped.

These reforms soon brought peace among the people, making them more happy and content. He used this interval of peace to build up his territorial defenses. Asa's actions towards his mother are important (1 Kings 15:13), for, although family is important, allegiance to God is more so. He removed his mother from being queen "because she had made an idol in a grove; and Asa destroyed her idol, and burnt it by the brook Kidron."

The Kings of Judah	
King (* righteous)	Reign
Rehoboam	22 yrs
Abijam	3 yrs
* Asa	41 yrs
* Jehoshaphat	25 yrs
Jehoram	8 yrs
Ahaziah	1 yr
Athaliah	7 yrs
* Joash (Jehoash)	40 yrs
* Amaziah	29 yrs
* Uzziah (Azariah)	52 yrs
* Jotham	16 yrs
Ahaz	16 yrs
* Hezekiah	29 yrs
Manasseh	55 yrs
Amon	2 yrs
* Josiah	31 yrs
Jehoahaz	3 mos
Jehoiakim	11 yrs
Jehoiachin	3 mos
Zedekiah	11 yrs

Babylon took Judah captive 3 times during Jehoiakim's, Jehoiachin's, and Zedekiah's reigns.

There was war between Asa, king of Judah, and Baasha, king of Israel, all their days. Baasha made a fortress at Ramah in order to prevent anyone from "go[ing] out or com[ing] in to Asa king of Judah." Fearing the loss of the temple's treasures again, Asa sent them through his servants to Ben-hadad, the king of Syria in Damascus. He also reminded Ben-hadad of the treaty between Judah and Syria, and asked him to help him defeat the Israelites. He did so, causing Baasha to retreat to his own land. Asa tore down the fortress at Ramah and used the materials to build two cities (1 Kings 15:16–24).

— Jehoshaphat (914 BC), the son of Asa, reigned righteously for 25 years. He was 35 years old when he began to reign, and "he walked in all the ways of Asa his father; he turned not aside from it, doing that which was right in the eyes of the Lord." But, as with his father, he did not remove the "high places" because "the people offered and burnt incense yet in the high places." Note that 2 Chronicles 17:6 says he did remove the high places. Both books agree that Jehoshaphat removed "the remnant of the sodomites, which remained in the days of his father Asa" (1 Kings 22:41–46).

As a result of his consistent righteousness, the Lord established his kingdom with peace, riches, and "honour in abundance." 2 Chronicles 17 says "his heart was lifted up in the ways of the Lord," and "in the third year of his reign" he sent his princes and Levites around the kingdom to teach the people concerning the "law of the Lord" (2 Chron. 17:3–9).

Jehoshaphat's priests taught the people

President Ezra Taft Benson taught, "Often we spend great effort in trying to increase the activity levels in our stakes. We work diligently to raise the percentages of those attending sacrament meetings. We labor to get a higher percentage of our young men on missions. We strive to improve the numbers of those marrying in the temple. All of these are commendable efforts and important to the growth of the kingdom. But when individual members and families immerse themselves in the scriptures regularly and consistently, these other areas of activity will automatically come. Testimonies will increase. Commitment will be strengthened. Families will be fortified. Personal revelation will flow"[3].

Elder Boyd K. Packer said, "True doctrine, understood, changes attitudes and behavior. The study of the doctrines of the gospel will improve behavior quicker than a study of behavior will improve behavior. Preoccupation with unworthy behavior can lead to unworthy behavior. That is why we stress so forcefully the study of the doctrines of the gospel"[4].

Elder Packer also said, "And there you have it—your commission, your charter, your objective. ... You are to teach the scriptures. ... If your students are acquainted with the revelations, there is no question—personal or social or political or occupational—that need go unanswered. Therein is contained the fulness of the everlasting gospel. Therein we find principles of truth that will resolve every confusion and every problem and every dilemma that will face the human family or any individual in it"[5].

- **2 Chronicles 20** This was a period of terrible anxiety for the people of Judah, as three nations had declared war on them. The outcome seemed bleak for King Jehoshaphat and his people, who were greatly outnumbered. But Jehoshaphat taught his people to rely on the Lord for their safety, and the threat was overcome.

— vv. 3–4   **Jehoshaphat asks the people of Judah to humble themselves before the Lord.** He sought the Lord in prayer and proclaimed a fast throughout all Judah. In response, the people of Judah gathered themselves together, to ask for help from the Lord.

— vv. 12–13   **They humbly seek the Lord's help.** "All Judah stood before the Lord, with their little ones, their wives, and their children" to ask for the Lord's help. Their words reveal their humility: "O our God, wilt thou not judge [destroy] them? for we have no might against this great company that cometh against us; neither know we what to do: but our eyes are upon thee."

— vv. 14–17   **The Lord answers that He will protect them.** The answer came through the prophet Jahaziel, who assured them that the battle was the Lord's, and he would protect them. "Thus saith the Lord unto you, Be not afraid nor dismayed by reason of this great multitude; for the battle is not yours, but God's." "Ye shall not need to fight in this battle: set yourselves, stand ye still, and see the salvation of the Lord … O Judah and Jerusalem."

— v. 20   **Jehoshaphat counseled his people to believe in the Lord and to follow his prophets** so that they might be established and prosper.

— v. 21   **Jehoshaphat appointed singers to praise the Lord rather than fight.** He instructed them to "praise the beauty of holiness, as they went out before the army" and to sing "Praise the Lord; for his mercy endureth for ever."

— vv. 22–24   **The Lord protected them by causing their attackers to war among themselves and destroy one another.** "And when Judah came toward the watch tower in the wilderness, they looked unto the multitude, and, behold, they were dead bodies fallen to the earth, and none escaped."

In our own dispensation, the United States of America had been a nation for less than a century when civil war divided the country. During that time, President Abraham Lincoln appealed to the nation to return to God:

Abraham Lincoln said, "It is the duty of nations as well as of men to own their dependence upon the overruling power of God, to confess their sins and transgressions in humble sorrow, … and to recognize the sublime truth, announced in the Holy Scriptures and proven by all history, that those nations only are blessed whose God is the Lord;. ... We have been the recipients of the choicest bounties of Heaven; ... But we have forgotten God

... and we have vainly imagined, ... that all these blessings were produced by some superior wisdom and virtue of our own ... It behooves us, then, to humble ourselves before the offended Power"[6].

— **Joram (Jehoram)** (893 BC), the son of Jehoshaphat, reigned for 8 years. He was 32 years old when he began to reign. He was not a righteous king. His wife was Athaliah, a daughter of Omri, the wicked king of Israel at the time. "And he walked in the way of the kings of Israel ... and he did evil in the sight of the Lord." But again, for the sake of His promises to David, the Lord allowed this wicked king to reign in Judah. But during his reign "Edom revolted from under the hand of Judah, and made a king over themselves" (2 Kings 8:16–20).

— **Ahaziah** (885 BC), the son of Jehoram, reigned for only 1 year. He was only 22 at the time he became king. He was the son of Athaliah, who was the daughter of Ahab, the wicked king of Israel at the time. "And he walked in the way of the house of Ahab, and did evil in the sight of the Lord, as did the house of Ahab: for he was the son in law of the house of Ahab."

He joined with Joram (the son of Ahab) in battling the Syrians, and when Joram was wounded in that battle Ahaziah visited him (2 Kings 8:25–29). Unfortunately, Joram was about to die at the hands of Jehu, who was seeking to wipe out the family of Ahab in Israel. He attacked while Ahaziah was there to visit Joram, and after Jehu shot and killed Joram, he also shot and mortally wounded Ahaziah. He died soon afterward when he fled to Megiddo. (2 Kings 9:23–28).

— **Athaliah** (884 BC), the wife of Jehoram and mother of Ahaziah, reigned for 7 years. She was a daughter of the wicked King Omri of Israel. This means she was also the sister of the even more wicked King Ahab of Israel. Like her brother, Athaliah was ambitious for power. So, when she saw that her son Ahaziah was dead, she destroyed all the remaining royal seed in Judah, and reigned herself for awhile. Unfortunately for her, "Jehosheba, the daughter of king Joram, sister of Ahaziah, took Joash the son of Ahaziah ... [and] hid him ... and his nurse, in [her] bedchamber ... so that he was not slain" (2 Kings 11:1–3). He was only an infant at the time.

— **Jehoash (Joash)** (878 BC), the son of Ahaziah, was only 7 when he began to reign, but he reigned in right- eousness for 40 years. The child Joash was kept hidden for 6 years while Athaliah reigned over the land. Then the priest Jehoiada (who was privy to the young king's whereabouts) "sent and fetched the rulers over hundreds, with the captains and the guard, and brought them to him into the house of the Lord, and made a covenant with them, and took an oath of them in the house of the Lord, and shewed them the king's son." He gave them the spears and shields of King David that were stored in the temple, and commanded them to protect the young king as they anointed him (2 Kings 11:4–11).

Then Jehoiada "brought forth the king's son, and put the crown upon him, and gave him the testimony; and they made him king, and anointed him; and they clapped their hands, and said, God save the king." When Athaliah heard all this commotion, she came to the temple and saw that "the king stood by a pillar, as the manner was, and the princes and the trumpeters by the king, and all the people of the land rejoiced, and blew with trumpets: and Athaliah rent her clothes, and cried, Treason, Treason." The guards then pursued her out of the temple and slew her with swords (2 Kings 11:12–16, 20).

Jehoiada the priest "made a covenant between the Lord and the king and the people, that they should be the Lord's people." After receiving this covenant, "all the people of the land went into the house of Baal, and brake it down; his altars and his images brake they in pieces thoroughly, and slew Mattan the priest of Baal before the altars." These were the remnants of Athalia's wicked reign. Then the priest brought the new child-king Joash down from the temple and placed him in the king's house, "and he sat on the throne of the kings" (2 Kings 11:17–21).

Athaliah sees Joash crowned king

Jehoash (Joash) did "that which was right in the sight of the Lord all his days" by following all that the priest Jehoiada taught him. But he did not remove all the "high places" because "the people still sacrificed and burnt incense in the high places." Joash attempted to repair "breaches" of the temple by using the money in the temple treasury and all the money donated by the people to the temple to pay for the repairs. But by the time that Jehoash was 30 "the priests had not repaired the breaches of the house." He urged them to delay no longer and they organized an effort to collect into one place "all the money that was brought into the house of the Lord." This was used to pay "carpenters and builders, that wrought upon the house of the Lord, and [the] masons, and hewers of stone, and to buy timber and hewed stone to repair the breaches of the house of the Lord … ." (2 Kings 12:2–16).

When the king of Syria planned to attack Judah Jehoash sent to the king of Syria all the precious contents of the temple and his own house, plus all the money in the temple treasury, as a ransom to prevent the attack. Then he left the city for his own protection. And while away, his servants entered into a conspiracy and slew him at Millo (2 Kings 12: 17–21).

Joash used donations to repair the temple

— **Amaziah** (841 BC), son of Joash, was 25 years old when he began to reign in Judah, and he reigned 29 years. Like his father before him, "he did that which was right in the sight of the Lord." However, like his father, he did not remove the "high places" because "as yet the people did sacrifice and burnt incense on the high places." (2 Kings 14:1–4).

Just as soon as "the kingdom was confirmed in his hand, … he slew his servants which had slain the king his father" (v. 5). But in obedience to the law of Moses, he did not slay the children of the murderers. He enjoyed military victories in Edom and Selah. Then, after 29 years of ruling, he became aware of a conspiracy against him and fled to Lachish. But it was of no use, because his conspirators followed him there and killed him (2 Kings 14:6–7, 17–20). Just as had happened to his father, he was assassinated by traitors.

— **Uzziah (Azariah)** (811 BC), the son of Amaziah, began reigning when he was only 16 years old, but he reigned for 52 years. He "did that which was right in the sight of the Lord, according to all that his father Amaziah had done; [except] that the high places were not removed" because "the people sacrificed and burnt incense still on the high places" (2 Kings 15:1–4). Uzziah (Azariah) had the misfortune of becoming "a leper unto the day of his death," forcing him to live in a "several" [separate] house. Thus incapacitated and separated from his people, his son Jotham took care of him and "judg[ed] the people of the land" while his father yet lived (2 Kings 15:5–7).

— **Jotham** (758 BC), the son of Uzziah (Azariah), was 25 years old when he began to reign, and he reigned in righteousness for 16 years. He "did that which was right in the sight of the Lord: he did according to all that his father Uzziah had done." Like his father and grandfather before him, he did not remove the "high places" because the people were still using them. But "he built the higher gate of the house of the Lord." During his reign, Rezin the king of Syria, and Pekah the son of Remaliah began to attack Judah (2 Kings 15:32–38).

— **Ahaz** (742 BC), the son of Jotham, was 20 years old when he began to reign, and he reigned for 16 years. He was not righteous, doing "not that which was right in the sight of the Lord his God." In fact, he may have been worse than all previous kings. He behaved like the kings of Israel in his idol worship, even making "his son to pass through the fire," which means that he offered him as a living sacrifice to the god Molech. He also "sacrificed and burnt incense in the high places, and on the hills, and under every green tree" (2 Kings 16:1–4).

Finding himself under attack from Syria and Israel, he "took the silver and gold that was found in the house of the Lord, and in the treasures of the king's house, and sent it for a present to the king of Assyria," asking him to help him by attacking Syria, which he did (2 Kings 16:5–9).

King Ahaz then went to Damascus to meet Tiglath-pileser king of Assyria. While there, he saw a pagan altar that he liked very much. He sent the design of it to Urijah the priest, who then built an altar in Jerusalem "according to all that king Ahaz had sent from Damascus" (2 Kings 16:8–11). When Ahaz returned, he moved the brazen altar of the Lord from in front of the temple and replaced it with his new altar. He also destroyed the brazen sea and changed the order of sacrifice in the temple. (2 Kings 16:12–20).

— **Hezekiah** (726 BC), the son of Ahaz, was 25 when he began to reign, and he reigned in righteousness for 29 years. Unlike several generations of kings before him, "he removed the high places, and brake the images, and cut down the groves, and brake in pieces the brasen serpent that Moses had made: for [in] those days the children of Israel did burn incense to it: and he called it Nehushtan [a "thing of brass"]" (2 Kings 18:1–4). By this he probably meant that it was not a god to be worshiped but only a "thing of brass" that symbolized something else. To worship it was inappropriate.

Hezekiah "trusted in the Lord God of Israel; so that after him was none like him among all the kings of Judah, nor any that were before him. For he clave to the Lord, and departed not from following him, but kept his commandments, which the Lord commanded Moses. And the Lord was with him; and he prospered whithersoever he went" (2 Kings 18:5–7).

Israel is taken captive into Assyria. Though his father had subjected Judah to Assyria, Hezekiah "rebelled against the king of Assyria, and served him not." He also "smote the Philistines, even unto Gaza, and the borders thereof." Then, in the fourth year of Hezekiah's reign, "Shalmaneser king of Assyria came up against Samaria (the kingdom of Israel), and besieged it. And at the end of three years they took it. … And the king of Assyria did carry away Israel unto Assyria … because they obeyed not the voice of the Lord their God, but transgressed his covenant, and all that Moses the servant of the Lord commanded, and would not hear them, nor do them" (2 Kings 18:8–12).

Having taken Israel captive, Sennacherib king of Assyria next attacked "all the fenced cities of Judah, and took them." But he had not yet conquered Jerusalem. So "Hezekiah … sent to the king of Assyria [in] Lachish, saying, I have offended; return from me: that which thou puttest on me will I bear. And the king of Assyria appointed unto Hezekiah king of Judah three hundred talents of silver and thirty talents of gold."

To meet this tribute, Hezekiah gave him all the silver in the house of the Lord, and the treasures of the king's house. He also "cut off the gold from the doors of the temple of the Lord, and from the pillars which [he] had overlaid [with gold], "and gave it to the king of Assyria." (2 Kings 18:13–16).

— **Manasseh** (697 BC), the son of Hezekiah, was 12 when he began to reign, and reigned 55 years (2 Kings 21:1–7). He was extremely wicked, doing "that which was evil in the sight of the Lord," and adopting "the abominations of the heathen, whom the Lord cast out before the children of Israel" (v. 2) He restored all the "high places" that his father Hezekiah had destroyed—rearing up altars for Baal, and making groves for the sensual rites of Ashteroth worship—and worshiping "all the host of heaven, and served them" (v. 3). Even worse, he built altars to Baal in the house of the Lord, and "altars for all the host of heaven in the two courts of the house of the Lord" (vv. 4–5). He also offered up his own son as a sacrifice to Molech by making him "pass through the fire" (v. 6). He also "observed times, and used enchantments, and dealt with familiar spirits and wizards: he wrought much wickedness in the sight of the Lord" (v. 6). This wicked king "shed innocent blood very much, till he had filled Jerusalem from one end to another" (v. 16), making him perhaps the most wicked king who ever ruled Judah.

— **Amon** (642 BC), the son of Manasseh, was 22 when he began to reign, and reigned 2 years (2 Kings 21:19). Like his father, he was thoroughly wicked, and "served the idols that his father served, and worsh- ipped them: And he forsook the Lord God of his fathers, and walked not in the way of the Lord" (vv. 21–22). He was assassinated by his own servants after a very brief two-year reign.

— **Josiah** (640 BC), the son of Amon, was only 8 when he began to reign, due to the sudden and unexpected death of his father. He reigned 31 years in right- eousness (2 Kings 22:1), being the last of all the kings of Judah who was righteous. Like his great- grandfather Hezekiah, Josiah sought to repair and restore the temple.

Book of the law found in the temple

While doing so, they found the book of the law in the temple. After reading it, Josiah sorrowed greatly for the wickedness of his ancestors. He determined to read the book to his people, and after doing so they placed themselves under covenant to keep the commandments of the Lord. Josiah proceeded to destroy all worship of false gods, drive out the sodomites, and put to death idolatrous priests. Because of his righteousness, Huldah the prophetess prophesied great blessings on Josiah personally, but predicted wrath that "shall not be quenched" upon the people of Judah for their wickedness (2 Kings 22:17). Unfortunately, Josiah died too early while fighting against Pharaoh Necho of Egypt (2 Chronicles 35:21–24).

— **Jehoahaz** (609 BC), the son of Josiah, was 23 when he began to reign. He reigned only 3 months (2 Kings 23:31) and was then taken to Egypt. Unlike his father, he "did that which was evil in the sight of the Lord" (v. 32). Pharaoh-nechoh took him off the throne of Judah "in bands" to assure that he could not reign, and then placed Judah under a heavy tribute of silver and gold (v. 33).

— **Jehoiakim** (609 BC), was another son of Josiah whose original name was Eliakim. He was 25 when Pharaoh Necho placed him on the throne of Judah and changed his name to Jehoiakim. He reigned for 11 years (2 Kings 23:36). He paid the heavy tax Judah owed to Egypt by taxing his people heavily. Also unlike his father before him, he "did that which was evil in the sight of the Lord" (v. 37). The armies of Nebuchadnezzar overran Jerusalem during his reign, and took some of its people captive into Babylon. Jehoiakim remained on the throne in servitude to Babylon for three years, then rebelled. This not only cost him his life, but also set the stage for a second devastating attack on Jerusalem.

— **Jehoiachin** (598 BC), the son of Jehoiakim, was 18 when he began to reign, and reigned for only 3 months (2 Kings 24:8) before he was deported to Babylon. Like his father and grandfather before him, he "did that which was evil in the sight of the Lord" (v. 9). During his reign, the armies of Nebuchadnezzar came again and besieged Jerusalem (v. 10). To stop the seige, Jehoiachin "went out to the king of Babylon, he, and his mother, and his servants, and his princes, and his officers: and the king of Babylon took him in the eighth year of his reign" (v. 12). He also took "all the treasures of the house of the Lord, and the treasures of the king's house, and cut in pieces all the vessels of gold which Solomon king of Israel had made in the temple of the Lord" (v. 13).

This deportation was more extensive than the first one. Nebuchadnezzar carried away 10,000 captives, including "all the princes, and all the mighty men of valour, … and all the craftsmen and smiths: none remained, save the poorest sort of the people of the land" (v. 14). This number included 7,000 "men of might, … and craftsmen and smiths a thousand, all that were strong and apt for war" (2 Kings 24:10–16). Among these rulers and most promising citizens of Judah were Ezekiel, Daniel, and Daniel's young friends. All of them were taken away into Babylon.

— **Zedekiah** (598 BC), was also a son of Jehoiakim, whose original name was Mattaniah (v. 17). He was placed on the throne by Nebuchadnezzar when his brother Jehoiachin was taken captive into Babylon. He was 21 when he began to reign, and reigned 11 years (2 Kings 24:18). Like his brother and father, he "did that which was evil in the sight of the Lord" (v. 19). And like his father Jehoiakim, he foolishly rebelled against the king of Babylon. (2 Kings 24:17–20), bringing about a third and final siege of Jerusalem that lasted two years (2 Kings 25:1–2). The siege produced extreme famine in the city, and "all the men of war fled by night" while Zedekiah "went the way toward the plain" (v. 4).

Nebuchadnezzar's forces "pursued after the king, and overtook him in the plains of Jericho," where he had no defense because "all his army were scattered from him" (v. 5). They brought Zedekiah captive "up to the king of Babylon [in] Riblah" (v. 6). There they "slew the sons of Zedekiah before his eyes, and put out the eyes of Zedekiah, and bound him with fetters of brass, and carried him to Babylon" (v. 7).

The army of Nebuchadnezzar then entered into the defenseless city of Jerusalem (v. 8). They "burnt the house of the Lord, and the king's house, and all the houses of Jerusalem, and every great man's house"(v. 9). They "brake down the walls of Jerusalem round about" (v. 10). And then they took "the rest of the people that were left in the city, and the fugitives that fell away" to the king of Babylon, who carried them away captive into Babylon (v. 11). The only people they left behind were "the

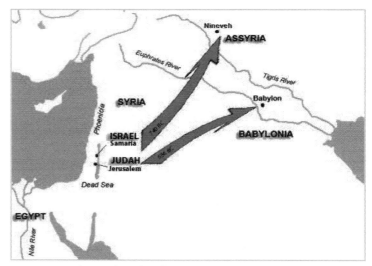

Both Israel and Judah were carried away captive

poor of the land to be vinedressers and husbandmen" (v. 12).

As booty, Nebuchadnezzar's army carried away "the pillars of brass that were in the house of the Lord, and the bases, and the brasen sea that was in the house of the Lord," all of which were cut into pieces and taken to Babylon (v. 13). They also took "the pots, and the shovels, and the snuffers, and the spoons, and all the vessels of brass wherewith they ministered, … the firepans, and the bowls, and such things as were of gold, … and of silver" (vv. 14–15). The sum of these things was so vast that it was "without weight" (v. 16). The pillars were 18 cubits high, with a 3-cubit brass chapiter on top, along with "the wreathen work, and pomegranates upon the chapiter round about" (v. 17).

Last of all, they took "Seraiah the chief priest, and Zephaniah the second priest, and the three keepers of the door," plus "an officer that was set over the men of war, and five men of them that were in the king's presence, which were found in the city, and the principal scribe of the host, which mustered the people of the land, and threescore men of the people of the land that were found in the city," and they "slew them at Riblah in the land of Hamath" (vv. 18–21). "So Judah was carried away out of their land" (v. 21).

Notes

1.   *The Articles of Faith*, 322–323.
2.   Douglas, ed., *The New Bible Dictionary*, s.v. "Shishak".
3.   *The Teachings of President Ezra Taft Benson*, 44.
4.   "Little Children," General Conference address, October 1986; or *Ensign*, November 1986, 17.
5.   Address to full-time educators in the Church Educational System, October 14, 1977.
6.   "A Proclamation by the President of the United States of America," cited in Richardson, *Messages and Papers of the Presidents* [Washington, D.C.: United States Congress, 1897], 164–165.

CHAPTER 28

The Prophet Elijah

(1 Kings 17–22; 2 Kings 1–2)

ഇറ്റ

INTRODUCTION

The Message and Purpose of the Prophets

The story of 1 and 2 Kings is the steady decline and destruction of both Israel and Judah. The story is made more poignant by the fact that they had both entered into a covenant relationship with Jehovah who promised to bless them with prosperity, security, and freedom if they honored their covenants. But they had also been fore- warned that if they broke their covenants, God would allow them to be cursed, smitten, and eventually scattered by the nations that surrounded them.

Israel's part of the covenant was to keep the law of Moses. However, all of Israel's kings and most of Judah's kings led their people into a course of serious apostasy. They broke their covenants with impunity and worshiped the gods of their neighbors. As the previous chapter made clear, the Lord extended His mercy multiple times in an effort to encourage them to repent and return to their covenants. But in the end, it was all in vain, and both Israel and Judah ended up fully conquered and carried away captive into foreign lands.

JOSÉ DE RIBERA, 1638

The Prophet Elijah

Did God intend all of this to happen? No. It could have been otherwise. But there is no doubt that He knew what they would do, and in that sense God was fully aware of the historical process and making plans for His people, both then and in the latter days. He maintains active involvement in the affairs of His people through his prophets. In this chapter we will examine the life and teachings of one of those prophets—Elijah—who issued a challenge that illustrates this principle: "How long halt ye between two opinions? If the Lord be God, follow him" (1 Kings 18:21).

THE PROPHET ELIJAH

● **1 Kings 17:1; 2 Kings 1:8 Who was Elijah?** "Elijah" means "My God is Jehovah." He was a Tishbite—not a local person. This verse says that a Tishbite was "of the inhabitants of Gilead," and some scholars believe this means the Gilead beyond the Jordan River in the tribal lands of Gad[1]. But other scholars believe that Elijah came from Tishbeh, in upper Galilee[2]. We learn in 2 Kings 1:8 that he was a "hairy man" who wore a girdle of leather ("garment of skins"). Calling him "a hairy man" means he was dressed in a rough garment, probably made of either goat's or camel's hair—perhaps an animal's skin with the hair still on it.

Elijah Seals the Heavens

● **1 Kings 16:28–33 The conditions in the kingdom of Israel during the time of Elijah.** The ruler of the northern kingdom of Israel at this time was the wicked King Ahab, who followed his powerful and wicked father, Omri, to the throne. His own wicked tendencies were compounded by his marriage to a Phoenician princess named Jezebel. Ahab adopted her practice of Baal worship, and encouraged his people to join him in the worship of this false god. Baal, Asherah, and Ashtoreth were among these false deities. The most offensive aspects of the worship of Baal and Ashtoreth were the immoral fertility rites, which were usually performed at outdoor shrines in groves prepared for that very purpose, usually on mountain-tops.

● **1 Kings 17:1 Elijah sealed the heavens because of the wickedness of Ahab and his people.** President Joseph Fielding Smith said: "The first appearance of Elijah we read of is in the 17th chapter of 1st Kings, when he came before the king and said, 'As the Lord God of Israel liveth, before whom I stand, there shall not be dew nor rain these years, but according to my word.' There is something very significant in that edict … . The reason I put emphasis upon this is to impress you with the sealing power by which Elijah was able to close the heavens, that there should be no rain or dew until he spoke"[3].

Elijah was fed by ravens

● **1 Kings 17:2–7 The Lord then commanded Elijah to flee to the Brook Cherith, where He fed Elijah by sending ravens with food.** He fled eastward to a spot "before" the river Jordan (v. 3). There he could drink water from the brook, and the Lord promised to feed him with food provided by ravens (v. 4). W. Cleon Skousen said: "We do not know which of the Jordan tributaries the brook Cherith might have been, but apparently it was an obscure and isolated place where Elijah could hide safely without being accidentally discovered by soldiers, shepherds or passers-by. It was also a desolate place where no animal life existed, therefore Elijah was completely dependent upon the Lord for his sustenance" (*The Fourth Thousand Years* [1966], 336).

Elijah was fed there both morning and evening by this process for awhile (vv. 5–6). But then the brook "dried up, because there had been no rain in the land" (v. 7).

MIRACLES FOR THE WIDOW OF ZAREPHATH

● **1 Kings 17:8–9 After the Brook Cherith dries up, the Lord prepares a widow to help Elijah.** Zarephath was on the coast of the Mediterranean between Tyre and Sidon, in what is now Lebanon and was then Phoenicia, outside the boundaries of Israel. This was the very same country that Jezebel came from—enemy territory for the prophet Elijah (v. 9). Grain and oil were among the major exports of Zarephath. The fact that the widow had little of these two necessities of life indicates how severe and widespread the drought was.

● **1 Kings 17:10–12 Elijah asks the starving widow to feed him.** Elijah's request was not a selfish one, but rather a test of her faith. She was gathering sticks from the street to make a small fire to cook her last bit of flour ("meal"). Elijah called to her as asked, "Fetch me, I pray thee, a little water in a vessel, that I may drink" (v. 10). Though she was suffering herself, she went immediately to fetch it. But as she did, Elijah asked another favor of her: "Bring me, I pray thee, a morsel of bread in thine hand" (v. 11). Only then did she explain her desperate circumstances. "As the Lord thy God liveth, I have not a cake, but an handful of meal in a barrel, and a little oil in a cruse: and, behold, I am gathering two sticks, that I may go in and dress it for me and my son, that we may eat it, and die" (v. 12).

Elijah asks the widow to feed him

● **1 Kings 17:13–16 Elijah promises that her that her barrel of flour and cruse of oil will not fail for the duration of the famine if she feeds him.** The key was that she was to feed make "a little cake first, and bring it unto me, and after make for thee and for thy son" (v. 13). To do this was to put both her and her son's life in danger. But Elijah promised her that "the barrel of meal shall not waste, neither shall the cruse of oil fail, until the day that the Lord sendeth rain upon the earth" (v. 14). Her obedient response showed her great faith in these words of the prophet. And because she passed the test, Elijah's promises to her were fulfilled (vv. 15–16). Jesus spoke of the faith of this woman during his earthly ministry (Luke 4:25–26).

Elder Jeffrey R. Holland said: "[The widow's response when Elijah asked her for food was an] "expression of faith—as great, under these circumstances, as any I know in the scriptures … Perhaps uncertain what the cost of her faith would be … , she first took her small loaf to Elijah, obviously trusting that if there were not enough bread left over, at least she and her son would have died in an act of pure charity"[4].

President Ezra Taft Benson said: "When we put God first, all other things fall into their proper place or drop out of our lives. Our love of the Lord will govern the claims for our affection, the demands on our time, the interests we pursue, and the order of our priorities ... May God bless us to put [him] first and, as a result, reap peace in this life and eternal life with a fulness of joy in the life to come"[5].

Bishop Vaughn J. Featherstone made an impressive promise concerning food storage in the Welfare Session of General Conference in April, 1974. He spoke of the faith of people with limited means who make the attempt to obtain their food storage as they have been commanded. And he used the Widow of Zarephath's experience to illustrate it.

> A year ago I had the privilege of staying with a family in a foreign country. In this country, income tax is 52%, sales tax is 17.65%—69.65% of their wages are spent in these taxes. As I sat down to the meal with them, and we asked the sweet little family how much they had to spend on food each month, the mother replied that she was spending $18 for her month's food bill. I reviewed this in my mind quickly. I had been into a store and priced groceries. They were not unlike those here in the United States—the grocery prices. And as we sat down and I calculated the cost of the meal we were eating, it could not possibly have cost less that $10 or $12. We were eating more than half of their entire month's allowance for food in one meal, and my heart wept within me. But I knew the Lord would not leave her withholden from a blessing. And I said to her, "How much are you putting on your year's supply of food?" and she said: "We're putting away one can of vegetables each month." Do you know how long it will take her to get a year's supply of food? Never. Never in this life. But I want you to know when the need comes and that woman goes down to her shelves and pulls off a can, another can will take its place.

> I met another great stake president and his wife in a distant city from here. They weren't making it too well. On Sunday morning as I got up with the head of this large family, the wife came and sat down with me and she mentioned the fact they weren't making it too well, and she said: "You know, we've had many experiences this past summer that have been great blessings to me and testimonies. We've had special guests and we've needed

> something, and there wasn't anything left in the basement, but I thought, 'I'll go down again and take a look,' and I've gone down in the basement and there was another can of applesauce, another bottle of tomato juice on the shelf, and I used those." And then she said: "When I heard you were coming, I didn't know what we'd do to feed you breakfast on Sunday morning—something special." She said: "I knew that we didn't have anything in the cupboards, and I thought, 'Well, I know there isn't anything in the basement, but I'll go down and take one last check.'" And she said: "I went back down in the basement, and there was another can of applesauce and another bottle of tomato juice on the front of the shelf." I believe, brethren, the Lord would do that for such souls.

> Now, I think that as we keep our year's supply of food, we need not fear, no matter what the problems are—whether we share with our neighbors or not—I want you to know that as you keep the commandment, the cruse of oil will never fail.[6]

● **1 Kings 17:17–24 Elijah subsequently raises her son from the dead.** Sometime after the miracle of the unfailing meal and oil, the widow's young son became deathly ill—so ill, in fact, that "there was no breath left in him" (v. 17). The widow was greatly distressed, and cried out to Elijah, "What have I to do with thee, O thou man of God? art thou come unto me to call my sin to remembrance, and to slay my son?" (v. 18). This was a plea for help rather than a criticism.

She believed, and had staked her life and the life of her son on the idea that sheltering a prophet would bring blessings and protection. Now instead, her son lay dead, and she did not understand why.

LOUIS HERSENT, c. 1862

Elijah said to her, "Give me thy son. And he took him out of her bosom, and carried him up into a loft, where he abode, and laid him upon his own bed" (v. 19). Then he prayed for the Lord's help with these words: "O Lord my God, hast thou also brought evil upon the widow with whom I sojourn, by slaying her son?" (v. 20). Then he followed the strange procedure of bending over the child three times as he sought to restore his life (v. 21). Elisha did a similar thing in restoring a dead child (2 Kings 4:34), as did Paul when raising Eutychus (Acts 20:10). But we have no record of the Savior do- ing this when He raised the dead. It may be that this phrase simply means he prayed three times before the miracle occurred, but we have no way to know.

Elijah revived the widow's son

Elijah prayed, "O Lord my God, I pray thee, let this child's soul come into him again" (v. 21). And the Lord answered his prayer as "the soul of the child came into him again, and he revived" (v. 22). Then Elijah "took the child, and brought him down … and delivered him unto his mother" (v. 23). She already knew that Elijah was a prophet, but now all doubt and fear flew away and she rejoiced.

ELIJAH CHALLENGES AHAB AND JEZEBEL

Elijah Bravely Visits Ahab

● **1 Kings 18:1 In the third year of the famine, the Lord commanded Elijah, "Go [show] thyself [to] Ahab; and I will send rain upon the earth."** This was a dangerous thing to do because Ahab was seeking to kill him for closing the heavens in the first place. It took a great deal of courage to obey the Lord in this matter.

● **1 Kings 18:2–16 Elijah promises Obadiah that he will appear before Ahab.** Obadiah was the governor of King Ahab's house. It was his responsibility to arrange the king's appointments, which is why Elijah told Obadiah to set up an interview with the king (v. 3). Whether this Obadiah was the same as the author of the Old Testament book of the same name is not known, but it seems doubtful. This Obadiah was not preaching repentance as a prophet (like Elijah) would do, but he "feared the Lord greatly." And despite the persecution of the prophets by Jezebel, he secretly hid 100 of the sons of the prophets in a cave and brought food and water to sustain them (vv. 4, 13).

The fact that King Ahab and his governor Obadiah were forced to hunt for water and grass like the rest of the Israelites, demonstrates how severe the famine had become (vv. 5–6). Because Elijah had produced this distress by sealing the heavens from rain, he was a wanted man in Ahab's court. Ahab even went so far as to extract promises from the heads of surrounding nations that they were not hiding Elijah and that they did not know of his location (v. 10). If a person reported seeing Elijah and the prophet had disappeared by the time Ahab got there, Ahab killed the person who made the report (vv. 11–16). Elijah promised Obadiah that he would appear before Ahab (v. 15), and if he failed to do so then Obadiah would be slain.

● **1 Kings 18:17–18 Ahab blames Elijah for Israel's suffering.** When Elijah appeared before Ahab, he said, "Art thou he that troubleth Israel?" (v. 17). But Elijah put the accountability for the drought right where it belonged: "I have not troubled Israel; but thou, and thy father's house, in that ye have forsaken the commandments of the Lord, and thou hast followed Baalim" (v. 18).

Elijah Challenges the Priests of Baal

● **1 Kings 18:19–20 Elijah invites 850 false priests to a contest on Mount Carmel.** This included 450 "prophets of Baal" (Ahab's god), and another 400 "prophets of the groves ... which eat at Jezebel's table" (v. 19). Ahab eagerly gathered all these prophets and the people of Israel together on Mount Carmel (v. 20). The contest that Elijah proposed—to see whose god could produce fire—would appeal to the prophets of Baal since their god, the "Sun god," could surely send down fire if anyone could.

When the people gathered to hear Elijah speak, he asked them, "How long halt ye between two opinions?" (v. 21). "Literally, [the phrase means] 'How long hop ye about upon two boughs?' This is a metaphor taken from birds hopping about from bough to bough, not knowing on which to settle ... They dreaded Jehovah, and therefore could not totally abandon him; they feared the king and queen, and therefore thought they must embrace the religion of the state. Their conscience forbade them to do the former; their fear of man persuaded them to do the latter; but in neither were they heartily engaged ... "[7].

Jesus taught the same principle. The word "mammon" refers to worldliness (Matthew 6:24). Elder Neal A. Maxwell said: "The stirring words of various prophets ... urge us to choose, to decide, and not to halt. ... Elijah's message has tremendous relevancy today, for all must finally choose between the gods of this world and the God of eternity"[8].

● **1 Kings 18:21–29 Elijah challenges the priests of Baal fail to produce fire.** He pointed out that he alone was a prophet of Jehovah, while Baal's prophets numbered 450 (v. 22). He invited them to prepare a sacrifice on top of wood "and put no fire under," while he did the same thing with his sacrifice (v. 23). Then they could call upon their gods while he called upon Jehovah to produce fire for their sacrifices, and "the God that answereth by fire, let him be God." The people thought it was a good idea (v. 24).

The proposed contest drew upon the trickery used regularly by the priests of Baal when trying to convince people that Baal's power was real. They were so unscrupulous that they rigged their altars with fires beneath them to make the sacrifices appear to ignite spontaneously. One ancient writer said he "had seen under the altars of the heathens, holes dug in the earth with funnels proceeding from them, and communicating with openings on the tops of the altars. In [these holes] the priests concealed fire, which, communicating through the funnels with the holes, set fire to the wood and consumed the sacrifice; and thus the simple people were led to believe that the sacrifice was consumed by a miraculous fire"⁹. This time, however, they would have no opportunity to rig their sacrifice beforehand.

Prophets of Baal in a frenzy on their altar

Elijah invited the priests of Baal to go first because "ye are many" (v. 25). This they did, "call[ing] on the name of Baal from morning even until noon, saying, O Baal, hear us. But there was no voice, nor any that answered. And they leaped upon the altar which was made" (v. 26). Elijah mocked them, saying, "Cry aloud: for he is a god; either he is walking, or he is pursuing or he is in a journey, or peradventure he sleepeth, and must be awaked" (v. 27). This produced a wild frenzy among Baal's prophets, as "they cried aloud, and cut themselves after their manner with knives and lancets, till the blood gushed out upon them" (v. 28). But it was all to no avail, because "when midday was past, and they prophesied until the time of the offering of the evening sacrifice, that there was neither voice, nor any to answer, nor any that regarded" (v. 29).

"It seems that the priests of Baal employed the whole day in their desperate rites. The time is divided into two periods: 1. From morning until noon; this was employed in preparing and offering the sacrifice, and in earnest supplication for the celestial fire. Still there was no answer, and at noon Elijah began to mock and ridicule them, and this excited them to commence anew. They con- tinued from noon till the time of offering the evening sacrifice, dancing up and down, cutting themselves with knives, mingling their own blood with their sacrifice, praying, supplicating, and acting in the most frantic manner"¹⁰.

- **1 Kings 18:30–35 Elijah drenches his own sacrifice.** First, he repaired the old altar to Jehovah on Mount Carmel that had fallen into disrepair (v. 30). He used "twelve stones, according to the number of the tribes of the sons of Jacob" to "buil[d] an altar in the name of the Lord" (vv. 31–32). Then, with great drama, and so that there could be no doubt whatsoever that he was not engaging in trickery, "he made a trench [around] the altar" (v. 32). Then, after he had laid the wood and the sacrifice on the altar, he said, "Fill four barrels with water, and pour it on the burnt sacrifice, and on the wood"— thoroughly soaking it (v. 33). Then he had them drench it again, not once but twice more (v. 34). So much water was poured on the sacrifice that it "ran round about the altar; and he filled the trench also with water" (v. 35).

- **1 Kings 18:36–39 Elijah calls down fire from heaven.** Elijah's purpose in challenging the priests of Baal was to show that Jehovah was the only true God of Israel (vv. 36–37). He did not spend all day calling upon God in a public and showy manner, but waited until "the time of ...

evening sacrifice" (v. 36). Then he prayed unto God to send down fire so that "this people may know that thou art the Lord God, and that thou hast turned their heart back again" (v. 37). The result was immediate. "The fire of the Lord fell, and consumed the burnt sacrifice, and the wood, and the stones, and the dust, and licked up the water that was in the trench" (v. 38). The people fell to the ground in fear, crying, "The Lord, he is the God" (v. 39).

"The fire proceeding from Jehovah, was not a natural flash of lightning, which could not produce any such effect, but miraculous fire falling from heaven ... the supernatural origin of which was manifested in the fact that it not only consumed the sacrifice with the pile of wood upon the altar, but also burned up...the stones of the altar and the earth that was thrown up to form the trench, and licked up the water in the trench. Through this

The fire of the Lord fell on the sacrifice

miracle Jehovah not only accredited Elijah as His servant and prophet, but proved Himself to be the living God, whom Israel was to serve; so that all the people who were present fell down upon their faces in worship."[11]

- **1 Kings 18:40 Elijah slays all the false prophets of Baal.** He commanded the people to "take the prophets of Baal; let not one of them escape," then "brought them down to the brook Kishon, and slew them there."

- **1 Kings 18:41–46 Elijah then unsealed the heavens.** He went up to the top of Mount Carmel and knelt down to pray (v. 42). He sent his servant to watch the skies, and at first the servant reported, "There is nothing," but he told him to look again seven more times (v. 43). On the seventh try, the servant reported that "there ariseth a little cloud out of the sea, like a man's hand" (v. 44). This was

Elijah prayed earnestly for rain

enough for Elijah to warn King Ahab to "prepare thy chariot, and get thee down, that the rain stop thee not" (v. 44). Meanwhile, the skies became "black with clouds and wind," and torrents of rain began to fall (v. 45). Ahab returned to Jezreel, but Elijah ran to get to the gates of Jezreel first (v. 46).

ELIJAH FLEES FOR HIS LIFE TO MT. SINAI

After this great miracle, Elijah expected the northern kingdom to repent of its evil ways. Ahab was affected, but his wife Jezebel only became more angry.

- **1 Kings 18:13 Jezebel is an enemy to righteousness.** She had already slain as many prophets of Jehovah as she could capture. Many more would have perished were it not for the protection offered them by Ahab's governor Obadiah.

- **1 Kings 19:1–9 She swears to slay Elijah in revenge for the death of her priests (vv. 1–2).** Elijah fled for his life, coming first to Beersheba in southern Judah, where he left his servant behind (v. 3). He continued on into the wilderness, and sat down under a juniper tree in a state of great depression (v. 4).

Elijah was so discouraged at this point that he "requested for himself that he might die; and said, It is enough; now, O Lord, take away my life; for I am not better than my fathers" (v. 4). He fell asleep in great sorrow, but was awakened when "an angel touched him, and said unto him, Arise and eat. And he looked, and, behold, there was a cake baken on the coals, and a cruse of water at his head. And he did eat and drink, and laid him down again" (vv. 5–6). The angel returned and bid him to eat again "because the journey is too great for thee" (v. 7).

Elijah then continued on "forty days and forty nights unto Horeb the mount of God (Mount Sinai)" in southern Arabia (v. 8). This was the place where Moses had spoken with Jehovah and received the law. It was a sacred place, and there Elijah expected to commune with the Lord. "And he came thither unto a cave, and lodged there" (v. 9).

An angel feeds Elijah in the wilderness

GUSTAVE DORÉ, 1896

- **1 Kings 19:10 Elijah feels that he is the only Israelite left who worships the true God.** This, despite the people's response to God's spectacular display of power. He was truly discouraged, and when the Lord asked him why he had come to this place, he said, "I have been very jealous for the Lord God of hosts: for the children of Israel have forsaken thy covenant, thrown down thine altars, and slain thy prophets with the sword; and I, even I only, am left; and they seek my life, to take it away."

Elder Joseph Fielding Smith said: "When he was there, the Lord called upon him and asked him what he was doing there; and in his sorrow, because of the hardness of the hearts of the people, he told the Lord the condition, that he alone remained, that they sought his life to take it away. But the Lord showed him that there were others who had remained true unto him, even 7,000"[12].

Elder Boyd K. Packer said:

> The prophets, as they walk and live among men, are common, ordinary men. Men called to apostolic positions are given a people to redeem. Theirs is the responsibility to lead those people in such a way that they win the battles of life and conquer the ordinary temptations and passions and challenges. And then, speaking figuratively, it is as though these prophets are tapped on the shoulder and reminded: "While you carry such responsibility to help others with their battles, you are not excused from your own challenges of life. You too will be subject to passions, temptations, challenges. Win those battles as best you can."

> Some people are somehow dissatisfied to find in the leading servants of the Lord such ordinary mortals. They are disappointed that there is not some obvious mystery about those men; it is almost as if they are looking for the strange and the occult. To me, however, it is a great testimony that the prophets anciently and the prophets today are called out from the ranks of the ordinary men. It should not lessen our faith, for example, to learn that Elijah was discouraged at times, even despondent.[13]

The Still, Small Voice of God

- **1 Kings 19:11–13 The Lord comforts Elijah through a "still, small voice" on Mount Sinai.** The Lord commanded Elijah to "go forth, and stand upon the mount before the Lord," where would teach Elijah (and us) an important principle about answers to prayer. Three great things occurred. First, "a great and strong wind rent the mountains, and brake in pieces the rocks … but the Lord was not in the wind" (v. 11). And, "after the wind an earthquake; but the Lord was not in the earthquake" (v. 11). And finally, "a fire; but the Lord was not in the fire" (v. 12). Elijah was well-enough acquainted with revelation to know that none of these manifestations constituted the "voice of the Lord" that he needed to hear. It was only after these things that "a still small voice" came, and when he heard it, Elijah "wrapped his face in his mantle, and went out, and stood in the entering in of the cave" to hear the word of the Lord (v. 13).

  - **1 Nephi 17:45 God's voice is described as a "feeling" in the Book of Mormon.** Nephi exhorted his brethren that they had not only "seen an angel," but had "heard his voice from time to time; and he hath spoken unto you in a still small voice, but ye were *past feeling, that ye could not feel his words*" (emphasis added). By this we learn that the voice of God is discerned more as a feeling than an actual voice. We must grow into the ability to discern such things, because it is not the natural way that we communicate as mortals. But numerous people who have had near-death experiences report that in the spirit world communication does not require words; they may be used, but a purer form of communication occurs spirit-to-spirit without the need for words. When God communicates with us, it is spirit-to-spirit, and we must be ready and able to discern such messages.

  - **3 Nephi 11:3 God's voice is gentle, yet piercing.** As the Nephites gathered together at the temple in Bountiful after great destructions had come upon the land, "they heard a voice as if it came out of heaven," but "cast their eyes round about, for they understood not the voice which they heard." It was described as "not a harsh voice, neither … a loud voice; nevertheless, and notwithstanding it being a small voice it did pierce them that did hear to the center, insomuch that there was no part of their frame that it did not cause to quake; yea, it did pierce them to the very soul, and did cause their hearts to burn." From this we learn that God does not shout, nor does He need to do so. He speaks gently, yet His voice can pierce our souls.

President Ezra Taft Benson said: "Do you take time to listen to the promptings of the Spirit? Answers to prayer come most often by a still voice and are discerned by our deepest, innermost feelings. I tell you that you can know the will of God concerning yourselves if you will take the time to pray and to listen"[14].

Elder Boyd K. Packer said: "Inspiration comes more easily in peaceful settings. Such words as quiet, still, peaceable, Comforter abound in the scriptures: 'Be still, and know that I am God.' (Ps. 46:10). And the promise, 'You shall receive my Spirit, the Holy Ghost, even the Comforter, which shall teach you the peaceable things of the kingdom.' (D&C 36:2). Elijah felt a great wind, an earthquake, a fire. The Lord was not in any of them; then came 'a still small voice.' (1 Kings 19:12)"[15].

President Gordon B. Hinckley said: "Now, let me just say, categorically, that the things of God are understood by the Spirit of God, and one must have and seek and cultivate that Spirit, and there comes understanding and it is real. I can give testimony of that. ... I think the best way I could describe the process is to liken it to the experience of Elijah as set forth in the book of First Kings. Elijah spoke to the Lord, and there was a wind, a great wind, and the Lord was not in the wind. And there was an earthquake, and the Lord was not in the earthquake. And there was a fire, and the Lord was not in the fire. And after the fire a still, small voice, which I describe as the whisperings of the Spirit"[16].

The "still, small voice" of the Spirit is not the only way that God communicates with His children. There are more dramatic forms as well. But the majority of the revelations we receive will come in this manner. We must cultivate our ability to discern it.

- **1 Kings 19: 13–14, 18 There are still many faithful people in Israel.** When the Lord asked Elijah why he had come to Mount Sinai (v. 13), Elijah complained that "the children of Israel have forsaken thy covenant, thrown down thine altars, and slain thy prophets with the sword; and I, even I only, am left; and they seek my life, to take it away" (v. 14). He felt all alone in his righteousness and that he had failed as a prophet. But the Lord assured him that "I have left me seven thousand in Israel, all the knees which have not bowed unto Baal, and every mouth which hath not kissed him" (v. 18). Though a nation may become thoroughly corrupt and overwhelmed with wickedness, yet there may still be believers among them who keep the commandments and seek the will of the Lord. Elijah was not alone, nor was his work yet done.

FINAL ASSIGNMENTS FOR ELIJAH

- **1 Kings 19:15, 17 The Lord is God of many nations.** This is illustrated by Elijah's instruction to anoint Hazael as the new king of Syria (v. 15) and Jehu as the new king of Israel (v. 16). This, despite the fact that these two nations were at war with one another, and "him that escapeth the sword of Hazael shall Jehu slay: and him that escapeth from the sword of Jehu shall Elisha slay" (v. 17).

● **1 Kings 19:16, 19–21 The Lord calls Elisha to be a prophet.** Elijah was instructed to anoint Elisha as a "prophet in thy room" (v. 16). Elijah went forward with this assignment and found Elisha "plowing with twelve yoke of oxen before him" (v. 19). Elijah called Elisha to his prophetic office by "cast[ing] his mantle upon him," symbolizing that Elisha was called to be his successor (v. 19). Elisha asked for a brief time to say goodbye to his parents and to give his possessions to the needy, which he did (v. 20). "Then he arose, and went after Elijah, and ministered unto him" (v. 21).

Elijah casts his mantle upon Elisha

THE HOLMAN BIBLE, 1890

Elisha was probably wealthy because he owned twelve yokes (pairs) of oxen, eleven of which yokes would have been driven by servants. He himself only drove the twelfth team. The feast he prepared from two oxen would also indicate his wealth. Burning his equipment to make the sacrificial meal symbolized Elisha's forfeiting of worldly wealth as he accepted his prophetic office.

AHAB AND JEZEBEL MEET THEIR DEMISE

● **1 Kings 20:1–29 Ben-hadad, king of Syria, unsuccessfully waged war against Israel.** The chapter begins with a recitation of insulting letters sent back and forth between the kings of these two nations. When the king of Syria said that Samaria (Israel) would be an insignificant reward for his people after he conquered it, the king of Israel responded "Let not him that girdeth on his harness boast himself as he that putteth it off" (v. 11). This was like saying "Don't boast of the deed until it is done."

The king of Syria also said that "The Lord is God of the hills, but ... not ... of the valleys" (v. 28). "There seems to be an allusion here to the opinion, prevalent among all heathen nations, that the different parts of the earth had different divinities. They had gods for the woods, for the mountains, for the seas, for the heavens, and for the lower regions. The Syrians seem to have received the impression that Jehovah was specially the God of the mountains; but he manifested to them that he ruled everywhere"[17]. The Syrians attempted to conquer Israel twice, but failed because Israel was protected by the power of the Lord.

● **1 Kings 20:30–34 Ahab preserves the life of Ben-hadad, king of Syria.** As he was being defeated, Ben-hadad fled to the city of Aphek to hide (v. 30). Eventually, he and his servants "put sackcloth on [their] loins, and ropes upon [their] heads, and [went] out to the king of Israel," hoping that he would spare their lives (v. 31). When Ahab heard the request, he referred to Ben-hadad as his brother and "caused him to come up into the chariot" (v. 33). Ben-hadad promised to restore to Israel "the cities, which my father took from thy father," and also to allow Israel to "make streets for thee in Damascus, as my father made in Samaria." Ahab was pleased with this covenant, and sent him away alive (v. 34).

● **1 Kings 20:35–43 Ahab prescribes the nature of his own death.** The Lord was displeased with Ahab's letting Ben-hadad go because He had ordered him slain, and a prophet was sent to declare the price he would pay for disobedience. First the prophet engaged in symbolic acts to test the people's obedience: He commanded a man to slay him, which the man refused to do (v. 35). Then, he prophesied that because the man had disobeyed him, "as soon as thou art departed from me, a lion shall slay thee. And as soon as he was departed from him, a lion found him, and slew him" (v. 36). The prophet then asked another man to "smite him," and the man obediently did so (v. 37). Some people were willing to be obedient to the prophets, others were not.

The prophet then disguised himself and waited by the side of the road for the king. When the king passed by him, he called out to him and asked for the king's judgment of a circumstance. "Thy servant went out into the midst of the battle; and, behold, a man … brought a man unto me, and said, Keep this man: if by any means he be missing, then shall thy life be for his life." Then, he said, he got busy and lost track of the man and "he was gone" (v. 40). Ahab declared, "So shall thy judgment be; thyself hast decided it"—he would have to pay with his life for letting the man go (v. 40).

In this encounter with the prophet of the Lord, Ahab unwittingly pronounced his own doom. The prophet removed his disguise and declared to the king, "Thus saith the Lord, Because thou hast let go out of thy hand a man whom I appointed to utter destruction, therefore thy life shall go for his life, and thy people for his people" (v. 42). Ahab returned to his home "heavy and displeased" (v. 43). And the prophecy was fulfilled in the next battle with the Syrians (1 Kings 22:34–35).

Ahab and Jezebel Shed Innocent Blood

● **1 Kings 21:1–16 They kill Naboth to obtain his vineyard.** Ahab coveted Naboth's beautiful vineyard. He offered to buy it at an apparently fair price, but Naboth could not sell it. His land had been inherited from his forefathers, and the law of Moses did not permit the sale of one's inheritance, except in cases of extreme destitution. Hence Naboth's reply: "The Lord forbid it me" (v. 3).

Ahab returned to his house "heavy and displeased" at Naboth's refusal to sell him the land. "And he laid him down upon his bed, and turned away his face, and would eat no bread" (v. 4). Ahab's tantrum gives insight into his character. The king already owned ten-twelfths of the land of Israel, but he was miserable because he could not get everything he wanted. His wife Jezebel asked, "Why is thy spirit so sad, that thou eatest no bread?" (v. 5). And when he told her, she boldly declared, "Dost thou now govern the kingdom of Israel? arise, and eat bread, and let thine heart be merry: I will give thee the vineyard of Naboth the Jezreelite" (vv. 6–7).

Jezebel "wrote letters in Ahab's name, and sealed them with his seal, and sent the letters unto the elders and to the nobles that were in his city, dwelling with Naboth," proclaiming a fast and commanding these leaders to "set two men, sons of Belial, before him, to bear witness against him, saying, Thou didst blaspheme God and the king. And then carry him out, and stone him, that he may die" (v. 10). The phrase "sons of Belial," was a figure of speech applied to evil persons, liars, thieves, murderers. They did as the "king" commanded them, stoning Naboth to death outside the city and reporting back to Jezebel that the deed was done (vv. 11–14). She then proclaimed to Ahab, "Arise, take possession of the vineyard of Naboth the Jezreelite, which he refused to give thee for money: for Naboth is not alive, but dead" (v. 15). Ahab gladly arose and took possession of it (v. 16).

● **1 Kings 21:17–26 Through Elijah, the Lord condemns Ahab and Jezebel to death.** There was nobody Ahab detested more than Elijah, his "enemy" (v. 20). Ahab's death in battle had already been declared by another prophet (1 Kings 20:43), but now Elijah was sent to declare that "in the place where dogs licked the blood of Naboth shall dogs lick thy blood, even thine" (v. 19). Furthermore, the Lord declared through Elijah that Ahab would lose all of his posterity (v. 21). And as for Jezebel, the Lord declared that "The dogs shall eat Jezebel by the wall of Jezreel" (v. 23). These were awful condemnations, but richly deserved, because "there was none like unto Ahab, which did sell himself to work wickedness in the sight of the Lord, whom Jezebel his wife stirred up. And he did very abominably in following idols, according to all things as did the Amorites, whom the Lord cast out before the children of Israel" (vv. 25–26).

● **1 Kings 21:17–29 Ahab repents in sackcloth and ashes.** When Ahab heard Elijah's prophecies, "he rent his clothes, and put sackcloth upon his flesh, and fasted, and lay in sackcloth, and went softly" (v. 27). And because he so humbly repented, the "evil" that was declared concerning his posterity was delayed until Ahab's son was king (vv. 27–29). Nevertheless, the predictions concerning his and his wife's manner of death remained and were fulfilled with exactness.

The Death of Ahab and Jezebel

● **1 Kings 22:1–14 Jehoshaphat and Ahab joined forces against Syria.** The friendship between Ahab, king of Israel, and Jehoshaphat, king of Judah, may have developed because Jehoram, Jehoshaphat's son, had married Ahab's daughter Athaliah. This friendship did not please the Lord, and Jehoshaphat was severely rebuked for encouraging it (2 Chronicles 19:1–3).

Righteous Jehoshaphat (king of Judah) asked for a prophet of God to give them guidance concerning whether they should go to war (vv. 5–7). There is one—Micaiah—but Ahab hates him because he prophesies evil concerning him. He prefers false prophets who bring him good news (v. 8). Ahab and Jehoshaphat were considering whether they should combine to fight against the Syrians. Ahab's false prophets, or counselors, said yes, but Micaiah said no. "As the Lord liveth, what the Lord saith unto me, that will I speak" (v. 14). When the king asked him whether they should go to war, and Micaiah responded "Go and prosper," it was said with great sarcasm in order to let King Ahab know that it was contrary to Micaiah's true advice (v. 15). Hence the King's response in verse 16: "How many times shall I adjure thee that thou tell me nothing but that which is true in the name of the LORD?"

● **1 Kings 22:23–24 The "lying spirit" of Ahab's prophets was not given to them by God.** The message of these verses is not literally true. The Lord does not place a lying spirit in any man. The Hebrew expression means that the Lord "hath permitted or suffered a lying spirit to influence thy prophets." When Micaiah said this to the king, "Zedekiah the son of Chenaanah went near, and smote Micaiah on the cheek, and said, Which way went the Spirit of the LORD from me to speak unto thee?" (v. 24). Ahab's court had no respect for a true prophet's words and only wanted prophecies that pleased them.

● **1 Kings 22:25–29 The two kings fight against Syria despite Micaiah's counsel.** He assured them that his words would be fulfilled even if they took him (Micaiah) and "put [him] in the prison, and feed him with bread of affliction and with water of affliction" until they returned "in peace" from their battles (vv. 25–27). "And Micaiah said, If thou return at all in peace, the Lord hath not spoken by me [I am not a prophet]. And he said, Hearken, O people, every one of you" (v. 28). Nevertheless, the two kings proceeded into battle (v. 29).

● **1 Kings 22:30–40 Ahab disguises himself but is killed as Micaiah had prophesied.** Typically in battle, the kings wore their robes to clearly identify them as kings, which offered them some protection from being killed. But in this battle, Ahab told Jehoshaphat, "I will disguise myself, and enter into the battle; but put thou on thy robes. And the king of Israel disguised himself, and went into the battle" (v. 30). In the meantime, the king of Syria had commanded his forces to slay the king of Israel (v. 31).

GUSTAVE DORÉ, 1896

King Ahab is killed in battle

When they saw Jehoshaphat in his robes, "they turned aside to fight against him: and [he] cried out" (v. 32), and realizing that it was not the king of Israel, they stopped pursuing him (v. 33).

As the battle continued, "a certain man drew a bow at a venture" (meaning without aiming at a particular target), "and smote the king of Israel between the joints of the harness"—the spaces where one piece of armor joined another (v. 34). Ahab had his chariot driver take him out of the battle because he was wounded, but he remained in his chariot watching as the battle raged on. By evening, he was dead, "and the blood ran out of the wound into the midst of the chariot" (v. 35). With their king now dead, the army returned, "every man to his city, and every man to his own country" (v. 36).

● **1 Kings 22:38 Dogs lick up his blood exactly as prophesied.** King Ahab's body was returned to Samaria and buried (v. 37). And, as someone washed out his chariot and his armor, "the dogs licked up his blood ... according unto the word of the Lord which he spake."

● **2 Kings 9:30–37 Jezebel is later also killed exactly as prophesied.** The Lord had anointed Jehu to rule in Israel and to destroy the entire family of Ahab and Jezebel. When Jehu came and Jezebel heard of it, "she painted her face, and tired [covered] her head, and looked out at a window" (v. 30). When Jehu rode up to the window he demanded of those inside, "Who is on my side? who?" (v. 32). In fear of him, the "two or three eunuchs"

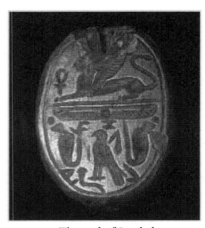

The seal of Jezebel

inside threw her out the window, and Jehu "trode her under foot" of his horses (v. 33). He went into the palace to eat and drink and invited those there to "go, see now this cursed woman, and bury her: for she is a king's daughter" (v. 34). But when they went out to bury her, "they found no more of her than the skull, and the feet, and the palms of her hands" because the dogs had taken her carcase and eaten it (v. 35). Thus was the word of the Lord, spoken through Elijah, that "dogs [shall] eat the flesh of Jezebel" literally fulfilled. She was so badly torn asunder that people could not recognize the corpse as being Jezebel (v. 37).

- **2 Kings 10:1–7 Jehu beheads 70 of Ahab's sons.** Ahab had 70 sons throughout Samaria, any one of whom might have succeeded to the throne. But the Lord had declared that Ahab would have no male posterity beyond one generation. Jehu wrote letters to all those that had care of or contact with any of Ahab's sons asking if any of them intended to encourage them to fight for their father's throne (vv. 2–3). "But they were exceedingly afraid, and said, Behold, two kings stood not before him [Jehu]: how then shall we stand?" and they wrote back to him saying they would do whatever he asked them to do (vv. 4–5). He commanded them to "take … the heads of … your master's sons, and come to me to Jezreel by to morrow this time" (v. 6). This they did, "and slew seventy persons, and put their heads in baskets, and sent him them to Jezreel" (v. 7). The only son of Ahab left to reign was Ahaziah.

Unrighteousness after Ahab

- **1 Kings 22:51–53 Ahaziah, son of Ahab, rules wickedly just as his father had done.** Learning nothing from the prophetic end of his father's wicked life, he continued to "walk … in the way of his father, and in the way of his mother, and … served Baal, and worshipped him, and provoked to anger the Lord God of Israel, according to all that his father had done."

- **2 Kings 1:1–8 The Moabites rebel against Israel after the death of Ahab.** Years earlier David had conquered them. The Moabites now saw an opportunity to break away from the Israelites, and they were determined to make the most of it. Their king, a man named Mesha, was so proud of the Moabites' rebellion that he wrote about it upon a large black stone, which has been discovered in our day by archaeologists. More details of the rebellion are found on this stone than are recorded in the Bible. Mesha recorded on the stone the account of hundreds of cities being added to his kingdom and how he built reservoirs, aqueducts, and fortifications.

King Ahaziah sought help in these battles from a heathen god named Baalzebub—"Lord of the flies"—a name also frequently given to Satan. Elder Bruce R. McConkie said: "This name for Satan signifies his position as the prince or chief of the devils. It is the same name (Baalzebub) as was given to an ancient heathen god. (2 Kings 1:3). In their rebellion against light, the ancient Jews applied the name Beelzebub to Christ (Matt. 10:25), and also said that he cast out devils by the power of Beelzebub. (Matt. 12:22–30)"[18].

As a result of this seeking after a heathen god, Elijah prophesied the king's death (v. 4). When word of this prophecy reached Ahaziah, he asked who had uttered it, and the answer was, "He was an hairy man, and girt with a girdle of leather about his loins" (v. 8). By this description, Ahaziah knew that it was Elijah.

- **2 Kings.1:9–12 Ahaziah sends soldiers to capture Elijah, but Elijah calls down fire from heaven to consume them.** The first captain of fifty men demanded that Elijah come with him to the king, but Elijah destroyed all of them with fire (vv. 9–10). Ahaziah then sent a second captain and fifty men, who, when they also demanded that Elijah come with them, were also destroyed by fire (vv. 11–12).

- **2 Kings 1:13–15 The third captain of fifty sent to Elijah humbles himself and is preserved.** Knowing what had befallen his predecessors, he "fell on his knees before Elijah, and besought him, and said unto him, O man of God, I pray thee, let my life, and the life of these fifty thy servants, be precious in thy sight" (v. 13). Elijah took the matter to the Lord, who advised him, "Go down with him: be not afraid of him. And he arose, and went down with him unto the king" (vv. 14–15).

Fire destroys those sent to seize Elijah

- **2 Kings 1:16–17 Elijah condemns Ahaziah to death, and he dies.** No doubt, King Ahaziah thought he would put Elijah to death, but instead it was he who died. Elijah condemned him for "enquir[ing] of Baal-zebub the god of Ekron" rather than turning to the God of Israel for his protection, and declared, "therefore thou shalt not come down off that bed on which thou art gone up, but shalt surely die" (v. 16). And "he died according to the word of the Lord which Elijah had spoken" (v. 17).

ELIJAH'S FINAL DAYS

Visiting the Prophets

- **2 Kings 2:1–3 Elijah visits the prophets at Bethel during his final journey.** The Lord intended to "take up Elijah into heaven by a whirlwind," but first he went with Elisha to Gilgal (v. 1). There he asked Elisha to stay because "the Lord hath sent me to Bethel," but Elisha said, "as thy soul liveth, I will not leave thee." So they went down to Bethel together (v. 2). As they approached this sacred site, "the sons of the prophets that were at Bethel came forth to Elisha, and said unto him, Knowest thou that the Lord will take away thy master from thy head to day? And he said, Yea, I know it; hold ye your peace" (v. 3).

These "sons of the Prophets" were part of a group of prophets "living together for instruction and worship" (*LDS Bible Dictionary*, 770). They married and had children and worked for their own livelihood (2 Kings 4:1). They are first mentioned at the time of the rise of Saul (1 Sam. 10:10), and David also contacted them (1 Sam. 19:19–20). We might conclude that Elijah and Elisha were part of this group (2 Kings 2:3, 5; 4:38; 6:1–7). And if Elijah was part of this group, they probably had the Melchizedek priesthood and ordinances among them.

They assisted the great prophets like Elijah and Elisha in all their duties. We see some of them officiating as prophets themselves, as with the prophet who prophesied the death of Ahab (1 Kings 20:35–43) and the prophet sent by Elisha to Ramoth-gilead to anoint Jehu king over Israel (2 Kgs. 9:1–10). Some of them we know by name, such as Micaiah (1 Kings 22:8). During the time of Elijah and Elisha they were found at various places, including, as we learn in this part of the scriptures, Gilgal, Bethel, and Jericho.

In the days of Ahab, this group was well known and influential. Jezebel hated and sought to destroy them, killing many of them. Her persecutions produced the death of so many of the prophets that Elijah thought he was the only one left (1 Kings 19:10). But by the time of Elisha's ministry, they had recovered to the point that they needed a larger place in which to dwell (2 Kings. 6:1–6).

● **The importance of Bethel—the "House of the Lord."** We see again in these verses the importance of Bethel as a holy place where the Lord communed with His prophets. It already had a long and venerable history.

— Genesis 12:6–8   Abraham received visions of God at Bethel when he entered Canaan.

— Genesis 13:3–4   Abraham received more visions there after leaving Egypt.

— Genesis 28:10–22   Jacob also received his first vision of the Lord at Bethel.

— Genesis 35:9–15   Jacob received more heavenly visions there upon returning.

The meaning of the word "Beth-el" is "house of the Lord." Thus, the place was like a temple to the righteous who lived in that day. And it is not surprising that the sealing keys that Elijah possessed are associated with this "house of the Lord."

Elijah Parts the Waters of the Jordan River

● **2 Kings 2:4–6 Elijah and Elisha visit the prophets at Jericho.** Once again, Elijah sought to leave Elisha with his fellow prophets while he prepared for his translation into heaven. He said to Elisha, "tarry here, I pray thee; for the Lord hath sent me to Jericho. And [Elisha] said, As the Lord liveth, and as thy soul liveth, I will not leave thee. So they came to Jericho" (v. 4).

As at Gilgal and Bethel, there were "sons of the prophets" at Jericho, and they came out to greet Elijah and Elisha. And like the prophets at Bethel, they already knew that Elijah was going to be translated. They said to Elisha, "Knowest thou that the Lord will take away thy master from thy head to day? And he answered, Yea, I know it; hold ye your peace" (v. 5). Once again, Elijah sought to persuade Elisha to stay with the prophets while he traveled on to "Jordan," but Elisha would not leave him (v. 6). He clearly wanted the benefit of every possible hour of instruction and inspiration from Elijah before the mantle fell entirely upon him.

● **2 Kings 2:7–8 Elijah parts the waters of the Jordan River and crosses it on dry ground.** As Elijah and Elisha approached the Jordan River, "fifty men of the sons of the prophets ... stood to view afar off" (v. 7). Elijah then took his mantle, wrapped it together into a bundle, "and smote the waters, and they were divided hither and thither, so that they two went over on dry ground" (v. 8). This had not been done since the day when Joshua brought the children of Israel into the promised land. It clearly indicated that Elijah, as the Lord's chief prophet, had power over elements.

Elijah Is Translated

● **2 Kings 2:9–10 Elisha requests a double-portion of Elijah's spirit.** After crossing the Jordan River, "Elijah said unto Elisha, Ask what I shall do for thee, before I be taken away from thee. And Elisha said, I pray thee, let a double portion of thy spirit be upon me" (v. 9). He would soon be asked to step into the prophetic shoes of Elijah, and that was not an easy act to follow. Anyone would feel intimidated. But Elisha's request was not just for the same spirit of Elijah, but a "double portion" of it. Elijah responded, "Thou hast asked a hard thing: nevertheless, if thou see me when I am taken from thee, it shall be so unto thee; but if not, it shall not be so" (v. 10). This test of whether the Lord would permit him to see Elijah's translation would indicate whether his faith was sufficient to obtain the desired gift.

● **2 Kings 2:11 Elijah is translated while Elisha watches.** "A chariot of fire, and horses of fire" appeared and took Elijah "up by a whirlwind into heaven." We can speculate as to whether this description is literal or figurative, but I prefer to interpret it as figurative—an attempt by the writer to describe something he could not explain because it was beyond earthly things. A "chariot" and "horses" were the means by which rapid travel was accomplished in those days, and whether there was a literal chariot and horses or not, the point is that he

Elijah was translated in a chariot of fire

rapidly ascended. Joseph Smith described a conduit or tube ("whirlwind") of light through which Moroni ascended on the night he appeared in Joseph's bedroom (JS-History 1:43). And since the glory of such beings is so bright, the writer describes it as being "fire." Joseph Smith said it was "lighter than at noonday" (JS-History 1:30). Elijah was translated rapidly into heaven in the midst of such great light.

The Prophet Joseph Smith said:

> Many have supposed that the doctrine of translation was a doctrine whereby men were taken immediately into the presence of God, and into an eternal fullness, but this is a mistaken idea. Their place of habitation is that of the terrestrial order, and a place prepared for such characters He held in reserve to be ministering angels unto many planets, and who as yet have not entered into so great a fullness as those who are resurrected from the dead. "Others were tortured, not accepting deliverance, that they might obtain a better resurrection." (Heb. 11th chap., part of the 35th verse).

> Now it was evident that there was a better resurrection, or else God would not have revealed it unto Paul. Wherein then, can it be said a better resurrection. This distinction is made between the doctrine

of the actual resurrection and translation: translation obtains deliverance from the tortures and sufferings of the body, but their existence will prolong as to the labors and toils of the ministry, before they can enter into so great a rest and glory.[19]

THE MISSION OF ELIJAH

The Sealing Powers

We usually think of the sealing powers of a prophet as those needed to seal a family together forever. And this is correct. But the sealing powers of Elijah are much broader. They permit a prophet to seal and unseal things on earth. For example:

— Elijah sealed up the heavens against rain (1 Kings 17:1).

— Elijah later called down torrents of water on dry land (1 Kings 18:1, 41–46).

● **What is this "sealing" power?**

— They are the keys of sealing both on earth and in the "gates of hell" (spirit world). (Matthew 16:13–19).

— They must be exercised by "him who is anointed, unto whom I have appointed this power and the keys of this priesthood" (D&C 132:19).

— The action must be ratified by the Holy Spirit. This is what the word "seal" actually means—to verify the act as being legitimate in the eyes of God (D&C 132:19).

— They have the power to seal anything on earth or in heaven (D&C 132:19). For example:

■ They have power to seal a person's coming forth in the first resurrection.

■ They have power to place a person's name in the Lamb's Book of Life, signifying the inheritance of the celestial kingdom.

■ They have power to seal a person up unto eternal life, where they will inherit "thrones, kingdoms, principalities, and powers, dominions, all heights and depths."

■ They have power to ensure that we can "pass by the angels, and the gods, which are set there, to [our] exaltation and glory in all things."

■ They have power to bequeath a fulness of glory, including "a continuation of the seeds [the ability to create offspring] forever and ever."

■ They have the power to place upon a person anything "in time, and through all eternity; and shall be of full force when they are out of the world."

— Those who are thus sealed "shall ... be gods, because they have no end; therefore shall they be from everlasting to everlasting, because they continue; then shall they be above all, because all things are subject unto them. Then shall they be gods, because they have all power, and the angels are subject unto them" (D&C 132:20).

— These keys must be exercised "by revelation and commandment" through the Lord's prophet "whom [He has] appointed on the earth to hold this power" (D&C 132:7).

— There "is never but one on the earth at a time on whom this power and the keys of this priesthood are conferred" (D&C 132:7).

— Anything not sealed by this power—"all covenants, contracts, bonds, obligations, oaths, vows, performances, connections, associations, or expectations"—will be "of no efficacy, virtue, or force in and after the resurrection from the dead; for all contracts that are not made unto this end have an end when men are dead" (D&C 132:7).

— These restrictions apply to all things on this earth, including the marriage covenants we make. "Therefore, if a man marry him a wife in the world, and he marry her not by me nor by my word, and he covenant with her so long as he is in the world and she with him, their covenant and marriage are not of force when they are dead, and when they are out of the world" (D&C 132:15).

● **Matthew 16:19 The Lord promised the sealing keys to his apostles,** saying, "Whatsoever thou shalt bind on earth shall be bound in heaven: and whatsoever thou shalt loose on earth shall be loosed in heaven."

● **Matthew 17:1–3 Elijah conferred these keys upon Peter, James and John one week later on the Mount of Transfiguration.** The Savior took the First Presidency of the Church in his day— Peter, James, and John—"up into an high mountain apart, and was transfigured before them: and his face did shine as the sun, and his raiment was white as the light" (vv. 1–2). Then there also appeared "Moses and Elias talking with him" (v. 3). We learn later that this "Elias" was Elijah. And they did more than talk. They conferred their respective keys: keys of the gathering (Moses) and the keys of sealing (Elijah) upon Peter, James and John.

The question is, "Why didn't the Savior merely give them the keys since He holds all keys?" And the answer is that this is the way the Lord establishes a new dispensation and Church. He brings back those who held the keys previously and has them confer them upon the new apostles and prophets. He did it that way with the original New Testament Church, and he did it that way in the Kirtland Temple in the latter days.

The Prophet Joseph Smith said: "The priesthood is everlasting. The Savior, Moses, and Elias [Elijah] gave the keys to Peter, James, and John, on the Mount when they were transfigured before him"[20].

Why Elijah and Moses Were Translated

Another significant point to notice is that these two individuals—Moses and Elijah— were translated at the end of their ministries. There was a very important reason for this. Had they been only spirits, they could not have tangibly placed their hands upon the heads of Peter, James, and John to perform this ordinance. They had not yet been resurrected since the Lord's death and resurrection had not occurred by then. So it was necessary to translate them, which allowed them to remain in their bodies, until this ordinance was completed.

President Joseph Fielding Smith said:

> From that we understand why Elijah and Moses were preserved from death: because they had a mission to perform, and it had to be performed before the crucifixion of the Son of God, and it could not be done in the spirit. They had to have tangible bodies.

> Christ is the first fruits of the resurrection; therefore if any former prophets had a work to perform preparatory to the mission of the Son of God, or to the dispensation of the meridian of times, it was essential that they be preserved to fulfill that mission in the flesh. For that reason Moses disappeared from among the people and was taken up into the mountain, and the people thought he was buried by the Lord. The Lord preserved him, so that he could come at the proper time and restore his keys, on the heads of Peter, James, and John, who stood at the head of the dispensation of the meridian of time. He reserved Elijah from death that he might also come and bestow his keys upon the heads of Peter, James, and John and prepare them for their ministry.[21]

- **D&C 133:55 Elijah and Moses were resurrected at the time of the Savior's resurrection.** Matthew tell us that after Christ's resurrection "the graves were opened; and many bodies of the saints which slept arose" (Matthew 27:52). And this verse in the Doctrine and Covenants teaches that those who rose from the dead included Moses, Elijah, John the Baptist, Abraham, Isaac, and Jacob.

- **Matthew 17:4–13 The sacredness of what Elijah and Moses conferred upon the apostles.** Recognizing the temple implications of what they received, Peter proposed that they build three "tabernacles" on the mount—"one for thee, and one for Moses, and one for Elias" (v. 4). While there, they heard the voice of God the Father speaking out of the cloud that had overshadowed them, saying, "This is my beloved Son, in whom I am well pleased; hear ye him" (v. 5). They were probably instructed in some of the principles of eternal sealings, and Jesus cautioned them not to teach them to others "until the Son of man be risen again from the dead" (v. 9). No such teachings were given to the early Church in general until after the 40-day ministry of the resurrected Christ.

The Sealing Powers in the Latter-days

- **Malachi 4:5–6; 3 Nephi 25:5–6 Elijah's mission is essential to the earth's purpose.** Malachi made this clear when he said, "And he [Elijah] shall turn the heart of the fathers to the children, and the heart of the children to their fathers, *lest I come and smite the earth with a curse*" (emphasis added). This statement concerning Elijah's mission is so important that it is the only scripture that can be found in all four of the standard works—the Bible, the Book of Mormon, the Doctrine and Covenants, and the Pearl of Great Price.

- **JS-History 38–39; D&C 2 Elijah's role was emphasized from the very beginning of the Restoration.** When Moroni visited the Prophet Joseph Smith, he quoted Malachi, saying, "Behold, I will reveal unto you the Priesthood, by the hand of Elijah the prophet, before the coming of the great and dreadful day of the Lord" (v. 38). Then he quoted the next verse differently than it appears in the book of Malachi: "And he shall plant in the hearts of the children the promises made to the fathers, and the hearts of the children shall turn to their fathers. If it were not so, *the whole earth would be utterly wasted at his coming*" (v. 39, emphasis added).

President Joseph Fielding Smith said: "If Elijah had not come … all the work of past ages would have been of little avail, for the Lord said the whole earth, under such conditions, would be utterly wasted at his coming. Therefore his mission was of vast importance to the world. It is not the question of baptism for the dead alone, but also the sealing of parents and children to parents, so that there should be a "whole and complete and perfect union, and welding together of dispensations, and keys, and powers, and glories," from the beginning down to the end of time … . Why would the earth be wasted? Simply because if there is not a welding link between the fathers and the children—which is the work for the dead—then we will all stand rejected; the whole work of God will fail and be utterly wasted. Such a condition, of course, shall not be"[22].

The Prophet Joseph Smith said:

DAGUERREOTYPE, 1844, NAUVOO, ILLINOIS

The Bible says, "I will send you Elijah the Prophet before the coming of the great and dreadful day of the Lord; and he shall turn the hearts of the fathers to the children, and the hearts of the children to the fathers, lest I come and smite the earth with a curse." [Malachi 4:5–6.]

Now, the word turn here should be translated bind, or seal. But what is the object of this important mission? or how is it to be fulfilled? The keys are to be delivered, the spirit of Elijah is to come, the Gospel to be established, the Saints of God gathered, Zion built up, and the Saints to come up as saviors on Mount Zion.

But how are they to become saviors on Mount Zion? By building their temples, erecting their baptismal fonts, and going forth and receiving all the ordinances, baptisms, confirmations, washings, anointings, ordinations and sealing powers upon their heads, in behalf of all their progenitors who are dead, and redeem them that they may come forth in the first resurrection and be exalted to thrones of glory with them; and herein is the chain that binds the hearts of the fathers to the children, and the children to the fathers, which fulfills the mission of Elijah. And I would to God that … we might go into [the temple], and go to work and improve our time, and make use of the seals while they are on earth.

The Saints have not too much time to save and redeem their dead, and gather together their living relatives, that they may be saved also, before the earth will be smitten, and the consumption decreed falls upon the world.[23]

President Joseph Fielding Smith said: "Now you get a glimpse of what is meant in this scripture which says that the whole earth would be smitten with a curse if Elijah did not first come … There is power in the Church for salvation and exaltation, and the Lord, when he comes, will not find it necessary to smite this earth with a curse, because that sealing power is here … so that all men who will may receive salvation and exaltation and the sealing powers. Thanks be unto God that he sent Elijah into the world to bestow these blessings"[24].

● **D&C 110:13–15 The keys of Elijah were restored to Joseph Smith and Oliver Cowdery in the Kirtland Temple on 3 April 1836.** They report that after their vision of the Savior had closed, "another great and glorious vision burst upon us; for Elijah the prophet, who was taken to heaven without tasting death, stood before us, and said: Behold, the time has fully come, which was spoken of by the mouth of Malachi— testifying that he [Elijah] should be sent, before the great and dreadful day of the Lord come—To turn the hearts of the fathers to the children, and the children to the fathers, *lest the whole earth be smitten with a curse*" (emphasis added). Moses also restored his keys on this occasion.

The Prophet Joseph Smith said: "'Elijah was the last prophet that held the keys of the priesthood, and who will, before the last dispensation, restore the authority and deliver the keys of the priesthood, in order that all the ordinances may be attended to in righteousness. ... Why send Elijah? Because he holds the keys of the authority to administer in all the ordinances of the priesthood; and without the authority is given, the ordinances could not be administered in righteousness"[25].

President Joseph Fielding Smith said: "What was the promise made to the fathers that was to be fulfilled in the latter-days by the turning of the hearts of the children to their fathers? It was the promise of the Lord made through Enoch, Isaiah, and the prophets, to the nations of the earth, that the time should come when the dead should be redeemed. And the turning of the hearts of the children is fulfilled in the performing of the vicarious temple work and in the preparation of their genealogies ... In the present dispensation we are privileged to perform ordinances for the dead which were denied them when living, notwithstanding their faithfulness and obedience to the gospel in their day"[26].

The Prophet Joseph Smith said concerning the spirit, power, and calling of Elijah:

DAGUERREOTYPE, 1844, NAUVOO, ILLINOIS

> The spirit, power, and calling of Elijah is, that ye have power to hold the key of the revelations, ordinances, oracles, powers and endowments of the fulness of the Melchizedek priesthood and of the kingdom of God on the earth; and to receive, obtain, and perform all the ordinances belonging to the kingdom of God, even unto the turning of the hearts of the fathers unto the children, and the hearts of the children unto the fathers, even those who are in heaven. ...
>
> I wish you to understand this subject, for it is important; and if you receive it, this is the spirit of Elijah, that we redeem our dead, and connect ourselves with our fathers which are in heaven, and seal up our dead to come forth in the first resurrection ... We want the power of Elijah to seal those who dwell on earth to those who dwell in heaven. This is the power of Elijah and the keys of the kingdom of Jehovah.[27]

Notes

1. Clarke, *The Holy Bible…with a Commentary and Critical Notes* [1832], 2:452.

2. Keil &Delitzsch, *Commentary on the Old Testament,* 10 vols. [1996], 3:1:234.

3. *Doctrines of Salvation*, comp. Elder Bruce R. McConkie, 3 vols. [1954–56], 2:102.

4. In Conference Report, Apr. 1996, 39; or *Ensign*, May 1996, 29.

5. In Conference Report, Apr. 1988, 3, 6; or *Ensign*, May 1988, 4, 6.

6. General Conference address, Welfare Session, April 6, 1974.

7. Clarke, Clarke, *Bible Commentary*, 6 vols. [n.d.], 2:457.

8. *That My Family Should Partake* [1974], 22.

9. Clarke, *Bible Commentary*, 6 vols. [n.d.], 2:459.

10. Clarke, Clarke, *Bible Commentary*, 6 vols. [n.d.], 2:457.

11. Keil and Delitzsch, *Commentary on the Old Testament*, 10 vols. [1996], 3:1:249.

12. *Doctrines of Salvation*, 2:106.

13. *The Holy Temple* (1980), 102.

14. In Conference Report, Oct. 1977, 46; or *Ensign*, Nov. 1977, 32.

15. "Reverence Invites Revelation," *Ensign*, Nov. 1991, 21.

16. In Conference Report, Oct. 1996, 71; or *Ensign*, Nov. 1996, 51.

17. James M. Freeman, *Manners and Customs of the Bible* [1996], 165.

18. *Mormon Doctrine*, 2nd ed. [1966], 75.

19. *History of the Church*, 4:210.

20. *Teachings of the Prophet Joseph Smith*, sel. Joseph Fielding Smith [1976], 158.

21. *Doctrines of Salvation*, 2:110–111.

22. *Doctrines of Salvation*, 2:121.

23. *History of the Church*, 6:183–184.

24. *Doctrines of Salvation*, 2:122.

25. *Teachings of the Prophet Joseph Smith*, 172.

26. *Doctrines of Salvation*, 2:154–155

27. *Teachings of the Prophet Joseph Smith*, 337–338.

CHAPTER 29

The Prophet Elisha

(2 Kings 3–13)

℘℃℞

INTRODUCTION

The Book of Second Kings

- **Author:**   Unknown

- **Position:**   The books of First and Second Kings are combined as one in the Hebrew Bible but are separated in the Greek Bible, a convention retained in the Latin and English versions.

- **Purpose:**   Along with First Kings, to provide a contrast of the pervasive wickedness of the people and their kings (with the notable exceptions of Hezekiah and Josiah) and the glorious devotion and righteousness of the prophets of God—Elijah, Elisha, and Isaiah.

- **Time Span:**   The time of transition of prophetic leadership from Elijah to Elisha (ca. 851 BC). to the destruction of Jerusalem by Nebuchadnezzar of Babylon (around 587 BC).

- **Length:**   25 chapters

- **Key Sections:**   — Chapters 1–13   Transition of leadership from Elijah to Elisha; Elisha's ministry

  — Chapters 13–17   Kings contend for supremacy until the Ten tribes are carried away captive into Assyria.

The Prophet Elisha

PROVIDENCE LITHOGRAPHIC CO. 1898

— Chapters 18–23   Reformation under the righteous leadership of Hezekiah and then Josiah in Judah.

— Chapters 24–25   The rule of Zedekiah and the Babylonian captivity.

● **Cross References:** The destruction of Jerusalem and the captivity of Judah by the Babylonians corresponds to the period of time when the Book of Mormon account begins (1 Nephi 1:4; 5:12–13; Omni 1:15; Helaman 6:10; 8:21).

ELISHA INHERITS ELIJAH's MANTLE

Who Was Elisha?

● **2 Kings 3:11 Elisha "poured water on the hands of Elijah."** In those days, servants poured water over the hands of their masters after each meal so he could clean them. This expression indicates that Elisha was the servant and disciple of Elijah.

Elijah casts his mantle upon Elisha

● **1 Kings 19:16, 19–21 The Lord calls Elisha to be a prophet.** Elijah was instructed to anoint Elisha as a "prophet in thy room" (v. 16). Elijah went forward with this assignment and found Elisha "plowing with twelve yoke of oxen before him" (v. 19). Elijah called Elisha to his prophetic office by "cast[ing] his mantle upon him," symbolizing that Elisha was called to be his successor (v. 19). Elisha asked for a brief time to say goodbye to his parents and to give his possessions to the needy, which he did (v. 20). "Then he arose, and went after Elijah, and ministered unto him" (v. 21).

Elisha was probably wealthy because he owned twelve yokes (pairs) of oxen, eleven of which yokes would have been driven by servants. He himself only drove the twelfth team. The feast he prepared from two oxen would also indicate his wealth. Burning his equipment to make the sacrificial meal symbolized Elisha's forfeiting of worldly wealth as he accepted his prophetic office.

Prophetic Succession

There were, in those days, many prophets of Jehovah located at Gilgal, Bethel, and Jericho. When their lives were threatened by Jezebel, the righteous man Obadiah brought them food and water to sustain them in the cave where they were hiding (1 Kings 18:2–16). And Elijah and Elisha visited all three of these groups just before Elijah was translated (2 Kings 2:1–5). They lived together "for instruction and worship"[1]. They married and had children and worked for their own livelihood (2 Kings 4:1). They are first mentioned at the time of the rise of Saul (1 Sam. 10:10), and David also contacted them (1 Sam. 19:19–20). We might conclude that Elijah and Elisha were part of this group (2 Kings 2:3, 5; 4:38; 6:1–7). And if they were among this group, they probably had the Melchizedek priesthood and ordinances among them.

They assisted the great prophets like Elijah and Elisha in all their duties. We see some of them officiating as prophets themselves, as with the prophet who prophesied the death of Ahab (1 Kings 20:35–43) and the prophet sent by Elisha to Ramoth-gilead to anoint Jehu king over Israel (2 Kgs. 9:1–10). Some of them we know by name, such as Micaiah (1 Kings 22:8). But while they were holy men, they were not designated as the Lord's priesthood leader among the people, as were Elijah and Elisha. And none of them were "in line" to succeed Elijah when he was translated. That honor fell to Elisha, whom the Lord had specifically chosen and Elijah had anointed to be his successor.

The situation is similar, yet different, today. While all of the Apostles are prophets who hold all the keys of the kingdom, only the President of the Church, who is the senior living Apostle, may use these keys or authorize others to use them on behalf of the entire Church (D&C 28:1–7; D&C 132:7). This would be similar to Elijah and Elisha's relationship to the rest of the prophets in their day.

While Elisha was anointed privately, there is a clear and public procedure by which a prophet is chosen today (D&C 43:2–3, 7, 11). The Prophet Joseph Smith wrote concerning this while he was incarcerated at Liberty Jail:

January 16th, 1839

"Brothers H.C. Kimball and B. Young:

"Joseph Smith, Jun., Sidney Rigdon and Hyrum Smith, prisoners for Jesus' sake, send greeting … Inasmuch as we are in prison, for a little season, if need be, the management of the affairs of the Church devolves on you, that is the Twelve …

"It will be necessary for you to get the Twelve together, ordain such as have not been ordained, or at least such of them as you can get, and proceed to regulate the Elders as the Lord may give you wisdom … Brethren, we remain yours in hope of eternal life,"

Sidney Rigdon
Joseph Smith Jr.
Hyrum Smith

"N.B. Appoint the oldest of those of the Twelve, who were first appointed, to be the president of your quorum"[2]

As a result of the post-script of this letter, Brigham Young was sustained by the Apostles as the president of their quorum because he had been serving longer than any other living and faithful apostle at that time.

President Joseph Fielding Smith explained: "There is no mystery about the choosing of the successor to the President of the Church. The Lord settled this a long time ago, and the senior Apostle automatically becomes the presiding officer of the Church, and he is so sustained by the council of the Twelve which becomes the presiding body of the Church when there is no First Presidency. The president is not elected, but he has to be sustained both by his brethren of the council and by the members of the Church"[3].

President Gordon B. Hinckley explained how this procedure was followed when he was ordained and set apart as the prophet and President of the Church following the death of President Howard W. Hunter:

> With President Hunter's passing, the First Presidency was dissolved. Brother Monson and I, who had served as his counselors, took our places in the Quorum of the Twelve, which became the presiding authority of the Church.
>
> [A few days later] all of the living ordained Apostles gathered in a spirit of fasting and prayer in the upper room of the temple. Here we sang a sacred hymn and prayed together. We partook of the sacrament of the Lord's supper, renewing in that sacred, symbolic testament our covenants and our relationship with Him who is our divine Redeemer. The Presidency was then reorganized, following a precedent well established through generations of the past [this precedent is explained in the preceding statement by President Joseph Fielding Smith]. There was no campaigning, no contest, no ambition for office. It was quiet, peaceful, simple, and sacred. It was done after the pattern which the Lord Himself had put in place.[4]

ELISHA BEGINS HIS MINISTRY

- **2 Kings 2:12–13 The mantle falls upon Elisha.** As Elijah was translated, Elisha cried out, "My father, my father, the chariot of Israel, and the horsemen thereof," then took hold of his clothing and "rent them in two pieces"—a way of bearing witness to a significant event. Then he took up "the mantle of Elijah that fell from him, and went back, and stood by the bank of Jordan" (v. 13). Elijah's cloak, or mantle, was a symbol of his authority. Possession of it symbolized that Elijah's former authority now rested on Elisha.

- **2 Kings 2:14–15 Elisha parts the waters of the Jordan River.** As his first prophetic act, "he took the mantle of Elijah that fell from him, and smote the waters," and "they parted hither and thither: and Elisha went over" (v. 14). The sons of the prophets observed this miracle and declared, "The spirit of Elijah doth rest on Elisha," and they "came to meet him, and bowed themselves to the ground before him" (v. 15).

- **2 Kings 2:16–18 The men of Jericho search unsuccessfully for Elijah's body.** The men of the city of Jericho (presumably not the prophets, since they knew Elijah was to be translated), then asked Elisha if they should go to look for Elijah's body. They were concerned that it might have been "cast ... upon some mountain, or into some valley." Elisha told them "Ye shall not send" (v. 16). But they could not take "no" for an answer and continued to beg Elisha for permission to send a search party until he was "ashamed" [weary] of their requests. He said: "Send," and they sent out 50 men who searched for 3 days without success (v. 17). And when they returned to Jericho empty-handed, "he said unto them, Did I not say unto you, Go not?" (v. 18).

- **2 Kings 2:19–22 Elisha heals the waters of a briny pool.** The men of Jericho then asked for a miracle from Elisha. The city was pleasant enough, but its water was not, and as a result the ground was barren (v. 19). Elisha called for a new container with "salt therein, and they brought it to him" (v. 20). Then he cast the salt into the pool, saying, "Thus saith the Lord, I have healed these waters; there shall not be from thence any more death or barren land" (v. 21). The use of salt to purify this water made this miracle all the more impressive because salt normally corrupts rather than purifies water. But "the waters were healed unto this day," as Elisha had declared (v. 22).

GUSTAVE DORÉ, 1896

She-bears kill young mockers of Elisha

● **2 Kings 2:23–25 Young men mock Elisha and are killed by bears.** Elisha traveled north toward Bethel, "and as he was going up by the way, there came forth little children out of the city, and mocked him, and said unto him, Go up, thou bald head; go up, thou bald head" (v. 23). The word that the King James Version translates "little children" means "young," not necessarily "little," and can be translated "young man"—one old enough to go to battle. It is not likely that little children would have been punished so severely.

Elisha turned around and looked at them "and cursed them in the name of the Lord." Two she bears came immediately out of the woods and killed 42 of them. There is no indication here that Elisha directed the bears—only that they came forth after his curse.

"Is it not possible that these 42 were a set of unlucky young men, who had been employed in the wood, destroying the whelps of these same she-bears, who now pursued them, and tore them to pieces, for the injury they had done? … The mention of she-bears gives some colour to [this] conjecture … At the time when these young fellows insulted the prophet, the bears might be tracing the footsteps of the murderers of their young, and thus came upon them in the midst of their insults … If the conjecture be correct, the bears were prepared by their loss to execute the curse of the prophet, and God's justice guided them to the spot to punish [their] iniquity …"[5]

THE WAR WITH MOAB

● **2 Kings 3:1–3 The Idolatry of Jehoram.** Joram or Jehoram was not so ungodly as his father Ahab and his mother Jezebel. He had the statue or pillar of Baal, which his father had erected in Samaria, removed. He did not succeed, however, in exterminating Baal worship. It continued in Samaria, which is not surprising since his mother Jezebel, a fanatical worshiper of Baal, was living throughout his entire reign.

● **2 Kings 3:4–10 Judah, Israel, and Edom unite in war against Moab.** Jehoshaphat, king of Judah, had maintained friendly relations with Ahab (1 Kings 22:4) and wanted to maintain them with his son Jehoram. This was one way to do that. These three nations joined in a march toward Moab, but ran out of water after seven days (v. 9).

- **2 Kings 3:11–15 Jehoshaphat seeks the advice of a true prophet of God before going to battle.** Because Jehoshaphat was a true worshiper of Jehovah, the kings went to Elisha, who was irritated by the presence of Jehoram, the wicked king of Israel. Elisha sarcastically advised him to seek the counsel of the false prophets of his father (v. 13). He also said: "As the LORD of hosts liveth, before whom I stand, surely, were it not that I regard the presence of Jehoshaphat the king of Judah, I would not look toward thee, nor see thee" (v. 14).

- **2 Kings 3:16–19 The prophet Elisha commands them to do four things as they go through the land of Moab.**

  1. They were to "make this valley full of ditches" from which they and their animals can miraculously obtain water, because "ye shall not see wind, neither shall ye see rain" (vv. 16–17).

  2. They were to cut down all trees that could be used to build fortifications (v. 19).

  3. They were to destroy the wells that provided the life-giving waters of the land (v. 19).

  4. They were to throw rocks on the fields (v. 19).

  The reasoning was that the defeated enemy would have to spend all its time trying to recover from these ravages rather than preparing to wage war again.

- **2 Kings 3:20–24 Moab is deceived by the appearance of red trenches of water.** When they saw them in the morning sun, they thought their enemies had massacred one another. But when they marched into the Israelite camp they were surprised and routed. They retreated to their capitol city, a fortress on a high hill, where the armies of Israel surrounded them.

- **2 Kings 3:26–27 Mesha, the king of Moab, offered his firstborn son as a sacrifice to Chemosh (Molech) when he realized he could not escape his enemies.** He made this offering on the top of the wall of the city, in full view of his enemies. They were so repulsed by this that they went home, leaving the king of Moab with the impression that his god had saved him. This was a big mistake, because it emboldened him to attack them again (2 Kings 13:20).

ELISHA'S PRIESTHOOD POWER

Elisha Performs Many Miracles

- **2 Kings 4:1–7 He multiplies a widow's oil.** The wife of one of the "sons of the prophets" spoke to Elisha, saying, "Thy servant my husband is dead; and thou knowest that thy servant did fear the Lord: and the creditor is come to take unto him my two sons to be bondmen" (v. 1). She had nothing in the house but a pot of oil (v. 2). So Elisha told her to "borrow thee vessels ... of all thy neighbours, even empty vessels; borrow not a few" (v. 3). The she was to pour oil "into all those vessels, and ... set aside [those which are] full" (v. 4). She did this, and filled every vessel before the oil ran out (vv. 5–6). "Then she came and told the man of God. And he said, Go, sell the oil, and pay thy debt, and live thou and thy children of the rest" (v. 7).

● **2 Kings 4:8–17 He promises a son to a Shunammite woman who showed her love for God by her kindness to Elisha.** "The aliyah, 'chamber,' (mentioned in verse 10) is an upper room of an Eastern house, being sometimes built on the roof, and sometimes making a second story to the porch, to which it has access by stairs. It is hence called … 'the chamber over the gate.' … [Here] it is called a chamber 'in the wall' … It is usually well furnished, and kept as a room for the entertainment of honored guests"[6].

Elisha called for her and she stood in his door (v. 15). Then he promised, "About this season, according to the time of life, thou shalt embrace a son. And she said, Nay, my lord, thou man of God, do not lie unto thine handmaid" (v. 16). This response to Elisha's prophecy was not one of doubt but of hope. In essence she was saying, "May your words not be a lie," or "May your words come true." And they did, because "the woman conceived, and bare a son" (v. 17).

● **2 Kings 4:18–37 He raises her son from the dead.** As the child grew, he followed his father into the field where he worked with the reapers (v. 18). Then, on a particular day, he cried unto his father, "My head, my head" and was carried by one of the workers back to his mother (v. 19). The child "sat on her knees till noon, and then died" (v. 20). She then took the body and "laid him on the bed of the man of God, and shut the door upon him, and went out" (v. 21). Elisha was at Mount Carmel, so she rode quickly to find him (vv. 22–26). "And when she came to the man of God [at] the hill, she caught him by the feet" (v. 27). She complained that when Elisha had promised her a son, she had told him, "Do not deceive me," but now the child lay dead (v. 28). Elisha commanded his servant Gehazi to take the prophet's staff and ride quickly to where the child lay "and lay my staff upon the face of the child" (v. 29).

Elisha raised a dead boy to life

The woman refused to leave without Elisha, so he also "arose, and followed her" (v. 30). But before they could get there, Gehazi arrived first and "laid the staff upon the face of the child; but there was neither voice, nor hearing" (v. 31).

When Elisha arrived, he found the child "dead, and laid upon his bed" (v. 32). He went into the room alone with the child, where he "lay upon the child, and put his mouth upon his mouth, and his eyes upon his eyes, and his hands upon his hands: and he stretched himself upon the child; and the flesh of the child waxed warm" (v. 34). After a brief pause, he again "stretched himself upon him: and the child sneezed seven times, and … opened his eyes" (v. 35). He called Gehazi and the woman to come in, then invited the woman to "Take up thy son" (v. 36). She bowed before the prophet in gratitude, then "took up her son, and went out" (v. 37).

● **2 Kings 4:38–41 He renders poisonous food harmless.** Elisha traveled on to Gilgal, where another group of the sons of the prophets resided. There was a great drought upon the land, so Elisha decided to feed them from a pot of seethed herbs (v. 38). He sent one of them out "into the field to gather herbs, and [he] found a wild vine, and gathered thereof wild gourds his lap full, and came and shred them into the pot of pottage," not knowing what they were (v. 39). As they began to eat, they cried out to Elisha that "there is death in the pot. And they could not eat thereof" (v. 40). Elisha cast "meal" into the pot and healed it, and afterward "there was no harm in the pot" (v. 41).

- **2 Kings 4:42–44 He multiplies food for the hungry in a time of famine.** These were difficult times, so when "there came a man from Baal-shalisha, and brought the man of God bread of the firstfruits, twenty loaves of barley, and full ears of corn in the husk thereof" it was reason for rejoicing, and Elisha said, "Give unto the people, that they may eat" (v. 42). There were at least 100 men present, and the server of meals protested that he could not feed them all. But Elisha said again, "Give the people, that they may eat: for thus saith the Lord, They shall eat, and shall leave thereof" (v. 43). "So he set it before them, and they did eat, and left thereof, according to the word of the Lord" (v. 44).

- **2 Kings 6:1–7 He causes an iron ax head to float on water.** The sons of the prophets needed an additional place to dwell, so they determined to make a new place by the Jordan River. While cutting down wood for this project, a young man became distressed when he lost a neighbor's axe head in the Jordan River. Iron was very scarce in Israel and therefore very valuable. He cried unto Elisha, "Alas, master! for it was borrowed" (v. 5). Elisha went to the place where it fell into the water, cut down a stick, and placed it into the water, and in response "the iron did swim," and the young gratefully took up the iron axe head (vv. 6–7).

THE STORY OF NAAMAN

The Power of Faith and Obedience

- **2 Kings 5:1 Naaman was captain of the host of the king of Syria—and he had leprosy.** He is described here as "captain of the host of the king of Syria, … a great man … and honourable," because through him the Lord had delivered Syria from its enemies. He was also "a mighty man in valour, but he was a leper."

- **2 Kings 5:2–4 A young Israelite girl told Naaman's wife about the prophet Elisha.** She was there because the Syrians had taken her captive. Now, just like Joseph in Egypt, she played a significant role in this miracle. She was a young servant girl for Naaman's wife, and said to her mistress, "Would God my lord were with the prophet that is in Samaria! for he would recover Young Israelite girl tells about Elisha him of his leprosy" (v. 3). This was reported to Naaman.

- **2 Kings 5:5–8 Naaman goes to Israel to seek Elisha's help.** Naaman made contact with Elisha who invited him to come to him and be healed. Then he asked the king of Syria for permission to go and seek this help, and the king said "go" and offered to send a letter to the king of Israel to explain what was happening. Namaan also took gifts for the king of Israel—"ten talents of silver, and six thousand pieces of gold, and ten changes of raiment" (v. 5). When he brought these to the king of Israel, he was very suspicious and "rent his clothes," but granted Namaan permission after

Elisha said to him, "let him come now to me, and he shall know that there is a prophet in Israel" (v. 8).

● **2 Kings 5:9–12 Elisha instructs Naaman to dip himself seven times in the Jordan River.** Naaman arrived at Elisha's home "with his horses and with his chariot, and [he] stood at the door of the house" (v. 9). But Elisha did not come out to greet him. Instead, he "sent a messenger unto him, saying, Go and wash in Jordan seven times, and thy flesh shall come again to thee, and thou shalt be clean" (v. 10). Naaman was accustomed to great public shows of deference, and he was offended that Elisha did not do some great and public thing to heal him. And he was further offended that Elisha told him to wash himself in the muddy Jordan River. After all the mighty rivers of Damascus were much more impressive and cleaner (v. 11). Could he not "wash in them, and be clean?" And "he turned and went away in a rage" (v. 12).

Young Israelite girl tells about Elisha

● **2 Kings 5:13–14 Naaman's servant convinces him to obey, and he is healed.** Fortunately, Naaman had level-headed servants who reasoned with him. They said, "My father, if the prophet had bid thee do some great thing, wouldest thou not have done it? how much rather then, when he saith to thee, Wash, and be clean?" (v. 13). It was a simple thing and not much trouble. So Naaman "went … down, and dipped himself seven times in Jordan, according to the saying of the man of God: and his flesh came again like unto the flesh of a little child, and he was clean" (v. 14).

Rex D. Pinegar asked, "Are we not sometimes like Naaman, looking for big or important things to do and bypassing simple things which could change our lives and heal us of our afflictions?"[7]

President Gordon B. Hinckley said, after recounting the story of Naaman, "The way of the gospel is a simple way. Some of the requirements may appear to you as elementary and unnecessary. Do not spurn them. Humble yourselves and walk in obedience. I promise that the results that follow will be marvelous to behold and satisfying to experience."[8]

● There are many events in scripture where doing that which seemed simple had significant consequences:

— Numbers 21:4–9   Moses and the serpent on a pole.

— 1 Nephi 17:41   Nephi's comments on the simpleness of this requirement.

— Alma 33:19–20   Alma's comments on the simpleness of this requirement.

— 1 Nephi 16:28–29   Nephi and the Liahona.

— Alma 37:38–46   Alma's comments on the simpleness of this device.

Elder Boyd K. Packer said:

> The Lord no doubt was more interested in obedience than he was with bathing.
>
> We who travel about the Church know that our members are looking anxiously for guidance in times of great spiritual peril. "When," they wonder, "will the prophets show us how to escape the spiritual leprosy to which we are very exposed?"
>
> Recently in California, one of the priesthood leaders asked, "What are the brethren doing to establish industries and store supplies in the Salt Lake Valley so that we can be secure if we must come there for protection in this time of peril?"
>
> My answer was, "Nothing."
>
> How much like Naaman we become, waiting to be bidden to do some great thing, when the prophets of the Lord have already spoken—when the instruction has already been given with the assurance that if we will follow them, we, with our families, will be secure from the spiritual diseases which now are among us.[9]

● **2 Kings 5:15–16 Elisha refuses Naaman's offer of a reward for this miracle.** He returned to the prophet's home with "all his company, and … stood before him: and he said, Behold, now I know that there is no God in all earth, but in Israel: now therefore, I pray thee, take a blessing of thy servant" (v. 15). But Elisha refused, saying, "As the Lord liveth, before whom I stand, I will receive none. And he urged him to take it; but he refused" (v. 16). Elisha's priesthood was given to him for service, not for profit. Had he accepted the gift, he would have been guilty of priestcraft.

President David O. McKay said: "Priesthood means service; it is not given just as an honor. I congratulate you and commend you that you are worthy to receive it, but it is given to you for service, and you act as an authorized representative of our Lord Jesus Christ in whatever position you may be assigned"[10].

● **2 Kings 5:17–19 Naaman's understanding of Jehovah was very limited.** Namaan next asked for "two mules' burden of earth? for thy servant will henceforth offer neither burnt offering nor sacrifice unto other gods, but unto the Lord" (v. 17). He wished to use it to worship the Lord when he returned home. And although this was pointless, Elisha did not scold him. He recognized that his understanding of the gospel was limited and he said, "Go in peace" (v. 18).

"It is very evident from Naaman's explanation, 'for thy servant,' etc., that he wanted to take a load of earth with him out of the land of Israel, that he might be able to offer sacrifice upon it to the God of Israel, because he was still a slave to the polytheistic superstition, that no god could be worshiped in a proper and acceptable manner except in his own land, or upon an altar built of the earth of his own land. And because Naaman's knowledge of God was still adulterated with superstition, he was not yet prepared to make an unreserved confession before men of his faith in Jehovah as the only true God, but hoped that Jehovah would forgive him if he still continued to join outwardly in the worship of idols, so far as his official duty required"[11].

● **2 Kings 5:21–27 Elisha's servant, Gehazi, is cursed with leprosy after seeking to obtain a reward from Naaman.** Elisha's servant Gehazi wanted the reward that Naaman had offered to Elisha. So he ran after him when he departed and told a lie in order to obtain it (vv. 21–22). He said, "Behold, even now there be come to me from mount Ephraim two young men of the sons of the prophets: give them, I pray thee, a talent of silver, and two changes of garments" (v. 22). Naaman, still very thankful for the healing of his leprosy, gave him instead two talents and two changes of garments (v. 23). After stashing these goods in his house, Gehazi returned to Elisha, who asked, "Whence comest thou, Gehazi? And he said, Thy servant went no whither" (v. 25). But Elisha had already discerned through the Spirit what he had done. He asked, "Is it a time to receive money, and to receive garments, and oliveyards, and vineyards, and sheep, and oxen, and menservants, and maidservants?" (v. 26). And then he cursed Gehazi with the leprosy that had been cleansed from Naaman "for ever," and Gehazi "went out from his presence a leper as white as snow" (v. 27).

Elisha was asking, "Is this the time, when so many hypocrites pretend to be prophets from selfishness and avarice, and bring the prophetic office into contempt with unbelievers, for a servant of the true God to take money and goods from a non-Israelite for that which God has done through him, that he may acquire property and luxury for himself?. … It was not too harsh a punishment that the leprosy taken from Naaman on account of his faith in the living God, should pass to Gehazi on account of his departure from the true God. For it was not his avarice [greed] only that was to be punished, but the abuse of the prophet's name for the purpose of carrying out his selfish purpose, and his misrepresentation of the prophet"[12].

● **There are many examples in the scriptures of such priestcraft.**

— Jude 1:11	The prophet Balaam succumbed to the temptation to use priesthood power for personal gain.
— Alma 1	Nehor did the same in the Book of Mormon.
— 2 Ne. 26:29–31	Nephi called such things priestcraft and said the Lord forbids it.
— 1 Cor. 9:18	Paul said that if one charged for his service in the priesthood, he would abuse his power in the gospel.
— Matt. 10:8	Jesus taught, "Freely ye have received, freely give" (Matthew 10:8). It is, after all, by divine power that men are able to perform priesthood miracles.

Elisha understood this truth perfectly, but Gehazi saw a chance for personal gain slipping away and let his greed overpower his good judgment.

Elisha Is Protected by the "Lord's Host"

● **2 Kings 6:8–10 Elisha helps the king of Israel in a war against Syria, through revelation.** Whenever the king of Syria chose a place to camp his warriors, Elisha revealed the location to the king of Israel, saying, "Beware that thou pass not such a place; for thither the Syrians are come down" (v. 9). By following these instructions the king of Israel prevailed "not once nor twice" (v. 10).

● **2 Kings 6:11–14 The king of Syria sends an army to capture Elisha.** Syria had attacked Israel several times but was always defeated. When it finally came to the attention of the king of Syria that his soldiers were losing because of the prophetic power of Elisha, he sent a large army to destroy Elisha. They located him in Dothan where they surrounded the city so he could not escape.

● **2 Kings 6:15–16 Elisha's servant panics when he sees the Syrian army surrounding them.** He had arisen early and beheld the Syrian host surrounding the city with "horses and chariots" (v. 15). He cried out to Elisha, "Alas, my master! how shall we do?" Elisha calmly responded, "Fear not, for they that be with us are more than they that be with them" (v. 16).

Elisha prays, "Open his eyes"

● **2 Kings 6:17 Elisha prays that his servant's eyes might be opened, saying, "Lord, I pray thee, open his eyes, that he may see.** And the Lord opened the eyes of the young man; and he saw: and, behold, the mountain was full of horses and chariots of fire round about Elisha."

Elder Dallin H. Oaks said: "When I read this wonderful story as a boy, I always identified with the young servant of Elisha. I thought, If I am ever surrounded by the forces of evil while I am in the Lord's service, I hope the Lord will open my eyes and give me faith to understand that when we are in the work of the Lord, those who are with us are always more powerful than those who oppose us"[13].

● **D&C 84:87–88 God has made similar promises to His servants in our own day.** "Behold, I send you out to reprove the world of all their unrighteous deeds, and to teach them of a judgment which is to come. And whoso receiveth you, there I will be also, for I will go before your face. I will be on your right hand and on your left, and my Spirit shall be in your hearts, and mine angels round about you, to bear you up."

The Prophet Joseph Smith related this vision in Kirtland: "I saw Elder Brigham Young standing in a strange land, in the far south and west, in a desert place, upon a rock in the midst of about a dozen men of color, who appeared hostile. He was preaching to them in their own tongue, and the angel of God standing above his head, with a drawn sword in his hand, protecting him, but he did not see it. … My scribe also received his anointing with us, and saw, in a vision, the armies of heaven protecting the Saints in their return to Zion, and many things which I saw"[14].

President Gordon B. Hinckley said: "We have not as yet carried the gospel to every nation, kindred, tongue, and people. But we have made great strides. We have gone wherever we are permitted to go. God is at the helm, and doors will be opened by His power according to His divine will. Of that I am confident. Of that I am certain"[15].

● **2 Kings 6:18–23 Elisha asks God to blind the Syrian army, which He does (v. 18).** Then Elisha led them away from Dothan and into Samaria (v. 19). There he asked the Lord to open their eyes (v. 20). And now, since they were right in the midst of Israel, the king of Israel wanted very much to attack and destroy them (vv. 20–21). But Elisha said that instead they should "set bread and water before them, that they may eat and drink, and go to their master" (v. 22). The king of Israel did so, and then sent them home, and "the bands of Syria came no more into the land of Israel" (v. 23).

PROPHECIES ARE FULFILLED

Prophecies of Food and Famine

● **2 Kings 6:24–33 A crushing famine in Samaria.** The king of Syria surrounded the city of Samaria, bringing on a crushing famine (vv. 24–25). It was so severe that the people resorted to cannibalism. For example, as the king passed by, one woman complained that she had given her son to be boiled but her neighbor reneged in her promise to do the same (vv. 26–29). This so upset the king that he rent his coat and swore to kill Elisha for not ending it (vv. 30–33).

The king is repulsed by cannibalism

● **2 Kings 7:1, 3–10, 16 A prophecy of food in the midst of famine.** Elisha then prophesied to the starving people of Samaria that "To morrow about this time shall a measure of fine flour be sold for a shekel, and two measures of barley for a shekel, in the gate of Samaria" (v. 1). This would have seemed impossible. But three lepers, standing at the gate of the city, decided to go to the Syrian forces surrounding Samaria in order to obtain food (vv. 3–4). And "when they were come to the utter-Most part of the camp of Syria, behold, there was no man there. For the Lord had made the host of the Syrians to hear a noise of chariots, and a noise of horses, even the noise of a great host" (vv. 5–6). This caused them to rise up and flee, leaving "their tents, and their horses, and their asses, even the camp as it was, and fled for their life" (v. 7).

The lepers spoiled the contents of two tents—eating and drinking and taking gold and silver jewelry—then told the rulers of Samaria what had happened (vv. 8–9). The citizens of Samaria then went out and "spoiled the tents of the Syrians. So a measure of fine flour was sold for a shekel, and two measures of barley for a shekel, according to the word of the Lord" (v. 16).

● **2 Kings 8:1–6 Elisha prophesies a seven-year famine.** Elisha warned the woman whose son he had raised to "go thou and thine household, and sojourn wheresoever thou canst sojourn: for the Lord hath called for a famine; and it shall also come upon the land seven years" (v. 1). This she did, living in the land of the Philistines for seven years (v. 2). At the end of those seven years, she returned and "cr[ied] unto the king for her house and for her land" (v. 3). It so happened that when she arrived, Gehazi, the servant of Elisha was telling the

Lepers found the Syrian camp empty

king how Elisha had raised a dead body to life (vv. 4–5). Gehazi then said, "My lord, O king, this is the woman, and this is her son, whom Elisha restored to life" (v. 5). So the king restored to her all that she previously had (v. 6).

Prophecies Concerning Syria

During the ministry of Elisha, the kingdoms of Syria, Israel, and Judah all experienced war and unrest because of their wickedness (2 Kings 8:7–29; 2 Chronicles 22:1–4). The names and records of these kings was summarized previously in chapter 27. But we will review some of those events here to place them into their context during the life of Elisha.

● **2 Kings 8:7–15 Elisha prophecies the death of Ben-hadad and the brutal reign of Hazael.** The Syrian leaders were well acquainted with the prophet Elisha, because they knew about Naaman's miraculous healing. They also remembered Elisha's leading a contingent of the Syrian army into captivity single-handedly and then releasing them (2 Kings 6:18–23). By these things, they knew that he was a true prophet of God.

Ben-hadad, the king of Syria, was jubilant when he heard that Elisha was in Damascus. Perhaps the prophet of God would tell him whether he would recover from his disease. The king sent Hazael with gifts to enquire of the prophet (vv. 7–9). Elisha informed Hazael that Ben-hadad's disease was not fatal, but he would soon die by other means (v. 10). Elisha then began to weep because he knew all the evil that Hazael would soon do to Israel, including setting their strong holds on fire, slaying their young men with the sword, dashing their children, and ripping up their pregnant women (vv. 11–12). Hazael denied that he could ever do such things, but Elisha said, "The Lord hath shewed me that thou shalt be king over Syria" (v. 13). Upon his return to Ben-hadad, Hazael smothered him with a thick, wet cloth and then became the king (vv. 14–15). He ruled Syria for 42 bloody and brutal years in which he did Israel much harm, fulfilling Elisha's prophecy concerning him.

DESTRUCTION OF THE POSTERITY OF AHAB

● **2 Kings 8:16–23 Jehoram, king of Judah, marries Athaliah, the daughter of Ahab, king of Israel, and his wife Jezebel.** Athaliah, like her mother, was an evil woman who worshiped the gods of Baal. She helped corrupt the Kingdom of Judah as her mother had done to the Kingdom of Israel (vv. 16–18). Because of the wickedness of Jehoram, the Lord would not support him during his administration, and he was greatly afflicted. Edom revolted, as did Libnah, against his rule (vv. 20–22). Jehoram finally died of a terrible disease after reigning only 8 years (v. 17; 2 Chronicles 21:18–20).

The Rise of Jehu in Israel

● **1 Kings 19:16 Elisha finishes Elijah's work.** One of the last commissions the Lord had given Elijah was to anoint Jehu as king of Israel. Since he was not able to do this before he was translated, Elisha performed the anointing for him.

● **2 Kings 9:1–13 Elisha sends a young prophet to anoint Jehu king of Israel.** He also prophesied the end of the house of Ahab. The young man Elisha sent was from the "sons of the prophets" and held the proper priesthood (v. 1). Elisha instructed him to take Jehu aside into an "inner chamber," pour oil on his head, and say, "Thus saith the Lord, I have anointed thee king over Israel." Then he was to open the door, and flee, and tarry not (vv. 2–3). The young prophet did so, adding a prophecy concerning the end of the posterity of Ahab, which he—Jehu—was commanded to undertake (vv. 4–9). This was to include Jezebel, the wife of Ahab, of whom he prophesied, "the dogs shall eat Jezebel in the portion of Jezreel, and there shall be none to bury her." And he opened the door, and fled (v. 10).

After the prophet left, the other men in the house asked Jehu, "Is all well?" and he told them he had been anointed to be king of Israel (vv. 11–12). At this point, they laid their coats down at his feet as a symbol of their loyalty and recognition of his authority (v. 13).

● **2 Kings 9:8–10 Jehu immediately begins to obliterate the family of Ahab and Jezebel,** vowing to fulfil the prophecies first made by Elijah and later reiterated by the young prophet at Ramoth-gilead concerning Ahab, Jezebel, and their posterity (1 Kings 21:17–29).

● **2 Kings 9:14–16 Jehu finds Joram and Ahaziah in Naboth's vineyard.** Joram was king of Israel and the son of Ahab. Ahaziah was king of Judah and a nephew of Ahab. Both were therefore slated to be slain by Jehu. It so happened that both kings were in Jezreel at this time—Joram to be healed of his wounds, and Ahaziah to visit Joram. This was the same spot where some years earlier Jezebel arranged to have Naboth killed, and Elijah prophesied the destruction of Ahab and his family.

● **2 Kings 9:17–27 Jehu's army kills them both as part of this purging.** Joram, king of Israel, was slain very near Naboth's vineyard (v. 24; 2 Chronicles 22:5–8). Ahaziah, king of Judah, fled but was wounded and then died at Megiddo (v. 27; 2 Chronicles 22:9).

- **2 Kings 9:30–35 Jehu next slays Jezebel at Jezreel.**
Even in her old age Jezebel tried to misuse feminine
charm and lots of makeup to get Jehu to spare
her. She put on makeup and fixed her hair before
appearing at the window of her palace (v. 30).

"When Jehu entered the palace gate, she cried
out to him, 'Is it peace, thou Zimri, murderer of
his lord?' (v. 31) She addressed Jehu as Zimri the
murderer of the king, to point to the fate which
Jehu would bring upon himself by the murder of
the king, as Zimri had already done (vv. 32–33) …

"But Jehu did not deign to answer the worthless
woman; he simply looked up to the window and
inquired: 'Who is with me? who?' Then two, three
chamberlains looked out (of the side windows),
and by Jehu's command threw the proud queen
out of the window, so that some of her blood
spurted upon the wall and the horses (of Jehu),
and Jehu trampled her down, driving over her with
his horses and chariot"[16].

Jezebel was tossed out the window

- **2 Kings 9:34–37 The prophecy of Elijah concerning Jezebel is literally fulfilled.** When Jehu's
men returned to bury her, only her skull, her feet, and the palms of her hands could be found
(vv. 34–35). When they returned and reported
this to Jehu, he said, "This is the word of the Lord,
which he spake by his servant Elijah the Tishbite,
saying, In the portion of Jezreel shall dogs eat the
flesh of Jezebel" (v. 36; 1 Kings 21:23). "And the
carcase of Jezebel shall be as dung upon the face of
the field in the portion of Jezreel; so that they shall
not say, This is Jezebel" (v. 37).

- **2 Kings 10:1–14 Jehu then went on to kill all
that remained of Ahab's family.** Ahab had seventy
sons in Samaria. Jehu wrote letters to all the rulers
of Jezreel, challenging them to defend the right of
these sons to rule Israel, but they were "exceedingly
afraid," saying,

"Behold, two kings stood not before him: how then
shall we stand?" (vv. 1–4). Instead, they sent a letter
back to Jehu, saying, "We are thy servants, and will
do all that thou shalt bid us; we will not make any
king: do thou that which is good in thine eyes"

Jezebel's head, feet, & palms were found

(v. 5). He answered that "If ye be mine, and if ye will hearken unto my voice, take ye the heads of the men your master's sons, and come to me to Jezreel by to morrow this time" (v. 6).

This they did, beheading all 70 of these sons and putting their heads in baskets which they sent to Jehu (v. 7). He stacked these heads up in two heaps by the city gate and declared to the people, "Know now that there shall fall unto the earth nothing of the word of the Lord, which the Lord spake concerning the house of Ahab: for the Lord hath done that which he spake by his servant Elijah" (v. 10). And thus did Jehu slay "all that remained of the house of Ahab in Jezreel, and all his great men, and his kinsfolks, and his priests, until he left him none remaining" in Israel (v. 11).

Jehu then left for Samaria, and along the way he came across "the brethren of Ahaziah king of Judah, and said, Who are ye? And they answered, We are the brethren of Ahaziah; and we go down to salute the children of the king and the children of the queen" (v. 13). They had no idea that all of Ahab's kin were dead. And because they were also kindred of Ahab, Jehu commanded, "Take them alive. And they took them alive, and slew them at the pit of the shearing house, even two and forty men; neither left he any of them" (v. 14). And thus did Jehu slay all of Ahab's descendants that remained in the land of Judah also.

● **2 Kings 10:18–28 Jehu also destroyed the religion of Baal.** He proclaimed a solemn feast to Baal and then destroyed all the worshipers and images that gathered together for the feast. In doing so, he obtained favor in God's eyes. He worked this deception by saying to the people, "Ahab served Baal a little; but Jehu shall serve him much" (v. 18). He called together "all the prophets of Baal, all his servants, and all his priests … [for] a great sacrifice to … Baal" and warned that whoever of this group did not come would be executed (v. 19). Understandably, every worshiper of Baal came and filled the house of Baal "from one end to another" (v. 21). He placed vestments upon them and made sure that none of them was a worshiper of the Lord (vv. 22–23). Then he placed a guard around the building who were charged with not letting any of those inside escape alive (v. 24). Then, after a sacrifice had been made to Baal, he ordered everyone in the house to be slain, which they were (v. 25). Finally, they went into the house of Baal and removed all the images out of it and burned them (v. 26). This included the great image of Baal and the entire building—all were destroyed (vv. 26–27). And by this means, "Jehu destroyed Baal out of Israel" (v. 28).

The Decline of Jehu

● **2 Kings 10:28–31 The Lord promised Jehu that his posterity to the fourth generation would sit on the throne of Israel.** But Jehu did not continue to keep the Lord's commandments, and the Northern Kingdom declined rapidly under Jehu and his son, Joahaz (815–802 BC).

"Jehu is promised the possession of the throne to the fourth generation of his sons for having exterminated the godless royal house of Ahab … The divine sentence, 'because thou hast acted well to do right in mine eyes, (because thou) hast done as it was in my heart to the house of Ahab,' refers to the deed as such, and not to the subjective motives by which Jehu had been actuated. For it is obvious that it had not sprung from pure zeal for the honour of the Lord, from the limitation added in verse 31: 'but Jehu did not take heed to walk in the law of Jehovah with all his heart, and did not depart from the sins of Jeroboam'"[17].

In other words, the house of Ahab had reached such a state of wickedness that it deserved destruction. Jehu was the means of bringing about the Lord's will in this regard. But that does not mean the Lord was pleased with his brutal methods or his wickedness.

- **2 Kings 10:32–33 Because of all this wickedness, the scattering of Israel began to loom in the distance.** The scriptures say that "In those days the Lord began to cut Israel short" (v. 32), meaning He began to allow them to lose territory. Hazael, the king of Syria, "smote them in all the coasts of Israel" (v. 32), and all the territory east of the Jordan River (v. 33).

MIXED-RIGHTEOUSNESS IN JUDAH

- **2 Kings 11:1–3 Jehoash (Joash) was preserved from death during the reign of Athaliah.** Athaliah had killed all the heirs to the throne in order to reign herself in Judah. But Jehoash escaped through the intervention of his aunt.

- **2 Kings 11:4–12; 2 Chronicles 23:1–3 After hiding Jehoash in the temple for six years, Jehoiada the priest brings him forth and anoints him king.** After deciding to make the child's existence known, he sent the king's bodyguard throughout the land of Judah to gather in the Levites and chief rulers to sustain Jehoash as king of Judah. They came and gladly sustained a descendant of David to sit on the throne of Judah.

Jehoiada crowns the boy-king Jehoash

- **2 Kings 11:13–20 Athaliah calls it treason and is slain.** "As soon as Athaliah heard the loud rejoicing of the people, she came to the people into the temple, and when she saw the youthful king in his standing-place surrounded by the princes, the trumpeters, and the whole of the people, rejoicing and blowing the trumpets, she rent her clothes with horror, and cried out, conspiracy, conspiracy! ... Jehoiada then commanded the captains ... those placed over the army, (the armed men of the Levites), to lead out Athaliah between the ranks, and to slay every one who followed her ... "[18].

- **2 Kings 11:21—12:17 Jehoash was only seven years old at the time he began to reign, but reigned as Judah's king for 40 years.** He reigned righteously as long as he received wise advice from the high priest, Jehoiada, which he followed (2 Chronicles 24:4, 7, 13–27). During that period of time, the temple was repaired through donations made by the people. But sadly, Jehoash did not continue in righteousness.

- **2 Kings 12:18–21 After Jehoiada's death Jehoash becomes weak and wicked.** He allowed heathen rituals to be performed in Judah again. He also sought to appease Hazael, king of Syria, by sending him sacred things from the temple (v. 18). The Lord sent prophets to testify against him and to call the people of Judah to repentance. One such prophet was Zechariah, son of Jehoiada the priest. Jehoash had him killed along with the other sons of Jehoiada. Then, because Jehoash had murdered the sons of Jehoiada, some of his own servants slew him while he lay on his bed.

CONTINUED WICKEDNESS IN ISRAEL

● **2 Kings 13:1–13 Jehoahaz and Jehoash (Joash), his son, continue the wickedness of Israel's kings.** The Jehoash (Joash) mentioned here is not the same Jehoash (Joash) who was king of Judah discussed above. There were two kings by the same name. Jehoash (Joash) who became king of Israel, the Northern Kingdom, was the son of Jehoahaz and helped deliver Israel from the Syrians.

Josephus said concerning Jehoahaz, King of Israel: "He did not [properly] imitate his father, but was guilty of as wicked practices as those that first had God in contempt: but the king of Syria [Hazael] brought him low, and by an expedition against him did so greatly reduce his forces, that there remained no more of so great an army than ten thousand armed men, and fifty horsemen. He also took away from him his great cities, and many of them also, and destroyed his army. And these were the things that the people of Israel suffered, according to the prophecy of Elisha, when he foretold that Hazael should kill his master, and reign over the Syrians and Damascenes. But when Jehoahaz was under such unavoidable miseries, he had recourse to prayer and supplication to God, and besought him to deliver him out of the hands of Hazael, and not overlook him, and give him up into his hands"[19].

Keil and Delitzsch explained:

> In this oppression Jehoahaz prayed to the Lord … and the Lord heard this prayer, because He saw their oppression at the hands of the Syrians, and gave Israel a saviour, so that they came out from the power of the Syrians and dwelt in their booths again, as before, (i.e. were able to live peaceably again in their houses, without being driven off and led away by the foe). The saviour … was neither an angel, nor the prophet Elisha, … nor a victory obtained by Jehoahaz over the Syrians, … but the Lord gave them the saviour in the two successors of Jehoahaz, in the kings Jehoash [Joash] and Jeroboam, the former of whom wrested from the Syrians all the cities that had been conquered by them under his father (v. 25), while the latter restored the ancient boundaries of Israel (14:25). According to vv. 22–25, the oppression by the Syrians lasted as long as Jehoahaz lived; but after his death the Lord had compassion upon Israel, and after the death of Hazael, when his son Ben-hadad had become king, Jehoash recovered from Ben-hadad all the Israelitish cities that had been taken by Syrians.[20]

THE DEATH OF ELISHA

● **2 Kings 13:13–19 Elisha prophesies on his deathbed that Israel will defeat the Syrians.** Elisha fell deathly sick, and Jehoash (Joash), king of Israel, sought an audience with the prophet, perhaps feeling that Elisha alone held the key to Israel's future safety. He came to Elisha's bedside and wept over him (v. 14).

Elisha responded by inviting Jehoash (Joash) to open a window and shoot an arrow toward the east (vv. 15–17). The arrow symbolized the Lord's deliverance of Israel from the Syrians. Elisha also told the king to shoot some arrows into the ground, which he did (vv. 18–19). "The shooting of the arrows to the earth was intended to symbolize the overthrow of the Syrians"[21]. The king shot only three arrows. For this Elisha chastised him, saying that had Jehoash (Joash) shot five or six times he would have smitten the Syrians to destruction (2 Kings 13:19).

THE HOLMAN BIBLE, 1890

Elisha told Joash to shoot arrows

Another Miracle after Elisha's Death

● **2 Kings 13:20–21 Elisha dies, and his bones revive another dead man.** Elisha did not recover of his illness, but died and was buried. It was the same year as when "bands of the Moabites invaded the land at the coming in of the year" (v. 20). During that invasion, as they were burying another man and became concerned about a "band of men" coming toward them, they quickly "cast the man into the sepulchre of Elisha: and when the man was let down, and touched the bones of Elisha, he revived, and stood up on his feet" (v. 21). Even in death, Elisha's great miracles continued.

Notes

1. LDS Bible Dictionary, 770.
2. Orson F. Whitney, *Life of Heber C. Kimball* [1945], 237–239.
3. *Doctrines of Salvation*, comp. Elder Bruce R. McConkie, 3 vols. [1954–56], 3:156.
4. In Conference Report, Apr. 1995, 92; or *Ensign*, May 1995, 69.
5. Smith and Sjodahl, *Doctrine and Covenants Commentary*, rev. ed. [1972], 2:486.
6. Freeman, *Manners and Customs of the Bible*, 171.
7. In Conference Report, Oct. 1994, 106; or *Ensign*, Nov. 1994, 80.
8. In Conference Report, Oct. 1976, 143; or *Ensign*, Nov. 1976, 96.
9. Regional Representatives' Seminar, 3 Apr. 1970.
10. In Conference Report, Apr. 1957, 94.
11. Keil and Delitzsch, *Commentary on the Old Testament*, 10 vols. [1996], 3:1:320.
12. Keil and Delitzsch, *Commentary on the Old Testament*, 3:1:322–23
13. In Conference Report, Oct. 1992, 54; or *Ensign*, Nov. 1992, 39.
14. *History of the Church*, 2:381.
15. In Conference Report, Oct. 1995, 93; or *Ensign*, Nov. 1995, 70–71.
16. Keil & Delitzsch, Commentary, 3:1:345.
17. Keil and Delitzsch, *Commentary on the Old Testament*, 3:1:354–55.
18. Keil and Delitzsch, *Commentary on the Old Testament*, 3:1:362–363.
19. *Antiquities*, bk. 9, chap. 8, par. 5.
20. *Doctrine and Covenants Commentary*, rev. ed. (1972), 3:1:375.
21. Keil and Delitzsch, *Commentary on the Old Testament*, 3:1:377.

CHAPTER 30

The Temple of Solomon

(1 Kings 5–9; 2 Chronicles 29–34)

ℬↃℭℛ

SOLOMON BUILDS A TEMPLE

We studied the life of King Solomon earlier in chapter 26. It was during his reign that the Temple of Solomon was built. This chapter deals entirely with that temple, which served the people of Judah (and Israel for awhile) for hundreds of years. It was present during the entire ministries of Elijah and Elisha, and survived right up until the day when Nebuchadnezzar captured Jerusalem, destroyed it, and carried away its inhabitants into Babylon.

Solomon built a beautiful House of the Lord

The Sacred Location of Solomon's Temple

Solomon built the house of the Lord at Jerusalem on Mount Moriah (1 Kings 6:1; 2 Chronicles 3:2). The location was significant. It was built over the threshing floor (solid rock surface) of Araunah on Mt. Moriah.

This sacred rock on Mt. Moriah, called es-Sakhara today, sits at the summit of Mt. Moriah. The temple of Solomon (and later, the Dome of the Rock) was built over it (see images on next page). Over time, the Israelites built several walls around the rock, then filled the resulting cavities in with earth to form platforms upon which the temple and other buildings could be constructed (see bottom right image on next page).

— This is the same rock on which Abraham nearly sacrificed his son Isaac.

— This was the site of the City of Salem, where Melchizedek was king.

— The people of Salem were eventually translated.

— Tradition holds that there was also a temple at this site in the city of Salem.

— David built an altar on this rock during his days as king (2 Samuel 24:18–25).

— These are the same mountains upon which Christ was eventually crucified.

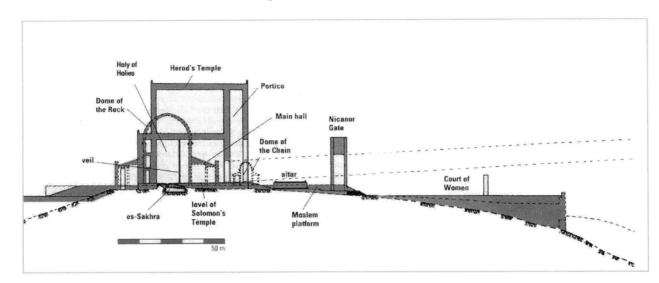

The rock of Abraham was located in the holy of holies of Solomon's Temple. The ark of the covenant rested upon it, with its lid (the "mercy seat" being the most sacred spot in Israel. It symbolized the coming sacrifice of our Father's Only Begotten Son which offered mercy to all of Israel if they kept the Lord's commandments.

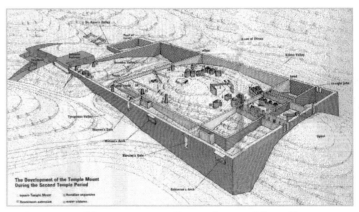

Images used by permission. Copyright 1996 Leen Ritmeyer

The Construction of Solomon's Temple

Solomon began to build the temple in the second day of the second month, in the fourth year of his reign.

● **1 Kings 5:17–18 Building a platform on the temple mount.** Mount Moriah, in its natural state, was not well suited for a temple on its summit. It descended steeply into valleys on three sides and had a peak to the north. The only flat surface was the threshing floor of Araunah and that was only about the size of a good-sized room. Solomon built a large platform on top of this mountain and then erected the temple on top of that platform (see image above right). All parts of the building were pre-built elsewhere and then brought to the temple block where they were fitted together.

● **1 Kings 5:17–18 The manpower required for the temple project.** Solomon used conscripts from Tyre (provided by Hiram, King of Tyre) as well as Israelite laborers to build the temple. The number of workers was huge.

— Solomon enlisted 30,000 men from all the tribes to cut timber—10,000 at a time.

— He enlisted 70,000 men to "[bear] burdens"—meaning to haul stones—to form the temple platform and fill in the spaces necessary to form the platform.

— He enlisted another 80,000 "hewers" to quarry, shape, finish, and place the huge stones.

— He enlisted 3,300 foremen, engineers and superintendents to supervise the work.

— He taxed the entire economy of Israel to provide food and other necessities for the workmen and to pay for the building materials.

The Architecture of the Temple of Solomon

● **1 Kings 6:2 The temple was patterned after the wilderness tabernacle that Moses had built.** But there were also important differences, mostly in its size and the materials with which it was built.

— It was twice as long, twice as wide and three times as high—90 feet long, 30 feet wide, and 45 feet high (see temple layout on the following page).

— The front entrance faced east. It was very ornate and impressive, with a huge porch as wide as the temple and extending 30 feet out into the courtyard (2 Chron. 3:4). The floor of the porch was overlaid with gold.

— The high roof of the porch rested on two massive brass pillars each 27 ft high and 18 ft in circumference.

— At the top of each pillar was an enlarged capital decorated with lily leaves. This was overhung with wreaths of 200 bronze pome- granates. These pillars had names. The pillar on the north side was called Boaz while the one on the south side was called Jachin. It is assumed these pillars were hollow.

— The temple's entrance consisted of two great doors made of thick olive wood planks. They were elaborately carved, with gold foil laid over the carving, and they swung on gold hinges.

3-D view of Solomon's Temple

The Holy Place in Solomon's Temple

— The Holy Place was 60 feet long and the Holy of Holies was 30 feet long.

— The Holy Place floor was overlaid with gold and the walls of carved cedar were decorated with gold and precious stones. Instead of a single candlestick with seven branches as was used in the tabernacle, there were ten candlesticks of pure gold, five on the right and five on the left, which flooded the Holy Place with brilliant light. Along the north wall was a golden table of shew bread. At the far end of the room, next to the partition leading into the Holy of Holies, stood the golden altar of incense.

A Comparison of the Wilderness Tabernacle and Solomon's Temple

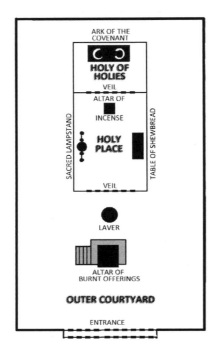

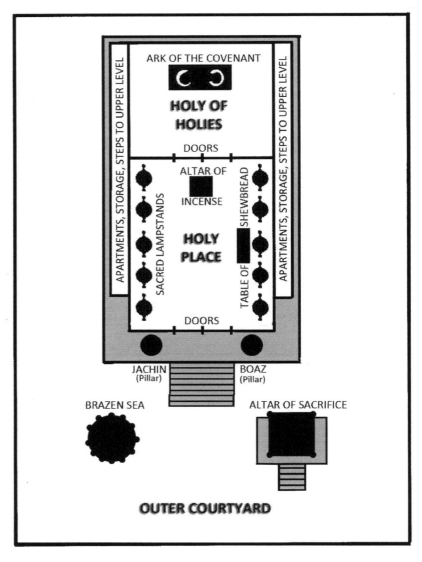

The Temple of Solomon was twice the size of the tabernacle and had an upper floor where the temple veil was most likely located. The lower floor used doors between the holy place and the holy of holies. It also had a brazen sea on the backs of 12 oxen, a larger altar of sacrifice, and ten sacred lampstands rather than just one.

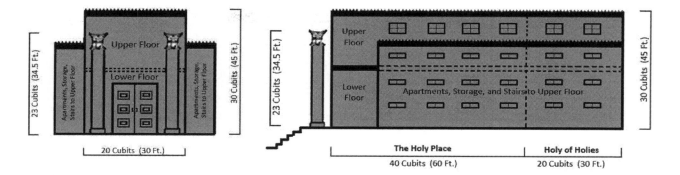

Upper Floor

Lower Floor

23 Cubits (34.5 Ft.)

30 Cubits (45 Ft.)

20 Cubits (30 Ft.)

Apartments, Storage, Stairs to Upper Floor

Upper Floor

Lower Floor

Apartments, Storage, and Stairs to Upper Floor

23 Cubits (34.5 Ft.)

30 Cubits (45 Ft.)

The Holy Place
40 Cubits (60 Ft.)

Holy of Holies
20 Cubits (30 Ft.)

— At the far end of the Holy Place a partition divided it from the Holy of Holies. This consisted of two doors, which, like the main doors of the temple, were made of heavy planks of olive wood, beautifully carved and overlaid with gold and hung on gold hinges. They were also protected by a gold chain which hung across them.

— At the center of the Holy of Holies sat the rock that was once the threshing floor of Araunah and on which the fire of the Lord had consumed David's sacrifice. The ark of the covenant rested there beneath the wings of two magnif- icent cherubim (winged angels).

The lid of the ark was called the mercy seat

— The cherubim, each 15 feet tall with 7½ foot wings that spread out in each direction, were placed so that their inside wings touched each other over the spot where the ark of the covenant rested, and their outside wings touched the north and south walls. These huge figures were also made of olive wood and overlaid with gold.

— The lid of the ark of the covenant was called the "mercy seat"—the place where the Lord Jehovah came to commune with His prophets. He showed mercy by coming to His people, but also would be the source of mercy through His atonement. Thus, there is great symbolism in naming His place in the temple the "mercy seat."

— The walls of the Holy of Holies were elaborately carved and then the entire interior was gold-plated, including the floor.

● **1 Kings 7:23–26 Solomon's "molten sea" rested on the backs of twelve oxen.** This round font measured 10 cubits (nearly 15 feet) in diameter, 30 cubits (45 feet) in circumference, and 5 cubits (7½ feet) deep (v. 23). It was a handbreadth in thickness, with a brim shaped like the brim of a cup, with decorative lilies (v. 26) and two rows of 300 "knops," 10 of them for each cubit of circumference (v. 24). It contained "two thousand baths" (approxi- mately 16,500) gallons of water (v. 26).

The entire font sat upon "twelve oxen, three looking toward the north, and three looking toward the west, and three looking toward the south, and three looking toward the east … [with] their hinder parts … inward" (v. 25). Baptismal fonts in latter-day temples are frequently patterned after Solomon's molten sea.

- **There were also ten large brass lavers (basins) on wheels which could be moved around the courtyard and used for washing and cleansing in connection with sacrifices.** Thus, we can conclude that the brazen sea was used for something else—probably baptisms, which were practiced in ancient Israel.

The Mysterious Upper Floor of Solomon's Temple

- **1 Chronicles 28:11; 2 Chronicles 3:9 The "upper chambers" of Solomon's temple.** Solomon's temple, which was 45 feet in height, was not one story, but two. The plans that King David gave to Solomon for the temple included "upper chambers." Very little can be found about these rooms in the Bible, but it must have been a most important and sacred place because we are told that Solomon "overlaid the upper chambers with gold."

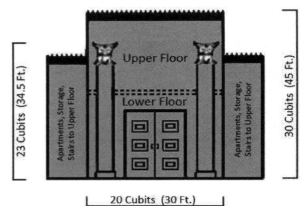

Annex rooms built on the outside of the temple, came only part-way up the side of the temple.
The entrance to the Upper House was not through the regular entrance to the temple but through doors on these side chambers, accessed by stairways built into the thickness of these walls.

Josephus said: "There was another building erected over it [that is, over the first floor], equal to it in its measures. … He also built around the temple thirty small rooms … Above these were other rooms, and others above them … so that these reached to a height equal to the lower part of the house: for the upper part had no buildings about it. … The king also had a fine contrivance for an ascent to the upper room over the temple, and that was by steps in the thickness of its walls; for it [the upper house] had no large door on the east end, as the lower house had, but the entrances were by the sides, through very small doors"[1].

- **D&C 124:37–39 The purpose of Solomon's temple included the endowment.** The Lord said, "How shall your washings be acceptable unto me, except ye perform them in a house which you have built to my name?" (v. 37). "For … this cause I commanded Moses that he should build a tabernacle, that they should bear it with them in the wilderness, and [David and Solomon] to build a house in the land of promise, that those ordinances might be revealed which had been hid from before the world was" (v. 38). The Lord says that temples are for anointings, washings, baptisms for the dead, solemn assemblies, memorials (covenants) of sacrifices, endowments, and oracles (conversations with God) "in your most holy places" where we receive statutes, judgments, and revelations (v. 39). For these purposes, "my people are always commanded to build [temples] unto my holy name" (v. 39). It was no different in

Solomon's day than it is in ours. But very few were worthy of such things in Solomon's day, and if it was done it was most likely done privately in the upper chambers. In the Bible, we hear only about the preparatory ordinances performed in the courtyard and the lower floor of the temple.

● **2 Chronicles 3:14 A veil was built for Solomon's temple.** "He made the vail of blue, and purple, and crimson, and fine linen, and wrought cherubims thereon." The question is, "Where was it used?" In the lower house, elaborately carved doors separated the Holy Place and Holy of Holies. Some authorities speculate it was placed over the opening of the two doors whenever they were left ajar, but there is nothing in the scriptures to indicate this.

Josephus says the dimensions of the upper floor were identical with the lower floor—one room 60 ft long (comparable to the Holy Place on the first floor), and a room 30 ft long (compar- able to the Holy of Holies on

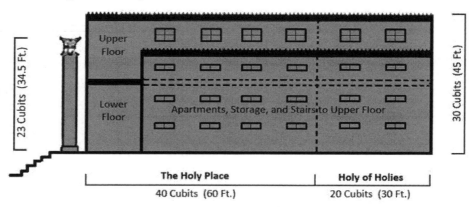

the first floor). If the upper cham- bers of Solomon's temple were used for the higher ordinances then the proper place for the temple veil would have been between the terrestrial and celestial rooms on the upper floor, as in modern temples.

SOLOMON DEDICATES THE COMPLETED TEMPLE

● **1 Kings 6:11–13 The Lord gives Solomon a revelation of encouragement during the difficult days of building the temple.** We can only imagine the difficulty of building such a large and complex building, managing literally tens of thousands of workers who shaped and placed the massive stones and finished the interior with preciseness.

The Lord said to Solomon, "Concerning this house which thou art in building, if thou wilt walk in my statutes, and execute my judgments, and keep all my commandments to walk in them; then will I perform my word with thee,

which I spake unto David thy father: And I will dwell among the children of Israel, and will not forsake my people Israel."

- **1 Kings 8:1–4 After seven years of construc- tion, the temple is ready for dedication.** Solomon assembled the elders of Israel—all the heads of the tribes—in Jerusalem. It was a sacred feast in "the month Ethanim, which is the seventh month" (v. 2). The twelve leaders of the tribes of Israel "took up the ark," and then "brought up the ark of the Lord … and all the holy vessels that were in the tabernacle" to place them in the finished temple.

THEBIBLEREVIVAL.COM. #7

- **1 Kings 6:16, 19 The ark of the covenant belongs in the "most holy place."** The Holy of Holies, both floor and walls, was covered with "boards of cedar" (v. 16). The floor consisted largely of the rock upon which Abraham nearly sacrificed Isaac and upon which David offered sacrifice which was lit by fire from heaven. There, on that sacred rock, Solomon planned to "set … the ark of the covenant of the Lord" (v. 19). The ark was a tangible symbol of the presence of the Lord in the temple, and of God's revelations and blessings.

- **1 Kings 8:5–9 Solomon and the multitude offer sacrifice, then place the ark in its place.** With the ark before them, they sacrificed "sheep and oxen, that could not be told nor numbered for multitude" (v. 5). Then they took the ark of the covenant and put it in "the most holy place, even under the wings of the cherubims" (v. 6). Then they took out the staves (rods) that had been used to carry the ark, symbolizing that it had reached its final resting place and would not be moved again. These were placed in the Holy Place, where the Bible says "they are unto this day" (v. 8).

THE HOLMAN BIBLE, 1890

The ark contained sacred objects such as "the two tables of stone, which Moses put there at Horeb" (v. 9), a pot of manna, and the rod of Aaron, which had miraculously blossomed in the wilderness.

- **1 Kings 8:22 Solomon dedicates the temple unto the Lord.** "Solomon stood before the altar of the Lord in the presence of all the congregation of Israel, and spread forth his hands toward heaven." Note that as the king does this he is acting as a prophet and a priest as well.

- **1 Kings 8:23–30 A portion of his dedicatory prayer.** Solomon's dedicatory prayer has become the model for all temple dedications in our day, including the first temple in our dispensation— the Kirtland Temple. His words are beautiful, thanking God for His mercy to Israel and extolling His greatness and power.

"And he said, Lord God of Israel, there is no God like thee, in heaven above, or on earth beneath, who keepest covenant and mercy with thy servants that walk before thee with all their heart:

"Who hast kept with thy servant David my father that thou promisedst him: thou spakest also with thy mouth, and hast fulfilled it with thine hand, as it is this day.

"Therefore now, Lord God of Israel, keep with thy servant David my father that thou promisedst him, saying, There shall not fail thee a man in my sight to sit on the throne of Israel; so that thy children take heed to their way, that they walk before me as thou hast walked before me.

"And now, O God of Israel, let thy word, I pray thee, be verified, which thou spakest unto thy servant David my father.

"But will God indeed dwell on the earth? behold, the heaven and heaven of heavens cannot contain thee; how much less this house that I have builded?

JAMES J. TISSOT, 1904

"Yet have thou respect unto the prayer of thy servant, and to his supplication, O LORD my God, to hearken unto the cry and to the prayer, which thy servant prayeth before thee to day:

"That thine eyes may be open toward this house night and day, even toward the place of which thou hast said, My name shall be there: that thou mayest hearken unto the prayer which thy servant shall make toward this place.

"And hearken thou to the supplication of thy servant, and of thy people Israel, when they shall pray toward this place: and hear thou in heaven thy dwelling place: and when thou hearest, forgive."

This is only a portion of the prayer. A more complete version is found in 2 Chronicles 6.

● **2 Chronicles 7:1–3 Fire from heaven consumes Solomon's sacrifice upon the altar.** Immediately after Solomon's prayer had ended, "fire came down from heaven, and consumed the burnt offering and the sacrifices; and the glory of the Lord filled the house" (v. 1). The first symbolized the Lord's acceptance of Solomon's sacrifice for all Israel, and the cloud symbolized the Lord's acceptance of the temple and His presence therein. The cloud was so thick that "the priests could not enter into the house of the Lord, because the glory of the Lord had filled the Lord's house" (v. 2; 1 Kings 8:10–11).

THE HOLMAN BIBLE, 1890

"And when all the children of Israel saw how the fire came down, and the glory of the Lord upon the house, they bowed themselves with their faces to the ground upon the pavement, and worshipped, and praised the Lord, saying, For he is good; for his mercy endureth for ever" (v. 3).

- **1 Kings 8:56–61 Solomon admonishes and blesses his people.** He reminded the people that "there hath not failed one word of all his good promise, which he promised by the hand of Moses his servant" (v. 56). He pleaded with them to live their lives so that "The Lord our God be with us, as he was with our fathers: let him not leave us, nor forsake us" (v. 57). To do this, he reminded them, we must "incline our hearts unto him, [and] walk in all his ways, and … keep his commandments, and his statutes, and his judgments, which he commanded our fathers" (v. 58).

Solomon wished that "these my words, wherewith I have made supplication before the Lord, be nigh unto the Lord our God day and night, that he maintain the cause of his servant, and the cause of his people Israel at all times, as the matter shall require" (v. 59), and "That all the people of the earth may know that the Lord is God, and that there is none else" (v. 60). Then he concluded with an admonition: "Let your heart therefore be perfect with the Lord our God, to walk in his statutes, and to keep his commandments, as at this day" (v. 61).

- **1 Kings 9:1–5 The Lord appears to Solomon to accept the temple and bless him.** Solomon had received a personal visitation once before at Gibeon, when he asked the Lord for wisdom at the beginning of his reign. Now, "the Lord appeared to Solomon the second time" to accept the temple and bless him. The Lord said, "I have heard thy prayer and thy supplication, that thou hast made before me: I have hallowed this house, which thou hast built, to put my name there for ever; and mine eyes and mine heart shall be there perpetually.

"And if thou wilt walk before me, as David thy father walked, in integrity of heart, and in uprightness, to do according to all that I have commanded thee, and wilt keep my statutes and my judgments: Then I will establish the throne of thy kingdom upon Israel for ever, as I promised to David thy father, saying, There shall not fail thee a man upon the throne of Israel" (vv. 4–5).

- **1 Kings 9:6–9 A solemn warning to Solomon concerning wickedness.** In hindsight, we know that Solomon would turn to idol worship in his old age in order to please his many wives. Thus, this warning was very much needed, both for the king and for the people of Israel.

The Lord warned, "if ye shall at all turn from following me, ye or your children, and will not keep my commandments and my statutes which I have set before you, but go and serve other gods, and worship them: Then will I cut off Israel out of the land which I have given them; and this house, which I have hallowed for my name, will I cast out of my sight; and Israel shall be a proverb and a byword among all people" (vv. 6–7).

Furthermore, the temple, which at this time was glorious and holy, would become defiled and destroyed. "And … every one that passeth by it shall be astonished, and shall hiss; and they shall say, Why hath the Lord done thus unto this land, and to this house? And they shall answer, Because they forsook the Lord their God, who brought forth their fathers out of the land of Egypt, and have taken hold upon other gods, and have worshipped them, and served them: therefore hath the Lord brought upon them all this evil" (vv. 8–9).

THE HOUSE OF THE LORD AFTER SOLOMON

The history of the temple after Solomon is mostly a sad one. In the long line of kings of Judah, only two—Hezekiah and Josiah—made major efforts to maintain the temple and to turn the hearts of the people back to their temple covenants.

PROVIDENCE LITHOGRAPHIC CO., 1896

— **Solomon** ended his life caught up in wealth and idolatry because he had broken commandments he had been given directly from the Lord (1 Kings 11:2–11). Early in his reign, Solomon married the daughter of the king of Egypt, which was probably a political marriage to protect him from invasion by the Egyptians (1 Kings 3:1). The Joseph Smith Translation says "the Lord was not pleased with Solomon" because of this marriage, and thereafter blessed him "for the people's sake only" (JST 1 Kings 3:1). He went on to marry other non-Israelite women, for he "loved many [foreign] women" (1 Kings 11:1).

This may be an understatement. He had 700 wives and 300 concubines (1 Kings 11:1, 3). Eventually, he began to worship his wives' many gods and declined in righteousness (1 Kings 11:5–8). To support the building of the temple, his palace, and his empire, Solomon imposed heavy taxation and forced labor on his people, creating great resentment (1 Kings 12:1–29). Then he died after reigning 40 years over all of Israel and left his son Rehoboam sitting on the throne.

— **Rehoboam,** the son of Solomon, also disobeyed God and led his people into idolatry during his 22-year reign.

— **Abijam** (957 BC), son of Rehoboam, "walked in all the sins of his father, which he had done before him: and his heart was not perfect with the Lord his God" (1 Kings 15:3). He reigned for only 3 years.

— **Asa** (955 BC), son of Abijam, reigned for 41 years and was righteous in the beginning. He launched an all-out campaign to complete the job his father had begun (2 Chronicles 14:1–16:14). He tore down idolatrous altars and images and began to eliminate the male and female prostitutes who attended the pagan temples, groves, altars, and shrines. He did not, however, remove the "high places" where Baal was worshiped. And unfortunately, he lacked faith in his later years. He

The Kings of Judah

King (* righteous)	Reign
Rehoboam	22 yrs
Abijam	3 yrs
* **Asa**	41 yrs
* **Jehoshaphat**	25 yrs
Jehoram	8 yrs
Ahaziah	1 yr
Athaliah	7 yrs
* **Joash (Jehoash)**	40 yrs
* **Amaziah**	29 yrs
* **Uzziah (Azariah)**	52 yrs
* **Jotham**	16 yrs
Ahaz	16 yrs
* **Hezekiah**	29 yrs
Manasseh	55 yrs
Amon	2 yrs
* **Josiah**	31 yrs
Jehoahaz	3 mos
Jehoiakim	11 yrs
Jehoiachin	3 mos
Zedekiah	11 yrs

Babylon took Judah captive 3 times during Jehoiakim's, Jehoiachin's, and Zedekiah's reigns.

desecrated the temple by bringing in the idols which his father had dedicated, and the things which he himself had dedicated (1 Kings 15:9–15).

Righteous King Jehoshaphat

— **Jehoshaphat** (914 BC), the son of Asa, reigned righteously for 25 years. He was 35 years old when he began to reign, and "he walked in all the ways of Asa his father ... doing that which was right in the eyes of the Lord." But, as with his father, he did not remove the "high places" because "the people offered and burnt incense yet in the high places." Jehoshaphat removed "the remnant of the sodomites, which remained in the days of his father Asa" (1 Kings 22:41–46).

Jehoshaphat taught the law to the people

As a result of his consistent righteousness, the Lord established his kingdom with peace, riches, and "honour in abundance." And "in the third year of his reign" he sent his princes and Levites around the kingdom to teach the people concerning the "law of the Lord" (2 Chronicles 17:3–9).

2 Chronicles 20 This was a period of terrible anxiety for the people of Judah, as three nations had declared war on them. The outcome seemed bleak for King Jehoshaphat and his people, who were greatly outnumbered. But Jehoshaphat taught his people to rely on the Lord for their safety, and the threat was overcome.

■ Jehoshaphat asked the people of Judah to humble themselves before the Lord. (vv. 3–4). He sought the Lord in prayer and proclaimed a fast throughout all Judah. In response, the people of Judah gathered themselves together, to ask for help from the Lord.

■ They humbly sought the Lord's help (vv. 12–13). "All Judah stood before the Lord, with their little ones, their wives, and their children" to ask for the Lord's help. Their words reveal their humility: "O our God, wilt thou not judge [destroy] them? for we have no might against this great company that cometh against us; neither know we what to do: but our eyes are upon thee."

■ The Lord answered that He would protect them (vv. 14–17). The answer came through the prophet Jahaziel, who assured them that the battle was the Lord's and he would protect them. "Ye shall not need to fight in this battle: set yourselves, stand ye still, and see the salvation of the Lord." Believing this, Jehoshaphat counseled his people to believe in the Lord and to follow his prophets so that they might be established and prosper (v. 20).

- Jehoshaphat appointed singers to praise the Lord rather than fight. He instructed them to "praise the beauty of holiness, as they went out before the army" and to sing: "Praise the Lord; for his mercy endureth for ever" (v. 21).

- The Lord protected them by causing their attackers to war among themselves and destroy one another. "And when Judah came toward the watch tower in the wilderness, they looked unto the multitude, and, behold, they were dead bodies fallen to the earth, and none escaped" (vv. 22–24).

— **Joram (Jehoram)** (893 BC), the son of Jehoshaphat, <u>was not a righteous king</u>. His wife was Athaliah, a daughter of Omri, the wicked king of Israel at the time. He was 32 years old when he began to reign, and reigned wickedly for 8 years.

— **Ahaziah** (885 BC), the son of Jehoram, <u>emulated the sins of Ahab, the wicked king of Israel</u>. He was the son of Athaliah, who was the daughter of Ahab, who reigned in Israel at the time. Ahaziah was only 22 when he became king, and reigned for only 1 year. He was killed by Jehu, who was seeking to wipe out the family of Ahab in Israel (2 Kings 9:23–28).

— **Athaliah** (884 BC), <u>the wife of Jehoram and mother of Ahaziah, reigned wickedly</u> for 7 years. She was a daughter of the wicked King Omri of Israel. This means she was also the sister of the even more wicked King Ahab of Israel. Like her brother, Athaliah was ambitious for power. So, when she saw that her son Ahaziah was dead, she destroyed all the remaining royal seed in Judah, and reigned herself for awhile. Unfortunately for her, "Jehosheba, the daughter of king Joram, sister of Ahaziah, took Joash the son of Ahaziah … [and] hid him … and his nurse, in [her] bedchamber … so that he was not slain" (2 Kings 11:1–3). He was only an infant at the time.

Righteous King Joash

— **Jehoash (Joash)** (878 BC), the son of Ahaziah, <u>reigned in righteousness for 40 years</u>. He was only 7 when he began to reign, having been kept hidden for 6 years while Athaliah reigned over the land. Then the priest Jehoiada brought him out of hiding and anointed him (2 Kings 11:4–11). When Athaliah saw what was happening, she "rent her clothes, and cried, Treason, Treason." The guards then pursued her out of the temple and slew her with swords (2 Kings 11:12–16, 20).

- Jehoiada the priest "made a covenant between the Lord and the king and the people, that they should be the Lord's people." After receiving this covenant, "all the people of the land went into the house of Baal, and brake it down; his altars and his images brake they in pieces thoroughly, and slew Mattan the priest of Baal before the altars." These were the remnants of Athalia's wicked reign. Then the priest brought the new child- king Joash down from the temple and placed him in the king's house, "and he sat on the throne of the kings" (2 Kings 11:17–21).

- Jehoash (Joash) did "that which was right in the sight of the Lord" by following all that the priest Jehoiada taught him. But he did not remove all the "high places" because "the people still sacrificed and burnt incense in the high places."

■ <u>Joash attempted to repair "breaches"</u> <u>of the temple</u> by using the money in the temple treasury and all the money donated by the people to the temple to pay for the repairs. But by the time that Jehoash was 30 "the priests had not repaired the breaches of the house." He urged them to delay no longer and they organized an effort to collect into one place "all the money that was brought into the house of the Lord." This was used to pay "carpenters and builders, that wrought upon the house of the Lord, and [the] masons, and hewers of stone, and to buy timber and hewed stone to repair the breaches of the house of the Lord … ." (2 Kings 12:2–16).

Josiah sought to repair the temple

■ Later, however, when the king of Syria planned to attack Judah, Jehoash sent to the king of Syria all the precious contents of the temple and his own house, plus all the money in the temple treasury, as a ransom to prevent the attack. Then he left the city for his own protection. And while away, his servants entered into a conspiracy and slew him at Millo (2 Kings 12:17–21).

— **Amaziah** (841 BC), son of Joash, like his father before him, <u>"did that which was right in the</u> <u>sight of the Lord."</u> However, like his father, he did not remove the "high places" because "as yet the people did sacrifice and burnt incense on the high places." (2 Kings 14:1–4). Just as soon as "the kingdom was confirmed in his hand, … he slew his servants which had slain the king his father. But in obedience to the law of Moses, he did not slay the children of the murderers. He was only 25 when he became king. After 29 years of rule, he became aware of a conspiracy against him and fled to Lachish. But it was of no use, because his conspirators followed him there and killed him (2 Kings 14:6–7, 17–20). Just as had happened to his father, he was assassinated by traitors.

— **Uzziah (Azariah)** (811 BC), the son of Amaziah, began reigning when he was only 16 years old and reigned for 52 years. He <u>"did that which was right in the sight of the Lord …</u> [except] that the high places were not removed" because "the people sacrificed and burnt incense still on the high places" (2 Kings 15:1–4). Uzziah (Azariah) had the misfortune of becoming "a leper unto the day of his death," forcing him to live in a "several" [separate] house. Thus incapacitated and separated from his people, his son Jotham took care of him and "judg[ed] the people of the land" while his father yet lived (2 Kings 15:5–7).

— **Jotham** (758 BC), the son of Uzziah (Azariah), was 20 years old when he began to reign. He <u>reigned in righteousness for 16 years, and "built the higher gate of the house of the Lord."</u>

But like his father and grandfather before him, he did not remove the "high places" because the people were still using them (2 Kings 15:32–38).

— **Ahaz** (742 BC), the son of Jotham, <u>desecrated the temple and "shut up [its] doors"</u> (2 Chronicles 28:24). He was 20 years old when he began to reign, and reigned for 16 years in wickedness. In fact, he may have been worse than all previous kings. He behaved like the kings of Israel in his idol worship, even making "his son to pass through the fire," which means that he offered him as a living sacrifice to the god Molech. He also "sacrificed and burnt incense in the high places, and on the hills, and under every green tree. (2 Kings 16:1–4). Finding himself under attack from Syria and Israel, he "took the silver and gold that was found in the house of the Lord, and in the treasures of the king's house, and sent it for a present to the king of Assyria," asking him to help him by attacking Syria, which he did (2 Kings 16:5–9).

King Ahaz then went to Damascus to meet Tiglath-pileser king of Assyria. While there, he saw a pagan altar that he liked very much. He sent the design of it to Urijah the priest, who then built an altar in Jerusalem "according to all that king Ahaz had sent from Damascus" (2 Kings 16:8–11). When Ahaz returned, he moved the brazen altar of the Lord from in front of the temple and replaced it with his new altar. He also destroyed the brazen sea and changed the order of sacrifice in the temple. (2 Kings 16:12–20).

Righteous King Hezekiah

— **Hezekiah** (726 BC), the son of Ahaz, <u>cleaned and restored the temple</u>. Only 25 when he began to reign, he reigned in righteousness for 29 years. Unlike several generations of kings before him, "he removed the high places, and brake the images, and cut down the groves, and brake in pieces the brasen serpent that Moses had made: for [in] those days the children of Israel did burn incense to it." Hezekiah called it Nehushtan [a "thing of brass"]" (2 Kings 18:1–4). By this he probably meant that it was not a god to be worshiped but only a "thing of brass" that had no life or power. Hezekiah "trusted in the Lord God of Israel; so that after him was none like him among all the kings of Judah, nor any that were before him. For he clave to the Lord, and departed not from following him, but kept his commandments, which the Lord commanded Moses. And the Lord was with him; and he prospered whithersoever he went" (2 Kings 18:5–7).

   ▪ <u>2 Chronicles 29:6–10</u> Hezekiah opened the doors of the temple that his father had shut and ordered the priests and Levites to cleanse and sanctify it. Man years of neglect and unrighteousness had left the temple desecrated and in disrepair. His fathers had "shut up the doors of the porch, and put out the lamps, and have not burned incense nor offered burnt offerings in the holy place unto the God of Israel" (vv. 6–7). He pointed out that the Lord had abandoned Judah because of its wickedness "and he hath delivered them to trouble, to astonishment, and to hissing, as ye see with your eyes. For, lo, our fathers have fallen by the sword, and our sons and our daughters and our wives are in captivity for this" (vv. 8–9). He said, "It is in mine heart to make a covenant with the Lord God of Israel, that his fierce wrath may turn away from us" (v. 10).

- <u>D&C 97:15–17</u> In our own dispensation, the Lord has said, "Inasmuch as my people build a house unto me in the name of the Lord, and do not suffer any unclean thing to come into it, that it be not defiled, my glory shall rest upon it; Yea, and my presence shall be there, for I will come into it, and all the pure in heart that shall come into it shall see God. But if it be defiled I will not come into it, and my glory shall not be there; for I will not come into unholy temples."

- <u>D&C 109:20-21</u> The Lord later commanded "that no unclean thing shall be permitted to come into thy house to pollute it" (v. 20). If people transgress, "they may speedily repent and return unto [God], and find favor in [His] sight, and be restored to the blessings which [He] hast ordained to be poured out upon those who shall reverence [Him] in [His] house" (v. 21).

- <u>2 Chronicles 29:20-21, 29–31</u> As part of the cleansing of the temple and of the people, "Hezekiah … rose early, and gathered the rulers of the city, and went up to the house of the Lord" where they offered "seven bullocks, and seven rams, and seven lambs, and seven he goats, for a sin offering for the kingdom, and for the sanctuary, and for Judah" (vv. 20–21). "And when they had made an end of offering, the king and all that were present with him bowed themselves, and worshipped" (v. 29). They sang praises to the Lord, using the words of David and Asaph the seer (v. 30). Then Hezekiah invited the people to "bring sacrifices and thank offerings into the house of the Lord," which "as many as were of a free heart" did (v. 31).

- <u>2 Chronicles 30:1, 6–9</u> On this occasion, Hezekiah "sent to all Israel and Judah, and wrote letters also to Ephraim and Manasseh" to invite them "to the house of the Lord at Jerusalem, to keep the passover unto the Lord God of Israel" (v. 1). Many of the citizens of Israel had already been taken captive into Assyria, but he was reaching out to "the remnant of you, that are escaped out of the hand of the kings of Assyria," saying, "turn again unto the Lord God of Abraham, Isaac, and Israel, and he will return to the remnant of you" (v. 6). He urged them, "be not ye like your fathers, and like your brethren, which trespassed against the Lord God of their fathers, who therefore gave them up to desolation, as ye see" (v. 7). And "be ye not stiffnecked, as your fathers were, but yield yourselves unto the Lord, and enter into his sanctuary, which he hath sanctified for ever: and serve the Lord your God, that the fierceness of his wrath may turn away from you" (v. 8). He promised them that if they would "turn again unto the Lord, your brethren and your children shall find compassion before them that lead them captive, so that they shall come again into this land: for the Lord your God is gracious and merciful, and will not turn away his face from you, if ye return unto him" (v. 9).

- <u>2 Chronicles 30:10-11</u> Hezekiah's letters "passed from city to city through the country of Ephraim and Manasseh even unto Zebulun," but unfortunately "they laughed them to scorn, and mocked them" (v. 10). Nevertheless, a few individuals "of Asher and Manasseh and of Zebulun humbled themselves, and came to Jerusalem" (v. 11).

- 2 Kings 18:10-12 Because of the wickedness of the people, the remainder of the kingdom of Israel, who did not go to Jerusalem to repent, was taken captive several years later. The captive Israelites became the lost ten tribes.

- 2 Kings 18:13–16 Hoping to avert war, "Hezekiah … sent to the king of Assyria [in] Lachish, saying, … that which thou puttest on me will I bear. And the king of Assyria appointed unto Hezekiah king of Judah three hundred talents of silver and thirty talents of gold." To meet this tribute, Hezekiah gave Sennacherib all the silver in the house of the Lord, and the treasures of the king's house. He also "cut off the gold from the doors of the temple of the Lord, and from the pillars which [he] had overlaid [with gold], and gave it to the king of Assyria." (2 Kings 18:13–16). But ultimately, it was not enough.

- 2 Chronicles 32:1-5, 30 Having taken Israel captive, Sennacherib king of Assyria next attacked "all the fenced cities of Judah, and took them." But he had not yet conquered Jerusalem. To help defend Jerusalem against attacks by the Assyrians, King Hezekiah diverted the water of the spring of Gihon to the pool of Siloam, inside the city walls². This was done by digging a conduit (tunnel) for the water through about 1770 feet of limestone rock. Hezekiah then ordered that the fountains outside the city be covered to deny the Assyrians easy access to the water. Without this water inside the walls of the city, the people of Jerusalem would not have survived the siege by the Assyrians. He also "built up all the wall that was broken, and raised it up to the towers, and another wall without, and repaired Millo (a tower) in the city of David, and made darts and shields in abundance" (v. 5).

- 2 Chronicles 32:6-8 After Hezekiah made preparations for war "he set captains of war over the people, and gathered them together to him in the street of the gate of the city, and spake comfortably to them" (v. 6). Hezekiah said, "Be strong and courageous, be not afraid nor dismayed for the king of Assyria, nor for all the multitude that is with him: for there be more with us than with him: With him is an arm of flesh; but with us is the Lord our God to help us, and to fight our battles. And the people rested themselves upon the words of Hezekiah king of Judah" (vv. 7–8). Thus, we learn from Hezekiah the proper relationship between trusting in our own efforts and trusting in the Lord.

- 2 Chronicles 32:9-17 Having surrounded them with his army, Sennacherib sent his servants to speak to the people in Jerusalem. He asked them "Whereon do ye trust, that ye abide in the siege in Jerusalem?" suggesting that Hezekiah had persuaded them to doom themselves to die by famine and thirst, saying, "The Lord our God shall deliver us out of the hand of the king of Assyria" (v. 11). He reminded them that he had conquered many other lands, whose gods could not protect them, and they should not expect that "your God should be able to deliver you out of mine hand" (vv. 13–17). The servants of Sennacherib "cried with a loud voice" in the Jewish language "unto the people of Jerusalem that were on the wall, to affright them, and to trouble them; that they might take the city" (v. 18). And thus, just as Satan does, they tried to convince them that God could not or would not help them.

- ■ 2 Chronicles 32:20 Hezekiah and the prophet Isaiah "prayed and cried to heaven" (v. 20). Hezekiah took the letter to the house of the Lord "and spread it before the Lord." Then he prayed, saying, "O Lord of hosts, God of Israel, that dwellest between the cherubims, thou art the God, even thou alone, of all the kingdoms of the earth: thou hast made heaven and earth. Incline thine ear, O Lord, and hear; open thine eyes, O Lord, and see: and hear all the words of Sennacherib, which hath sent to reproach the living God. Of a truth, Lord, the kings of Assyria have laid waste all the nations, and their countries, And have cast their gods into the fire: for they were no gods, but the work of men's hands, wood and stone: therefore they have destroyed them. Now therefore, O LORD our God, save us from his hand, that all the kingdoms of the earth may know that thou art the LORD, even thou only" (Isaiah 37:14–20).

- ■ 2 Chronicles 32:21–22 The Lord answered Hezekiah's prayer through the prophet Isaiah: "Therefore thus saith the Lord concerning the king of Assyria, He shall not come into this city, nor shoot an arrow there, nor come before it with shields, nor cast a bank against it. By the way that he came, by the same shall he return, and shall not come into this city, saith the Lord. For I will defend this city to save it for mine own sake, and for my servant David's sake" (Isaiah 37:33–35). Then "the angel of the Lord went forth, and smote in the camp of the Assyrians"— all 185,000 of them—so that "when they arose early in the morning, behold, they were all dead corpses" (Isaiah 37:36). Sennacherib himself returned and dwelt at Nineveh, where, while worshiping "in the house of Nisroch his god, that Adrammelech and Sharezer his sons smote him with the sword … his son reigned in his stead" (Isaiah 37:37–38). "Thus the Lord saved Hezekiah and the inhabitants of Jerusalem from the hand of Sennacherib the king of Assyria … and guided them on every side" (2 Chronicles 32:22).

- ■ D&C 109:24-28 Hezekiah and his people received the Lord's protection because of their righteousness, which was demonstrated by their worship at the temple. In his dedicatory prayer at the Kirtland Temple, the Prophet Joseph Smith promised, "no weapon formed against them shall prosper; that he who diggeth a pit for them shall fall into the same himself; [and] no combination of wickedness shall have power to rise up and prevail over thy people upon whom thy name shall be put in this house; And if any people shall rise against this people, [the Lord's] anger [will] be kindled against them; And if they shall smite this people [the Lord] wilt smite them; [He] wilt fight for [His] people as [He] didst in the day of battle, that they may be delivered from the hands of all their enemies."

— **Manasseh** (697 BC), the son of Hezekiah, was 12 when he began to reign, and reigned 55 years (2 Kings 21:1–7). He was extremely wicked, adopting "the abominations of the heathen, whom the Lord cast out before the children of Israel" (v. 2) He built altars to Baal inside the house of the Lord, and "altars for all the host of heaven in the two courts of the house of the Lord" (vv. 4–5). He restored all the "high places" that his father Hezekiah had destroyed—rearing up altars for Baal, and making groves for the sensual rites of Ashteroth worship—and worshiping "all the host of heaven, and served them" (v. 3). He also offered up his own son as a sacrifice to Molech by making him "pass through the fire" (v. 6). He also "observed times, and used enchantments, and dealt with familiar spirits and wizards: he wrought much wickedness in the sight of the Lord" (v. 6). This wicked king "shed innocent blood very much, till he had filled Jerusalem from one end to another" (v. 16), making him perhaps the most wicked king who ever ruled Judah.

— **Amon** (642 BC), the son of Manasseh, like his father, was thoroughly wicked, and "served the idols that his father served, and worshipped them" (vv. 21–22). He was 22 when he began to reign, but was assassinated by his own servants after a very brief two-year reign (2 Kings 21:19, 23).

Righteous King Josiah

— **Josiah** (640 BC), the son of Amon, was only 8 when he began to reign, due to the sudden and unexpected death of his father. He reigned 31 years in righteousness (2 Kings 22:1), being the last of all the kings of Judah who was righteous. Like his great-grandfather Hezekiah, Josiah sought to repair and restore the temple.

Book of the law found in the temple

■ While doing so, they found the book of the law in the temple (2 Chronicles 34:14). After read- ing it, Josiah sorrowed greatly for the wicked- ness of his ancestors. He determined to read the book to his people, and after doing so they placed themselves under covenant to keep the commandments of the Lord. Josiah proceeded to destroy all worship of false gods, drive out the sodomites, and put to death idolatrous priests (2 Chronicles 34:14–24).

■ 2 Chronicles 34:22-25 Because of his righteousness, Huldah, a prophetess, prophesied great blessings on Josiah personally, but predicted wrath upon the people of Judah for their wickedness. The Lord said he would "bring evil upon this place, and upon the inhabitants thereof, even all the curses that are written in the book which they have read before the king of Judah: Because they have forsaken me, and have burned incense unto other gods, that they might provoke me to anger with all the works of their hands; therefore my wrath shall be poured out upon this place, and shall not be quenched."

■ 2 Chronicles 34:26, 28 Huldah had more glorious promises for Josiah: "Thus saith the Lord God of Israel … Behold, I will gather thee to thy fathers, and thou shalt be gathered to thy grave in peace, neither shall thine eyes see all the evil that I will bring upon this place, and upon the inhabitants of the same."

■ 2 Chronicles 35:20-24 The fulfillment of this promise came very soon thereafter when Josiah was killed in battle. Josiah had finished his work on the temple and went out to battle Necho king of Egypt (v. 20). Necho had no quarrel with Josiah; he was coming to conquer others (v. 21). "Nevertheless Josiah would not turn his face from him, but disguised himself, that he might fight with him, and hearkened not unto the words of Necho … and came to fight in the valley of Megiddo" (v. 22). Unfortunately, Josiah was mortally wounded in the battle and died, and "all Judah and Jerusalem mourned for Josiah" (vv. 23–24). He did not live long enough to see the destruction and captivity of Judah.

■ 2 Chronicles 34:29-30 When Josiah heard the condemnation of his people because of their wickedness, he called them to the temple and read the scriptures to them. He hoped to turn them from their condemnation. They were blessed to have the scriptures among them, and Josiah hoped that by reading them they would realize their need for repentance. Also, having heard the Lord's words to the prophets, they would be accountable for their own destiny.

President Spencer W. Kimball said, "The Lord is not trifling with us when he gives us these things, for 'unto whomsoever much is given, of him shall be much required.' (Luke 12:48.) Access to these things means responsibility for them. We must study the scriptures according to the Lord's commandment (3 Ne. 23:1–5); and we must let them govern our lives" ("How Rare a Possession—the Scriptures!" Ensign, Sept. 1976, 5).

■ 2 Chronicles 34:31-33 While Josiah and his people were at the temple, they made a covenant with the Lord "to keep his commandments, and his testimonies, and his statutes, with all [their] heart, and with all [their] soul, to perform the words of the covenant which [were] written in [the] book" (v. 31). Josiah then held them accountable for this covenant (v. 32), and "took away all the abominations out of all the countries that pertained to the children of Israel, and made all that were present in Israel to serve, even to serve the Lord their God. And all his days they departed not from following the Lord, the God of their fathers" (v. 33).

— **Jehoahaz** (609 BC), the son of Josiah, was 23 when he began to reign. Unlike his father, he "did that which was evil in the sight of the Lord" (2 Kings 23:32). He reigned only 3 months (v. 31) and then Pharaoh-nechoh of Egypt took him off the throne of Judah "in bands" to assure that he could not reign, and laced Judah under a heavy tribute of silver and gold (v. 33).

— **Jehoiakim** (609 BC), was another son of Josiah whose original name was Eliakim. Also unlike his father before him, he "did that which was evil in the sight of the Lord" (v. 37). He was 25 when Pharaoh Necho placed him on the throne of Judah and changed his name to Jehoiakim. He reigned for 11 years (2 Kings 23:34, 36). He paid the heavy tax Judah owed to Egypt by taxing his people heavily. The armies of Nebuchadnezzar overran Jerusalem during his reign, and took some of its people captive into Babylon. Jehoiakim remained on the throne in servitude to Babylon for three years, then rebelled. This not only cost him his life, but also set the stage for a second devastating attack on Jerusalem.

— **Jehoiachin** (598 BC), the son of Jehoiakim, was 18 when he began to reign, and like his father and grandfather before him, <u>"did that which was evil in the sight of the Lord"</u> (2 Kings 24:9). He reigned for only 3 months (v. 8) before he was deported to Babylon along with "his mother, and his servants, and his princes, and his officers" (v. 12). <u>Nebuchadnezzar also took "all the treasures of the house of the Lord,</u> and the treasures of the king's house, and <u>cut in pieces all the vessels of gold</u> which Solomon king of Israel had made in the temple of the Lord" (v. 13).

— **Zedekiah** (598 BC), was also a son of Jehoiakim, whose original name was Mattaniah (2 Kings 24:17). Like his brother and father, he <u>"did that which was evil in the sight of the Lord"</u> (v. 19). He was placed on the throne by Nebuchadnezzar when his brother Jehoiachin was taken captive into Babylon. He was 21 when he began to reign, and reigned 11 years (v. 18). Like his grandfather Jehoiakim, he foolishly rebelled against the king of Babylon (vv. 17–20), bringing about a third and final siege of Jerusalem that lasted two years (2 Kings 25:1–2). The siege produced extreme famine in the city, and "all the men of war fled by night" while Zedekiah "went the way toward the plain" (v. 4). But Nebuchadnezzar's forces "pursued after the king, and overtook him in the plains of Jericho," the brought him captive "to the king of Babylon [in] Riblah" (v. 6). There they "slew the sons of Zedekiah before his eyes, and put out the eyes of Zedekiah, and bound him with fetters of brass, and carried him to Babylon" (v. 7).

THE DESTRUCTION OF THE TEMPLE OF SOLOMON

● **2 Kings 25:8–21 Nebuchadnezzar destroys Solomon's temple.** His army entered into the defenseless city of Jerusalem (v. 8). They "burnt the house of the Lord, and the king's house, and all the houses of Jerusalem, and every great man's house"(v. 9). They "brake down the walls of Jerusalem round about" (v. 10). And then they took "the rest of the people that were left in the city, and the fugitives that fell away" to the king of Babylon, who carried them way captive into Babylon

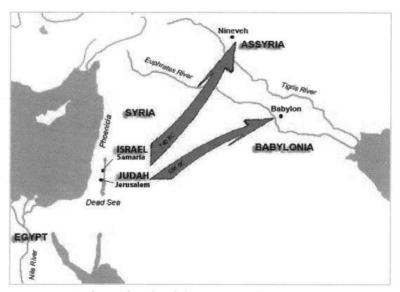

Both Israel and Judah were carried away captive

(v. 11). The only people they left behind were "the poor of the land to be vinedressers and husbandmen" (v. 12).

As booty, Nebuchadnezzar's army carried away "the pillars of brass that were in the house of the Lord, and the bases, and the brasen sea that was in the house of the Lord," all of which were cut into pieces and taken to Babylon (v. 13). They also took "the pots, and the shovels, and the snuffers, and the spoons, and all the vessels of brass wherewith they ministered, ... the firepans, and the bowls, and such things as were of gold, ... and of silver" (vv. 14–15). The sum of these things was so vast that it was "without weight" (v., 16). The pillars were 18 cubits high, with a 3-cubit brass chapiter on top, along with "the wreathen work, and pomegranates upon the chapiter round about" (v. 17).

Last of all, they took "Seraiah the chief priest, and Zephaniah the second priest, and the three keepers of the door," plus "an officer that was set over the men of war, and five men of them that were in the king's presence, which were found in the city, and the principal scribe of the host, which mustered the people of the land, and threescore men of the people of the land that were found in the city," and they "slew them at Riblah in the land of Hamath" (vv. 20–21). "So Judah was carried away out of their land" (v. 21).

Chapter 31

The Wisdom of Solomon

(Proverbs; Ecclesiastes)

෪෨ඏ

Solomon Was Wiser than Other Men

In the beginning of his reign, Solomon was wiser than other men. When the Lord asked him "what [shall I] give thee," he responded, "Give … thy servant an understanding heart to judge thy people, that I may discern between good and bad: for who is able to judge this thy so great a people?" (1 Kings 3:5, 9).

The Lord answered this request by giving Solomon "wisdom and understanding exceeding much, and largeness of heart, even as the sand that is on the sea shore" (1 Kings 4:29).

The classic example is the story of two women, harlots, who came to him claiming that a child was theirs. Understanding perfectly the love of a mother, Solomon ordered his servants to cut the child in half, whereupon one of the women cried out, "O my lord, give her the living child, and in no wise slay it. But the other said, Let it be neither mine nor thine, but divide it." Solomon then declared "Give her [the woman who asked him to spare the child] the living child, and in no wise slay it: she is the mother thereof" (1 Kings 3:16–28).

GUSTAVE DORÉ, 1896

Solomon's wisdom "excelled the wisdom of all the children of the east country, and all the wisdom of Egypt. For he was wiser than all men … and his fame was in all nations round about. … And there came of all people to hear the wisdom of Solomon, from all kings of the earth, which had heard of his wisdom" (1 Kings 4:30–31, 34). Among these visitors was the Queen of Sheba, who exclaimed, "It was a true report that I heard in mine own land of thy acts and of thy wisdom. Howbeit I believed not the words, until I came, and mine eyes had seen it: and, behold, the half was not told me: thy wisdom and prosperity exceedeth the fame which I heard" (1 Kings 10:6–7).

THE PROVERBS OF SOLOMON

The Bible tells us that Solomon spoke 3,000 proverbs and 1,005 songs. In speaking his words of wisdom, Solomon used symbols, images, metaphors, similes, and many other literary methods to illustrate his advice. "He spake of trees, from the cedar tree that is in Lebanon even unto the hyssop that springeth out of the wall: he spake also of beasts, and of fowl, and of creeping things, and of fishes" (1 Kings 4:32–33).

The Book of Proverbs

- **Author:**   Solomon and successors who carried on the wisdom literature tradition.

- **Position:**   Proverbs is one of the 11 books of the Old Testament that belong to the Hagiographa ("sacred writings") of the Jewish canon, along with the books of Ruth, Chronicles (counted as one book), Ezra-Nehemiah (also counted as one book), Esther, Job, Psalms, Ecclesiastes, Song of Solomon, Lamentations, and Daniel.

- **Purpose:**   The Proverbs of Solomon (together with the pronouncements of the "Preacher" in the Book of Ecclesiastes) are a vast collection of wisdom in the form of maxims, exhortations, and poems concerning life. Solomon was enormously prolific, speaking 3,000 proverbs and 1,005 songs.

- **Time Span:**   The reign of Solomon from around 1015 BC until his death around 975 BC.

- **Length:**   31 chapters

- **Key Sections:**

— Chapters 1–9	Wisdom of the genuine kind.
— Chapters 10–24	Contrasting right & wrong ways to live.
— Chapters 25–29	Proverbs copied by scribes during the reign of Hezekiah, king of Judah.
— Chapters 30–31	Writings of Agur and Lemuel, including the latter's portrait of the ideal wife.

The Nature of the Proverbs

The book of Proverbs is classified as wisdom literature. It contains various collections of proverbs, wise sayings, and some poems. Most were written mainly to get younger people to accept counsel from those with more experience, especially their parents and the Lord. Though Solomon "spake three thousand proverbs" (1 Kings 4:32), only some of those sayings are included in the book of Proverbs.

The book of Proverbs contains sayings by more than just Solomon—it is composed of proverbs written by various authors at different times. But of these, only Solomon is known to us. Although

Solomon and the other authors of this book were not all prophets, much of what they wrote was inspired by the Lord. Their writings generally reflect a belief that true wisdom comes from God.

SELECTED WISDOM FROM PROVERBS

There are hundreds of proverbs in the Book of Proverbs, and no attempt will be made here to review them all. Instead, I have selected out several that deal with a dozen main themes. I encourage the reader to spend some extended time reading these proverbs in their entirely. The beauty of the language and the wisdom of the sayings are wonderful.

Proverbs on Wisdom

● **Proverbs 1:1–7 Wisdom is not the same thing as being "learned."** (See also 2 Nephi 9:28–29; Proverbs 9:9–10). Solomon defines wisdom as all of the following:

GUSTAVE DORÉ, 1896

Solomon wrote down words of wisdom

— To know wisdom and instruction; to perceive the words of understanding (v. 2).

— To receive the instruction of wisdom, justice, and judgment, and equity (v. 3).

— To give subtlety (understanding) to the simple (unknowledgeable) (v. 4).

— To give to the young man knowledge and discretion (v. 4).

— To hear and increase learning (v. 5).

— To attain unto wise counsels (v. 5).

— To understand a proverb, and the interpretation (v. 6).

— To understand the words of the wise, and their dark sayings (v. 6).

Solomon concludes by saying that "the fear of the Lord is the beginning of knowledge: but fools despise wisdom and instruction" (v. 7).

● **Proverbs 2:1–5 God will reward those who earnestly seek wisdom.** Speaking to his "son," Solomon says that the secret to understanding the things of God is to "receive my words, and [keep] my commandments, ... [to] incline thine ear unto wisdom, and apply thine heart to understanding, ...[to seek] after knowledge, and ... understanding" (vv. 1–3). If we treasure these things "as silver, and ... as ... hid[den] treasures," then we will truly "understand the fear of the Lord, and find the knowledge of God" (vv. 4–5).

- **Proverbs 2:6–9 God is the source of wisdom.** The Lord gives "wisdom … knowledge and understanding. He layeth up sound wisdom for the righteous: he is a buckler to them that walk uprightly. He keepeth the paths of judgment, and preserveth the way of his saints" (vv. 6–8). If we seek wisdom from him, we will "understand righteousness, and judgment, and equity; yea, every good path" (v. 9).

- **Proverbs 2:16–19 Wisdom will protect us from evil.** A wise man will avoid "the strange woman, [and] the stranger which flattereth with her words;" those who "forsaketh the guide of her youth, and forgetteth the covenant of her God" (vv. 16–17). The result of these behaviors is death: "None that go unto her return again, neither take they hold of the paths of life" (vv. 18–19). Note that evil is depicted as an evil woman, whereas wisdom is frequently depicted by Solomon as a righteous woman.

- **Proverbs 3:13–15 Wisdom is more valuable than earthly treasures.** "Happy is the man that findeth wisdom, and the man that getteth understanding" (v. 13). Wisdom is "better than the merchandise of silver, and the gain thereof than fine gold, … more precious than rubies: and all the things thou canst desire," none of which can be compared to the value of wisdom (vv. 14–15).

- **Proverbs 3:16–18 Wisdom leads to every other desirable blessing.** "Length of days is in her right hand; and in her left hand riches and honour. Her ways are ways of pleasantness, and all her paths are peace. She is a tree of life to them that lay hold upon her: and happy is every one that retaineth her" (see also Ecclesiastes 7:12).

- **Proverbs 15:31–33 The difficulties of life provide wisdom and understanding.** A wise man "heareth the reproof of life" (v. 31), through which he "getteth understanding" (v. 32), while "he that refuseth instruction despiseth his own soul" (v. 32). "The fear of the Lord" (trust in Him) helps us receive "the instruction of wisdom" and "humility," which always must come before we can receive "honour" (v. 33).

Learning to trust in God's words

- **Proverbs 4:7 "Wisdom is the principal thing; therefore get wisdom."** We are prone to seek after knowledge, which is not an evil thing, but Solomon counsels us, "with all thy getting get understanding." Otherwise, as Paul said, we will be "ever learning, and never able to come to the knowledge of the truth" (2 Timothy 3:7).

Trusting in the Lord

- **Proverbs 3:5–6 "Trust in the Lord with all thine heart.** … In all thy ways acknowledge him, and he shall direct thy paths." This is a hard principle to learn, but it is the secret to peace of mind and sufficient faith in God to receive the miracles we seek. One of the most precious things I possess is a framed embroidery of these verses which a faithful ward member gave me at a time of great trial in my life. I have found this scripture to be a source of great peace in every circumstance of life.

- **Proverbs 30:5 God is a "shield unto them that … trust in him."** Solomon reminds us that "every word of God is pure," and can be absolutely trusted. If we believe this, then there is no difficulty that need overwhelm us.

Obedience

- **Proverbs 15:5 Fools reject counsel.** Solomon spoke frequently in the proverbs about the foolishness of youth (see, for example, Proverbs 1:7–27). He concludes such counsel with this simple couplet: "A fool despiseth his father's instruction: but he that regardeth reproof is prudent."

- **Proverbs 3:11–12 "Whom the Lord loveth he correcteth;** even as a father the son in whom he delighteth." We should not see the difficulties that arise from our unwise choices as a sign of God's rejection. They are, rather, the ministrations of a wise Parent who wants us to learn from our own experience how to discern between good and evil.

- **Proverbs 6:23 The laws of God are a "light."** The commandments are "a lamp" to guide us, and when the Lord reproves us He is attempting to instruct us in the "way of life."

- **Proverbs 12:15 A fool's way is right in his own eyes,** while "he that hearkeneth unto counsel is wise." There is nothing so impenetrable as the mind of somebody who thinks he is right and will not consider the possibility of error or the need for correction.

Maintaining Righteousness

- **Proverbs 4:14–19 Do not enter the path of the wicked,** but "avoid it, pass not by it, turn from it, and pass away" (vv. 14–15). The wicked "sleep not, except they have done mischief; and their sleep is taken away, unless they cause some to fall" (v. 16). "They eat the bread of wickedness, and drink the wine of violence" (v. 17). "The way of the wicked is as darkness: they know not at what they stumble" (v. 19). By comparison, "the path of the just is as the shining light, that shineth more and more unto the perfect day" (v. 18).

JAMES J. TISSOT, 1904

The way of the wicked leads to death

- **Proverbs 4:24–27 Stay on the straight path of righteousness.** "Put away from thee a froward (stubborn or contrary) mouth, and perverse lips put far from thee" (v. 24). "Let thine eyes look right on, and let thine eyelids look straight before thee" (v. 25). "Ponder the path of thy feet, and let all thy ways be established" (v. 26). And along the pathway through life, "Turn not to the right hand nor to the left: remove thy foot from evil" (v. 27).

- **Proverbs 6:16–19 Seven things the Lord hates.** "These six things doth the Lord hate: yea, seven are an abomination unto him:"

  — A proud look.

  — A lying tongue.

  — Hands that shed innocent blood.

  — An heart that deviseth wicked imaginations.

  — Feet that be swift in running to mischief.

  — A false witness that speaketh lies.

  — He that soweth discord among brethren.

He that soweth discord

- **Proverbs 10:3 The righteous will have the necessities of life.** "The Lord will not suffer the soul of the righteous to famish: but he casteth away the substance of the wicked."

- **Proverbs 10:27–32 The results of righteousness compared to unrighteousness.**

  — The righteous enjoy prolonged days, while the years of the wicked are shortened.

  — The righteous have hope and gladness, while the expectation of the wicked perishes.

  — The righteous receive strength, while destruction comes to the workers of iniquity.

  — "The righteous shall never be removed: but the wicked shall not inhabit the earth."

  — The righteous speak wisdom, but "the froward tongue shall be cut out."

  — "The lips of the righteous know what is acceptable: but the mouth of the wicked speaketh frowardness (contention)." (See also Proverbs 11:1–4; Proverbs 19:16).

- **Proverbs 15:8–9 The Lord loves the righteous but despises wickedness.** The false worship and idolatry of the wicked are "an abomination to the Lord: but the prayer of the upright is his delight" (v. 8). The Lord "loveth him that followeth after righteousness" (v. 9).

- **Proverbs 23:7 As a man thinketh in his heart, so is he.** This is one of the most famous of Solomon's proverbs, which reminds us that a man might saying anything while "his heart is not with thee." We need to pay attention to what people *do* rather than just what they *say*.

- **Proverbs 7:4–27 Stay away from "strange" (immoral) women.** Solomon here personifies righteousness and wickedness as women, as he counsels, "Say unto wisdom, Thou art my sister; and call understanding thy kinswoman: That they may keep thee from the strange woman, from the stranger which flattereth with her words" (vv. 4–5).

He then gives the example of a "young man void of understanding" that he observed through his window (vv. 6–7). Enticed by a harlot, "he goeth after her straightway, as an ox goeth to the slaughter" (v. 22). Like "a dart strik[ing] through his liver" or "a bird [hastening] to the snare," he is oblivious to the fact that he is losing his life (v. 23).

Solomon begs young people to "hearken unto me … and attend to the words of my mouth. Let not thine heart decline to her ways, go not astray in her paths. For she hath cast down many wounded: yea, many strong men have been slain by her. Her house is the way to hell, going down to the chambers of death" (vv. 24–27).

Immorality leads to death

- **Proverbs 5:3–5 Those who embrace immoral women go down to hell.** Solomon observes that "the lips of a strange woman drop as an honeycomb, and her mouth is smoother than oil: But her end is bitter as wormwood, sharp as a two-edged sword. Her feet go down to death; her steps take hold on hell."

Righteous Communication

- **Proverbs 11:13 Righteous people keep confidences.** "A talebearer revealeth secrets: but he that is of a faithful spirit concealeth the matter."

- **Proverbs 12:22 The Lord abhors lying and delights in truth.** "Lying lips are abomination to the Lord: but they that deal truly are his delight."

- **Proverbs 12:25 The results of speaking kindly.** "Heaviness in the heart of man maketh it stoop: but a good word maketh it glad."

- **Proverbs 15:1 "A soft answer turneth away wrath:** but grievous words stir up anger."

  President Gordon B. Hinckley said: "We seldom get into trouble when we speak softly. It is only when we raise our voices that the sparks fly and tiny molehills become great mountains of contention"[3].

- **Proverbs 15:23 The importance of well-chosen words.** "A man hath joy by the answer of his mouth: and a word spoken in due season, how good is it!"

- **Proverbs 16:23–24 Pleasant words are sweet to the soul.** "The heart of the wise teacheth his mouth, and addeth learning to his lips. Pleasant words are as an honeycomb, sweet to the soul, and health to the bones."

- **Proverbs 16:27–28 Gossipers create dissension and destroy relationships.** "An ungodly man diggeth up evil: and in his lips there is as a burning fire. A froward (contentious) man soweth strife: and a whisperer separateth chief friends."

- **Proverbs 18:8 The words of talebearers.** "The words of a talebearer are as wounds, and they go down into the innermost parts of the belly." (See also Proverbs 25:18).

- **Proverbs 19:5, 9 Liars will be punished.** "A false witness shall not be unpunished, and he that speak- eth lies shall not escape. A false witness shall not be unpunished, and he that speaketh lies shall perish."

- **Proverbs 21:23 Wise people choose their words carefully.** "Whoso keepeth his mouth and his tongue keepeth his soul from troubles."

Gossipers create dissension

- **Proverbs 17:28 He who remains silent is thought to be wise.** "Even a fool, when he holdeth his peace, is counted wise: and he that shutteth his lips is esteemed a man of understanding." (See also Proverbs 29:11).

- **Proverbs 22:10 Scorners create dissension.** "Cast out the scorner, and contention shall go out; yea, strife and reproach shall cease."

Avoiding Anger

Solomon repeatedly suggests that the key to avoiding anger is patience—waiting and thinking before responding to offenses that may come.

- **Proverbs 14:29 Wise people are slow to anger.** "He that is slow to wrath is of great understanding: but he that is hasty of spirit exalteth folly."

- **Proverbs 15:18 Angry people cause problems; wise people solve them.** "A wrathful man stirreth up strife: but he that is slow to anger appeaseth strife."

- **Proverbs 16:32 He who is slow to anger is strong.** "He that is slow to anger is better than the mighty; and he that ruleth his spirit than he that taketh a city.

Grievous words stir up strife

Pride

● **Proverbs 8:13 The Lord hates pride.** Those who "fear the Lord" (worship Him) should "hate evil: pride, and arrogancy, … the evil way, and the froward mouth," because these are things the Lord also hates.

President Ezra Taft Benson said:

> The central feature of pride is enmity—enmity toward God and enmity toward our fellowmen. Enmity means "hatred toward, hostility to, or a state of opposition." It is the power by which Satan wishes to reign over us.
>
> Pride is essentially competitive in nature. We pit our will against God's. When we direct our pride toward God, it is in the spirit of "my will and not thine be done." As Paul said, they "seek their own, not the things which are Jesus Christ's" (Philippians 2:21).
>
> Our will in competition to God's will allows desires, appetites, and passions to go unbridled (Alma 38:12; 3 Nephi 12:30).
>
> The proud cannot accept the authority of God giving direction to their lives (Helaman 12:6). They pit their perceptions of truth against God's great knowledge, their abilities versus God's priesthood power, their accomplishments against His mighty works.
>
> Our enmity toward God takes on many labels, such as rebellion, hard-heartedness, stiff-neckedness, unrepentant, puffed up, easily offended, and sign seekers. The proud wish God would agree with them. They aren't interested in changing their opinions to agree with God's…
>
> Pride is a damning sin in the true sense of that word. It limits or stops progression (Alma 12:10–11). The proud are not easily taught (1 Nephi 15:3, 7–11). They won't change their minds to accept truths, because to do so implies they have been wrong.[4]

● **Proverbs 13:10 Pride leads to contention.** In fact, Solomon says that "*only* by pride cometh contention" (emphasis added).

President Ezra Taft Benson said, "Another face of pride is contention. Arguments, fights, unrighteous dominion, generation gaps, divorces, spouse abuse, riots, and disturbances all fall into this category of pride. Contention in our families drives the Spirit of the Lord away. It also drives many of our family members away. … Pride adversely affects all our relationships—our relationship with God and His servants, between husband and wife, parent and child"[5].

● **Proverbs 16:18–19 Pride leads to destruction.** "Pride goeth before destruction, and an haughty spirit before a fall. Better it is to be of an humble spirit with the lowly, than to divide the spoil with the proud."

Family Relationships.

● **Proverbs 6:20–23 Following parental counsel.** "My son, keep thy father's commandment, and forsake not the law of thy mother: Bind them continually upon thine heart, and tie them about thy neck" (vv. 20–21). Parental counsel will guide us through life, keep us safe, and continually "talk with thee" (v. 22). Their commandments are "a lamp," and their law is "light," while their reproof guides us in "the way of life" (v. 23).

EDWARD HALLOWAY, THE BIBLE AND ITS STORY, 1908

The counsel of wise parents

● **Proverbs 10:1 Wise children make parents happy.** "A wise son maketh a glad father: but a foolish son is the heaviness of his mother." (See also Proverbs 17:25).

● **Proverbs 22:6 Train children while they are young.** "Train up a child in the way he should go: and when he is old, he will not depart from it."

Elder Richard G. Scott said: "You must be willing to forgo personal pleasure and self- interest for family-centered activity, and not turn over to church, school, or society the principal role of fostering a child's well-rounded development. It takes time, great effort, and significant personal sacrifice to 'train up a child in the way he should go.' But where can you find greater rewards for a job well done?"[6].

● **Proverbs 19:18 Chasten and discipline your children.** "Chasten thy son while there is hope, and let not thy soul spare for his crying." (See also Proverbs 23:13–14).

● **Proverbs 29:15, 17 An un-trained child shames its mother.** "The rod and reproof give wisdom: but a child left to himself bringeth his mother to shame." "Correct thy son, and he shall give thee rest; yea, he shall give delight unto thy soul."

● **Proverbs 31:10–31 A virtuous woman is more precious than rubies.** Solomon lists the characteristics that he includes in the descriptive term "virtuous":

— She can be trusted (v. 11).

— She works willingly (v. 13).

— She is compassionate (v. 20).

— She is strong and honorable (v. 25).

— She speaks with wisdom and kindness (v. 26).

— She is a dedicated wife and mother (v. 28).

— She obeys the Lord (v. 30).

GEORGES VAN DER STRAETEN, THE BIBLE AND ITS STORY, 1908

More precious than rubies

Friendship

- **Proverbs 13:20 Warnings about unrighteous friends.** "He that walketh with wise men shall be wise: but a companion of fools shall be destroyed." (See also Proverbs 22:24–25).

- **Proverbs 17:17 Characteristics of good friends.** "A friend loveth at all times, and a brother is born for [to help with] adversity." (See also Proverbs 27:9).

- **Proverbs 18:24 How to obtain true friends.** "A man that hath friends must shew himself friendly: and there is a friend that sticketh closer than a brother."

Diligent Labor

- **Proverbs 19:15 Laziness results in deprivation.** "Slothfulness casteth into a deep sleep; and an idle soul shall suffer hunger."

- **Proverbs 20:4 The sluggard ends up with nothing.** "The sluggard will not plow by reason of the cold; therefore shall he beg in harvest, and have nothing."

- **Proverbs 10:4–5 Wise people work diligently.** "He becometh poor that dealeth with a slack hand: but the hand of the diligent maketh rich. He that gathereth in summer is a wise son: but he that sleepeth in harvest is a son that causeth shame."

A. GRAY, THE BIBLE AND ITS STORY, 1908

Solomon observes a "field of sloth"

- **Proverbs 24:30–34 Laziness brings poverty.** "I went by the field of the slothful, and by the vineyard of the man void of understanding; And, lo, it was all grown over with thorns, and nettles had covered the face thereof, and the stone wall thereof was broken down. Then I saw, and considered it well: I looked upon it, and received instruction. Yet a little sleep, a little slumber, a little folding of the hands to sleep: So shall thy poverty come as one that travelleth; and thy want as an armed man."

The Pursuit of Riches

- **Proverbs 16:8 Righteousness is more important than wealth.** "Better is a little with righteousness than great revenues without right." (See also Proverbs 15:16).

- **Proverbs 22:1 A good name is better than riches.** "A good name is rather to be chosen than great riches, and loving favour rather than silver and gold."

- **Proverbs 22:2 The Lord is God of both rich and poor.** "The rich and poor meet together: the Lord is the maker of them all."

- **Proverbs 23:4–5 Don't work for riches, which fly away.** "Labour not to be rich" and "cease from thine own wisdom" (arrogance). "Wilt thou set thine eyes upon that which is not? for riches certainly make themselves wings; they fly away as an eagle toward heaven."

Elder Boyd K. Packer said: "We come into mortal life to receive a body and to be tested, to learn to choose. We want our children and their children to know that the choice of life is not between fame and obscurity, nor is the choice between wealth and poverty. The choice is between good and evil, and that is a very different matter indeed. When we fully understand this lesson, thereafter our happiness will not be determined by material things. We may be happy without them or successful in spite of them. ... Our lives are made up of thousands of everyday choices. Over the years these little choices will be bundled together and show clearly what we value"[7].

- **Proverbs 11:24–25 The generous prosper.** Some people "scatter" their wealth and yet "increase" in it. Others "with-holdeth more than is meet," and yet "tendeth to poverty." Those that are "liberal" (generous) "shall be made fat: and he that watereth shall be watered also himself."

The Generous Prosper

- **Proverbs 13:7 The management of riches determines wealth.** There are those that "maketh [themselves] rich, yet [have] nothing," while others "maketh [themselves] poor, yet [have] great riches." Managing what we have is what makes us secure and happy.

- **Proverbs 22:7 The rich rule the poor.** "The rich ruleth over the poor, and the borrower is servant to the lender."

- **Proverbs 30:8–9 Having too much or too little.** Solomon says, "give me neither poverty nor riches; feed me with food convenient for me: Lest I be full, and deny ... the Lord ... or lest I be poor, and steal, and take the name of my God in vain."

Happiness and Good Humor

- **Proverbs 15:13 The importance of a good attitude and sense of humor.** "A merry heart maketh a cheerful countenance: but by sorrow of the heart the spirit is broken." (See also Proverbs 17:22).

Elder Hugh B. Brown said: "I would like to have you smile because after all we must keep a sense of humor whatever comes. I think of all the people in the world we should be the happiest. We have the greatest and most joyous message in the world. I think when we get on the other side, someone will meet us with a smile (unless we go to the wrong place and then someone will grin), so let us be happy. But let our happiness be genuine—let it come from within"[8].

F. WRIGHT/THE BIBLE AND ITS STORY, 1908

- **Proverbs 29:18 "Where there is no vision, the people perish."** This can be interpreted in an earthly sense—that unless we have a vision for ourselves and our work it will all be random and uninspired. But it can also be said about spiritual things—that without prophets to guide us we will soon sink into apostasy and misery.

THE BOOK OF ECCLESIASTES

- **Author:** A traditional view has been to interpret "The words of the Preacher, the son of David, king in Jerusalem" (Eccl. 1:1) and "I the Preacher was king over Israel in Jerusalem" (Eccl. 1:12) as referring to Solomon, son of David. However, this attribution could refer to a successor king as well.

- **Position:** Ecclesiastes is one of the 11 books of the Old Testament that belong to the Hagiographa ("sacred writings") of the Jewish canon, along with the books of Ruth, Chronicles (counted as one book), Ezra-Nehemiah (also counted as one book), Esther, Job, Psalms, Proverbs, Song of Solomon, Lamentations, and Daniel. The word ecclesiastes is based on the Greek rendering of the Hebrew word koheleth, meaning preacher.

- **Purpose:** To provide a cogent and soul-searching contrast between a worldly perspective marked by impermanence and a godly view, in which the eternal destiny of man is anchored in the fear of God and obedience to His commandments.

- **Time Span:** The reign of Solomon extended from around 1015 B.C. until his death around 975 B.C. The writing of Ecclesiastes, however, appears to have occurred much later (around 300 B.C. to 250 B.C).

- **Length:** 12 chapters

- **Key Sections:** — Chapters 1–10   An intricate exploration of the theme "all is vanity" (Eccl. 1:2).

   — Chapters 11–12   The summum bonum of life: to do good, fear God, and keep his commandments.

SELECTED WISDOM FROM ECCLESIASTES

- **Eccl.** 1:12 "The Preacher" is probably Solomon. The writer of the book is referred to as "the Preacher," but it was probably Solomon. We draw this conclusion from this verse which says, "I the Preacher was king over Israel in Jerusalem." It could have been David, since he also ruled over all of Israel from Jerusalem, but all the others ruled only a portion of the people—either Judah (from Jerusalem) or Israel (from Samaria). And none of the other kings of Judah or Israel was well-known for writing down his words of wisdom and philosophy. Thus, the Preacher is probably Solomon.

The Preacher's Search for Life's Meaning

The first 10 chapters of Ecclesiastes explore the theme "all is vanity." And the first five of those speak of how pointless and monotonous life can be unless we have a higher purpose than just living through each day.

- **Eccl. 1:1–11 All is vanity (pointless).** The Preacher complains that all work seems pointless (v. 3). One generation after another comes to earth and leaves with the earth hardly taking notice because it "abideth forever" (v. 4). The sun rises and falls and rises again (v. 5). The wind blows in all directions (v. 6). Rivers run to the sea, yet the sea never seems to be full because the waters eventually return to where they started (v. 7). Everything requires labor, yet we can never see all nor hear all that we want to (v. 8). "There is no new thing under the sun" because everything that has happened in the past happens again now, and everything we do now will be repeated in the future (v. 9). The Preacher asks, "Is there any thing whereof it may be said, See, this is new?" then answers "no" because "it hath been already of old time, which was before us" (v. 10). And the memory of things slips away, both past and present, rendering them also pointless (v. 11). This is a depressing way to begin the book, but it establishes the foundation upon which "the meaning of life" can be discussed.

- **Eccl. 1:13–18 He sought wisdom but found only vanity (pointlessness), vexation, and sorrow.** He gave his heart to the search for the meaning of life, which search God has "given to the sons of man to be exercised therewith" (v. 13). He had considered "all the works that are done under the sun," and found that all of them consist of "vanity and vexation of spirit" (v. 14). "That which is crooked cannot be made straight: and that which is wanting cannot be numbered" (v. 15). He had become greatly wealthy and obtained "more wisdom than all they that have been before me in Jerusalem" (v. 16). He had used this wealth and wisdom "to know wisdom, and to know madness and folly," but found that "this also is vexation of spirit" (v. 17). "For in much wisdom is much grief: and he that increaseth knowledge increaseth sorrow" (v. 18). (See also Eccl. 2:12–18; Eccl. 12:8–12).

- **Eccl. 2:1–11 He could not find contentment in pleasure, culture, or riches.** He thought he might find meaning in mirth and the enjoyment of pleasure, but "behold, this also is vanity" (v. 1). He also tried giving himself to wine and laying hold on folly to see if that might be "good for the sons of men" (v. 3). "I made me great works; I builded me houses; I planted me vineyards" (v. 4). "I made me gardens and orchards, and I planted trees in them of all kind of fruits" (v. 5). "I made me pools of water, to water therewith the wood that bringeth forth trees" (v. 6). "I got me servants and maidens, and had servants born in my house; also I had great possessions of great and small cattle above all that were in Jerusalem before me" (v. 7). "I gathered me also silver and gold, and the peculiar treasure of kings and of the provinces: I gat me men singers and women singers, and the delights of the sons of men, as musical instruments, and that of all sorts" (v. 8).

In summary, he was "great, and increased more than all that were before [him] in Jerusalem," while at the same time retaining his great wisdom (v. 9). He saw whatever he wanted to see, and "withheld not [his] heart from any joy; for [his] heart rejoiced in all [his] labour" (v. 10). Yet, he says, "I looked on all the works that my hands had wrought, and on the labour that I had laboured to do: and, behold, all was vanity and vexation of spirit, and there was no profit under the sun" (v. 11).

Riches can lead to contention and envy

The Preacher continues with a list of complaints about the pointlessness of life. We will only summarize them here, but the reading of these entire chapters may be profitable for anyone who struggles with these seeming inequities.

— Eccl. 2:19–23 His labor was in vain, for the fruits of it would be left to another.

— Eccl. 3:16–22 All men must die and return to dust, just as beasts do.

— Eccl. 4:1–3 He was disheartened by the oppressions and injustices of life.

— Eccl. 4:4–6 A man travails and does "every right work," only to be envied by others.

— Eccl. 4:7–8 People with no family continue to labor just for themselves.

— Eccl. 4:15–16 Numberless ancestors are forgotten, just as we will be in the future.

Maintaining a Proper Perspective on Life

The Preacher now shifts from his list of complaints to a series of observations about life. He begins by telling us that, no matter what happens in life, we should "fear (worship) God" (Eccl. 5:7). Then he gives us some sound advice about how to react to the apparent injustice and inequality of life.

— Eccl. 5:8 God will judge those who oppress others.

— Eccl. 5:9 "The profit of the earth is for all," and even kings must rely on the earth.

— Eccl 5:10–12 The possession of wealth does not bring peace of mind.

— Eccl 5:13–14 It is "a sore evil" to hoard riches, because "those riches perish."

— Eccl 5:14–16 A child is born with "nothing in his hand" and "naked," and we will leave the earth just as we came.

— Eccl. 6 Unless a man's soul is filled with good, riches, honor, and posterity are of no advantage to him.

— Eccl. 8:8   No man can stop his spirit from leaving at death; death comes to all.

— Eccl. 8:11   Because punishment for evil is not executed speedily, the wicked fully set their hearts to do evil.

— Eccl. 8:12–13   Yet, in the end, righteousness is rewarded and wickedness punished.

● **Eccl. 3:1–8 "To every thing there is a season, and a time to every purpose under heaven":**

— A time to be born, and a time to die.

— A time to plant, and a time to pluck up that which is planted.

— A time to kill, and a time to heal.

— A time to break down, and a time to build up.

— A time to weep, and a time to laugh.

— A time to mourn, and a time to dance.

— A time to cast away stones, and a time to gather stones together.

— A time to embrace, and a time to refrain from embracing.

— A time to get, and a time to lose.

— A time to keep, and a time to cast away.

— A time to rend, and a time to sew.

— A time to keep silence, and a time to speak.

— A time to love, and a time to hate.

— A time of war, and a time of peace.

● **Eccl. 4:9–10 Two are better than one because they can help each other.** "Two are better than one … For if they fall, the one will lift up his fellow: but woe to him that is alone when he falleth; for he hath not another to help him up."

Elder Marvin J. Ashton said:

> Someone has said, "A friend is a person who is willing to take me the way I am." Accepting this as one definition of the word, may I quickly suggest that we are something less than a real friend if we leave a person the same way we find him. …
>
> No greater reward can come to any of us as we serve than a sincere "Thank you for being my friend." When those who need assistance find their way back through and with us, it is friendship in action. When the weak are made strong and the strong stronger through our lives, friendship is real. If a man can be judged by his friends, he can also be measured by their heights. …
>
> Yes, a friend is a person who is willing to take me the way I am but who is willing and able to leave me better than he found me.[9]

- **Eccl. 5:2 Be not rash with thy mouth toward God.** "Be not rash with thy mouth, and let not thine heart be hasty to utter any thing before God: for God is in heaven, and thou upon earth: therefore let thy words be few."

- **Eccl. 5:12 Riches do not bestow peace of mind.** "The sleep of a labouring man is sweet, whether he eat little or much: but the abundance of the rich will not suffer him to sleep."

- **Eccl. 5:18–19 We should be content with what God has given.** We are free to enjoy the fruits of our labor, because they are God-given and considered to be "[our] portion." Rich or poor, God expects us "to take [our] portion, and to rejoice in [our] labour; this is the gift of God."

- **Eccl. 7:1 A good name is better than precious ointment.** That is to say, a good name is more precious and valuable, and should be guarded with the utmost care. Also, we honor our parents best by bringing honor to their names by the way be behave.

- **Eccl. 7:1 The day of death is better than the day of one's birth.** Though men fear death, yet what lies beyond this earth is so glorious that "eye hath not seen, nor ear heard, neither have entered into the heart of man, the things which God hath prepared for them that love him" (1 Corinthians 2:9). And the day of our "birth" into the Spirit World will be filled with the same joy that accompanied our entrance into this life.

- **Eccl. 7:16 Do not be over-righteous or over-wise.** The warning is that if we do this, we will "destroy [ourselves]." Why? Because any kind of "holier-than-thou" attitude is the result of pride, and "pride leadeth to a fall."

- **Eccl. 8:1–5 We should obey the law and our political leaders.** Solomon says flatly, "I counsel thee to keep the king's commandment, and that in regard of the oath of God" (v. 2). Thus, we do not have to violate the laws of the land to keep our covenants. Political leaders have power, and challenging them is dangerous (vv. 3–4). If we do as they command, we "shall feel no evil thing," and "a wise man's heart discerneth both time and judgment" for when we should speak up or not (v. 5).

We should obey the law and our rulers

- **Eccl. 8:16–17 Man cannot comprehend the ways of God.** For one thing, they are too many—God, "neither day nor night seeth sleep with his eyes" (v. 16). Try as we might, we can never comprehend all that he has done, is doing, and will do for the benefit of his children on this earth (v. 17).

- **Eccl. 9:1 All things are in the hands of God.** Though we may fear for the future, we should remember "that the righteous, and the wise, and their works, are in the hand of God," and we need not worry.

- **Eccl. 9:7–10 We should make the most of each day of life,** for no one knows when death will come, and "there is no work, nor device, nor knowledge, nor wisdom, in the grave, whither thou goest" (v. 10).

- **Eccl. 9:11–12 We are all subject to the vagaries of life.** "The race is not [always] to the swift, nor the battle to the strong, neither yet bread to the wise, nor yet riches to men of understanding, nor yet favour to men of skill; but time and chance happeneth to them all" (v. 11). Just as fishes caught in a net or birds in a snare, "so are the sons of men snared in an evil time, when it falleth suddenly upon them" (v. 12).

- **Eccl. 11:9 Rejoice in thy youth, but do not sin.** "Rejoice, O young man, in thy youth; and let thy heart cheer thee in the days of thy youth, and walk in the ways of thine heart, and in the sight of thine eyes: but know thou, that for all these things God will bring thee into judgment."

- **Eccl. 12:1–7 Youth think that death will never come; but it will.** He advises them to "remember … thy Creator in the days of thy youth, while the evil days come not, nor the years draw nigh, when thou shalt say, I have no pleasure in [life]" (v. 1). When we are young, it seems that "the sun, or the light, or the moon, or the stars, be not darkened, nor the clouds return after the rain" (v. 2).

GEORGE F. WATTS, 1878

The carefree folly of youth

But soon enough, troubles will come, and the scenes we see when we "look out of the windows [will] be darkened" (v. 3). Under the oppressions of life, "fears shall be in the way, and … desire shall fail: because man goeth to his long home [the grave], and the mourners go about the streets" (vv. 4–5). "Then shall the dust return to the earth as it was: and the spirit shall return unto God who gave it" (v. 7).

The Preacher's Conclusions Concerning Life

- **Eccl.** 12:13–14 The conclusion of the whole matter. Having given us both sides of the story of life—its seeming pointlessness and its joys and opportunities and future promised rewards—the Preacher finishes his book with an upbeat conclusion:

"Let us hear the conclusion of the whole matter: Fear God, and keep his command- ments: for this is the whole duty of man. For God shall bring every work into judgment, with every secret thing, whether it be good, or whether it be evil."

OTHER WISDOM LITERATURE

The Song of Solomon

Though it is full of sensuous and sexual imagery, from a religious perspective, the Song of Solomon can be interpreted as an allegory of God's love for Israel and/or for His church. This, indeed, is how many orthodox Christians explain it. The Joseph Smith Translation manuscript states that "The Songs of Solomon are not inspired writings," yet, the Prophet actually quoted the Song of Solomon (6:10) in his inspired dedicatory prayer for the Kirtland Temple, referring to the Church's coming forth "fair as the moon, clear as the sun, and terrible as an army with banners"(D&C 109:73–74; also 105:31–32).

- **Author:** It is doubtful that Solomon was the author.

- **Position:** Song of Solomon is one of the 11 books of the Old Testament that belong to the Hagiographa ("sacred writings") of the Jewish canon, along with the books of Ruth, Chronicles (counted as one book), Ezra-Nehemiah (also counted as one book), Esther, Job, Psalms, Proverbs, Ecclesiastes, Lamentations, and Daniel.

- **Purpose:** Depends entirely on how it is viewed (see introduction above).

- **Time Span:** Uncertain.

- **Length:** 8 chapters

- **Key Sections:** The book is a continuous sequence of pronouncements, images, metaphors, and similes concerning a love relationship.

Ecclesiasticus

- **The Book of Ecclesiasticus is part of the Apocrypha, which is included in the Catholic bible but not in the King James Version.** It contains the wisdom of a man named Jesus, son of Sirach, who is apparently one of the wise men in Israel that are referred to in the book of Proverbs. Because it does not appear in the King James Bible, we will not discuss it here other than to say that it part of the "wisdom literature" of the ancients.

Notes

1. *Antiquities of the Jews*, Book 8. chapter 3:2.
2. *Bible Dictionary*, "Hezekiah's Tunnel," 702.
3. In Conference Report, Apr. 1971, 82; or *Ensign*, June 1971, 72.
4. In Conference Report, Apr. 1989, 3–5; or *Ensign*, May 1989, 4, 6.
5. In Conference Report, Apr. 1989, 5; or *Ensign*, May 1989, 6.
6. In Conference Report, Apr. 1993, 43; or *Ensign*, May 1993, 34.
7. In Conference Report, Oct. 1980, 28–29; or *Ensign*, Nov. 1980, 21.
8. *The Abundant Life* [1965], 83.
9. In Conference Report, Oct. 1972, 32, 35; or *Ensign*, Jan. 1973, 41, 43.

Job's Adversity and Triumph

(Job)

୫୦୯୧

THE STORY OF JOB

Job is one of the world's greatest stories. Victor Hugo called it "perhaps the greatest masterpiece of the human mind."[1] Thomas Carlyle said it is "one of the grandest things ever written."[2] And H. H. Rowley considered it "the greatest work of genius in the Old Testament."[3]

The central questions raised by the book of Job are mostly "why" questions:

— Why do bad things happen to good people?

— Why do good things happen to bad people?

— Does God cause bad things to happen?

— Can God prevent bad things?

— If so, why doesn't He?

The book of Job "narrates the afflictions that befell a righteous man, and discusses the moral problem such sufferings present … The book of Job does not entirely answer the question as to why Job (or any human) might suffer pain and the loss of his goods. It does make it clear that affliction is not necessarily evidence that one has sinned. The book suggests that affliction, if not for punishment, may be for experience, discipline, and instruction"[4].

The Book of Job

● **Author:**   Unknown

● **Position:**   Job is one of the 11 books of the Old Testament that belong to the Hagiographa ("sacred writings") of the Jewish canon, along with the books of Ruth, Chronicles (counted as one book), Ezra-Nehemiah (also counted as one book), Esther, Psalms, Proverbs, Ecclesiastes, Song of Solomon, Lamentations, and Daniel.

● **Purpose:**		The book of Job is a poetic drama of great intensity and meaning about the human condition: the misery and lowliness of man in comparison with the majesty and supremacy of God; the trials of life as a test of man's integrity and loyalty to his Creator (and not necessarily as evidence of unrighteousness); and the divine spark of testimony within man that God lives and guides man toward a better state based on his obedience, patience, and willingness to endure to the end.
● **Time Span:**		Unspecified.
● **Length:**		42 chapters
● **Key Sections:**	— Chapters 1–3	Opening prologue and framework.
	— Chapters 4–18	Job's three friends discuss implications of his suffering.
	— Chapter 19	Job declares his faith in God and his enduring testimony.
	— Chapters 20–28	Job continues his dialogue with his friends.
	— Chapters 29–31	Job reviews his condition.
	— Chapters 31–37	Elihu's sermon on man's weakness and God's majesty.
	— Chapters 38–41	God speaks with Job and gives a divine perspective.
	— Chapter 42	Job repents and is blessed.

JOB'S CHARACTER AND FAITH

Considering the unbelievable things that happened to him, we might ask, "Was Job a real person or just a metaphor for suffering?" Ezekiel considered him to be real (Ezekiel 14:14, 20), as did James (5:10–11). And the Lord compared Joseph Smith to Job, as we will discuss later.

According to the Bible, Job lived in the land called Uz (Job 1:1), which was a large region east of the Jordan River incorporating several political entities from as far north as Damascus (the Aramaens or Syrians) to Edom in the south.

Scholars disagree on the date when Job lived. Some say he lived during the time of the patriarchs (Abraham, Isaac, Jacob) while others suggest dates as late as the time of Malachi. Given his wealth and influence, it is more likely that he lived during or shortly after the days of Solomon, when Israel and its people prospered.

- **Job 1:1 Job was a righteous man.** The Bible describes him as a "man [that] was perfect and upright, and one that feared God, and eschewed evil" (vv. 1, 8). The Hebrew word translated "perfect" is *tmm* or *tam* and literally means complete or finished. It also means "blameless, innocent, sincere, quiet, peaceful, pious, pure, healthy" and even upright, honest, and loyal. The phrase "perfect and upright" means that he was blameless and just—spiritually and morally upright. Eschewed translates the Hebrew word *sur*, which means "to turn away from." Thus, Job shunned evil.

- **Job 1:2–5 Job was a wealthy man, blessed of God.** Job had a large family—seven sons and three daughters (v. 2). He was extremely prosperous, being called "the greatest of all the men of the east" (v. 3). His possessions included 7,000 sheep, 3,000 camels, 500 yoke of oxen (1,000 oxen), 500 asses, and "a very great household" (v. 3). Yet, he was not caught up in his wealth, graciously sharing all that he had with his family (v. 4). He also made sacrifices every day for them, saying, "It may be that my sons have sinned, and cursed God in their hearts. Thus did Job continually" (v. 5).

Job was wealthy but charitable

- Other Information concerning Job's character and situation includes:

— Job 2:3	He had integrity.
— Job 4:3–4	He strengthened the weak.
— Job 23:10–12	He walked in the Lord's paths and esteemed His words.
— Job 29:1–11	His children were all around him.
— Job 29:21–25	Men respected him and often asked him for advice.
— Job 29:12–16	He was compassionate to the widow, poor, lame, and blind.
— Job 29:17	He opposed those who were unjust.
— Job 31:29–30	He was concerned for his enemies and forgave them.
— Job 1:8	He was perfect and upright, an honest person who feared God and shunned evil.

THE TRIALS OF JOB

Job's Faith Is Tested by Satan

- **Job 1:6 The assembly before Lord.** In both Job 1 and 2, we are told of assemblies of the "sons of God" (JST account says "children of God) "before the Lord" (1:6–12; 2:1–6). The place and time of these assemblies are not mentioned. However, the scene probably does not have reference to a meeting in heaven, but rather a meeting at the temple here on earth.

  Menahem Haran says that "in the Bible, the phrase 'before the Lord' can be considered an indication of the existence of a temple at the site, since this expression stems from the basic conception of the temple as a divine dwelling-place and actually belongs to the temple's technical terminology"[5].

  The phrase "sons of God" or "children of God" is a phrase used to refer to those who have made covenants with God (Moses 6:64–68; 8:12–15). So the assembly probably consisted of faithful Israelites who had come to the temple (perhaps Solomon's temple in Jerusalem) to carry out their religious devotions to God. While doing so, Satan came among them to tempt and distract them. It seems likely, though it is not stated, that Job was among the "sons of God" who had come to the temple.

Artist's idea of the meeting of God with Satan

CORRADO GIAQUINTO, 1750

  Job may have become the object of a conversation between the Lord and Satan as they observed him at the temple. But we might question whether God converses with the devil as described here. These verses may be a poetic way of setting the stage for what follows in Job's life—his afflictions, temptations, loss of worldly goods—rather than a reporting of an actual conversation.

  The Lord does not bargain with Satan or agree to his evil deeds; however, Satan is permitted by the Lord to afflict and torment man until Lucifer's allotted time on earth is done. Thus, Job's trials would be consistent with the concept that Satan was allowed by God to bring the afflictions upon Job, not because of a bargain God made with Satan, but because it fit God's purposes for Job. The same could be said of our own temptations and sorrows.

- **Job 1:7–12 Satan challenges the Lord to stop blessing Job, arguing that if he does, Job will turn against him.** He asked the Lord, "Doth Job fear God for nought?" (v. 9), or in other words, "is it any wonder?" "Hast not thou made an hedge about him, and about his house, and about all that he hath on every side? thou hast blessed the work of his hands, and his substance is increased in the land" (v. 10). He has it all; no wonder, then, that he is righteous. "But put forth thine hand now, and touch all that he hath, and he will curse thee to thy face" (v. 11). The Lord does not bargain with Satan, but as a test of Job's integrity he allows Satan to try him: "Behold, all that he hath is in thy power; only upon himself [physically] put not forth thine hand" (v. 12).

GUSTAVE DORÉ, 1896

Job receives word of his calamities

- **Job 1:13–19 In a single day, Job loses all his children and all his worldly wealth.** On a particular day when his children were all having dinner at the eldest son's house (v. 13), "there came a messenger unto Job," with the bad news that all his oxen and asses had been stolen by the Sabeans, who also slew all of Job's servants except for this one man who had escaped (vv. 14–15). And before that conversation was over, "there came also another, and said," that fire had fallen from heaven and burned up his sheep and the servants who tended them (v. 16). And yet another came and said that the Chaldeans had stolen all his camels and slain the servants who were with them (v. 17).

Even worse, while this last report was being given, "there came also another, and said, Thy sons and thy daughters were eating and drinking wine in their eldest brother's house: And, behold, there came a great wind from the wilderness, and smote the four corners of the house, and it fell upon the young men, and they are dead; and I only am escaped alone to tell thee" (vv. 18–19).

- **Job 1:20–22 Job falls down and worships God and blesses his name.** Job was suddenly destitute and alone, except for his wife. But rather than be angry, he "arose, and rent his mantle, and shaved his head, and fell down upon the ground, and worshipped [God]" (v. 20). He observed that "naked came I out of my mother's womb, and naked shall I return thither: the Lord gave, and the Lord hath taken away; blessed be the name of the Lord" (v. 21). And "in all [of] this Job sinned not, nor charged God foolishly" (v. 22). He firmly believed that everything he had received had been given to him by God, and that God had the right to take it from him.

- **Job 2:1–6 Satan is not impressed.** God observed that Job "still … holdeth fast his integrity, although thou [sought] to destroy him without cause" (v. 3). Notice that the Bible account makes it seem that the evil came from God, which it most certainly did not. This is apostate doctrine from the scribes who frequently ascribed evil to God when writing or translating Bible stories. Satan was not impressed, claiming that "all that a man hath will he give for his life" (v. 4), and if he were cursed in his "bone and his flesh, … he will curse thee to thy face" (v. 5). Knowing better about Job, God allowed him to be tested but would not allow Satan to take his life (v. 6).

- **Job 2:7–8 Job is afflicted with boils all over his body.** Anyone who has experienced even one boil knows how extremely painful it can be. So when we are told that Job received "sore boils from the sole of his foot unto his crown" (v. 7) we can only imagine the extreme pain he suffered.

He "took him a potsherd [piece of broken pottery] to scrape himself ... and ... sat down among the ashes" (v. 8).

"Sore boils, one of the symptoms of a terrible disease (perhaps elephantiasis), [had] attacked every portion of Job's body, forming large pustules which itched so greatly that a piece of pottery was used to scrape them. Job's face was so disfigured that his friends could not recognize him. Worms or maggots were bred in the sores ([Job] 7:5). His breath became so foul and his body emitted such an odor that even his friends abhorred him ([Job] 19:17–18), and he sought refuge outside the city on the refuse heap where outcasts and lepers lived. Pain was his constant companion ([Job] 30:17, 30), as were also terrifying nightmares ([Job] 7:14)"[6].

● **Job 3:1–4, 11–13 Job is suffering terribly.** He felt to curse "the day ... wherein I was born" (v. 3). "Let that day be darkness; let not God regard it from above, neither let the light shine upon it," he said (v. 4). He wished he had died at birth and "give[n] up the ghost when I came out of the belly" (v. 11). If so, he could have "lain still and been quiet, I should have slept ... [and] been at rest" (v. 13). "My soul is weary of my life," he said later (Job 10:1).

Job's Friends Accuse Him of Sin

● **Job 2:11–13 Three of Job's friends—Eliphaz, Bildad, and Zophar—arrive to comfort him.** They had heard of his troubles and came to "mourn with him and to comfort him" (v. 11). His face was so disfigured by the boils that they didn't recognize him at first, and when they saw his condition, "they lifted up their voice, and wept; and they rent every one his mantle, and sprinkled dust upon their heads toward heaven" (v. 12). They sat by his side for seven days and nights without saying a word, "for they saw that his grief was very great" (v. 13).

JAMES J. TISSOT, 1897–1904

Job's friends grieve with him for seven days

The chapters that follow (Job 4–37) contain a lengthy discussion between Job and his friends of the questions which were listed at the beginning of this chapter:

— Why do bad things happen to good people?

— Why do good things happen to bad people?

— Does God cause bad things to happen?

— Can God prevent bad things?

— If so, why doesn't He?

Time and space do not permit a lengthy discussion of all that Job and his friends said to one another. But the following summary captures the essence of the conversation.

- **Job 4–7 Eliphaz says Job has sinned and must look to God for deliverance.**

  — Job 4:7 He asked, "who ever perished, being innocent? or where were the righteous cut off?" He believed that Job had sinned somehow.

  — Job 6–7 Job bemoaned the burden God had given him, the unsympathetic response of his friends, and his wretched condition.

  — Job 6:15, 21 Job said to Eliphaz that his friends had shown him no mercy because "ye see my casting down, and are afraid" (v. 21). Could such things also happen to them? The thought was terrifying, and they sought to explain it by blaming Job for his condition.

Eliphaz accused Job of sinning

  — Job 6:24 Still, even though Job felt betrayed, he was willing to listen to his friend Eliphaz's counsel.

- **Job 8–10 Bildad says if Job were pure, God would heal him.** He was even bolder in his condemnation of Job than was Eliphaz.

  — Job 8:3–4 He asked, "Doth God pervert judgment? or doth the Almighty pervert justice?" (v. 3). He said that Job's children had sinned against God and "he [had] cast them away for their transgression" (v. 4).

"If you were pure, God would heal you"

  — Job 8:5–6 He told Job that if he would repent "betimes" (immediately) and "make thy supplication to the Almighty" and become "pure and upright," then the Lord "would awake for thee, and make the habitation of thy righteousness prosperous."

  — Job 8:20 He asserted again that "God will not cast away a perfect man, neither will he help the evil doers."

- **Job 11–14 Zophar chastises Job for asserting his innocence.**

  — Job 11:3 He accused Job of lying about his innocence, and said he was ashamed of him.

— Job 11:6 As a result, he suggested that Job was not receiving all the punishment that he deserved.

— Job 11:11 He said Job was vain—that he could not admit his faults.

— Job 11:13–16 He advised Job to prepare his heart, confess to God, and repent of his sins.

Zophar called Job a liar

- **We might ask, "With friends like these, who needs enemies?"** Their unsympathetic responses must have made Job feel very alone. Referencing this, the Lord said to Joseph Smith in Liberty Jail, "Thy friends do stand by thee, and they shall hail thee again with warm hearts and friendly hands. Thou art not yet as Job; thy friends do not contend against thee, neither charge thee with transgression, as they did Job" (D&C 121:9–10).

- **Job 15–21 Job's friends renew their criticism and speak of the awful state of the wicked.** In response, Job complained of their harshness, reasserted his innocence, and testified that though the wicked sometimes prosper, they will be brought down.

- **Job 22–28 Job's friends commence a third round of criticism.** Job maintained his innocence, reaffirmed his testimony that God will bring judgments upon the wicked, and extolled God's greatness.

- **Job 29–31 Job contrasts his past happiness and greatness with his present wretched condition** and invites God's critical examination and penalty if he is deserving of it. There is no vanity here. Job did not believe that he had sinned, but if he had, he was more than willing to accept God's punishment. He did not understand why all of this had happened to him, but he was willing to submit to God in all of it.

Elihu Speaks with Youthful Self-Righteousness

- **Job 32 Elihu offers his opinions.** We know very little about Elihu except that he was "the son of Barachel the Buzite, of the kindred of Ram" (v. 2), and was younger than Job and his friends (v. 4). "I am young," he said: "and ye are very old; wherefore I was afraid, and durst not shew you mine opinion" (v. 6). But now that it was his turn, he did not hold back. "There is a spirit in man: and the inspiration of the Almighty giveth [the spirit] understanding" (v. 8)—in other words, he was quite as able to receive inspiration as they were. "Great men are not always wise: neither do the aged [always] understand judgment," he said (v. 9). "I am full of the matter," he said, and "the spirit within me constraineth me" (v. 18). "It is ready to burst like new bottles" (v. 19). He could not wait to tell everybody how much he thought he knew and how wrong they were, notwithstanding their age and wisdom.

- **Job 32–37 Elihu reproves Job's friends but offers similar criticisms to Job.**

— Job 32:3 He was upset with Job's friends for condemning Job.

— Job 32:2 But he was also upset with Job for asserting his innocence and seeking to justify himself.

— Job 33:12, 14–16 He said that God is greater than man and reveals His wisdom and purposes in visions.

— Job 34:12, 21–34 He said that God would not afflict anyone unjustly. He sees all things and recompenses according to men's deeds.

Elihu criticized both Job and his friends

— Job 34:35–37 He said that Job did not understand because he lacked knowledge and wisdom, and "my desire is that Job may be tried unto the end because of his answers for wicked men" (v. 36).

— Job 35 He contrasted the weakness of man with the power of God, said that our behavior greatly affects others, and said we must learn to trust in God.

— Job 36 He claimed that those who are righteous are prospered while those who are wicked perish and die. How, then, can Job claim to be righteous?

Elihu's discourse reveals his youthful disdain for the words of his elders. Yet, he says very little that is different than what they had already said. It reads like a lengthy exercise in self-justification, mixed in with elaborate praise for the greatness and power of God. And in the end, we are left with the same basic questions.

When people prosper, we all too often assume it is because they are doing what's right. This grows out of a long-standing Christian tradition of the commonwealth—that God will prosper the righteous. And so, when people suffer, we also feel the need to look for "a reason" for it. We assume something is wrong whenever bad things happen to people. But this is not always the case.

Bruce Satterfield wrote:

> Job's friends tried to convince Job that his afflictions were the result of sin (Job 22). They tried desperately to get Job to confess and repent of his sins. But Job refuted their claim (Job 31). Job knew he has not sinned.
>
> One of the messages of the book of Job is that sin is not always the reason people suffer. The idea that afflictions are the result of sin was generated by the covenant relationship between Israel and God. Moses gave instructions to Israel that when they entered into the land of Canaan, they were to go to the sacred city of Shechem and enter into a covenant relationship with Jehovah (Deut. 27–28). As part of the ritual, the tribes of Israel were to literally yell out the designated blessings and curses that would come upon them for either their obedience or disobedience. A look at the various curses (Deut. 28:15–68) demonstrates that Israel would experience many calamities as a result of their disobedience. Israel entered into this covenant relationship after they entered the land of promise (Joshua 8:30–35). As a result whenever the covenant was broken by the people in general, the nation suffered various afflictions (e.g., famine, etc.). Because of this, the idea developed among them that

whenever one sins he is afflicted or punished by God. But the afflictions Israel was to experience as a result of a broken covenant were at a national level, not at the individual level. ...

Individual suffering is not necessarily an indication that the individual is being punished by God for their sins. The book of Job expressly refutes that idea.[7]

And the Prophet Joseph Smith said: "It is a false idea that the Saints will escape all the judgments, whilst the wicked suffer; for all flesh is subject to suffer, and 'the righteous shall hardly escape;' still many of the Saints will escape, for the just shall live by faith; yet many of the righteous shall fall a prey to disease, to pestilence, etc., by reason of the weakness of the flesh, and yet be saved in the Kingdom of God. So that it is an unhallowed principle to say that such and such have transgressed because they have been preyed upon by disease or death, for all flesh is subject to death; and the Savior has said, 'Judge not, lest ye by judged'"[8].

● **The Questions that arise, then, are these:**

1. <u>Why do the righteous, those who love and serve God, suffer?</u> Job was a "perfect and an upright man." Why then did the Lord permit Satan to afflict his righteous servant?

   Elder Bruce R. McConkie said: "The greatest trials of life are reserved for the Saints. They are the ones whom the world hates (Matt. 10:22), and they must overcome the world, if they are to gain the Lord's approval. They face all that the world faces in the way of mortal difficulties—sickness, disease, calamities, famine, pain, sorrow, death—and in addition their faith in Christ and his work is tested to see if they will serve the Lord at all hazards"[9].

2. <u>Who is responsible for man's troubles?</u> Is it the Lord who directs a plane into the mountainside? Does God cause highway collisions? Does he prompt young children to toddle into canals or cause us to suffer heart attacks?

President Spencer W. Kimball said:

Answer, if you can. I cannot, for though I know God has a major role in our lives, I do not know how much he causes to happen and how much he merely permits. Whatever the answer to this question, there is another I feel sure about. Could the Lord have prevented these tragedies? The answer is, Yes. The Lord is omnipotent, with all power to control our lives, save us pain, prevent all accidents, drive all planes and cars, feed us, protect us, save us from labor, effort, sickness, even from death, if he will. But he will not ...

If we looked at mortality as the whole of existence, then pain, sorrow, failure, and short life would be calamity. But if we look upon life as an eternal thing stretching far into the premortal past and on into the eternal post-death future, then all happenings may be put in proper perspective ... Are we not exposed to temptations to test our strength, sickness that we might learn patience, death that we might be immortalized and glorified?[10]

President Kimball also said:

Now, we find many people critical when a righteous person is killed, a young father or mother is taken from a family, or when violent deaths occur. Some become bitter when oft-repeated prayers seem unanswered. Some lose faith and turn sour when solemn administrations by holy men seem to be ignored and no restoration seems to come from repeated prayer circles. But if all the sick were healed, if all the righteous were protected and the wicked destroyed, the whole program of the Father would be annulled and the basic principle of the gospel, free agency, would be ended. No man would have to live by faith.

If pain and sorrow and total punishment immediately followed the doing of evil, no soul would repeat a misdeed. If joy and peace and rewards were instantaneously given the doer of good, there could be no evil—all would do good and not because of the rightness of doing good. There would be no test of strength, no development of character, no growth of powers, no free agency, only Satanic controls.[11]

The Extent of Job's Suffering

● **Job 1:13–17 Job lost all his servants, property, and income in a single day.** Can we even imagine such loss? Once one of the nation's wealthiest men, he was now destitute of all means of supporting himself or his family.

● **Job 1:18–19 He also lost all his children on that same day.** Even worse, he lost his entire family—seven sons and three daughters, their spouses, and all their grandchildren. He was not alone except for his wife.

● **Job 2:7 He suffered great physical illness and pain.** Job was smitten "with sore boils from the sole of his foot unto his crown" (Job 2:7). He said: "My flesh is clothed with worms and clods of dust; my skin is broken, and become loathsome" (Job 7:5) and "my face is foul with weeping, and on my eyelids is the shadow of death" (Job 16:16).

GUSTAVE DORÉ, 1896

● **Job 7:4, 13–14 His sleep was restless and filled with nightmares.** He wondered each night as he went to bed, "When shall I arise, and the night be gone?" (v. 4) but the nightmare never ended. "I am full of tossings to and fro unto the dawning of the day," he said (v. 4). Hoping to receive at least some comfort from sleep, instead he is tormented with frightening dreams (vv. 13–14).

● **Job 2:9 He suffered cruel accusations and loss of support from friends and family.** (The lengthy discussion of this above, and also Job 4:1, 7–8; 11:1–6; 19:13–22).

Job's suffering was extremely intense

● **Job 10:15 He was greatly confused about why he was suffering these trials.** "If I be wicked, woe unto me; and if I be righteous, yet will I not lift up my head. I am full of confusion; therefore see thou mine affliction."

- **Job 16:10–11 He was gawked at and mocked by those who observed his downfall.** "They have gaped upon me with their mouth; they have smitten me upon the cheek reproachfully; they have gathered themselves together against me," he complained (v. 10). "God hath delivered me to the ungodly, and turned me over into the hands of the wicked" (v. 11; see also Job 30:1, 8–10).

- **Job 19:6–8 He feared that God was not listening anymore.** "I cry out of wrong, but I am not heard," he complained (v. 7). He felt that God had "fenced up my way that I cannot pass, and he hath set darkness in my paths" (v. 8).

- **Job 23:3–4 He wished for an opportunity to ask God the central question: Why?** "Oh that I knew where I might find him! that I might come even to his seat! I would order my cause before him, and fill my mouth with arguments."

JOB'S FAITHFUL RESPONSES

- **Job 2:9–10 Job's wife is bitter, but he remains faithful.** We should not forget that she had suffered the same losses that Job suffered. It had turned her bitter. She said to Job, "Dost thou still retain thine integrity? curse God, and die" (v. 9). But Job would not. "Thou speakest as one of the foolish women speaketh," he said. "Shall we receive good at the hand of God, and shall we not receive evil? In all this did not Job sin with his lips" (v. 10)

BERNARD PICART, 1728

Job's wife also suffered, and was angry

Elder Richard G. Scott said: "When you face adversity, you can be led to ask many questions. Some serve a useful purpose; others do not. To ask, Why does this have to happen to me? Why do I have to suffer this now? What have I done to cause this? will lead you into blind alleys. It really does no good to ask questions that reflect opposition to the will of God. Rather ask, What am I to do? What am I to learn from this experience? What am I to change? Whom am I to help? How can I remember my many blessings in times of trial?"[12].

President Spencer W. Kimball said: "One time or another we all face adversity's chilling wind. One man flees from it, and like an unresisting kite falls to the ground. Another yields no retreating inch, and the wind that would destroy him lifts him as readily to the heights. We are not measured by the trials we meet, only by those we overcome"[13].

Elder Marvin J. Ashton said: "Adversity will surface in some form in every life. How we prepare for it, how we meet it, makes the difference. We can be broken by adversity, or we can become stronger. The final result is up to the individual ... There are some persons who in our human eyes seem to have more than their share of trouble, as we measure, but with God's help they are made special. They will not break. They will not yield"[14].

- **Job 5:6–7 Job believes that man experiences trouble to help him grow.** "Man is born unto trouble, as the sparks fly upward," he observes (v. 7). "Affliction cometh not forth of the dust, neither doth trouble spring out of the ground," he said. There had to be a purpose in it.

- **Job 5:8–15 Job is determined to plead his cause before God.** "I would seek unto God, and unto God would I commit my cause," he said (v. 8). He knows that God is great and extols His virtues: He "doeth great things and unsearchable; marvellous things without number" (v. 9). He "giveth rain upon the earth, and sendeth waters upon the fields" (v. 10). He "set[s] up on high those that be low; that those which mourn may be exalted to safety" (v. 11). "He disappointeth the devices of the crafty, so that their hands cannot perform their enterprise" (v. 12). "He taketh the wise in their own craftiness: and the counsel of the froward (contentious) is carried headlong"—"They meet with darkness in the daytime, and grope in the noonday as in the night" (vv. 13–14). "But he saveth the poor from the sword, from their mouth, and from the hand of the mighty" (v. 15). Surely, such a God would not purposefully punish him for no good reason.

- **Job 5:17–19 Joy comes after the trial of our faith.** Job observed wisely, "Behold, happy is the man whom God correcteth: therefore despise not thou the chastening of the Almighty: For he maketh sore, and bindeth up: he woundeth, and his hands make whole. He shall deliver thee in six troubles: yea, in seven there shall no evil touch thee."

- **Job 13:13–15 "Though he slay me, yet will I trust in him."** Job's faith is inspiring. He will not flinch in his faith in the Lord. "Let come on me what will," he said (v. 13). "Though he slay me, yet will I trust in him" (v. 15).

- **Job 14:13–15 Even while wishing for death, he expresses faith in the resurrection.** "O that thou wouldest hide me in the grave," he says to the Lord, wishing that his suffering would be behind him and that the Lord would take him in death according to his set time (v. 13). He knows that death is not the end, but a blessed relief from suffering.

Job testifies to his friends

"If a man die, shall he live again?" he asks. Yes, and after death he will patiently wait for the resurrection: "all the days of my appointed time will I wait, till my change come" (v. 14). And on that blessed day, "Thou shalt call, and I will answer thee: thou wilt have a desire to the work of thine hands" (v. 15).

● **Job 19:25–27 He knows that Christ is the source of resurrection.** "I know that my redeemer liveth," he testifies, "and that he shall stand at the latter day upon the earth" (v. 25). "And though after my skin [death] worms destroy this body, yet in my flesh shall I see God: Whom I shall see for myself, and mine eyes shall behold, and not another; though my reins [innards] be consumed within me" (vv. 26–27).

● **The resurrection is literal, not figuration as many Christians claim today.** Job saw it, and so did Ezekiel and the Prophet Joseph Smith.

Ezekiel's vision of the resurrection

The Prophet Joseph Smith said: "As concerning the resurrection, I will merely say that all men will come from the grave as they lie down, whether old or young; there will not be 'added unto their stature one cubit,' neither taken from it; all will be raised by the power of God, having spirit in their bodies, and not blood"[15].

The Prophet also said:

> Would you think it strange that I relate what I have seen in vision in relation [to] this interesting theme? Those who have died in Jesus Christ may Ezekiel's vision of the resurrection expect to enter into all that fruition of Joy when they come forth, which they have pursued here.

> So plain was the vision I actually saw men before they had ascended from the tomb as though they were getting up slowly. They take each other by the hand. It was my father and my son, my mother and my daughter, my brother and my sister. When the voice calls suppose I am laid by the side of my father. What would be the first joy of my heart? Where is my father, my mother, my sister? They are by my side. I embrace them and they me …

> All your losses will be made up to you in the resurrection provided you continue faithful. By the vision of the Almighty I have seen it … God has revealed his Son from the heavens and the doctrine of the resurrection also. We have a knowledge that those we bury here God [will] bring them up again, clothed upon and quickened by the spirit of the Great God.[16]

● **Job 27:2–6 Job's integrity despite his sufferings.** "All the while my breath is in me, and the spirit of God is in my nostrils; My lips shall not speak wickedness, nor my tongue utter deceit" he promises (vv. 3–4). He will not agree with his wife or his friends in their condemnations: "God forbid that I should justify you: till I die I will not remove mine integrity from me. My righteousness I hold fast, and will not let it go: my heart shall not reproach me so long as I live" (vv. 5–6).

Elder Joseph B. Wirthlin defined integrity: [Integrity is] "always doing what is right and good, regardless of the immediate consequences. It means being righteous from the very depth of our soul, not only in our actions but, more important, in our thoughts and in our hearts. Personal integrity implies such trustworthiness and incorruptibility that we are incapable of being false to a trust or covenant"[17].

GOD BLESSES JOB ABUNDANTLY

The Long-awaited Answer Comes

● **Job 38–41 Jehovah, speaking out of a whirlwind, questions Job** about the wonders of creation and illustrates the folly of any human attempt to criticize his doings.

— Job 38:1–7   Who created heaven and earth?

— Job 38:12   Who set the time of the days?

— Job 38:15   How is light withheld from the wicked?

— Job 38:17   How can you overcome death?

— Job 38:18   What is the breadth of the earth?

— Job 38:19   What is the dwelling place of light and darkness?

— Job 38:20   What are the limits of light and darkness?

— Job 38:22   What are the treasures of snow and hail?

● **Job 42:1–3, 6 Job acknowledges his limited understanding and God's omniscience.** "I know that thou canst do every thing," he confesses, "and that no thought can be withholden from thee" (v. 2). Men often speak counsel (reasons) without knowledge, and "therefore have I uttered that I understood not; things too wonderful for me, which I knew not" (v. 3). Job is embarrassed at his presumptive complaining, saying, "I abhor myself, and repent in dust and ashes" (v. 6).

● **Job 42:7–9 The Lord condemns Job's friends for their presumption and for their accusations.** "My wrath is kindled against thee," he said to Eliphaz, "and against thy two friends: for ye have not spoken of me [in His name] the thing that is right, as my servant Job hath" (v. 7). He commands them to repent by taking "seven bullocks and seven rams, and go to my servant Job, and offer up for yourselves a burnt offering; and my servant Job shall pray for you: for him will I accept" (v. 8). Otherwise he would punish them for their folly. This they did, and "the Lord also accepted Job" (v. 9).

Job prayed for and forgave his friends

● **Job 42:10 The Lord reverses Job's fortunes when he prays for his friends.** This was the final test for Job—whether or not he could forgive his friends. We are told that "the Lord turned the captivity of Job, when he prayed for his friends" (v. 10). This is reminiscent of the Lord's instruction in the Doctrine and Covenants: "I, the Lord, will forgive whom I will forgive, but of you it is required to forgive all men" (D&C 64:10). It is also consistent with His teachings on the Sermon on the Mount: "But if ye forgive not men their trespasses, neither will your Father forgive your trespasses" (Matthew 6:15).

● **Job 42:11 Job's friends and acquain- tances come to his aid.** This included "all his brethren, and all his sisters, and all they that had been of his acquaintance before." They came and ate with him and "bemoaned him, and comforted him over all the evil that the Lord had brought upon him." But equally important, "every man also gave him a piece of money, and every one an earring of gold." This became the basis for his economic recovery, and illustrates the importance of service. As President Kimball once said, "God does notice us, and he watches over us. But it is usually through another person that he meets our needs. Therefore, it is vital that we serve each other."[18]

Job's friends came to his aid temporally

● **Job 42:12–17 The Lord provides Job with twice what he had before,** "bless[ing] the latter end of Job more than his beginning: for he had fourteen thousand sheep, and six thousand camels, and a thousand yoke of oxen, and a thousand she asses" (v. 12). He also doubled his family, providing seven more sons and three more daughters to add to the ten that had been taken from him in death but would be his in the eternities (v. 13). "And in all the land were no women found so fair as the daughters of Job: and their father gave them inheritance among their brethren" (v. 15). "After this lived Job an hundred and forty years, and saw his sons, and his sons' sons, even four generations" (v. 16). Then, "Job died, being old and full of days" (v. 17).

THE PURPOSE OF ADVERSITY

The Reasons for Adversity

● **Job 23:6, 10–16 Trials refine and purify us.** Job asked whether God would use His great power to torment him, and responded "No; but he would put strength in me" (v. 6). He observed that God knew all the steps he would take in life, and "when he hath tried me, I shall come forth as gold" (v. 10). Job was trying to do what was right in the Lord's sight, and he had faith that "he [God] performeth the thing that is appointed for me" (v. 14). "For God maketh my heart soft, and [that is why] the Almighty troubleth me" (v. 16).

Elder Orson F. Whitney said: "No pain that we suffer, no trial that we experience is wasted. It ministers to our education, to the development of such qualities as patience, faith, fortitude and humility. All that we suffer and all that we endure, especially when we endure it patiently, builds up our characters, purifies our hearts, expands our souls, and makes us more tender and charitable, more worthy to be called the children of God ... and it is through sorrow and suffering, toil and tribulation, that we gain the education that we come here to acquire and which will make us more like our Father and Mother in heaven"[19].

● **Ether 12:6 We do not receive spiritual witnesses until after our faith is tried.** Moroni taught that "faith is things which are hoped for and not seen; wherefore, dispute not because ye see not, for ye receive no witness until after the trial of your faith."

● **JST Hebrews 11:40 Suffering made the righteous in the Old Testament perfect.** The Joseph Smith Translation corrects this verse, which is part of Paul's summary of the great examples of faith in the Old Testament, "God having provided some better things for them through their sufferings, for without sufferings they could not be made perfect."

● **Hebrews 5:8 Even Jesus had to learn "obedience by the things which he suffered" even though He was the Son of God.** Thus, apparently, there is no other way to learn the difference between good and evil but by experience and faith.

● **D&C 136:31 "My people must be tried in all things, that they may be prepared to receive the glory that I have for them ... and he that will not bear chastisement is not worthy of my kingdom."** This revelation to the prophet Brigham Young explained the reasons for their extreme suffering in Missouri and Illinois.

The Prophet Joseph Smith said: "God hath said that He would have a tried people, that He would purge them as gold"[20].

The Prophet also said: "You will have all kinds of trials to pass through. And it is quite as necessary for you to be tried as it was for Abraham and other men of God ... God will feel after you, and He will take hold of you and wrench your very heart strings, and if you cannot stand it you will not be fit for an inheritance in the Celestial kingdom of God.[21]

President Spencer W. Kimball said: "The Lord does not always heal the sick, nor save those in hazardous zones. He does not always relieve suffering and distress, for even these seemingly undesirable conditions may be part of a purposeful plan. Being human we would expel from our lives, sorrow, distress, physical pain, and mental anguish and assure ourselves of continual ease and comfort. But if we closed the doors upon such, we might be evicting our greatest friends and benefactors. Suffering can make Saints of people as they learn patience, long-suffering, and self-mastery. The sufferings of our Savior were part of his education"[22].

The Fifteen Fruits of Adversity

- **D&C 121:1–6 Joseph Smith's trials In Liberty Jail.** Other than the Master's suffering in Gethsemane, there is no better example in all of scripture than Job's. But another example may come near to it: the sufferings of Joseph Smith that culminated in his incarceration in Liberty Jail. Doctrine and Covenants 121 contains the soul-cry that he made to God in the midst of those trials:

  > O GOD, where art thou? And where is the pavilion that covereth thy hiding place?

  > How long shall thy hand be stayed, and thine eye, yea thy pure eye, behold from the eternal heavens the wrongs of thy people and of thy servants, and thine ear be penetrated with their cries?

  > Yea, O Lord, how long shall they suffer these wrongs and unlawful oppressions, before thine heart shall be softened toward them, and thy bowels be moved with compassion toward them?

  > O Lord God Almighty, maker of heaven, earth, and seas, and of all things that in them are, and who controllest and subjectest the devil, and the dark and benighted dominion of Sheol—stretch forth thy hand; let thine eye pierce; let thy pavilion be taken up; let thy hiding place no longer be covered; let thine ear be inclined; let thine heart be softened, and thy bowels moved with compassion toward us.

  > Let thine anger be kindled against our enemies; and, in the fury of thine heart, with thy sword avenge us of our wrongs.

  > Remember thy suffering Saints, O our God; and thy servants will rejoice in thy name forever.

- **D&C 121:7–46 The fruits of adversity.** The Lord's answer in the remainder of this revelation and in D&C 122 spells out 16 fruits that come from adversity. He assured Joseph with these comforting words: "My son, peace be unto thy soul; thine adversity and thine afflictions shall be but a small moment; And then, if thou endure it well, God shall exalt thee on high; thou shalt triumph over all thy foes" (vv. 7–8). And in the end "all these things shall give thee experience, and shall be for thy good" (D&C 122:7). I believe it is appropriate to review the fruits of adversity as we close this chapter on Job. I encourage the reader to review them using this summary.

- **From D&C 121, we read of the following fruits of adversity:**

— v. 7	Fruit # 1	Patience
— v. 8	Fruit # 2	Endurance
— v. 9	Fruit # 3	Friends
— v. 10	Fruit # 4	Faith
— vv. 26–29, 33	Fruit # 5	Knowledge
— v. 34–38	Fruit # 6	Priesthood Power through Humility

— v. 45	Fruit # 7	Charity
	Fruit # 8	Virtue
	Fruit # 9	Confidence
	Fruit #10	Wisdom
— v. 46	Fruit #11	Holy Ghost as a Companion
	Fruit #12	Eternal Exaltation

- **D&C 122 The Lord's response to Joseph Smith contains four more fruits:**

— vv. 1–3	Fruit #13	Respect, honor and loyalty from the righteous.
— v. 7	Fruit #14	Experience that will be "for thy good."
— v. 9	Fruit #15	The priesthood will remain with you.
— v. 9	Fruit #16	God will be with you "forever and ever."

- **The Prophet Joseph Smith was shaped by this experience,** and so can we if we are willing to endure our trials well.

The Prophet Joseph Smith said: "I am like a huge, rough stone rolling down from a high mountain; and the only polishing I get is when some corner gets rubbed off by coming in contact with something else, … knocking off a corner here and a corner there. Thus I will become a smooth and polished shaft in the quiver of the Almighty"[23].

President Brigham Young said: "Joseph could not have been perfected, though he had lived a thousand years, if he had received no persecution. If he had lived a thousand years, and led this people, and preached the Gospel without persecution, he would not have been perfected as well as he was at the age of thirty-nine years"[24].

The Prophet Joseph Smith said:

A religion that does not require the sacrifice of all things never has power sufficient to produce the faith necessary unto life and salvation; for, from the first existence of man, the faith necessary unto the enjoyment of life and salvation never could be obtained without the sacrifice of all earthly things. It was through this sacrifice, and this only, that God has ordained that men should enjoy eternal life; and it is through the medium of the sacrifice of all earthly things that men do actually know that they are doing the things that are well pleasing in the sight of God. When a man has offered in sacrifice all that he has for the truth's sake; not even withholding his life, and believing before God that he has been called to make this sacrifice because he seeks to do his will, he does know, most assuredly, that God does and will accept his sacrifice and offering, and that he has not, nor will not seek his face in vain. Under these circumstances, then, he can obtain the faith necessary for him to lay hold on eternal life. …

Those, then, who make the sacrifice, will have the testimony that their course is pleasing in the sight of God; and those who have this testimony will have faith to lay hold on eternal life, and will be enabled, through faith, to endure unto the end, and receive the crown that is laid up for them that love the appearing of our Lord Jesus Christ. ...

All the Saints of whom we have account, in all the revelations of God which are extant, obtained the knowledge which they had of their acceptance in his sight through the sacrifice which they offered unto him; and through the knowledge thus obtained their faith became sufficiently strong to lay hold upon the promise of eternal life, and to endure as seeing him who is invisible; and were enabled, through faith, to combat the powers of darkness, contend against the wiles of the adversary, overcome the world, and obtain the end of their faith, even the salvation of their souls.[25]

Notes

1. Victor Hugo, quoted in Henry H. Halley, *Pocket Bible Handbook* [1946], 232.
2. Thomas Carlyle, quoted in Henry H. Halley, *Pocket Bible Handbook* [1946], 232.
3. H. H. Rowley, *The Growth of the Old Testament* [1966], 143.
4. *LDS Bible Dictionary*, 713, 714.
5. *Temples and Temple Service in Ancient Israel* [1985], 26.
6. *The Westminster Study Edition of the Holy Bible* ... [1948], 641.
7. Lesson 32, "I Know That My Redeemer Liveth," one of a series of lessons on the Old Testament published online by *Meridian Magazine*, 2002.
8. *Teachings of the Prophet Joseph Smith*, sel. Joseph Fielding Smith [1976], 162–163.
9. *Doctrinal New Testament Commentary*, 3 vols. [1966–73], 3:319.
10. *Faith Precedes the Miracle* [1972], 96–97.
11. "Tragedy or Destiny," *Improvement Era*, Mar. 1966, 180, 210.
12. In Conference Report, Oct. 1995, 18; or *Ensign*, Nov. 1995, 17.
13. In General conference Address, October 1974; or *Ensign*, November 1974, 82.
14. In Conference Report, October 1980; or *Ensign*, November 1980, 54, 60.
15. Teachings of the Prophet Joseph Smith, 199–200.
16. In S.H. Faulring (Ed)., *The Diaries and Journals of Joseph Smith: An American Prophet's Record* [1989], 366–367.
17. In Conference Report, Apr. 1990, 38; or *Ensign*, May 1990, 30.
18. "The Abundant Life," *Ensign*, Oct. 1985, 3.
19. Quoted in Spencer W. Kimball, *Faith Precedes the Miracle*, 98.
20. *Teachings of the Prophet Joseph Smith*, 135
21. President John Taylor, In *Journal of Discourses*, 24:197.
22. *Improvement Era*, Mar. 1966, 210, 216.
23. *Teachings of the Prophet Joseph Smith*, 304.
24. In *Journal of Discourses*, 2:7.
25. Joseph Smith, comp., *Lectures on Faith* [1985], 58–60.

About the Author

Randal S. Chase spent his childhood years in Nephi, Utah, where his father was a dry land wheat farmer and a businessman. In 1959 their family moved to Salt Lake City and settled in the Holladay area. He served a full-time mission in the Central British (England Central) Mission from 1968 to 1970. He returned home and married Deborah Johnsen in 1971. They are the parents of six children—two daughters and four sons—and an ever-expanding number of grandchildren.

He was called to serve as a bishop at the age of 27 in the Sandy Crescent South Stake area of the Salt Lake Valley. He served six years in that capacity, and has since served as a high councilor, a stake executive secretary and clerk, and in many other stake and ward callings.

Regardless of whatever other callings he has received over the years, one was nearly constant: He has taught Gospel Doctrine classes in every ward he has ever lived in as an adult—a total of 35 years.

Dr. Chase was a well-known media personality on Salt Lake City radio stations in the 1970s. He left on-air broadcasting in 1978 to develop and market a computer-based management, sales, and music programming system to radio and television stations in the United States, Canada, South America, and Australia. After the business was sold in 1984, he supported his family as a media and business consultant in the Salt Lake City area.

Having a great desire to teach young people of college age, he determined in the late 1980s to pursue his doctorate, and received his Ph.D. in Communication from the University of Utah in 1997. He has taught communication courses at that institution as well as at Salt Lake Community College and Dixie State University for 21 years. He served as Communication Department chair and is currently a full-time professor at Dixie State University in St. George, Utah.

Concurrently with his academic career, Brother Chase has served as a volunteer LDS Institute and Adult Education instructor in the CES system since 1994, both in Salt Lake City and St. George, where he currently teaches a weekly Adult Education class for three stakes in the Washington area. He has also conducted multiple Church History tours and seminars. During these years of gospel teaching, he has developed an extensive library of lesson plans and handouts which are the predecessors to these study guides.

Dr. Chase previously published a thirteen-volume series of study guides on the Book of Mormon, Church History, the Old Testament, and the New Testament. The series, titled *Making Precious Things Plain,* along with four smaller study guides on Isaiah, Jeremiah, the story of the Nativity, and the final week of our Lord's atoning sacrifice, are designed to assist teachers and students of the gospel, as well as those who simply want to study on their own. Several of these books are also available in the Spanish language.